MARRIAGE & FAMILY

Cover Photo

Couples of every culture, language, and age can benefit from this book. Whether you are just considering marriage or already have grandchildren, you can improve the relationship between you and your mate, and learn new principles that will help you and others.

Contact Information

Order your copy from:

Resource and Development Ministries
1722 S. Glenstone, W-163
Springfield, Missouri 65804 U.S.A.

Telephone: 417-881-4698

Fax: 417-881-1037

E-mail: RDMlit@rdmlit.org

Web: www.rdmlit.org

Special thanks to BGMC for helping fund this project.

MARRIAGE & FAMILY
Student Manual

by
Dr. Wayde I. Goodall
with
Rosalyn R. Goodall

Instructional Design by
Dr. Quentin McGhee,
Senior Editor

Faith & Action Series

Resource and Development Ministries
1722 S. Glenstone, W-163
Springfield, Missouri 65804 U.S.A.

Photo Credits

We would like to thank the following for use of photos in this book:

TheBibleRevival.com for Figures 9.2, 10.3 and 11.4 from their "FREE Clip Art Collection" page,

Assemblies of God World Missions—Latin American Child Care for Figure 9.9a,

Assemblies of God World Missions—Kid's Quest for Figure 9.9b,

www.usaid.gov—photo by Ellyn W. Ogden, MPH, USAID for Figure 9.14,

The Oaks Fellowship, Red Oak, Texas—photos by Justin Mease for Figure 13.6.

Many photos in this book are purchased by license from DesignPics.com.

Other photos in this book are purchased by license from Photos.Com.

Copyright Information

The Holy Bible: New International Version, International Bible Societies, Grand Rapids, Michigan: Zondervan Publishing House, ©1984.

The Holy Bible: New Century Version, Dallas: Word Bibles, ©1991.

The Holy Bible: King James Version, Cleveland and New York: The World Publishing Company.

The Holy Bible: New American Standard Bible, Philadelphia and New York: A. J. Holman Company, ©1973.

First Edition 2006

Faith & Action Series—Marriage & Family, First Edition
©2006 RDM

Course # MIN3073

Item # 4431-37E0

Table of Contents

Page

List of Figures 6

Faith & Action Series Overview 8

Three-Year Bible School Plan 9

About This Book 10

Unit 1: Preparing for Marriage

1 How to Understand Marriage and the Family 16

2 How to Choose a Mate for Life 30

3 How to Plan the Engagement and Wedding 48

Unit 2: Adjusting to Marriage

4 How to Practice Good Communication 64

5 How to Approach Sexual Life in Marriage 80

6 How to Answer Three Key Questions 96

Unit 3: Relating in a Family Life

7 How to Be a Loving Husband 114

8 How to Be a Loving Wife 130

9 How to Be an Effective Father or Mother—Part 1 144

10 How to Be an Effective Father or Mother—Part 2 166

Unit 4: Succeeding as a Family

11 How to Overcome Threats to Your Family 192

12 How to Handle Tough Problems 216

13 How to Live the Latter Years 232

Appendix A: Websites to Help You Prevent and Conquer Internet Pornography 243

Appendix B: Creative Ways to Use This Book 243

Definitions 244

Scripture List 248

Bibliography 250

Endnotes 254

List of Figures

Page

Figure 1.2	Three actions of marriage	19
Figure 2.2	Fleshly love versus biblical love	31
Figure 2.3	First Corinthians 13:4-8 describes biblical love.	32
Figure 2.4	Dating: Its strengths and weaknesses	32
Figure 2.5	Courtship: Its strengths and weaknesses	33
Figure 2.6	Arranged engagements: strengths and weaknesses	34
Figure 2.8	Your body is the temple of the Holy Spirit (1 Cor. 6:19).	36
Figure 2.15	Questions to discern if a person is immature or mature	45
Figure 3.3	Tasks of a wedding coordinator or helper	52
Figure 3.4	Ways engaged couples can learn more about each other in three different situations	53
Figure 3.5	Eight questions to ask before setting the wedding date	54
Figure 4.2	The circle of communication	65
Figure 4.4	Proverbs warns of things to avoid when speaking.	68
Figure 4.5	Proverbs teaches things to practice when speaking.	68
Figure 4.7	Common mistakes women make in communicating	71
Figure 4.8	Common mistakes men make in communicating	72
Figure 4.9	List of some basic emotions and opposite emotions	73
Figure 4.10	Look for the cause of the conflict.	74
Figure 4.11	People make decisions in many ways.	74
Figure 4.12	A difference in values can cause conflict in marriage.	75
Figure 5.1	General sexual differences between men and women	82
Figure 6.5	Biblical examples of people who made decisions, based on the wrong reasons	99
Figure 6.7	Examine the priorities in your marriage.	100
Figure 6.8	Scriptures give us principles about things more valuable than money.	102
Figure 6.9	Scriptures give us principles about ungodly ways of getting money.	102
Figure 6.11	Sample budget plan for one month; how you will manage your income	104
Figure 6.14	Seven questions to discuss about the extended family	109
Figure 7.4	Practice chart on words of praise	122
Figure 9.3	Ways children grow mentally, physically, spiritually, and socially	148
Figure 9.6	Attitudes and skills related to money	153
Figure 9.7	Ten reasons for sex education in the home	154
Figure 9.8	Seven ways to teach your children about sexual matters	154
Figure 9.11	Children need various foods to grow in health.	158
Figure 9.13	Poor planning to get rid of sewage causes sickness.	161
Figure 10.4	Parents should teach their children to bear the fruit of good character.	169
Figure 10.5	Watch for signs that show your child is ready to develop a personal relationship with God.	170
Figure 10.7	Jacob used word pictures to encourage his children (Gen. 49:8-27).	174
Figure 10.9	A person's self-worth affects his actions and relations.	176
Figure 10.13	Example of random (occasional) rewards	186
Figure 10.14	The success of physical discipline decreases as a child's age increases.	187
Figure 11.11	The top five needs of most men and women.	204
Figure 11.14	Three common steps in the cycle of abuse	208
Figure 11.15	People become slaves by taking four steps over a period of time.	210
Figure 11.16	In a family, help for any problem comes after the valley of discussion.	211

Figure 11.18 Galatians 5:16-25 contrasts the emotions caused by the flesh and the Spirit. 213
Figure 11.19 Problems and solutions related to the threat of distance in a family 214
Figure 12.1 Stress varies with the events of life. 218
Figure 12.5 Eight ways to help children work through grief from the loss of a loved one 222
Figure 12.6 Divorce causes children to have many negative feelings. 223
Figure 12.9 Signs of stress and ways to lessen it 227

Figure 13.1 As we grow older we walk slower, but time seems to travel faster. 234

Faith & Action Series Overview

Bible	Theology	Church Ministries	General
Survey of the Old Testament	*Bible Doctrines Survey	Church Ministries	*Introduction to English
Survey of the New Testament	*Apologetics	Pastoral Ministry	*English Composition
Pentateuch	General Principles for Interpreting Scripture (Hermeneutics I)	Marriage & Family	*World Religions & Cults
Historical Books	Hermeneutics II	Evangelism & Discipleship	Cross-Cultural Communications
*Poetic Books	The Bible, God, & Angels (Theology I)	*Church Government	
Major Prophets	Man, Sin, Christ, & Salvation (Theology II)	*Church History	
*Minor Prophets	The Holy Spirit & His Work in the Church (Theology III)	*Principles of Teaching	
Life & Teachings of Christ (Synoptic Gospels)	Last Things (Eschatology) (Theology IV)	*Teaching Literacy	
John	Missions	*Leadership	
Acts of the Holy Spirit		*Biblical Counseling	
Romans & Galatians		Preach the Word (Homiletics I)	
Corinthians		Homiletics II	
Prison Epistles		Prayer & Fasting	
Pastoral Epistles		*Church Planting	
*Hebrews		Children's Ministry	
General Epistles			
Revelation & Daniel			

*Elective

Faith & Action Series
Three-Year Bible School Plan (97 credits)

First Year

First Semester

Course #	Title	Credits
BIB1013	Survey of the New Testament	3
BIB1023	Pentateuch	3
BIB1033	Synoptic Gospels	3
THE1012 MIN1022	*Bible Doctrines Survey or *Church Planting	2
THE1022	Hermeneutics I	2
GEN1012 MIN1032	*Introduction to English or *Teaching Literacy	2
		15

Second Semester

Course #	Title	Credits
BIB1043	Survey of the Old Testament	3
BIB1053	John	3
BIB1063	Acts	3
THE1032	The Bible, God, & Angels (Theo. I)	2
MIN1013	Homiletics I	3
MIN1042 GEN1022	*Evangelism & Discipleship or *English Composition	2
		16

Second Year

First Semester

Course #	Title	Credits
BIB2013	Romans & Galatians	3
BIB2023	Historical Books	3
THE2012	Man, Sin, Christ, & Salvation (Theo. II)	2
THE2022	Hermeneutics II	2
MIN2013	Homiletics II	3
BIB2072	Hebrews	2
THE2043	Missions	3
		18

Second Semester

Course #	Title	Credits
BIB2033	Corinthians	3
BIB2042	Prison Epistles	2
MIN2022	Prayer & Fasting	2
BIB2053 BIB2063	*Poetic Books or *Minor Prophets	3
THE2032	The Holy Spirit and His Work in the Church (Theo. III)	2
MIN2032	Church Ministries	2
MIN2042	*Principles of Teaching	2
		16

Third Year

First Semester

Course #	Title	Credits
BIB3012	Pastoral Epistles	2
BIB3023	General Epistles	3
BIB3033	Major Prophets	3
THE3012	Last Things (Eschatology) (Theo. IV)	2
MIN3013	Pastoral Ministry	3
GEN3013	Cross-Cultural Communications	3
		16

Second Semester

Course #	Title	Credits
BIB3043	Revelation & Daniel	3
MIN3023	Children's Ministry	3
MIN3033 MIN3043	*Leadership or *Biblical Counseling	3
MIN3052 MIN3062	*Church Government or *Church History	2
MIN3073	Marriage & Family	3
GEN3022 THE3022	*World Religions & Cults or *Apologetics	2
		16

*Elective

About This Book

1. **The Lesson** headings divide each chapter into two to four parts. Each of these parts or sections focuses on several principles related to one theme.

2. **The Lesson Goals** are listed at the beginning of each chapter. Also, when a lesson begins, the goal for that lesson is printed there. You will find that there is at least one goal for each lesson.

3. **Key Words** are defined in a section called "Definitions" at the end of the book. The symbol * comes before all words that are defined. To help some students, we have also defined a few words that are not key words.

4. **Teaching Method:** These courses are designed for the *guided discovery* method of learning. This method focuses on the student, rather than the teacher. When this course is used in a classroom, lectures are not intended. Rather, most of the class time should be used for students to discuss the questions in the margins and related questions from the teacher and other students. At least 25 percent of the student's grade should be on how faithfully the student has tried to answer questions *before* class.

   It is VERY important for each student to own his or her book. We encourage Bible schools to require students to buy their texts at the time they pay tuition. It is a shame for students to leave school without their books, because they need them for a lifetime of ministry. Owning the book enables a student to write notes in it and underline important ideas. Also, when students own their books, they do not waste class time by copying things that are already written in the text. Rather, they spend their time discussing questions related to the Bible and ministry.

   In a classroom the teacher and students should discuss key questions together. The best teachers never answer their own questions. Some students will complain at first when the teacher requires them to think, read, and search for answers. But a good teacher knows that children who are always carried never learn to walk. And students who are always told the answer learn to memorize, but not to think and solve problems. In many ways, a good teacher is like a coach—guiding others to succeed.

   The questions in this course are like a path that leads straight to the goal. If the questions are too hard for a student, the teacher can ask easier questions that are like stairs toward harder questions. Also, the teacher should ask questions that guide students to apply the text to local issues. Often, a good teacher will add a story or illustration that emphasizes a truth for students.

5. **Schedule:** Most *Faith & Action Series* courses have up to 40 sections. For a Bible school course, it is good to plan for 40 contact hours between the teacher and students. This allows one section for a class hour.

6. **The Questions:** Most questions in the margins are identified by the hammer ➚ and nail ➘ symbols. Questions are steps toward a goal. As a student answers the questions, he or she is sure to reach the goals. The hammer introduces *content questions* and the nail precedes *application questions*. Our logo for this book includes the hammer hitting the nail. A student must grasp content before being able to apply it. The answers to all content questions are in the text, near the question. We encourage students to answer nail or application questions from their local settings.

   In some books there is the symbol of a shovel ➘ before certain questions. Questions beside the shovel symbol are inductive questions. The word *induce* means "to lead." These questions lead students to discover truth for themselves. The shovel symbol alerts students that it is time to dig in and discover truth for themselves. *All students studying this course alone should complete the shovel questions.* Such students miss the 40 or more hours in a classroom that resident or extension students receive. The shovel questions will help these correspondence students get more out of the course. *When this book is used in a classroom setting, students will still benefit from answering the shovel questions. Teachers may require students to answer all shovel questions outside of class, or they may guide students to complete these questions in class; or they may replace some shovel questions with other work.*

7. **The Illustrations**, such as stories and examples, are preceded by the candle symbol 🕯 .

8. **Figures** include pictures, photos, charts, and maps. We number the figures in order throughout the chapter. For example, the first three figures in chapter one are numbered 1.1, 1.2, and 1.3. There is a List of Figures near the front of the book.

9. **The Test Yourself** questions come at the end of each chapter and are indicated by the balance symbol ⚖. There are always ten of these questions. As a rule, there are two test questions for each goal in the chapter. If students miss any of these questions, they need to understand why they missed them. Knowing why an answer is right is as important as knowing the right answer.

10. **Sample Answers** to the hammer questions, some comments on the nail questions, and answers for the Test Yourself questions are in the Teacher's Guide. Students should answer questions so they will grow and become strong in their mental skills.

11. **Bible quotations** are usually from the New International Version (NIV). We also use the New Century Version (NCV), New American Standard Bible (NASB), and the King James Version (KJV). We encourage students to compare biblical passages in several versions of the Bible.

12. **The Scripture List** includes key Scripture references in this course. It is located near the back of the book.

13. **The Bibliography** is near the endnotes page. It is a complete list of books the author refers to in this course. Some students will want to do further research in these books.

14. **Endnotes** identify the sources of thoughts and quotes. They are listed by chapter at the end of the book.

15. **The Unit Exams and Final Exam** are in the Teacher's Guide. In the Teacher's Guide there are also other useful items for the teacher and potential projects for the students.

16. **Course Description (MIN3073):** This is a practical survey of marriage and the family from A to Z. After a brief overview, the study focuses on such matters as: ways to choose a mate, guidelines for the engagement and wedding, communication principles, sexual fulfillment, making decisions, how to be a good spouse and parent, tough issues, and the final years.

17. **Course Goals**

    Chapter 1: Give an overview of marriage: its beginning, order, pattern, purposes, and stages.
    Chapter 2: Analyze three ways of choosing a mate, and the roles of love, friendship, and sexual purity in the process.
    Chapter 3: Describe the engagement period and wedding. Comment on local customs, a wedding helper, laws, finances, sexual issues, and social matters.
    Chapter 4: Explain communication principles related to listening, the role of feelings, avoiding common mistakes of men and women, and conflict.
    Chapter 5: Summarize keys to a fulfilling sexual relationship in marriage.
    Chapter 6: Identify principles for making good decisions about family matters.
    Chapter 7: Explain how a husband should relate to his wife, children, extended family, and work.
    Chapter 8: Explain how a wife should relate to her husband, children, extended family, and community.
    Chapter 9: Examine principles for parents to practice in relation to the mental and physical growth of children.
    Chapter 10: Summarize principles for parents to practice in relation to the spiritual, emotional, and social growth of children.
    Chapter 11: Describe how a family can overcome the threats of distance, adultery, abuse, and addiction.
    Chapter 12: Analyze how to deal with the tough family issues of grief and rebellion.
    Chapter 13: Explain the way relationships change as children mature. Include comments on the empty nest and grandparents.

18. **Authors**

Dr. Wayde I. Goodall and Rosalyn are missionaries with the Assemblies of God and work in areas of critical need in different locations of the world. He serves under the Executive Director of the world missions office. In the past, Dr. Goodall was the head of the Ministerial Enrichment Department of the Assemblies of God in Springfield, Missouri, for 5 years. He was appointed in 1994 to create this department and to be a "minister to the ministers" of the Assemblies of God, overseeing programs for marriage, family, and parenting to over 32,000 ministers within the denomination. While serving as the Executive Editor of Enrichment Journal, which he created, it received first place for clergy magazines in 1997 and 2000 from the Evangelical Press Association.

Wayde and Rosalyn are the founding pastors of Vienna Christian Center, in Vienna, Austria. In the United States they have served as senior pastors of congregations of several thousand attendees and received the Church Health Award from the Purpose Driven Church. Wayde was appointed to represent the Pentecostal/Charismatic churches of America on the Pulpit and Pew "think tank" at Duke University. He is a certified Congregational and Team Coach and works with church leaders in areas of spiritual and life balance.

Because of Wayde's extensive writing and pastoral experience he frequently teaches at colleges and seminaries. He is an adjunct professor at Asia Pacific Theological Seminary and the Assemblies of God Theological Seminary. He has also been a guest teacher at the Billy Graham Cove in North Carolina and served as Executive Director of Benevolence for Bethesda Ministries/Mission of Mercy. He and his wife, Rosalyn, are frequent speakers at churches, seminars, pastors and missionary retreats throughout the world. They have co/hosted on Christian television and have been interviewed by Focus on the Family for their radio programs.

Wayde holds Doctor of Ministry degrees from the Assemblies of God Theological Seminary and Northwest Graduate School of Ministry. He also holds a Master of Arts degree in counseling from Central Michigan University and a Bachelor of Arts degree in Bible and one in psychology from Southern California College (Vanguard University).

Dr. Goodall has written and co-authored 13 books, including *Why Great Men Fall, Conflict Management for Church Leaders, Marriage & Family, By My Spirit, The Fruit of the Spirit, The Choice, The Blessing, The Battle,* and *Back to the Word*, many of which are translated into several languages.

Rosalyn is a technical editor, writer, and educator and has served as a faculty member at Southwest Missouri State University for 5 years. Her ministry has included women's conferences, retreats, and educators training. Wayde and Rosalyn have viewed their ministry as a team effort for God's kingdom. They have two grown children, Jeremy and Kristin.

19. Contributors and Consultants

Dr. Quentin McGhee is the founder and director of the *Faith & Action Series*. He earned a B.A. from Southwestern College in Oklahoma City, and a B.S. from Oral Roberts University (ORU). Later he completed an M.Div. at the Assemblies of God Theological Seminary. There he taught beginning Greek and was selected by the faculty for "Who's Who Among Students in American Colleges and Universities." He earned a D.Min. from ORU in 1987. Dr. McGhee and his wife, Elizabeth, pioneered a church in Oklahoma. They went on to serve as missionaries in Kenya for 15 years. There they helped start many churches, developed an extension Bible school for full-time ministers, and assisted in curriculum development.

Darlene Sullivan Robison holds a B.A. in Biblical Studies from Central Bible College, and an M.A. in Christian Education and an M. Div. (emphasis in Cross-cultural Communications) from the Assemblies of God Theological Seminary. As an ordained minister and U.S. Missionary of the Assemblies of God, she serves in church planting and leadership training in major urban centers among culturally diverse communities. Currently, she serves on the National Church Planting Team that focuses on urban issues and developing church planters. Darlene has designed and implemented programs and curriculum for various groups—to reach communities for Christ. She spent many hours assisting with research and editing on this course. She says that the greatest highlights of her life include being daughter to Roy and Evelyn, wife to Timothy, and mother to Leslie and Daniel.

Dr. Marvin Glenn Gilbert is Dean of Post Graduate Studies at Cape Theological Seminary in South Africa. He and his wife, Rosie, have been married 33 years, and have two children, Stephen and Lisa.

His formal education includes a B.A. in Bible from Central Bible College, an M.S. in Psychology from Central Missouri State, and an Ed.D. in Counselor Education (minor in Family Relations) from Texas Tech.

Marvin has served as an Assemblies of God missionary for 20 years, taught Bible School classes, conducted many workshops or seminars on family matters and counseling, authored numerous articles for Pentecostal and psychological publications, and edited several books in the Discovery Series. He has co-authored three books: The Holy Spirit and Counseling: Volumes I and II—Theology and Theory and Application; and Successful Family Living: An African View, with Don Odunze, which has been a valuable resource for this *Faith & Action Series* course.

Cary Tidwell and his wife, Faye, served overseas as missionaries for 20 years. They began in West Africa, where they ministered in five countries. Then, for the next 13 years, Cary and Faye served in 12 European countries, directing the Eurasia Teen Challenge training ministry. Through their work of teaching, training, children's ministry, and seminars, Cary and Faye were able to proclaim the healing message of Jesus Christ to many lost, hurting, and lonely people. During their most recent term of missionary service, Cary was family life coordinator for the Assemblies of God World Missions outreach in Europe to American servicemen and their families on bases throughout the continent. In this position, he and Faye conducted marriage, family, and singles retreats, and taught as guest teachers in AG Bible schools in Europe.

Cary began ministry with the U.S. staff of AGWM as secretary and then director of Personnel and Family Life. In that position, he supervised the missionary application process and coordinated pastoral care of the missionary family. In his current position as administrator, Cary facilitates the ministries of AG missionaries around the world.

Trudy Moeckl has served as an Assemblies of God missionary since 1980, including terms in Africa and with International Service Ministries. Trudy began her ministry as a teenager, teaching small children in Sunday school, and continued to teach through Teen Challenge, while pastoring with her husband, Ken, and a 2-year MAPS assignment in Brussels, Belgium. In Tanzania, she trained teachers for children's ministry, developed a gazette for Sunday school teachers, and taught at the resident and night Bible schools. For the past 10 years, Trudy has served as Administrative Assistant, technical editor, and project coordinator of the *Faith & Action Series*. She has 2 B.A. degrees from North Central University and an M.A. from Assemblies of God Theological Seminary.

Unit 1: Preparing for Marriage

Welcome to our study on marriage and the family. This first Unit is important, because it lays the foundation for the entire course. Marriage is an old custom—as old as the human race. Since people have been marrying from the time of Adam and Eve, you would think that everyone understands marriage. But this is not true. Many people rush into marriage before they are ready. Some find that marriage is not what they expected. Many feel like they married the wrong person. Others divorce and start over again—often because of wrong ideas about marriage.

This unit is to help people prepare—*get ready* for married life.
- Do not worry about the future; prepare for it!
- It is better to prepare than to repair. It is better to prevent problems than to repent after they happen!
- "When you are thirsty, it is too late to start digging a well!"[1]

Chapter 1 gives an overview of marriage and the family. You will learn to:
- *Explain the beginning, plan, and order for marriage.*
- *Describe the three actions of God's pattern for marriage.*
- *Explain at least eight purposes of marriage and family.*
- *Contrast Stages One and Two of marriage.*
- *Describe seven characteristics of mature love.*

Chapter 2 describes how to choose a mate for life. We will enable you to:
- *Summarize the differences between biblical love and fleshly love.*
- *Analyze the strengths and weaknesses of three methods to choose a mate.*
- *Explain the roles of friendship and purpose in preparing for a mate.*
- *Summarize five reasons for sexual purity in preparing for a mate.*
- *Describe six keys to living sexually pure while preparing for a mate.*
- *Ask and answer questions on each of the 12 topics about choosing a mate.*

Chapter 3 discusses the engagement and wedding. We will guide you to:
- *Explain five principles to evaluate local customs.*
- *Describe matters to consider when choosing a wedding helper and a date for the wedding.*
- *Explain how to prepare for marriage matters that are legal or financial, including a new home.*
- *Summarize what a couple should learn about each other, sexual union, pregnancy, and sexual purity.*
- *Comment on the balance between being generous and sensible at the wedding celebration.*
- *Explain the balance between pleasing the new couple and pleasing others at the wedding.*

Chapter 1:
How to Understand Marriage and the Family

Introduction

Many centuries ago, Abraham set out on a journey with his family. God had promised:

Figure 1.1 Believers all over the world are a part of God's big, spiritual family.

²*"I will make you into a great nation and I will bless you; I will make your name great, and you will be a blessing. ³I will bless those who bless you, and whoever curses you I will curse; and all peoples on earth will be blessed through you"* (Gen. 12:2-3).

Two thousand years later, Paul wrote about the promise God gave Abraham. The apostle said that all who believe are part of Abraham's spiritual family. Consider Abraham:

⁶*"He believed God, and it was credited to him as righteousness."* ⁷*Understand, then, that **those who believe are children of Abraham**. ⁸The Scripture foresaw that God would justify the Gentiles by faith, and announced the gospel in advance to Abraham: "**All nations will be blessed through you**"* (Gal. 3:6-8).

Later, the apostle John saw a vision related to the growing family of Abraham. *"I looked and there before me was **a great multitude that no one could count, from every nation, tribe, people and language**, standing before the throne and in front of the Lamb"* (Rev. 7:9).

Like Abraham, we are on a journey with our families. Abraham's journey took him to a far-away land. Our journey is taking us toward our eternal home with God. The goal of this course is to help each family who studies become more pleasing to God. Our desire is that Christ will make our families a blessing to the world. We can read about the struggles Abraham had with his family. We can understand family struggles, because we have our own, and expect to have more. But, like Abraham, we walk in faith.

All believers are part of God's bigger, spiritual family. This family is *"a great multitude ... from every nation, tribe, people and language"* (Rev. 7:9). We are a family because we all have faith in Christ. We are all the children of Abraham.

Believers all over the world will study this course on the family. Whoever studies will have the chance to grow in their local family *and* in relation to the big family of God. We have a lot in common with each other, but there are also many differences. You will read some customs and illustrations that have little to do with your culture. When this happens, take some time to learn about your spiritual family in other parts of the world—and pray for them.

Lessons:

A Biblical Foundation
Goal A: *Explain the beginning, plan, and order for marriage.*
Goal B: *Describe the 3 actions of God's pattern for marriage.*

God's Purposes for the Family
Goal: *Explain at least 8 purposes of marriage and family.*

Three Stages of Growth in Marriage
Goal A: *Contrast Stages One and Two of marriage.*
Goal B: *Describe 7 characteristics of mature love.*

Key Words

marriage   polygamy   temperament
monogamy   intimacy

A Biblical Foundation
Goal A: *Explain the beginning, plan, and order for marriage.*
Goal B: *Explain the 3 actions of God's pattern for marriage.*

A. In the beginning God ordained marriage and the family.

What do you think of when you hear the word *marriage*? Some link marriage with "being in love." The word *marriage* causes others to think of a wedding. In many cases, governments have laws about marriage. These laws deal with issues like age, kinship, property, and divorce. Human laws are helpful, but the idea of marriage did not come from humans.

"In the beginning God created the heavens and the earth" (Gen. 1:1). He created the land and sea, the sun and moon, the plants and animals. And in the beginning, God created man and woman and joined them together in marriage. Marriage is God's idea.

This is why we let the Bible define *marriage* and *family*. Surely, the One who planned marriage should define it! The Bible teaches that marriage is a public commitment between a man and woman to become one and remain faithful to each other until death. A new family begins when a man and woman marry. The family grows as children are born or adopted into it.[1] Some families are large, but a family may be as small as two people.

Q 1 *Define marriage and family.*

God planned marriage and families to be the foundation for all societies throughout history. Today, in every culture of the world, there are marriages and families. Still, families often fall short of God's plan. Throughout this course, let us ask God for His grace to help our marriages and families become all that He desires.

Q 2 *Why do you think that marriage and family exist in the entire world?*

B. God's plan for marriage is that each man should have only one wife.

There are two major types of marriage in various cultures. The first is *monogamy*—a marriage between only one husband and one wife.[2] The second major type of marriage is *polygamy*—a marriage in which there is more than one husband, or more than one wife.[3] In the Old Testament, Jacob married Leah and her sister Rachel (Gen. 29:1-30). However, his desire was to marry only Rachel. It was Laban, an idolater and a cheat, who wanted Jacob to have more than one wife.

Q 3 *Define monogamy and polygamy.*

The Bible teaches that monogamy—a marriage between one man and one woman—is God's plan. This is clear from the story of the first family, Adam and Eve (Gen. 2:20-24). The Scripture tells us, [18]*"The LORD God said, 'It is not good for the man to be alone. I will make a helper suitable for him.'* ... [24]*For this reason a man will leave his father and mother and be united to his wife"* (Gen. 2:18, 24). It does NOT say, *"helpers* suitable for him" or "he shall be united to his *wives.*" God's plan has always been for one man and one woman to marry. Lamech, a murderer, was the first man in the Bible to marry a second wife (Gen. 4:19-24).

We see God's plan for one wife in His relationship to Israel. He desired Israel to be like a faithful wife to Him.[4] The Old Testament prophets often reminded Israel to be faithful to God. Hosea points out that God would have no other wife but Israel, just as Israel was to have no other husband but Jehovah.[5] We can find the same emphasis on one wife in Isaiah and Ezekiel (Isa. 54, 62:1-5; Ezek. 16).

Q 4 *If monogamy is God's plan, how do you explain polygamy in the Old Testament?*

The kings of Israel often married more than one wife. This fleshly behavior was against God's plan and standard taught in Genesis 2:24.[6] In fact, Solomon's many wives were the root of Israel's unfaithfulness to God. They led the king's heart into idolatry. The nation soon followed Solomon on this path of spiritual adultery.

The apostle Paul supports God's plan for one wife. He says that a deacon must be the husband of one wife. (1 Tim. 3:2, 12; Titus 1:6). Likewise, for a widow to receive support, she must have been married to only one husband (1 Tim. 5:9).

Jesus made it plain that God's plan was for a man to marry only one wife [4]*"At the beginning the Creator 'made them male and female,' [5]and said, 'For this reason a man will leave his father and mother and be united to his wife* [not wives!]'" (Matt. 19:4-5; Mark 10:6-7).[7] Likewise, the New Testament tells us that Jesus will marry only one bride, the Church.

C. God also blesses those who choose the single life (1 Cor. 7:1-11, 25-40).

Q 5 *State 2 reasons why some should not marry.*

God has given the gift of marriage to most people. He warns unmarried people to marry if they cannot control their sexual desires (1 Cor. 7:9). Still, marriage is not for everyone. God often approves long periods of singleness or a lifetime of singleness. First Corinthians 7 gives several reasons why a person may choose to be single.

- A gift and call for the single life (1 Cor. 7: 7)
- A present crisis (1 Cor. 7:26)
- An understanding that the time in this world is short (1 Cor. 7:29-31)
- A commitment to give undivided devotion to God (1 Cor. 7:28, 32-35)
- An absence of a desired believer to marry (1 Cor. 7:39; see also 2 Cor. 6:14-18)

A single life is not a second-class life. It is fully approved and blessed by God.

Each person should be given the opportunity to accept or reject marriage (1 Cor. 7:37, 39-40). Some unmarried people feel that they have not been given a choice. They would like to marry, but have not had the chance. Or perhaps they let an opportunity pass and now regret it. Perhaps they wonder if something is wrong with them since another has not chosen them for marriage. But God is not surprised by their lives. He has a purpose for everyone. If you are single, remain pure and faithful to God. Serve the Lord with all your heart. In the next chapter, we will consider how to choose and find a mate. But it is important to first seek God about whether to marry.

D. God gives order for marriage and family (Eph. 5:22–6:3; Gen. 1–2).

Q 6 *Explain the need for order in the family.*

Order is necessary in the world God has created. God has a plan of order for everything. He separated water from the dry land, and the night from the day. We need order in nature, and order in society; order in each nation, and order in each family—the smallest unit of society. If order fails in the home, then society is in danger. The Bible teaches at least three things about God's plan for order in a family.

Q 7 *Summarize God's plan for order in the family.*

1. The husband is the head of the wife. Husbands and wives are equal, but they have different roles. Remember the creation story. Adam and Eve were both made in the image of God. Both were given the right to rule over the earth. And both had to answer to God for their sin. But God gave the leadership role to the husband. He was created first. It was Adam who named the animals. And Adam showed his leadership when he called her *"woman"* and gave her the name *"Eve."*[8] God commands husbands to follow Christ's example as a loving leader.

2. The wife is to submit to her husband. The wife's role is not less than the husband's role, but it is different. A wife's submission is an attitude of respect for her husband and his leadership in the home. A wife feels, speaks, and thinks for herself as she contributes to the marriage. Her submission is like the Church's submission to Christ. It is a response to her husband's love (Eph. 5:22-24).

3. Children are to honor and obey their parents. This connects the generations of a family. Children imitate their parents. If parents honor *their* parents, then the children who watch will honor their own parents. As the proverb says, "Water runs down."[9] The command for children to honor parents comes with a promise of God's blessing (Eph. 6:2).

The order that God gives for the family is similar to all order—it contains authority and submission. But each person in the family is guided by love, respect, honor, and kindness.

E. God gives us a pattern for marriage that has three parts (Gen. 2:20-25).

*"For this reason a man will **leave** his father and mother and **be united** to his wife, and they will **become one flesh**"* (Gen. 2:24). Let us look at God's pattern for marriage based on this Scripture.

1. Leave father and mother. In the times of the Old Testament, it was common for the woman to leave her parents and go live with her husband's family. But the Bible says the man must also leave his parents. The husband and wife must make their own home. They need space and privacy to learn to make their own decisions. They need to form their own way of living and solving problems. It is hard to do this when the parents are always watching and wanting things done their way. Leaving can be hard for the bride and groom and their parents. But the parents must not come between the bride and groom. And the bride and groom must not rely too much on parents.

1. Leave

3. Become one flesh

2. Be united

Figure 1.2
Three actions of marriage[10]

Q 8 What are the 3 actions in God's pattern for marriage?

The distance between parents and the new couple will vary from family to family. When Rebekah left her family to marry Isaac, she traveled to another country. She probably never saw her family again (Gen. 24:3-6). But when Isaac married, he may have only moved to a different tent near his father (Gen. 24:67). Today, cultures may expect a new couple to live near or far from the parents. But the couple must move as far away physically as necessary to unite themselves as one. Some parents continue to demand first loyalty from their married children. They want the young wife and husband to obey them as if they were still children. A newly married couple may need to move far from parents like these. They must not let parents harm their marriage.

Some newly married people want to stay close to their parents and remain like little children. They want someone else to support them and make decisions for them. They want their parents to solve their problems. They want to please their parents more than they want to please their spouses. Parents may need to insist that this kind of couple moves away from them.

Families (including parents, uncles, aunts, grandparents, brothers, sisters, and cousins) can be a great source of strength and help. They can:

- help each other in times of trouble.
- share their talents and possessions to help each other prosper.
- understand and encourage each other in making decisions.
- help each other with work.
- help each other with children.

Q 9 Why do you think God wants the husband and wife to leave their parents?

Q 10 What does God mean by "leave"?

Q 11 How can a young couple remain close to their families and still "leave" them?

It is good for families to be together. But each couple needs privacy. And no family member must come between the husband and wife.

Leaving—no matter what the distance is—means that things will change between parents, sons, and daughters. The new marriage needs the loyalty and attention of the new couple. But God also taught us to honor our parents. So, we must not abandon our parents and larger family when we leave. As the husband and wife grow strong together, they will be able to help and honor their parents and larger families.

Q 12 *What is a sign that a husband has not obeyed God's command to leave his parents?*

When counseling couples, pastors often face people who want to call their mother or father before they make any decisions. Such people spend almost all their holidays and days off with their parents. When they always go "home," they do not build their own family traditions. When there is trouble or conflict in their home, they call their parents at once. God tells us to avoid depending too much on our parents. He says a man must leave his father and mother. The influence of parents is necessary in our lives when we are growing up. We should always respect and honor our parents. Still, we must grow in our ability to make our own decisions. When your duties to your parents, brothers, or sisters take *priority* over your own marriage and family, you are in trouble. Let go of parents, and become a new family with your mate and children.

A grandfather may need a cane to lean upon. He wants a strong stick—not one that is thin and weak. For if the cane breaks, the grandfather will fall. Likewise, we may need to lean on our children and their marriages when we become old, sick, lonely, or poor. We must help our children grow strong in their marriages, for their sake and for our own sake. If the marriage breaks, many are hurt.

Q 13 *Why should leaving be public and legal?*

Leaving is not a private matter. It must happen in a public and legal way. The community and the government should know a marriage has taken place. Then everyone knows to treat the couple as husband and wife; and the law will protect them. Their children will be recognized as members of a family. Abraham made a big mistake by trying to hide his marriage with Sarah (Gen.12:10-20). Later, Isaac made the same mistake (Gen. 26:1-11). The mistakes of Abraham and Isaac guide us to be sure people know we are married. A public and legal marriage brings many blessings.

Q 14 *What does it mean for a husband and wife to be united? Give an example.*

2. Be united. It is not enough to leave parents. God says the husband and wife must be united. The word *united* means "to be like two papers glued together." Nothing can get between the two papers. The glued papers cannot be separated unless each paper is torn.[11]

The husband and wife should be united. Nothing should get between them—not parents, not children, not another man or woman, not work, not ministry, not anger, not jealousy. The marriage should not be torn apart. A husband and wife cannot be torn apart without great damage to both. Jesus said that when a husband and wife are united in marriage, no one should try to separate them (Matt. 19:6).

United is a special kind of love. This love is bigger and stronger than the husband and wife's feelings. It is based on the decision to be faithful to each other. It is built on the promise to always do what is best for the one you married. *United* love inspires wedding vows like:

"I promise to be faithful to you; to love, serve, protect, and honor you, in sickness and health, in poverty or wealth; forsaking all other lovers and clinging only to you until death separates us."

I promise to be faithful to you; to love, serve, protect, and honor you, in sickness and health, in poverty and wealth; forsaking all other lovers and clinging only to you until death separates us.

Figure 1.3
Sample wedding vow

3. Become one flesh. This phrase speaks of the physical joining of husband and wife. *"The wife's body does not belong to her alone but also to her husband. In the same way, the husband's body does not belong to him alone but also to his wife"* (1 Cor. 7:4). The husband and wife are still two people. They still possess their own bodies and thoughts. But when their bodies join together in sexual union, they become one flesh (1 Cor. 7:5).

Q 15 *What things do a husband and wife share when they become one flesh?*

This joining is so private that it is hard to speak about it. God gave this sexual union to husbands and wives to help them be close to each other. Closeness needs to happen

How to Understand Marriage and the Family   21

with our thoughts and feelings as well as with our bodies. We refer to this closeness as *intimacy. The joining of bodies should happen in a way that will help husband and wife to be close physically, and also in other ways. The full meaning of *"one flesh"* is that the husband and wife share all of themselves. They share their possessions, their thoughts, their feelings, and their bodies. They do this without fear, knowing that they love each other as they love themselves. They have become *"one flesh."*

Summary. God's pattern for marriage includes three actions: leaving, being united, and becoming one flesh. Notice that children are not mentioned. God blessed Adam and Eve before He told them to have children (Gen. 1:28). A marriage is complete before God, even if no children are born.[12] But these three parts of marriage form a warm, safe dwelling place for the husband, the wife, and any child that may be born.

> GOD'S PATTERN FOR MARRIAGE INCLUDES THREE ACTIONS: LEAVING, BEING UNITED, AND BECOMING ONE FLESH.

Conclusion

Some may say, "God's plan for the family is impossible. God's ideas about marriage could only work in a perfect world. These are old ideas from an old time." It is true that marriage began long ago in the Garden of Eden. And it is true that the sin of Adam and Eve damaged marriage. Blame and shame came between Adam and Eve. Pain and sorrow filled childbirth. Hardship and sweat made work more difficult. One day, even murder came into their family. But God did not give up on people, and He did not give up on marriage or the family.

Thousands of years after Eden, someone asked Jesus about marriage. From Eden to the birth of Jesus, God had been watching the earth. He saw all of the adultery, *prostitution, polygamy, *homosexuality, divorce, abuse, and sadness. But when Jesus was asked about marriage, He said, [4]*"At the beginning the Creator 'made them male and female,'* [5]*and said, 'For this reason a man will leave his father and mother and be united to his wife, and the two will become one flesh'"* (Matt. 19:4-5). Jesus pointed us again to the beginning. What was good in Eden is still good for our world today. God still wants us to follow His plan. God's grace is our hope and our help.

God's Purposes for the Family
Goal: *Explain at least 8 purposes of marriage and family.*

A. Marriage and the family provide fellowship (Gen. 2:20-23).

God created Adam and put him in a perfect place. He had a beautiful garden to care for. He could talk to God at times. But there was not another human. God said, *"It is not good for the man to be alone"* (Gen. 2:18).

Q 16 *Why is it not good for a man to live alone?*

People need fellowship. We need to talk with another human, to share our thoughts and our feelings. We need to feel accepted and loved—to give to others and to receive from them. These types of fellowship make us feel complete and worthwhile.

Why did God wait to create the woman? Sometimes we do not understand how important something is until we do without it. Perhaps God wanted to teach the man that he needed the woman. Then the man would understand her great value. By the time God brought the woman to Adam, he was prepared to receive her joyfully.

A man's wife died. Then he understood the great value of his wife's friendship. In the morning, he fixed his own breakfast in silence. He drove to the special place where he and his wife liked to eat and talk, but he was lonely. In the evening, he started home to share a meal, and share his thoughts about his day. But he remembered that he would be alone. He longed to hear her voice, to feel her presence, and to share his thoughts with her. But there was only silence.[13]

Adam recognized something of himself in his wife. *"This is now bone of my bones and flesh of my flesh"* (Gen. 2:23). He could love her as he loved himself.[14] She was valuable to him.

B. Marriage and the family provide help.

Q 17 *What work did God give to both the man and the woman?*

God saw that it was not good for man to be alone. He made Eve to help Adam. Then, He gave them the commands to multiply, subdue the earth, and rule over the fish, birds, and land animals (Gen.1:26-28). Together they could fulfill the commands God gave them.

Q 18 *How is the word "helper" used in other places in the Old Testament?*

A helper is not an inferior person. The Old Testament uses the Hebrew word for *helper* 21 times. It is used twice for the woman. But it is used 15 times to describe God as the *helper* of his people.[15] Psalm 115:9-11 repeats three times, *"Trust in the LORD—he is their help and shield."* God is certainly not below those He helps. The woman, even though she is called *"helper,"* is not of less value than the man. Men and women are of equal value in the eyes of God.

An ancient proverb says that if God meant for woman to rule over man, He would have created her from the top of Adam's head. In contrast, if God had meant for woman to be a slave, He would have created her from the bottom of Adam's foot. But God made woman from a bone in man's side because He wanted her to be a helper who was equal to him.

Q 19 *Why do you think God created woman from man's rib, instead of his head or foot?*

C. Marriage produces children.

Q 20 *Is it God's plan for a marriage to produce children? Explain.*

God planned marriage to create children. God told Adam and Eve, *"Be fruitful and increase in number"* (Gen. 1:28). God could have chosen many ways for children to be born. But God decided that children needed a mother and a father. He made babies to depend on their parents. The Lord's plan is to bind a baby to a husband and wife who love each other and love their child. The child can receive the proper care, and grow up safely to become an adult. Then, that mature child can find a mate and produce more children. The earth continues to have people today. Although some adults die daily, new children continue to be born.

Q 21 *What physical and mental needs does a family fulfill?*

D. Marriage and the family provide for physical and mental needs.

Physical needs. As the husband and wife work together, they produce shelter, food, clothing, care, and protection for the family. Look around at those who are not part of a family. Orphans suffer. Widows may lack someone to care for them. If you come from a good family, remember its blessings. Stop for a minute and think of all the physical blessings you have because you are part of a family.

Figure 1.4 Baby turtles are left without parents. A large number die within the first hours after hatching.

Mental needs. A family plans for the educational needs of its members. Not all family members receive the same education. But most of the time, whatever education there is comes because of the family.

E. Marriage and the family provide for emotional needs.

Q 22 *A family provides emotional support in which 3 types of struggles?*

Likewise, the family provides for the emotional needs of its members. Every person has struggles in the difficult seasons of life. Things do not always go as planned. Sickness visits every home. We need a place of care, stability, and security. The Bible tells us that *"he who fears the LORD has a secure fortress, and for his children it will be a refuge"* (Prov. 14:26). Our family should feel that the home is a place of refuge and security. God created the family to provide help during financial pressures, emotional trials, and moral decisions. There are many struggles in life. But three common struggles are change, disappointment, and rejection (criticism).

How to Understand Marriage and the Family

1. **Change is a struggle.** Most people would like things to stay the same. But all of life includes change. We grow, have illnesses, make friends, and lose friends to death. We change jobs and locations. As parents, we go through the various seasons of life with our children. We are with them from the time they are babies until they become mature. As adults we go through seasons as well. Most people change from being single, to married, to parents, to middle-aged, to elderly, and perhaps to being a widow or widower. Each period of growth is unique and can be hard. Our family needs to be a group we can rely on—no matter which season of life we are going through. When life's changes come, the family should protect and support its members.

2. **Disappointment and failure cause many struggles.** As we mature, we need to understand that we cannot always win in life. We are disappointed when we do not get the job we applied for; when we do poorly at school; when we are not chosen for a team; or when our business fails. Things do not always happen as we desire. We can endure great disappointment in life when we have a family that prays for us and encourages us to keep trying. The Bible says; ⁹*"Two are better than one, because they have a good return for their work: ...* ¹²*A cord of three strands is not quickly broken"* (Eccl. 4:9, 12). Family members should pray for and encourage each other when a member has disappointment or failure.

3. **Rejection and criticism are common trials.** These can be among the hardest struggles in life. No one likes to be rejected, ridiculed, shamed, or criticized. Some of the most difficult rejection comes to children. Children often say cruel things. Children may criticize another child's size, color, parents, home, or even a handicap or illness. The sinful nature of every person appears in childhood. Most of us can remember painful times when we were embarrassed as a child. Someone said something about us—and it hurt. Having a home to go where we sense protection will help us through the "storm of rejection." At home we learn how to live together, to forgive one another, and to encourage each other.

Why is divorce so painful? Because the family that is meant to be a place of acceptance and love becomes a place of rejection and division. A broken family is like a broken roof—it does not protect well from the storm.

F. Marriage and the family enable members to learn how to live.

Families are learning centers. We learn the basic skills for life in the family: how to walk, talk, eat, work, rest, play, relate to people, worship, and make decisions. David wrote, *"Then our sons in their youth will be like well-nurtured plants, and our daughters will be like pillars carved to adorn a palace"* (Ps. 144:12). The Bible often compares the family to a growing garden or a pillar of strength. Children have a unique opportunity to grow and become strong before they leave the home. Paul wrote, *"Fathers, do not exasperate your children; instead, bring them up in the training and instruction of the Lord"* (Eph. 6:4). Training and instruction are to be in every home. Parents train their children about character, moral values, and relationships with God and others. Sons often become like their fathers. Daughters often become like their mothers. Children learn how to relate to a future spouse by watching their parents relate to each other. The home is a classroom where children learn by watching the examples of others. (We will study this in chapters 9 and 10.)

In the family, parents can learn as much as children. A father should learn to love and relate well to his wife and children. He should learn, through much effort and many mistakes, to be gentle, tolerant, kind, humble, and courteous with his family members. A wife should learn the best way to respond to, talk to, and please her husband. Parents should learn to teach, care for, and be examples for their children. As the children become teenagers, parents should learn new skills to love, listen, lead, communicate, counsel, and relate.

Q 23 *What are some types of change that most people face?*

Q 24 *What are some examples of emotional support in a family?*

Q 25 *What kinds of things do we learn in the home?*

Q 26 *What types of things do parents learn in the family?*

> **Parents need to ask themselves some important questions:**
> What am I learning from my family?
> What am I teaching my children about money, marriage, mercy, sexuality, character, integrity, work, and happiness?
> Am I teaching what I want them to learn?
> What do I want them to know—to leave home with?
> What do I want to pass on to the next generation?

Your home is a learning center. Through it, you may pass on your values to your children, grandchildren, and great-grandchildren.

G. Marriage and the family provide a place to learn to serve God.

Q 27 What are some ways that your family can serve God together?

The biblical basis for joy in the family is in Acts 16:34, *"He was filled with joy **because** he had come to believe in God—**he and his whole family.**"* Walking with God is the most important thing in life. When your whole family knows and loves the Lord, it fills a family with joy and unity. When you see your children sitting in church, worshiping or listening to the Word, rejoice! Families that pray together stay together.

Perhaps you have never thought of your family as a ministry team. Serving the Lord together as a family will bring joy and unite your family for a lifetime. *"You know that the **household** of Stephanas were the first converts in Achaia, and **they have devoted themselves to the service of the saints**"* (1 Cor. 16:15). The family of Stephanas ministered to the saints. They were all in the Lord's work. Your family can do the same thing through hospitality in your home, helping at the church, ministering to the poor, and giving of time and money to bless others. Your family can be a witness to your neighbors. No family is perfect, but your Christian family has light for the darkness and answers to the problems people face.

H. Marriage and the family provide a place to learn to be happy.

Q 28 What things can a family do to help each member learn to be happy?

The family is a place where people can relax and accept each other. In a family we have those who can comfort us about mistakes and hard times. It is a place where we can rest, laugh, get away from pressure, and enjoy life. But, too often these good things are missing in the home. The Bible tells husbands to *"Enjoy life with your wife"* (Eccl. 9:9). This verse in the Good News Bible says, *"Be happy with your wife and find your joy with the girl you married."* God wants the husband and wife to enjoy each other in marriage. God wants parents and children to enjoy each other and learn how to relax and laugh. He also wants all family members to learn how to accept each other's differences.

Q 29 What is the lesson of the story about "kissed by an angel"?

Pastor Charles Swindoll wrote about the power of love to make the home a happy place. In a seminary there was a young man with a large birthmark across his face. The red mark stretched from the eyelid, across his lips, and down his neck to his chest. The man made his living in front of people—even with that birthmark. Charles asked his friend how he overcame that mark. His response was amazing. He said, "Oh, it was my dad. You see, my dad told me from my earliest days, 'Son, that's where an angel kissed you, and he marked you just for me. You are very special, and whenever we are in a group, I'll know which one you are. You are mine.'" The friend continued, "I felt sorry for people who didn't have red marks across the front of their face." The home is the best place for a child to learn to tolerate self and others. And the home is the best place a child can learn when to laugh, what to joke about, and how to enjoy other people. Remember that the Bible says, *"A cheerful heart is good medicine"* (Prov. 17:22).[16]

Parents are to enjoy their children and realize that they are a gift from God. ³*"Sons are a heritage from the LORD, children a reward from him. ⁴Like arrows in the hands of a warrior are sons born in one's youth. ⁵Blessed is the man whose quiver is full of them"* (Ps. 127:3-5). Families are a place to celebrate and rejoice.

Conclusion

Figure 1.5 The family is one of God's first gifts to every child.

God's purpose for marriage and the family is to bless the people He has created. Families provide a place for love, provision, and care. God's plan is for every person in the world to belong to a family. The family is one of God's first gifts to every child. Genesis 1:31 says, *"God saw all that he had made, and it was very good."* When we see God's gracious purpose in creating the family, we can also say, "It is very good."

In this chapter, we have studied the ideal family: a husband and wife with children. No family is perfect, but any family can be helpful. Blended families are created when a spouse remarries after death or divorce. Either the man or woman has children who become part of a blended family. In single-parent families, children are raised by one parent. Other conditions can make it necessary for children to be raised by their extended family—uncles or aunts, or even non-family. Still, God meets us where we are. His Word gives wisdom for every situation. God invites every family to grow in grace—like the grace He gives as you study this course.

Three Stages of Growth in Marriage
Goal A: *Contrast Stages One and Two of marriage.*
Goal B: *Describe 7 characteristics of mature love.*

The Bible tells us, *"By wisdom a house is built, and through understanding it is established"* (Prov. 24:3). In other words, God wants you to be wise and understand how to build your marriage and family.

The wise couple will understand that there are common stages in a marriage. Many marriages fail because of ignorance. People enter marriage, but do not know how to succeed in it for life. Many believe that the emotion of romantic love will carry them through life. They do not realize that difficult times come to any marriage. After only a few weeks of marriage, some people say, "He (or she) has changed; this is not the person I married. I have no idea what went wrong!" Most of the time this occurs because people who were marrying did not really know each other. They did not want to see faults in each other, or they did not count the cost. Before marriage, people learn to please themselves or their families. But when two people marry, they must learn to please each other. The Bible tells us to *"Submit to one another out of reverence for Christ"* (Eph. 5:21). Many times married people refuse to learn to submit to one another. But a husband and wife should become closer through the **three stages of growth in marriage.**

A. Stage One: Getting to know your spouse

The Song of Solomon is mostly about the first stage of marriage. ²*"Like a lily among thorns is my darling among the maidens. ³Like an apple tree among the trees of the forest is my lover among the young men"* (Song of Songs 2:2-3). Often a new marriage is full of energy, *naiveté (innocence), and surprises. The early months of marriage are a time to learn about each other. Five sentences describe a couple during this first stage of marriage:

- **They are attracted to each other.** Their attention is focused on each other. The couple spends much time thinking about each other. They forget other things, and walk around smiling about the one they have married.

Q 30 ✎ *In your own words, summarize the feelings of Stage One in marriage.*

- **They see only the best in each other.** In the first stage of marriage, people tend to think of their partner on a high level. Solomon wrote: *"How beautiful you are, my darling! Oh, how beautiful! Your eyes behind your veil are doves"* (Song 4:1). During these early days, married partners praise and admire each other. Each is perfect in the other's eyes.
- **They submit to each other.** At first, new couples *give in* to each other, and *give up* their rights. They submit to each other to have harmony. They are tender with each other and like to be together. They care about each other's needs.
- **They enjoy each other.** Early in marriage the partners are very happy. They have a feeling of well-being. Everything seems great, and they are encouraged.

Solomon writes from this point of view throughout the Song of Songs. He feels all the emotion of Stage One: joy, happiness, and excitement. But there is one more sentence that describes this stage.

- **They ignore the faults of each other.** The fact is, at the beginning of a marriage, you really do not know the other person. You are in love with an ideal of him or her. You do not know what your spouse is really like, and you do not know your future. In those early months couples tend to ignore differences and overlook faults. They put odd things aside. Often, they ignore major problems.

This first stage of marriage does not last, because it *cannot* last. Sooner or later, couples become aware of differences and faults. They have different personalities, different *temperaments, and different responsibilities. The *honeymoon (first period of enthusiasm) will end, and they must go back to work. When this stage passes, we come to Stage Two.

B. Stage Two: Understanding and growing through differences

The man who wrote Song of Songs also wrote Proverbs 27. In Song of Songs, Solomon was saying, "You are perfect! You are flawless. There is nothing wrong with you. Marriage is great! I am in love!" After a time Solomon says this about his wife, [15]*"A quarrelsome wife is like a constant dripping on a rainy day;* [16]*restraining her is like restraining the wind or grasping oil with the hand"* (Prov. 27:15-16).

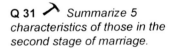

Q 31 Summarize 5 characteristics of those in the second stage of marriage.

What happened? It sounds like his joy in marriage and his joy about his wife disappeared. During this stage, delight *can* turn to confusion, bitterness, and tension. Here are five descriptions about what can happen to the husband and wife in Stage Two.

- **They become dull.** Routine and boredom become part of the couple's life. Most excitement is gone, like a Coke that had the lid left off of it. There is some loss of interest and some change in feelings. People do not care much about the way they look, because they cannot look perfect all the time. The honeymoon (first stage) is over, and now the partners begin to realize that marriage is like life—some days are wonderful, but many are slow, dull, routine, or even boring.
- **They argue.** The couple begins to quarrel over their differences. They no longer give up and give in. Strife enters the marriage.
- **They defend themselves.** The partners start protecting themselves. They are not as open and trusting as they were. They do not want the other to accuse them of their faults. They start protecting themselves. They excuse themselves and accuse their mate. Resentment and bitterness can build up. They can become defensive and unwilling to admit faults or to mature.
- **They criticize each other.** In the first stage, husbands, like Solomon, say, "Everything she does is right!" And "she is perfect!" Now, very

Figure 1.6 In Stage Two, respect can move out, as criticism moves in.

little seems right. What a change in attitude. The wife says, "I do not respect him anymore." Respect moves out and criticism moves in.
- **They become disappointed.** The couple's dreams are not coming true. Sometimes people have said, "I feel trapped," or "I would rather be single again than be married to this selfish person." Others have said, "I am not happy, and I know God wants me happy; so I should get a divorce." They are disappointed.

Many couples give up at this stage and seek divorce. Some make the mistake of trying to find feelings of love with another person. This unfaithfulness often destroys their marriage. Others become stuck in this stage of discouragement. They do not make the effort to work through this stage, and understand their spouse. Because of these five reactions, many never know how wonderful marriage can be. They do not cross over the valley of disappointment to the mountain of mature love.

Q 32 Why is Stage Two a dangerous time in marriage?

C. Stage Three: Mature love

Stage Three is described in 1 Corinthians 13—the "love chapter."

> ⁴*Love is patient, love is kind. It does not envy, it does not boast, it is not proud.* ⁵*It is not rude, it is not self-seeking, it is not easily angered, it keeps no record of wrongs.* ⁶*Love does not delight in evil but rejoices with the truth.* ⁷*It always protects, always trusts, always hopes, always perseveres.* ⁸*Love never fails* (1 Cor. 13:4-8).

In Stage Three, we see mature love. This is not *romantic feelings. It is mature love. Love is a decision to do the right thing, and say the right thing, and to be the right person. Let us look at **seven characteristics of mature love.**

1. Mature love is tender. Every marriage needs tenderness. We must be gentle and not judge each other. We must be careful with each other's feelings. We must be tender and avoid embarrassing our spouse. We realize that we are on the same team and we refuse to criticize or destroy each other.

Q 33 Describe mature love.

2. Mature love is responsible. We respect our spouse and treat him or her with thankfulness. We fulfill our duty to build a good marriage.

3. Mature love is accepting. The only way to make it to Stage Three is to know and accept our differences. We will never be alike, and that is good. God created every husband and wife unique. We know we have different personalities and temperaments—and different faults—and we still find a way to accept the one we married.

Q 34 Explain the proverb: "Before marriage keep both eyes open, but after marriage close one."

As a wise man said, "Before marriage keep both eyes open, but after marriage close one."

Even the best marriages will have stormy days. A grandmother—who was celebrating her 50th wedding anniversary—told the secret of her long and happy marriage. On her wedding day, she decided to make a list of *ten* of her husband's faults. Then for the sake of their marriage, she overlooked and forgave the faults. A guest asked the woman to explain some of the faults that she had chosen to overlook. The grandmother said that she never did make the list. But whenever her husband did something that made her mad, she said to herself, "Lucky for him that is one of the ten!"¹⁷ *"Accept one another, then, just as Christ accepted you, in order to bring praise to God"* (Rom. 15:7).

Q 35 Summarize the story about "that is one of the ten."

4. Mature love is secure. Mature love offers security that says, "No matter what happens, we will make it together." Spouses must feel that both will remain faithful if they lose a job, lose health, or fail to reach their goals. This commitment brings security to both husband and wife. It also brings a deep sense of security to the children. During difficult times, they should know that Mom and Dad would do whatever it takes to make the marriage succeed.

5. Mature love is truthful and open. Mature love is truthful. *"Love ... rejoices with the truth"* (1 Cor. 13:6). As couples, we must be open—honest with each other—and

Q 36 Describe love that is mature and open.

able to say what we feel. We must be truthful, but tender. The Bible calls this *"speaking the truth in love"* (Eph. 4:15).

The Bible instructs believers *to "confess your sins to each other and pray for each other so that you may be healed"* (James 5:16). There are many couples that need to be healed. Their marriage is sick. Many husbands and wives need to confess their sins (faults) to each other and pray for each other. How can a relationship be healed? Through confession and prayer. As a couple, we must be willing to reveal our thoughts. Reaching the third stage requires much honest communication. Mature love says, "This is where I am hurting." Or, "This is what I do not like." "This is what I need. What do you need?" "What is hurting you?" We need to stop hiding our feelings and opinions and be honest with each other.

Q 37 *Do you know adults who pout like Ahab? Explain.*

6. Mature love is humble. Some people sulk, pout, and brood. Ahab was like this when Naboth refused to sell him a vineyard. The king was so angry he would not talk. He lay on his bed and refused to eat (1 Kings 21:4). If a husband or wife refuses to talk, this can kill a marriage. Some people threaten to walk out. Others use sarcasm and ridicule to attack. Some people like to blame their spouse. If we waste time and energy trying to find out who is at fault, we cannot fix the problem. Some people are always trying to change their partner. These actions are a form of pride and judging—and they will hurt a marriage. In contrast, mature love is humble. It learns to walk away from actions that reveal the pride of the flesh.

7. Mature love is willing to grow. If our marriage is mature, we have made the decision to grow up. Many selfish, childish Christians are married.

> [15]*Instead, speaking the truth in love, we will in all things grow up into him who is the Head, that is, Christ.* [16]*From him the whole body, joined and held together by every supporting ligament, grows and builds itself up in love, as each part does its work* (Eph. 4:15-16).

Conclusion

Change in a person is seldom sudden. Change takes little steps and walks slowly. As a child can grow slowly from a baby to an adult, people can grow together in marriage. In the process, they fulfill God's plan for their lives. And they enjoy the friendship and wonder of being heirs together of the precious gift of life (1 Pet. 3:7).

 ## Chapter Summary

 **A Biblical Foundation**

Goal A: *Explain the beginning, plan, and order for marriage.*

In the *beginning* God ordained marriage and the family.

God's *plan* for marriage is that each man should have only one wife.

The biblical *order* for a family touches three areas. The husband is the head of the wife. The wife is to submit to her husband. Children are to honor and obey their parents.

Goal B: *Explain the 3 actions of God's pattern for marriage.*

Leave father and mother. Be united. Become one flesh.

How to Understand Marriage and the Family

 God's Purposes for the Family

Goal: *Explain at least 8 purposes of marriage and family.*

Marriage and the family provide fellowship, help, and children. A family provides for physical, mental, and emotional needs. The family is a place to learn how to live, learn to serve God, and learn to be happy.

 Three Stages of Growth in Marriage

Goal A: *Contrast Stages One and Two of marriage.*

Stage One is getting to know your spouse. Spouses are attracted to each other. They see only the best in each other, submit to each other, enjoy each other, and ignore the faults of each other.

Stage Two is understanding and growing through differences. Spouses become dull, argue, defend themselves, criticize each other, and become disappointed.

Goal B: *Describe 7 characteristics of mature love.*

Stage Three is mature love. It is tender, responsible, accepting, secure, truthful and open, humble, and willing to grow.

 Test Yourself: Circle the letter by the *best* completion to each question or statement.

1. How many people are in the smallest family?
a) 1
b) 2
c) 3
d) 4

2. In marriage, which of these phrases is TRUE?
a) A wife is equal to her husband.
b) A wife is worth less than her husband.
c) A wife is worth more than her children.
d) A wife is worth more than her husband.

3. A sign that a man has left his parents is that he
a) has moved a great distance away.
b) no longer cares about his parents.
c) cares as much for his parents as his wife.
d) puts his wife and children first.

4. To be safe and honorable, a marriage must be
a) inside of a church.
b) planned for 2 years.
c) legal and public.
d) large and expensive.

5. As a husband and wife unite and become one flesh, they share
a) the same name.
b) the same house.
c) their bodies.
d) everything.

6. Who said that it is not good for man to be alone?
a) God
b) Satan
c) Man
d) Woman

7. What should a family provide for its members?
a) Salvation from sin
b) Escape from trials
c) A college degree
d) Emotional support

8. Song of Songs describes which stage of marriage?
a) Stage One
b) Stage Two
c) Stage Three
d) Stage Four

9. In which stage of marriage do people defend themselves and criticize their spouses?
a) Stage One
b) Stage Two
c) Stage Three
d) Stage Four

10. Stage Three of marriage is best described by
a) Matthew 1:1-17.
b) 1 Corinthians 13:4-8.
c) Hebrews 11:1-6.
d) Revelation 22:1-10.

Chapter 2:
How to Choose a Mate for Life

Introduction

Ruth Bell married Billy Graham, the famous evangelist. As a little girl, Ruth was raised in China. When she became a teenager, she went to school in Korea. Ruth wanted to be missionary to Tibet. She did not expect to find a husband, but she spent some time thinking about the kind of husband she would require. She wrote something like this:

If I marry, he must be so tall on his knees that he reaches all the way to heaven. His shoulders must be broad enough to carry a family. His lips must be strong enough to smile, firm enough to say no, and tender enough to kiss. His love must be so deep that it takes its stand in Christ, and so wide that it reaches out to the lost of the world. He must be active enough to save souls and big enough to be gentle. He must be great enough to be thoughtful. His arms must be strong enough to carry a little child.[1]

Figure 2.1
Choose a mate who **loves God as much as you do.**

Ruth Bell's desires for her husband were met when she married Billy Graham. Before a marriage, it is wise to consider the type of husband or wife desired. In this chapter we will look at how to choose a mate for life.

Lessons:

Ways to Choose a Mate
Goal A: *Summarize the differences between biblical love and fleshly love.*
Goal B: *Analyze the strengths and weaknesses of 3 methods to choose a mate.*

Ways to Prepare for a Mate
Goal A: *Explain the roles of friendship and purpose in preparing for a mate.*
Goal B: *Summarize 5 reasons for sexual purity in preparing for a mate.*
Goal C: *Describe 6 keys to living sexually pure while preparing for a mate.*

Good Questions to Ask Before Choosing a Mate
Goal: *Ask and answer questions on each of the 12 topics about choosing a mate.*

 ## Key Words

dating
courtship

arranged marriage
romantic feelings

chaperoned
virginity

Ways to Choose a Mate
Goal A: *Summarize the differences between biblical love and fleshly love.*
Goal B: *Analyze the strengths and weaknesses of 3 methods to choose a mate.*

Background

People choose a mate in three different ways around the world: *dating, *courtship, and *arranged marriages. Those who date cannot imagine that someone else could help choose a spouse. Those with arranged marriages cannot imagine marrying without the wisdom of their family members. But happy marriages can result from any of the three ways of choosing. Wisdom is needed in all of these methods.

Q 1 *In which 3 ways do people select a mate to marry?*

Love is an important part of marriage. Jacob's love for Rachel was so great that working 7 years to get her seemed like only a few days to him (Gen. 29:20). But love is deeper than just a feeling. There is a fleshly type of love that causes one person to be attracted to another. For example, consider the way Amnon *fell in love* with Tamar. Read the complete story in 2 Samuel 13:1-39.

Q 2 *How was the love Amnon felt for Tamar different than the love needed for marriage?*

> ¹*In the course of time, Amnon son of David **fell in love** with Tamar, the beautiful sister of Absalom son of David.* ... ¹⁵*Then Amnon hated her with intense hatred. In fact, **he hated her more than he had loved her.** Amnon said to her, "Get up and get out!"* (2 Sam. 13:1, 15).

Amnon *fell out* of love as quickly as he *fell in* love. This shallow, fleshly love happens often between a man and a woman. Millions of people can testify that this *in love* feeling does not last more than about 1 year in a marriage. In fact, sometimes the *in love* feeling lasts only a few weeks! Many people divorce as soon as the *in love* feeling is gone. Then they *fall in love* again, only to find that the *in love* feeling is gone again after a short time. So it is important to base the decision to marry on more than *feeling in love*.

A person must discern between *romantic (emotional) feelings and deep, biblical love. Sexual attraction and romantic feelings are shallow. That is why so many people can be "in love" with each other for a brief time. They are confused about what biblical love is. It is good for a husband and wife to have romance and sexual attraction. But those feelings must mature and become a part of mature, biblical love. Then the couple can have a happy marriage that endures. Let us look at the differences between fleshly love and mature, biblical love.²

Q 3 *Summarize the differences between biblical love and fleshly love.*

Fleshly Love	Biblical Love
Highly emotional	Uses head as well as heart
Starts suddenly and often stops suddenly	Gives time for love to grow
Self-centered; focused on how this makes me feel	Focuses on what is best for the other person
May feel a strong urge for immediate sex or marriage	Can wait while knowledge grows
Idealistic; cannot see the faults of the other	Realistic; knows faults and loves anyway
Emotional unity leaves if they disagree	Relationship is not in danger when disagreement comes
Looks for constant proofs that love is still present	Security is based on commitment until death parts

Figure 2.2 Fleshly love versus biblical love

The love needed for marriage includes sexual and emotional feelings—but it must be much deeper. The Bible says that a husband must love his wife *"as Christ loved the church and gave himself up for her"* (Eph. 5:25). **Love that will last for a lifetime is more of a decision than a feeling.** Feelings come and go. First Corinthians 13 describes deep, biblical love.

Q 4 *State the 5 characteristics of biblical love that you like best.*

> *Love is patient,*
> *love is kind.*
> *It does not envy,*
> *it does not boast, ...*
> *It is not easily angered,*
> *it keeps no record of wrongs.*
> *Love does not delight in evil*
> *but rejoices with the truth.*
> *It always protects,*
> *always trusts,*
> *always hopes,*
> *always perseveres.*
> *Love never fails.*

Figure 2.3   First Corinthians 13:4-8 describes biblical love.

Q 5 ⬉ *What do you think is the best thing about dating? What is the greatest danger?*

Now let us study three paths that can lead to a good marriage. Keep in mind that biblical love can be present on any of the three paths for finding a mate.

A. Dating can lead to a good marriage.

In Western nations, choosing a spouse is usually a personal decision. Two unmarried people *date*. A date is usually centered on some social event. On their date, they may eat a meal together, spend time alone, attend a public event, or attend church. Unmarried people may have dates many times, with various people. They date until they *fall in love*. Then, they may decide to marry. Around the world, youth have learned about dating and being in love. These ideas have come by television, videos, DVDs, movies, popular music, books, and magazines. All of these emphasize being *in love*.

The accepted order for many in the world is:
- Two people should be in love before they marry.
- Only those two persons can decide if love is present in their relationship.
- Dating is the way young men and women develop this type of love relationship.[3]

Often, youth date with little or no input from those who are more mature.

Dating gives a lot of freedom to a man and a woman. A date does not mean a person is interested in marriage. People may date many different people before they meet someone they want to marry. Figure 2.4 summarizes some strengths and weaknesses of dating.

Good Things About Dating	Dangers of Dating
It helps men and women know and understand each other better.	It presents opportunity (and sometimes pressure) for sexual immorality.
It helps men and women learn what kind of person they enjoy being with.	It tends to focus on physical beauty and attraction.
It helps men and women eliminate those they do not wish to marry.	It gives opportunity for fleshly love to develop between two people who should not marry.
It helps men and women learn to talk to one another and develop socially.	Feelings can be hurt when one person decides to stop dating the other person.
It can be a lot of fun.	It may increase social pressure on those young people who do not date.

Figure 2.4   Dating: Its strengths and weaknesses

Q 6 ↗ *Summarize the 7 standards for dating. Illustrate or explain 2 of them.*

A believer whose culture practices dating should set standards to lessen the dangers.[4] Consider seven standards:
- Parents should decide the age for dating to begin. The young person must be old enough to have good judgment and to understand dating responsibilities.
- Date only Christians. This helps protect against marriage to an unbeliever.
- The parents should know the person their son or daughter is dating.
- Agree on dating activities. Places and activities should not hinder one's testimony.
- Avoid any expressions of affection that arouse sexual desire. Maintain sexual purity.
- Limit time alone.
- In public behavior, show respect for others.

Q 7 ↗ *How do some youth groups avoid the dangers of dating, but fulfill social needs?*

The dating path to marriage is not very old. Dating has caused many problems. A large percentage of the youth in America are no longer virgins because of dating. Many youth groups in American churches no longer encourage dating. In such churches, the youth do things as a group. This fulfills the social needs of youth. But a boy and girl do not go places alone. Thus, the youth have fun and fellowship, but they avoid the dangers of dating.

B. Courtship can lead to a good marriage.

Courtship is similar to dating—the man and woman choose to spend time together. They may spend time alone or with other friends. In courtship, the young man or woman only goes out alone with someone they may want to marry. The time together is for the purpose of deciding if they want to marry each other. In some cultures, courtship must be approved by the family and is *chaperoned—supervised and attended by an adult.

Q 8 *What do you think is the best thing about courtship? What is its greatest danger?*

Good Things About Courtship	Dangers of Courtship
It allows the couple to see if they enjoy and respect each other before marriage occurs.	Rejection after courtship can be painful.
It reduces the opportunity for sexual immorality.	There is still some danger of sexual sin.
It is serious about the decision to marry.	It can make a person feel judged rather than enjoyed.
It encourages people to spend their social time in groups of friends rather than alone.	It can limit a person's understanding of the differences in people, (unless a person develops social skills and studies people day by day).

Figure 2.5   Courtship: Its strengths and weaknesses

A young man courted his beloved for 2 years. He said, "This has helped to build a strong bond of understanding and expectations of each other. We talked a lot during those days. We talked about our hopes, our wishes, our school days, and our lives. We met almost every day of the week after work. After 15 years of marriage, I am still thankful for those 2 years of communication. They have added much to our bond together. Now, I am busy with the responsibilities of being a husband, father, church helper, and a manager at work. I realize that those 2 years were a privilege and a luxury!"[5]

C. Arranged engagements can lead to good marriages.

In most societies throughout history, parents chose mates for their children. Society has believed that parents gain wisdom through the years. This wisdom qualifies them to plan marriages. Today, around the world, the process for arranging marriages varies. In some places, the couple has little to say about the marriage. Perhaps they do not talk to each other until the wedding. But in most places, engagements are arranged between people who know each other. And the young person may be able to agree with or reject the parents' choice. Sometimes, the young person begins the process by asking parents to arrange a marriage to a certain person. These marriages can be happy marriages. Even those who did not know each other at all have learned to love each other after marriage. For example, the marriage between Isaac and Rebekah was arranged (Gen. 24). When parents plan a marriage, it unites two families, not just two people.[6] Still, it is possible for any type of marriage to unite two families.

Q 9 *What do you think is the best thing about arranged engagements? What is the greatest danger?*

In some cultures, marriage is linked to a *bride-price*. The groom must pay money or animals to the family of the bride. Laban required a bride-price for Rachel and Leah (Gen. 29). A bride-price is common when parents plan a marriage. But this old custom still exists in cultures where parents used to plan marriages. A bride-price shows that the groom values the bride. Also, the bride-price supports parents in their old age. In contrast, a bride-price may prevent a young man from marrying the young woman he chooses. Jacob worked 7 years to pay the bride-price for Rachel!

Q 10 *Is buying a ring for the bride like paying a bride-price? Explain.*

Q 11 *What are some strengths and weaknesses of a bride-price?*

There is a story about a man who gave eight cows for his bride, even though the father only required one. This caused the bride to stand up straighter than other women. She knew she had great worth in her husband's eyes.

In contrast to the bride-price is the *dowry*. This is wealth that the father of the bride gives her. This dowry gives some wealth to the new couple that marries. In this system, the bride brings the dowry with her into the marriage. After her marriage, Caleb gave his daughter, Acsah, a field and two springs (Judges 1:12-15).

Q 12 *How much should youth depend on parents in choosing a mate? Explain.*

Q 13 *Summarize the strengths and weaknesses of arranged engagements.*

The world is changing. In some nations, parents still plan the marriages for their children. But in most places, parents are planning fewer marriages than in the past. Today, the most common reason for marriage is romantic love. This is one reason that divorce is increasing. Around the world, youth are deciding whom they will marry. Still, wise youth always listen to the advice of their parents. One father told his son, "Never date a girl you would not marry. And when you date, treat the girl like you want a man to treat your sister." Years later, the son was glad he obeyed his father's wise words.

Good Things About Arranged Engagements	Dangers of Arranged Engagements
They draw from the wisdom of elders.	The elders may not be seeking what is best for the couple.
They have the approval of both families.	The couple may not be attracted to each other.
They may bring financial resources to the family.	The financial arrangements may bring great burdens.
They discourage divorce more than other methods.	There may be a great difference between age and interests of the man and woman.
They usually enforce sexual purity.	The standard of purity for the woman is often higher than the standard for the man.
Fewer people are left without spouses in these cultures.	Elders in the family may prevent the marriage that a couple desires.

Figure 2.6 Arranged engagements: Strengths and weaknesses

The person seeking a mate should be encouraged. A good marriage can happen in different ways. No matter what your culture or customs, God can bless you with a good spouse.

Ways to Prepare for a Mate
Goal A: Explain the roles of friendship and purpose in preparing for a mate.
Goal B: Summarize 5 reasons for sexual purity in preparing for a mate.
Goal C: Describe 6 keys to living sexually pure while preparing for a mate.

Setting
Most people will get married. But **all of us** will be unmarried for a time—*single for a few years. Some people are unmarried for a short time while they seek a mate. Others become single again through death or divorce. And some remain unmarried throughout their lives. In this lesson, we will consider direction for our lives when we are unmarried.

A. Prepare for a mate by making friends and having fellowship.
We all share Adam's need for friendship. Unmarried people have no spouse to fellowship with, but they must not ignore the need for friendship. Friendship is a need of all humans. A single person's life will become weak without friends.

Q 14 *How can an unmarried person fulfill the need for fellowship?*

The single person must seek and keep strong friendships. A person may find a good friend in a family member—such as a parent, brother, or sister. Or, outside the family, there are often deep friendships between those of the same faith. David and Jonathan were close friends (1 Sam. 20). The single person can find friends among believers—those who share common interests in things such as work, music, and recreation.

Most scholars think Paul was unmarried. Still, we know he developed many deep friendships.
- He became a friend to Priscilla and Aquila **through his work** as a tentmaker (Acts 18:1-3).

How to Choose a Mate for Life 35

- He had fellowship with people who **shared in his ministry**. Barnabas, Silas, Timothy, and Titus are examples of Paul's friends. The greetings in his letters reflect the many deep friendships he formed through shared ministry.
- Paul had friendships **within his family** (Rom. 16:7, 11, 21).
- Paul also had close relationships with those **to whom he ministered**. The Ephesian elders were very close to Paul. They wept together when he left for Jerusalem (Acts 20:13–21:14). Their love was deep and enduring. They pleaded with Paul to avoid his suffering and stay with them. It was so hard for Paul to bear that he cried out, *"Why are you weeping and breaking my heart?"* (Acts 21:13). The Bible does not mention that Paul had a wife, but his life was rich in friendship (1 Cor. 9:5-6; Rom. 16:1-16).

Q 15 *Name 4 areas of life in which Paul made friends.*

Some single people are always looking for a spouse. They are lonely and think that marriage is the only answer. They may not know that married people also feel lonely from time to time. But there are many opportunities for fellowship without being married.

Married people and churches sometimes forget the fellowship needs of a single person. Married couples fellowship with other married couples. The church often speaks of marriage and family. But the church may err by looking past the unmarried. Single people can feel ignored by married people and by the church. This should not be true among us. The family of God should be a place of fellowship for all who believe.

Figure 2.7 An unmarried person can find friends in many places.

B. Prepare for a mate by finding and fulfilling your purpose in life.

Q 16 *How can the church meet the fellowship needs of the unmarried?*

Most single people greatly desire to get married. They may dream of the future so much that they neglect the present. They may think too much about the day when their lives will be fulfilled in marriage. But wise singles understand that God has a purpose for *every* day. God desires all single people to accomplish His purposes. Living with a purpose makes a person feel valuable, satisfied, and fulfilled. **Single people who desire to marry should know that they are more attractive to others when they live with purpose.** This is very important. Those with a purpose are excited about life, and anointed by God. This draws others to them. A person who is "just waiting" seems desperate, empty, cold, and needy to others. Which kind of person would you choose to marry—one dreaming about the future, or one living every day with joy and purpose?

Q 17 *Why does one who lives for a purpose attract others?*

C. Prepare for a mate by discerning the reasons for sexual purity (1 Cor. 6:9-20).

Q 18 *What are 6 reasons why God does not approve any sex outside of marriage?*

God's plan is for a man and woman to become one flesh in marriage. He blesses marriage because it is His plan. There are several reasons why God blesses sexual relations **only** within marriage.

Q 19 *What sexual union does God bless?*

1. God commands sexual purity because of our relationship with Him.
Salvation impacts the whole person. It is not just our spirits that are saved. Our bodies are temples of the Holy Spirit.

Q 20 *How does sexual purity reflect our unity with Christ?*

Since our bodies are temples of the Holy Spirit, we must remain sexually pure. Sexual immorality—any sexual union outside of marriage—is a sin against the body and against Christ Himself. Our bodies are for Christ, not for sexual sins (1 Cor. 6:18-20).

36   Marriage & Family

Exodus 40:34-38　　　　1 Kings 8:6-13　　　　1 Corinthians 6:19
A **past** dwelling place　　A **past** dwelling place　　A **present** dwelling place
　　of the Spirit　　　　　　　of the Spirit　　　　　　　　of the Spirit

Figure 2.8　Your body is the temple of the Holy Spirit (1 Cor. 6:19).

Q 21 ➤ *How does sexual purity protect people from some diseases?*

2. Sexual purity protects from disease. People everywhere are learning that sex outside of marriage brings disease and death. Sexual diseases are spreading. AIDS is destroying families and entire nations. Doctors have no cure for AIDS or many sexual diseases. Yet God has told us how to avoid sexual diseases. Remain *chaste—sexually pure—if you are single. Remain faithful if you are married. Sexual purity protects people from many diseases. Through AIDS, one prostitute spread death to more than 300 men!

Q 22 ➤ *How has pregnancy outside of marriage affected your culture?*

3. Sexual purity protects fathers, mothers, and children. A man who is sexually pure and faithful never wonders if he has unknown children. He never lives with the guilt of leaving a woman or a child.

Sexual purity protects women. Single women who remain sexually pure never suffer from the heartbreak of children outside of marriage. A woman and her child are blessed when her pregnancy is within the dignity of marriage.

Every child needs a father and a mother. David said that *"**goodness and love**"* would follow him all the days of his life (Ps. 23:6). But **poverty and suffering** often follow the woman and child left by a lover outside of marriage. God's plan is not for *illegitimate, unwanted children (Heb. 12:8). The presence, protection, and provision of a father bless a child. Sexual purity brings God's blessings to all. The Lord's plan brings blessing and adds no sorrow!

Q 23 ➤ *Explain how sex outside of marriage harms the emotions.*

4. Sexual purity protects the emotions. A sexual union can affect a person's emotions forever. Many societies encourage a couple to try sex and live together—to see if they want to marry. But this is rebellion against God's wisdom. The commitment of marriage protects the emotions. Then, in security, the couple can learn to live and love each other. Sexual union without commitment often causes a person to feel insecure and of less value. Sex outside of marriage makes people feel cheap. Men, women, and children feel of little worth because of sex outside of marriage (See Prov. 6:26). They feel like *used goods* instead of feeling *new*. In contrast, remaining pure protects the way a person feels about self. Sexual purity raises a person's value in his or her own eyes, and in the eyes of others. Proverbs 31:10 states that a woman with virtue has great value. *"A wife of noble character who can find? She is **worth far more than rubies**."* Sexual purity protects the emotion of self-esteem.

Q 24 ➤ *Do you think casual sex hurts men and women in the same way?*

Casual sex between unmarried people deadens the emotions. A person is seen as an object to be used. The only thing important in casual sex is selfish desire. The user and the one being used cannot escape damage to their emotions. When two people have sex, they become one flesh (1 Cor. 6:16). This union unites bodies and emotions. Tearing this

How to Choose a Mate for Life

one flesh apart will cause damage, like tearing two pieces of paper apart that were glued together. A part of each must remain with the other.

Sex *before* marriage affects emotions *after* marriage. Guilt and feelings of betrayal may trouble the marriage. Sexual memories may cause a person to compare a spouse to a former sexual partner. The person who has had other sexual partners may have a harder time remaining faithful to a spouse. Jealousy and insecurity may come when a person learns a spouse has had past sexual partners. There are many negative emotions from sex outside of marriage. Sexual purity protects a person's emotional life.

5. Sexual purity leads to trust and security. When sex is only within marriage, there is no fear of disease. There is no guilt of infecting your spouse and children. If a child is conceived, the man is certain that he is the father. The woman is certain of support. And the child is certain who the parents are. *Intimacy—closeness—is strengthened by knowing that neither person had sex with anyone else. Neither spouse is compared with another person in the sexual union. They can each learn to please each other. A valuable and precious gift that you can give your future spouse is your *virginity—your sexual purity. Do not give this great gift away before marriage—save it for the special person you will love for a lifetime!

D. Prepare for a mate by remaining sexually pure.

Here are some keys to help you remain sexually pure.

1. Do not let the world squeeze you into its mold or pattern (Rom. 12:1-2). Sinners do whatever their lusts lead them to do. They approve of those who rebel against God. In contrast, Christians do not live by the world's standards. They follow God's plan.

2. Fulfill sexual desire in the way that God approves. The desire for food is a normal part of being human. But a person should not steal food; he should work to buy it. Likewise, sexual desire is normal. Work and plan for marriage. Then you can fulfill your sexual desires through God's plan.

3. Renew your mind (Rom. 12:1-2). There are two parts to this. *First,* we must protect our minds from the things that feed sexual desire. Many choices about entertainment increase sexual desire. We must control what we think, read, watch, and talk about. We must pull down bad thoughts and make them bow to Jesus (2 Cor. 10:5). Jesus wants to be Lord of our thoughts. Likewise, we must manage our time with others so that we avoid situations where sexual temptation is strong. *Second,* we must fill our minds with good things. Philippians 4:7-9 teaches us that thinking about noble and pure things helps us to guard our minds and hearts.

4. Use personal energy in good ways. The Bible warns men, *"Do not spend your strength on women, your vigor on those who ruin kings"* (Prov. 31:3). Many kings like Solomon wasted their strength in sex with many women. In contrast, a man should use his strength for good things—like work, worship, family, ministry, or community life. An idle mind is the devil's workshop. Do something good instead of something bad.

5. Walk in the Spirit and you will not fulfill the desires of the flesh (Gal. 5:16). Believers are not led by the sinful nature (the flesh), but by the Spirit (Rom. 8:4). If the Spirit causes you to feel guilty in an area of your life, repent and turn in a better direction. Submit to the Spirit. But reject guilt that is not from God. For example, do not feel guilty about what happens while you sleep! The body must have sexual release. Men's bodies produce sexual fluids that the body releases. Sexual tension builds in both men and women. Men and some women experience sexual release while they are sleeping (Lev. 15:16-17). This often comes with a dream. It is best to accept this as the way our bodies provide for sexual release. Dreams are mysterious. They are not always from God. A sexual dream does not always show a problem with character. If we are

Q 25 *How can sex before marriage affect sex after marriage?*

Q 26 *Explain the trust and security that comes from sexual purity.*

Q 27 *What pressures about sex does the single person face in your culture?*

Q 28 *Does God want people to enjoy sex? Explain.*

Q 29 *How can a person renew his mind?*

Q 30 *Why should a person not feel guilty about sexual dreams?*

seeking to keep a pure mind and body when we are awake, we do not need to accept guilt for sexual dreams. God made your body the way it is—He created your *plumbing!

Q 31 *If a person has repented and turned from sin, is guilt that remains from God or Satan? Explain.*

6. Accept grace for your past, and move forward in holiness. God is serious about sexual sin. Breaking His commands brings many bad results. But, thank God, His grace can cover sexual sins. First Corinthians 6:9-11 states,

> [9]*Neither the sexually immoral nor idolaters nor adulterers nor male prostitutes nor homosexual offenders* [10]*…will inherit the kingdom of God.* [11]***And that is what some of you*** ***were****. **But*** *you were* ***washed****, you were* ***sanctified****, you were* ***justified*** *in the name of the Lord Jesus Christ and by the Spirit of our God.*

God forgives all who repent and turn away from sin (1 John 1:9).

③ Good Questions to Ask Before Choosing a Mate
Goal: *Ask and answer questions on each of the 12 topics about choosing a mate.*

Setting

When he was young, a man decided not to marry until he met the perfect woman. Years later, he met her, but she was looking for the perfect man![7]

Know yourself before seeking a mate. Imagine a man shopping for clothing without knowing his size. How long should the garment be? How big around should it be to fit the man? First, he must be measured. Then he can find the right clothes. A person must know self in order to find the right mate or match. This lesson contains over **100 questions about choosing a mate**! Ask these questions to yourself before you ask them to another. In class, a teacher might like to have students ask these questions to each other.

Q 32 *If feelings alone may lead us astray, what can guide us to choose a good mate?*

Suppose Esther thinks Peter might be a good person to marry. How can she know? She should observe him in various situations. She should discover his reputation in the community and the church. If possible, she should talk with him a lot. She should ask questions, be a good listener, and share her views. There are over *100 questions* in this lesson. Any couple that is thinking about marriage should ask these questions to each other. It would be wise for the couple and a third person to discuss these questions.

Q 33 *What can churches do to help young people make good decisions about choosing a mate?*

A pastor or elder can use these 100 questions as a guide for *pre-marital counseling. A sensitive counselor will be aware when a person does not feel free to express true thoughts. A shy, timid person may need to discuss sexual issues with a person of the same sex, rather than with the pastor or future spouse. But the couple should be aware of the sexual issues each person will bring to marriage.

Q 34 *Why should questions be asked over time in several sessions?*

Pre-marital counseling should happen over several periods or sessions. This gives the couple time to think and talk about issues that arise. Some pastors will assign topics for the couple to discuss between counseling sessions. The pastor may discover things the couple has neglected. For example, he may assign them the task of preparing a budget. He may give a book or paper to read. He may have them spend more time with each other's family. (If you are asking these 100 questions to each other, you may also give yourselves homework to do.)

Q 35 *Which 3 guidelines for asking questions do you like best? Explain.*

Soon, we will give you the 100 questions to consider before choosing whom to marry. But first, consider these guidelines when you ask questions:

- Smile! Ask questions in a friendly, relaxed way.
- Do not ask one question after another, like you are throwing rocks or shooting bullets. Take time to talk between questions. Then the person will not feel like he or she is a target or taking a test.
- Ask questions that cannot be answered with one word.

- Ask the person's opinion. Most people would rather talk about themselves than listen.
- Begin with easy questions. Do not ask questions that are too personal at first.
- After asking a question, focus your complete attention on the person. Listen carefully.
- Do not talk too much. Give the other person time to talk.

A. Questions about the basics

Questions 1–7 help the pastor and couple know if they need more time before deciding to marry.

1. How long have you known each other?
2. How much time have you spent together?
3. How did you meet?
4. What kinds of things have you done together?
5. What do your families and friends think of your interest in each other? What are their concerns?
6. How involved is your family in this decision?
7. When do you want to get married?
8. What are the legal requirements you must meet?
9. What are your concerns as you think about marriage to this person? How does he/she treat you now?

Q 36 ↖ *Name, in order, the 5 things that are most important to you in a marriage.*

Figure 2.9 A pastor can use questions to guide a couple to discuss marriage.

B. Questions about spiritual life

1. Are both people believers?

    Read 2 Corinthians 6:14-16. Light must not marry darkness. Christians must marry Christians. As believers, we are different from those who do not know Jesus Christ. We have a different view of what is right and wrong. We have the Holy Spirit living in us. A Christian must never consider marrying an unbeliever.

2. Are you growing in your faith? What evidence is there that this is true?
3. What kind of character do you have?
4. Do you agree on the authority of Scripture for your lives today? Do you agree on the major doctrines of the Bible? If you disagree, what are you going to teach your children?

    The Bible gives specific instructions about how a husband is to treat his wife; how a wife is to treat her husband; how parents are to treat their children; and how children are to treat their parents (Eph. 5:21–6:4; Col. 3:17-21; 1 Pet. 3:1-7). The Bible is the highest court—both husband and wife must submit to it.

5. Do you know what the Bible teaches about marriage? (A counselor may need to give instruction.)
6. Have you prayed about this decision?
7. Where will you attend church?
8. How do you expect to help in the local church?

Q 37 ↖ *Should 2 believers marry who do not agree on major biblical doctrines? Explain.*

Figure 2.10 Believers who are considering marriage should discuss many topics in the Bible.

It can be difficult to discern a person's spiritual life. A person's deepest thoughts may be hidden. One way to discern the heart is to watch a person's actions and habits when he does not know you are watching.

Bernice gave nothing in the offering. But after church, she went to buy a Coke. Gifts were given for a family who lost their home in a fire. This young lady looked through

Q 38 ↖ *Bernice illustrates that you can learn much by _____.*

her things and gave her oldest dress to the family. Workers were needed to help prepare the church dinner. But this lady came after almost all the work was done. If you were thinking of marrying Bernice, what concerns might you have?

Q 39 *Why should a person not marry someone who angers easily and criticizes often?*

C. Questions about positive attitudes

1. Is the person critical?

    Is the person's attitude like a sunny day or a stormy day? Some people are angry with others most of the time. They criticize people often. Marrying someone like this will bring a critical nature into the home. Many times, a critical person is impossible to please and causes misery in the home. The person who criticizes others will criticize you. The person who is angry with others will be angry with you. Living with a critic is like living in a dark room. God wants each spouse to encourage the other.

2. Is the person happy?

    Remember that you cannot make anyone happy (including your spouse). Happiness is something that each person chooses or rejects. Do not think you will change a person's attitude *after* marriage. People resist change. Find a person who is *already* the kind of person you want to marry. Find someone who will encourage you, inspire you, listen to you, and speak the truth in love to you.[8]

Figure 2.11 Attitudes speak louder than words!

D. Questions about relationships

1. How does the person relate to others?

    We can learn a lot from watching how a person treats parents, brothers and sisters, friends, waiters, children, and other people. A person's respect (or disrespect) will move into a home at marriage. You can be sure that if a person is rude, mean, cold, or critical before marriage, this will continue in marriage.

2. Do you communicate well? Are you willing to work to become a better communicator?

    Communication is not only talking, but also listening. Communication includes seeking to understand a different point of view or opinion. Good communication is polite—kind and tactful, not rude. Communication is something that a couple can work on before marriage and continue to work on throughout their married life. Communication is hard for many men, but they can grow in this area if they try. Woman, do not marry someone who is as silent as a post!

Figure 2.12 A man can learn to communicate better if he tries!

E. Questions about emotional health

The purpose of these questions is to see if each person has a healthy self-image, or view of self.

1. What do you like about yourself? Would you like to change places with someone else? Explain.

2. What do you do when you become angry? Have you been angry with each other? Describe how you dealt with that conflict.

3. How do you feel about the idea of sharing your thoughts and feelings with each other?

4. What are five reasons you want to get married? (Marriage should not be to solve a personal problem, or to please someone else. Reasons like this are signs of danger.)

5. How do you handle change? (The ability to change or adapt is one of the greatest traits a person can bring to marriage.)[9]

6. How do you interact with your brothers and sisters?

How to Choose a Mate for Life

7. Describe your relationship with your parents. Does one or more of your parents try to control you? Explain.
8. Does the person you might marry show sorrow after doing wrong? Can he/she get past guilt?
9. Are you stable in your emotions? Are you very happy one day and very sad the next?
10. Are there any addictions or types of slavery present? (An addiction is a form of slavery—any behavior that hurts your health, work, or relationships, but you will not stop it.)
11. Describe how you make decisions. Tell about a decision you made this week. Tell about an important decision you made. How did you decide? (Can this person deal with reality? Does he/she consider results? Does he/she consider others? Is he or she unwise?)

Here is an example of how poor emotional health can hurt a marriage.

A young woman named Marna had a secret struggle. She felt worthless. When she was a child, her father had ignored her. Her mother was always too busy to listen to her talk. Now, Marna was an adult. But she was very quiet. No one asked her opinion. She was not brave enough to speak up. She had a great desire for someone to notice her.

Figure 2.13 Some people are addicts—bound by habits that hurt themselves and others close to them.

Then, one day, a young man did notice her. He never forgot to invite her to go with the group. He asked her questions and loved to hear her talk. She was filled with joy. He made her feel important, smart, and pretty. She expected him to always spend a lot of time talking to her. When they married, she thought all of her problems were over.

But her young husband had to work hard for many hours each day. As their talks became fewer, her old feelings began to return. She thought, "Maybe he does not have to work so hard. Maybe he is losing interest in me. I am not interesting. I am not valuable." She began to grow quiet and sad. She was not brave enough to talk to him. She feared he would say she was silly.

One day, her husband returned home and found her sick in bed. He was full of concern, so he fixed her some hot tea and brought it to her. As he sat by the bed and they talked, hope stirred in her heart. The next day she met him at the door, eager to return to their talks. But he was tired, and her hope died. But one thing did change. When the wife became desperate for attention, she would get sick. Each time, her husband would sit by the bed and talk. The wife began to be ill often. As the years went by, neither husband nor wife was satisfied. He longed for a healthy wife. And because of her deception, she could only receive his attention as pity.

Q 40 *Summarize how Marna's emotional needs hurt her marriage.*

Counselors would say that Marna brought emotional *baggage* into the marriage. *Baggage* may refer to such things as traditions, values, memories, and expectations. We will identify various types of baggage from time to time in this course. Baggage that people bring into a marriage may be cultural, emotional, mental, or spiritual.

Q 41 *Explain: sometimes people bring baggage into a marriage.*

F. Questions about expectations: what you expect in a marriage

Expecting too much in a marriage is dangerous. Remember the opening illustration of this lesson about the man who was looking for the perfect mate? Some people create ideas of the perfect spouse, the perfect marriage, and the perfect love. They imagine how perfect everything will be in their marriage. When they are attracted to someone, they feel like they have found perfection. Then, after marriage, they are disappointed. They feel like they have been deceived. Or they may feel like they have made a terrible mistake. They believe the perfect mate is out there somewhere, but now they feel trapped with less than the best. Or they seek a divorce so they can look again for the "perfect" marriage.

Q 42 *How do you think a person can have proper expectations of marriage?*

Perfection does not exist in people or in marriages. Married couples will experience anger, hurt, and loneliness. They will discover things about each other that they do

Figure 2.14 When two people marry, they are like two rivers that meet to form one river.

not like. They will disagree about the best way to do things. At times, each will have to lay aside personal ways and find a new way together. This is hard work. There are good days and there are bad days. If both spouses learn to love, there will be many more good days than bad.

Review the three stages of marriage in chapter 1. When two people marry, they are like two rivers that meet to form one river. The water will be rough as they first begin to flow together. But the further they flow, the smoother the waters become.

1. Do you believe marriage is a commitment until death?

    While in pre-marriage counseling, a couple stated that they wanted their marital vows to say "For better or worse, for richer or poorer, <u>until we no longer love each other</u>!" What is wrong with these vows? "Until we no longer love each other?" Love is a decision, and sometimes the emotions are absent (for many reasons). God wants us to understand that we fulfill our vows to our spouse <u>no matter how we feel</u>.

2. What are the reasons for people to divorce?
3. What is a good husband like? Describe him.
4. What is a good wife like? Describe her.
5. How much time do you think you will spend together?
6. What do you think you will do together during your free time?
7. Will there be times when each of you uses free time alone?
8. What do you think your financial standard of living will be?
9. What kinds of work do you expect your spouse to do?
10. Do you expect that both of you will earn money?
11. What kind of social standing do you want your spouse to have?
12. How do you think you will spend holidays?
13. How do you expect to interact with the family of your spouse?
14. How will your spouse show love and respect to you?
15. How do you think Ephesians 5:22-33 will be applied in your marriage?
16. How do you expect your spouse to show sorrow for hurting your feelings?
17. How will your husband/wife know that something is bothering you?
18. How much do you expect to share about your thoughts and feelings?
19. How will you make decisions about your life together?
20. Where will you live?
21. (This list can grow. Create new questions as you hear responses.)

G. Questions about physical health

1. Are you healthy?
2. Do you have any long-term health problems?
3. Are you free from sexual disease? Have you been tested?
4. Do you understand your own body and sexual functions? (Explain if necessary.)
5. What if one of you became crippled or very ill?

H. Questions about children

1. How many children would you like to have?
2. What are your plans for birth control?
3. Do you value boys and girls equally?
4. How soon after marriage do you want to have children?
5. Do you already have children? (If yes, will they be living with you? How do they feel about this marriage? How are you preparing them for this marriage?)
6. Who will discipline the children after marriage? How do you expect your spouse to interact with the children?
7. What is the proper way to discipline children? How did your parents discipline you?
8. Describe the kind of relationship you want your spouse to have with your children.
9. What kind of church do you want your children to attend?
10. What kind of education do you want for your children?
11. How do you want your children to interact with the rest of your family?
12. What if you cannot have children?

I. Questions about sexual issues

1. Does the person tempt you and try to satisfy sexual desires?

    First Peter 2:11 instructs us: *"Dear friends, I urge you, as aliens and strangers in the world, to abstain from sinful desires, which war against your soul."* Sexual desires can war against the mind, emotions, and will. They can make a person weak and unstable. Do not date or marry a person who lacks self-control. If the person lacks self-control before marriage, do not expect a change after marriage. Character remains the same after marriage.

2. What do you expect of your sexual life? Have you received education about sexual issues? (Even if people say "yes," give them good material to read. Follow up after they have read it. A good follow-up question is, "So, what did you think about ____ ____?")

3. What is your plan for remaining sexually pure until marriage? Have you followed your plan?

    Sex before marriage will cloud a person's judgment, cause guilt and worry, and will negatively affect a person's spiritual life.

4. Have you had a sexual experience with anyone? (If the answer is yes, you need to pursue the matter. How long ago? How does the other person feel about this? Help the couple develop a plan that will help them feel secure about each other's faithfulness.)

5. Do you have [or use] pornography of any kind? (This will harm healthy sexual attitudes.)

6. Have you ever been sexually abused? (If yes, this person will probably need more counseling to have a healthy sexual life in marriage. Make sure they get other material to read.) What effect do you think this will have on your sexual life?

7. Has either person been circumcised? What kind of issues will this bring to marriage? (Encourage them to seek help to deal with possible problems.)

8. Is the only purpose of sex to have children? Is it right to have fun with sex in marriage?

J. Questions about common values, and differences

For couples, common values and unity are like money they have saved. But differences can be like debts they owe. If they have saved a lot and owe little, they are more secure. When trouble comes, they can manage from their savings. But if they have only a little money and large debt, hard times can hurt them. Likewise, if they agree on most things, it is easy to talk their way through areas in which they disagree. But if they do not agree on most things, their marriage will be like a ship in a constant storm. So it is important to choose a mate that shares the values that are most important to you.[10]

Adjusting to differences is hard work. Many couples cannot handle the tension and strain—they become unhappy. But couples that have much in common can use their energy to work toward common goals. This is one reason to be careful about things like age differences in marriage. The further apart people are in age, the less they may have in common.

The questions that follow will help you discern areas where you agree or disagree. Also, these questions can help you prepare to adjust your habits and expectations. This will help prevent some problems for the future marriage. If you disagree with a person in many areas, you probably need to seek a different mate. Do not ignore differences that affect daily life. For example, a mate who talks too much can destroy the happiness of a mate who loves peace and quiet.

1. What are your ages?
2. Where did you grow up?
3. What is your ethnic/tribal background?
4. Are both parents still living?
5. Were you raised by both parents?
6. What are your political opinions?
7. What is the religious background of your family?
8. What is your family's social and financial background?
9. What is your level of education? What are your future plans for education?
10. How clean should a house be kept? What about personal cleanliness?
11. What foods do you like the best?
12. Do you like to take risks or be cautious?
13. Do you plan things in advance, or do you like to do things suddenly?
14. Would you rather be with lots of people or at home?
15. Are you quiet, or do you talk a lot?
16. Do you share your feelings easily, or are you very private?
17. How do you describe success? How important is it to you?
18. How important are the opinions of others?
19. What is the most important thing in a friendship?
20. What are three things that interest you most?
21. If you could have any job, which would you choose? Are you moving in that direction?
22. (This list can grow. The more things the couple have in common, the better their marriage will be.)

K. Questions about finances

1. Are you a hard worker?
2. Do you have any debts?

3. Do you have a job?

4. Do you practice self-control in buying? Or do you buy things you do not need?

5. What have you saved to bring into the marriage?

6. Do you have a budget?

7. How do you earn money? How much do you earn?

8. How will you make decisions about money?

9. How do you feel about loans and debt?

10. What are your financial goals?

11. How important are material things to you?

12. How would you describe a generous person? Are you generous?

13. Do you tithe? Have you ever made a faith promise to missions?

14. Should a husband and wife share all of their money and wealth? Will both of their names be on the deed to their home and land?

15. Who will manage the money in the family? Why? Will both know about family finances?

16. Do you have any gambling addictions? Do you put your money at any other high risk?

L. Questions about maturity

The best evidence of how people will act in the future is how they act now. Ask and answer the questions that follow to determine maturity.

Q 43 Summarize questions to discern mature and immature people.

Behaviors of an Immature Person	Behaviors of a Mature Person
Do I often feel inferior and unsure of myself?	Can I accept my weaknesses without feeling inferior?
Am I unable to see another person's point of view?	Can I get along with all kinds of people?
Do I dream, but lack actions to make dreams come true?	Can I see reality and deal with it?
Do I change opinions and actions—depending on who is around?	Am I honest about myself? Am I willing to share my thoughts and feelings?
Am I only concerned that I am understood? Am I self-centered?	Will I listen and try to understand? Am I sensitive to others? Do I consider how my actions will affect others?
Do I see myself as the victim? Do I blame others? Are my actions based on feelings, rather than a plan?	Can I learn from good and bad experiences? Do I see my faults? Do I think about results before acting?
Do I lord it over others, if given authority?	Am I kind to all? Do I show honor and respect to others?
Am I unreliable?	Am I dependable? Do I keep my promises?
Do I rebel against authority? Do I reject correction?	Do I submit to authority?
Do I give up easily? Am I a bad loser?	Am I steadfast, faithful, and persistent? Am I consistent?
Do I seek to control other people? Am I jealous?	Do I show and accept love?

Figure 2.15 Questions to discern if a person is immature or mature

Conclusion

Choosing a mate is one of the most serious decisions a person will make. The choice can make the difference between happiness and sorrow, between a godly home and a worldly home, between a healthy home and a broken home. The person you choose to marry can make the difference between prosperity and poverty—between dignity and shame. Take time to ask and discuss the 100 questions above before you marry. God will use these questions to help you be the right person—and find the right person to marry.

Chapter Summary

 **Ways to Choose a Mate**

Goal A: *Summarize the differences between biblical love and fleshly love.*

First Corinthians 13 describes biblical love, which is more of a decision than a feeling (Review Figures 2.2 and 2.3).

Goal B: *Analyze the strengths and weaknesses of 3 methods to choose a mate.*

Dating, courtship, and arranged engagements can lead to good marriages. Review Figures 2.4, 2.5, and 2.6 for the strengths and weaknesses of each method.

 Ways to Prepare for a Mate

Goal A: *Explain the roles of friendship and purpose in preparing for a mate.*

All humans need friends to prevent loneliness and to grow socially. A single person's life will become weak without friends.

God desires all single people to accomplish His purposes. Living with a purpose makes a person feel valuable, satisfied, and fulfilled—and more attractive to others.

Goal B: *Summarize 5 reasons for sexual purity in preparing for a mate.*

God commands sexual purity. It protects from disease. It protects the health of fathers, mothers, and children. Sexual purity protects the emotions, and leads to trust and security.

Goal C: *Describe 6 keys to living sexually pure while preparing for a mate.*

Do not let the world squeeze you into its mold. Fulfill sexual desire in the way that God approves. Renew your mind. Use personal energy in good ways. Walk in the Spirit and you will not fulfill the desires of the flesh. Accept grace for your past, and move forward in holiness.

 Good Questions to Ask Before Choosing a Mate

Goal: *Ask and answer questions on each of the 12 topics about choosing a mate.*

The 12 topics were: the basics, spiritual life, positive attitudes, relationships, emotional health, expectations, physical health, children, sexual issues, common values, finances, and maturity. Review the questions under each of these topics.

Test Yourself: Circle the letter by the *best* completion to each question or statement.

1. Which statement is TRUE about romantic love?
a) It is not desired in marriage.
b) It is enough for marriage.
c) It is based mostly on the Bible.
d) It is based mostly on the world.

2. Sexual sins are the most common in
a) dating relationships.
b) courting relationships.
c) arranged relationships.
d) marriage relationships.

3. Being together to see if marriage is suitable describes
a) dating relationships.
b) courting relationships.
c) arranged relationships.
d) friendship relationships.

4. An example of an arranged marriage is
a) Aquila and Priscilla.
b) Ananias and Sapphira.
c) Amnon and Tamar.
d) Isaac and Rebekah.

5. A biblical example of making many friends is
a) Thomas.
b) Herod.
c) Paul.
d) Peter.

6. A godly trait that attracts others to a relationship is
a) natural beauty.
b) much education.
c) believing in God.
d) fulfilling a purpose.

7. What is the greatest gift to give your spouse?
a) Many children
b) Great wealth
c) Sexual purity
d) Much wisdom

8. What is a key to sexual purity?
a) Avoid dating.
b) Walk in the Spirit.
c) Choose courtship.
d) Realize that sex is sinful.

9. One use of the 100 questions we studied is
a) an article for the newspaper.
b) pre-marital counseling.
c) a tool for evangelism.
d) a class for married couples.

10. A big key to finding the right mate is
a) common values.
b) the same education.
c) financial blessings.
d) different expectations.

Chapter 3:
How to Plan the Engagement and Wedding

Introduction

Engagement and wedding customs differ around the world. Some believers prefer the customs that come from their families. But all believers must consider what God says to His family. We must examine all our customs to see if they please our heavenly Father.

Q 1 *What advice would you give Joel?*

Joel did not know what to do. In the place where he lived, it was the family custom for the groom to buy beer for the father and his friends. At other weddings, he had seen his father and many others drunk during the wedding. This custom had come down from generation to generation. Joel knew that the Bible says to honor your father and mother. Likewise, he wanted to show respect for the local customs. Still, he knew that it was wrong to get drunk, and he did not feel right about using his money to buy the beer that would make them drunk. Many who came to the wedding would expect to drink all the beer they wanted. If Joel did not buy the beer, his father would become angry. Then, if Joel still did not agree, the father would probably buy the beer himself. Now you know the problem. What advice would you give Joel?

Figure 3.1
What advice would you give Joel?

Lessons:

Local Customs—A Time to Evaluate With Biblical Principles
Goal: *Explain 5 principles to evaluate local customs.*

The Engagement Period—A Time to Prepare, to Grow, and to Be Pure
Goal A: *Describe matters to consider when choosing a wedding helper and a date for the wedding.*
Goal B: *Explain how to prepare for marriage matters that are legal or financial, including a new home.*
Goal C: *Summarize what a couple should learn about each other, sexual union, pregnancy, and sexual purity.*

The Wedding Celebration—A Time to Plan With Balance
Goal A: *Comment on the balance between being generous and sensible at the wedding celebration.*
Goal B: *Explain the balance between pleasing the new couple and pleasing others at the wedding.*

     Key Words

| engagement | coordinator | dowry |
| custom | bride-price | birth control |

Local Customs—A Time to Evaluate With Biblical Principles
Goal: *Explain 5 principles to evaluate local customs.*

When families have done a certain thing for many years, it is accepted by society. It is hard to think that we might need to change. It is not the place of visitors or foreigners to evaluate the customs of others. Rather, believers in each local setting should search the Scriptures. Mature leaders, in the light of God's Word, must decide whether local customs contradict the Bible. The apostle Paul gives several principles to help all believers evaluate customs.

A. Principle: Believers should honor the Bible above customs.

For example, in some countries, customs teach a man and woman to have sex before marriage. But the Bible teaches that this is wrong. So all believers should obey the Bible and abstain from sex during the engagement period.

Consider another custom. The Bible teaches us to flee from the lusts of the flesh. But in some countries, friends plan a party for the engaged man to watch female dancers—who entice and seduce him. Some women have begun to copy this custom. They plan a party with the bride and several women. At this party, the women watch as a man dances and takes off his clothes. Believers should not have parties that feed lust.

No Christian should take part in ceremonies that relate to demons. Paul taught that it is wrong to offer food to idols. Why? Because there are demons behind idols (1 Cor. 10:18-22). So the wedding of a believer should not include any offerings to idols. Likewise, the wedding of a believer should not be related to the spirits of those who have died. For example, a meeting to seek communication with dead relatives is wrong. The Bible forbids God's people to seek any contact with the dead (Deut. 18:9-13). Demons deceive those who seek the dead.

Q 2 *In Matthew 15, what custom did the Pharisees practice that contradicted the Bible? What was the result?*

No believer should practice circumcision for a religious purpose. In the Old Testament, circumcision of males was a sign of the covenant God made with Israel. But in the New Testament, the emphasis is on circumcision of the heart, not the flesh (Rom. 2:28-29; Gal. 5:1-2, 6; 6:15). Under our new covenant, circumcision has no religious value. Doctors have discovered that there are good medical reasons for males to be circumcised. Circumcised males have a cleaner, healthier sex life. But neither the Bible nor medical science teaches that women should ever be circumcised. Some people circumcise females. This causes women to enjoy sex less than God intended. Also, it causes the men to suffer because the wives' sexual joy and desires do not match those of the men. Women who have been circumcised cannot fully enjoy the pleasure of the sexual experience that God intended. So female circumcision destroys the plan of God for men and women.

Q 3 *Why does a woman who was circumcised not enjoy sex with her husband?*

In one place, a church leader faced a problem. His daughter was getting close to the age of being married. It was the custom of his tribe to circumcise the young women. But as he studied the Bible, he saw that circumcision was for males, but never females. And he saw that circumcision of the flesh had religious value under the old covenant, but not under the new covenant. The pressure from his people was rising. But the leader took his stand to obey the Bible, not local customs. He refused for his daughter to be circumcised. His people followed him as the leader. He led them in the light of the Scriptures. Today, all of the young men and young women are very thankful! Why?

Q 4 *What should leaders do if local customs contradict the Bible?*

In another place, Dominic faced a hard decision. It was the custom of the mother-in-law to name the new baby. She did this by consulting the departed ancestors—the spirits of those who had died. The process was to hold the top of a short stick, while the bottom

49

Q 5 *What advice would you give Dominic? Explain.*

of the stick rested on the ground. Then the woman called out the name of an ancestor who had departed. She took her hand away from the stick to see if it would stand up alone. Time after time the stick would fall. But after many hours—perhaps even a few days—the stick would stand alone when the name of a certain ancestor was called. The local people believed that the spirit of the dead person was causing the stick to stand. Then, they would give the baby the name of the dead ancestor. Do you think the spirits of the dead are free to affect the lives of people today (Heb. 9:27; Luke 16:19-31)? What power do you think caused the stick to stand up by itself?

B. Principle: Honor local customs that do not contradict the Bible.

Q 6 *What are some customs in your area that the church could use to relate to unbelievers?*

Many believers honor customs related to Christmas, freedom, birthdays, and other special days. It is hard for sinners to listen to the gospel if the church stands against all local customs. In 1 Corinthians 9:19-23, Paul describes how he practiced the customs of many people. He knew that this helped others to listen to the gospel.

A city had no official celebration for the nations' freedom. There was a national holiday—but each family celebrated in its own way. A church in that town decided they would organize a celebration that everyone in town could attend. They cooked food and sold it at low prices. The leaders planned games for the children and music for all. A special speaker gave his testimony, relating his faith in God to freedom. The pastor gave an invitation, and many came forward to receive Jesus Christ as Savior. At the end of the day, there were beautiful *fireworks as the choir sang songs about freedom. Thousands of unbelievers in the city came to the celebration. They enjoyed the food, fellowship, and music. Many felt closer to the church. The event was so successful that the church continued with the plan each year. As a result, many new people have come into the church called James River Assembly of God in Springfield, Missouri.

Figure 3.2 In some cultures, people use fireworks to celebrate certain holidays.

*Diwali is a yearly festival time in India. In South India, it celebrates the victory of the Hindu god Shiva over the evil god Narakhasura. In North India, Diwali is the day when King Rama's coronation was celebrated after his epic war with Ravana, the demon king of Lanka. Each family lights little clay-pot lamps. They put them around their houses. These little lights appear all over each village. Also, people put new grass on their roofs. And they buy new clothes to celebrate the feast. It is a special time of year for the people of India. But it can be a lonely time for some believers.

Q 7 *What advice would you give the Prasad family?*

The Prasad family lives in a small village. There are no other believers nearby. Their friends and family have rejected them. At the time to celebrate Diwali, their house is the only dark house in the village. The other houses have pretty lamps glowing around them. Is there any way they can celebrate? The Christians in Europe found a way to celebrate during the pagan Festival of Winter. These European believers changed the meaning of the pagan symbols. They took the green tree the pagans used at their festival. They used candles on the tree, just like the unbelievers used. But when believers looked at the tree, they celebrated the birth of Christ. Should the Prasads put lamps around their house to worship Jesus during Diwali? Or will this be a bad testimony to others? Will the lamps be a link with their old way of Hinduism, or a bridge to reach their lost neighbors?[1]

A pastor named Philip was praying for God's direction about what to do. Near his church, a family was gathering. One of the children had died, and it was a local custom for many family members to gather for the funeral. Philip knew they would eat together,

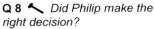

Q 8 *Did Philip make the right decision?*

How to Plan the Engagement and Wedding 51

cry together, and seek to comfort each other. He felt the Holy Spirit leading him to reach out to this family. But in the past, his church had ministered only to believers at the time of death. Believers did not assist any families that did not attend the church. Why? They did not want to give false hope to unbelievers. Still, Philip's heart was moved with compassion. After much prayer and counsel with his deacons, they agreed on a plan. The church gathered food to share with the family. Pastor Philip took the food and visited the home of the family. He told them that he and his church were very sad because the child had died. He said that since the family did not attend his church, he did not know the son who had died. Now, all they could do was place the child in the hands of God. Then, Philip asked if he could say a prayer for the family members who had gathered. They agreed, so he prayed that God would comfort them and that each would be ready to meet God at the time of death. As he left, Philip invited them to attend his church on Sunday. Through the food and the prayer, God touched the hearts of many family members. When Sunday came, several of them visited Philip's church and received Jesus as Savior. Philip was thankful that he found a way to honor their local custom.

C. Principle: Each believer should honor his conscience (Rom 14:14).

No believer should take part in a custom he thinks is wrong (Rom. 14:14, 23). Some Christians may practice a custom with a clear conscience. Another Christian may feel guilty if he does the same thing. If guilt feelings come, avoid the custom.

> NO BELIEVER SHOULD TAKE PART IN A CUSTOM HE THINKS IS WRONG

Q 9 *Do all believers agree on which customs are good? Explain.*

A wedding custom in some cultures is for <u>each man</u> present to kiss the bride in the way a brother would kiss a man on the cheek. Many of the believers in the church regularly kissed a bride's cheek with no guilt at all. But one man was uncomfortable with this tradition. Each time he kissed a bride's cheek, he wondered what it would be like to kiss her lips. So he stopped practicing this tradition because it troubled his conscience. Instead, he shook her hand, smiled, and nodded his head.

D. Principle: Avoid customs that cause other believers to stumble (Rom. 14:15-21).

You may be able to practice a custom with a clear conscience. But if your practice harms the faith of another, you must stop (Rom. 14:21).

A group of young believers gathered the food for the wedding of a friend. They stopped at a market that had delicious fruit. But Karome, one of the youngest, said, "The man who owns this market has dedicated it to a false god." Another responded, "My family always buys fruit here. This is the only place to get the traditional fruit that our friend wants for the wedding. The fruit tastes good. We trust in the true God, so we should not be concerned about false gods." The young people entered to speak to the owner. But Karome stood outside, refusing to enter. What should the others do?

Q 10 *What should believers do to help Karome?*

E. Principle: Do not judge other believers for customs they feel free to practice (Rom. 14:13).

One believer should not judge another for practicing or refusing certain customs. Believers can disagree about these things, if both are trying to obey the Bible. But they must not judge the one with whom they disagree (Rom. 14:13-23).

The tradition of the Christmas tree comes from an old, pagan religion. Some believers refuse to have a Christmas tree in their homes. But other believers bring in a tree and put a pretty star on top. This reminds them of the star that led the Wise Men to Bethlehem. Can we tell which of these believers loves God more?

Conclusion

Engagements and weddings are full of traditions. People like traditions—they help us feel connected with others. Traditions help us honor our forefathers. They help us establish our identity. But some traditions are a problem. We want to honor our customs, but we also want to honor Christ. We must cast aside or change traditions that dishonor God. But we can keep those traditions that do not contradict Scripture or conscience. We need wisdom from God. Paul's principles will help us make wise decisions about these matters.

At a wedding in the city, Sheila wanted to braid her hair in a special way. Some of her family members were from the village. She knew that they thought it was wrong to braid hair or wear jewelry. These believers from the village based their belief on 1 Timothy 2:9: *"I also want women to dress modestly, with decency and propriety, not with braided hair or gold or pearls or expensive clothes."* Do you think it is wrong for a bride to dress in a special way for a wedding? Does the way godly women wear their hair and clothes vary from place to place and century to century?

Q 11 ◤ *What advice would you give Sheila?*

The Engagement Period—A Time to Prepare, to Grow, and to Be Pure

Goal A: *Describe matters to consider when choosing a wedding helper and a date for the wedding.*
Goal B: *Explain how to prepare for matters that are legal or financial, including a new home.*
Goal C: *Summarize what a couple should learn about each other, sexual union, pregnancy, and sexual purity.*

Setting

The engagement period begins when there is an agreement that a man and woman will marry. It ends when the wedding is completed. There is a lot of work to do during the time of engagement. It can be joyful work, but there may be a lot of stress during this time. The Holy Spirit, thoughtful families, and helpful friends can help manage the stress and work. Let us consider several things to help people prepare for the wedding.

A. Prepare for the wedding by choosing a coordinator—a person to help you.

As people begin to prepare for the wedding, they may say HELP! The bigger the wedding, the more work there is to do. Help is very important in the days just before the wedding. The couple will feel better if they can get a wedding *coordinator—a person to help plan the wedding. The coordinator or helper may be a volunteer, or someone the couple pays to help.

Q 12 ◤ *What are some important things a wedding helper will do?*

> **Tasks of the Wedding Coordinator or Helper**
> 1. Represent you and your families with honor.
> 2. Listen carefully to what you and your families desire for the wedding.
> 3. Follow your instructions about food, photos, and other things.
> 4. Plan the order in which each thing should be done.
> 5. See problems when they are small, and solve them.
> 6. Spend only the amount of money you and your families decide.
> 7. Show patience and kindness to other workers.
> 8. Fulfill the responsibilities agreed on.

Figure 3.3 Tasks of a wedding coordinator or helper

How to Plan the Engagement and Wedding 53

B. Prepare for the wedding by learning more about your future mate.

The engagement period is a time to prepare many things. But it is also a time for the engaged man and woman to grow in their knowledge of each other. The more they understand each other, the more they can enjoy and please each other. Growing in knowledge also provides a chance to discover difficulties before the marriage. Breaking an engagement is a tough decision—but a broken engagement is better than a bad marriage. Many good things can come from learning more about your future mate.

Q 13 ⤢ *What good things come from growing in knowledge of your engaged partner?*

There are many customs around the world on how an engaged couple may relate. In some places, there is no personal relationship—as when parents arrange the marriage. In other places, the couple can spend time with each other if another adult is present. In some cases the couple has complete freedom. In all of these situations, getting to know each other helps the couple. Let us look at some ways in which couples can grow in their knowledge of each other.

Situation 1: If there is no personal time between those who plan to marry	
Action	**Topic**
Listen	• to what your parents and others say about the person you plan to marry. • to what his/her family says about the person. • to what children say about the person.

Watch	• to see how the person works.
	• to see if the person is neat and clean.
	• to see how the person treats animals and children.
	  (How someone treats the weakest shows if the person is kind.)
	• to see how the person worships God.
	• to see how the person's mother and father act.
	  (People often act like their parents.)
	• to see how the person acts when losing or winning at a game. Is the person angry? Proud?
	• to see what the person buys.

Pray	• to receive insight about the person. • to receive deliverance from any evil you or your family may not discover.

Q 14 ⤢ *In Situation 1, name 3 things a person should listen for.*

Situation 2: If there are adults *with* the couple who will marry *(Listen, watch, and pray as Situation 1 summarizes.)*	
Action	**Topic**
Talk	• about your childhood and ask about the person's childhood. • about current events and the person's opinion. • about your spiritual life and ask about the person's walk with God. • about your future dreams and ask what the future spouse hopes life will bring. • about all of the questions we gave you in chapter 2.
Visit	• the person's family—as much as possible.

Q 15 ⤢ *In Situation 2, what can you learn from visiting a person's family?*

Situation 3: If there is total freedom for the couple who will marry *(Listen, watch, pray, talk, and visit as Situations 1& 2 summarize.)*	
Action	**Topic**
Talk	• about personal matters, more than you could discuss when others may hear. • about your disappointments, and ask about the person's discouragements. • about children. (Take some children with you and watch the person's actions.)
Explore	• thoughts and ideas. Read a book together and discuss it. • new places, and observe the person's responses.
Pray	• read, and discuss the Bible together.

Q 16 ⤢ *In Situation 3, summarize some ways for two people to know each other better.*

Figure 3.4
Ways engaged couples can learn more about each other in three different situations

Q 17 *How could the couple from India have gained knowledge of each other before the wedding?*

A family from India moved to the United States. For 12 years the daughter went to American schools and learned American culture. But as she grew close to an age for marriage, her parents became concerned. They wanted her to marry an Indian man. So they arranged a marriage between their daughter and a young man living in India. The daughter wanted to be obedient. So she flew to India. Several days later she married the man she had just met.

To grow in knowledge of each other is an important task of the engagement time. Do not let romance, fear, or social customs prevent learning about each other *before* the wedding. Whatever limits a couple may have, they can find good ways to know each other better.

C. Prepare for the wedding by wisely choosing the date.

The date of the wedding is one of the most important things to plan. Figure 3.5 lists eight things to think about before choosing a wedding date.

Q 18 *Which 2 questions in Figure 3.5 do you think are the most important?*

1. When will legal requirements be fulfilled?
2. Is there a good financial plan for the couple to live?
3. When will a home be ready for the new couple?
4. How long will it take to prepare for the wedding?
5. Does the date avoid the monthly flow of the bride?
6. Will key family members and guests be able to come on this date?
7. Is the minister able to come on this date?
8. Is the building or land you need for the wedding open to you on this date?

Q 19 *What are some other questions to ask in your part of the world?*

Figure 3.5 Eight questions to ask before setting the wedding date

As we continue this lesson, we will look more closely at some of the things in Figure 3.5.

D. Prepare for a wedding by fulfilling the legal requirements.

Q 20 *Why should a couple fulfill the legal and/or cultural requirements for a marriage?*

Laws about marriage vary from place to place. Sometimes the couple must meet local requirements before a marriage is recognized. But almost all governments have their own rules. The engaged couple must know the laws in their area. God says we should obey the laws of our country (Rom. 13:1-7). There are few times that believers must choose between obeying God and man (Acts 4:1-20).

Q 21 *Why do many countries require health tests for the engaged couple?*

The laws of many countries require health tests for the engaged couple. Many diseases spread by sexual contact. It is important for a man and woman to know if they are engaged to someone with sexual diseases. When they join their bodies, the sick

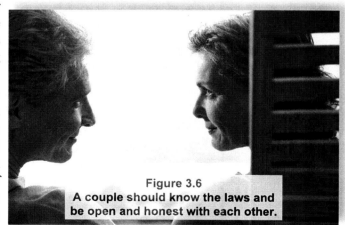

**Figure 3.6
A couple should know the laws and be open and honest with each other.**

person may cause the other person to be sick. The disease may then spread to their children before or at birth. A person with one of these diseases may not look sick, and may not know he or she has a sexual disease. Most often, sexual diseases come from sexual contact. Some get a sexual disease from their mothers at birth. Some get sexual

How to Plan the Engagement and Wedding   55

diseases through touching or receiving diseased blood. Medicine can cure some of these diseases, but not all of them. Many people die from sexual diseases, such as AIDS. Wise men and women **always** have health tests, even if their laws do not require it. Then, they share the written results of the health tests with each other. Neither person should hide a sexual disease when marriage is being considered. People with AIDS, or other serious sexual diseases, should discuss the problems these illnesses will cause in marriage. Some will decide not to marry.

E. Prepare for a wedding by settling financial matters for the marriage.

Early financial matters before the wedding may include things like debts, a bride-price, a dowry, or wedding rings. A couple must plan for these to have a good financial foundation for their marriage. As Scripture says, *"There is a time for everything"* (Eccl. 3:1).

Financial customs can be helpful. They help form strong relationships between families. They show how much a husband values his future wife. They help prevent divorce if the money or property given may not be returned. Some who give dowries think the money should help with a home or help with educational expenses. When practiced well, bride-price or dowry can bring dignity and respect to the wife. Good things can come from these customs.

Q 22 ⤢ What good things come from the customs of giving a bride-price or dowry?

Most wedding customs are meant to help people. But sin can twist any custom. Sadly, this is sometimes true of giving bride-price or dowry. Greed and pride cause some families to raise the bride-price. Too large a bride-price or dowry can cause problems.

Q 23 ⤢ How do pride and greed hurt the customs of giving a bride-price or dowry?

- The desire for a high bride-price may cause an unsuitable, bad marriage for a daughter. Her family may force her to marry the man who can pay the highest bride-price. But this man may not be the right age, or the right choice.
- A high bride-price places a burden of debt on the husband. Poverty or debt may weaken the marriage.
- Men who cannot afford a high bride-price may get discouraged. Without hope of doing things properly, the couple may choose to run away together or begin sexual relations without marriage.
- Some husbands who pay a high bride-price may demand too much from the wife, or treat her like property they bought.
- Greed also affects the practice of giving dowries. A groom's family may demand more dowry from the bride's family after the wedding. This dishonest family then treats the bride cruelly, until her family gives more money. Much sorrow can come from the abuse of bride-price and dowry.

Lowering bride-prices and dowries would solve some problems, but not all of them. Lower prices cannot solve the problem of a sinful heart. When a man bargains for a lower bride-price, he and his family may treat the bride poorly. They may value her by the amount they pay, not by her character and skills. No one who loves his daughter would want her to be in that kind of a family.

Q 24 ⤡ Can a family lower a marriage price without lowering the honor of their daughter? Explain.

Families of believers who choose to practice the custom of bride-price or dowry should consider these biblical principles:

- Seek wisdom in helping your children build their marriage (Prov. 24:3-4).
- Free your heart from greed (Prov. 22:1; 28:25).
- Seek to be generous and give honor (Prov. 22:9).
- Treat others as you would like to be treated. Do what is best for your children, and good things will come back to you (Matt. 7:12; Luke 6:38).
- Value each woman because she is created in God's image—not for the money she brings (Gen. 2; John 3:16).

Q 25 ⤢ What are 5 biblical principles for practicing bride-price or dowry?

Godly character and knowledge of the Bible guide us to honor God, the couple, and their families.

Q 26 *Why should a new married couple not depend too much on parents for finances?*

Matters such as debts, a dowry, bride-price, and wedding rings are only the beginning of financial concerns. In a new marriage, a couple must support themselves. They must not depend too much on their parents. Depending too much on their parents limits the couple's ability to grow as healthy adults. Family members who support the couple may demand too much. Some demands may hinder the couple's unity and respect for each other. The couple needs to know that they can provide for themselves before they marry. Later in this course, we will study about a family budget.

F. Prepare for a wedding by planning a home for the new couple.

Q 27 *What must a new home provide?*

A new couple needs a place of their own. They need space and privacy to begin their marriage. Their home does not need to be large or full of expensive things. But it should be safe and sufficient. The home needs the basic things for cooking, sleeping, sitting, and cleanliness. The couple themselves adds beauty to the home—with joy and thankfulness—whether they are rich or poor. This kind of home is always a good place to live.

Q 28 *Instead of a dowry, how do people in the West help a couple that marries?*

Westerners do not usually practice the customs of dowry or bride-price. But they know that young people who marry need financial help. Sometimes the parents will help buy land or a home. Friends plan parties and all the guests bring gifts. Later, all who are invited to the wedding bring a gift for the home of the new couple. At a big wedding, one couple received over 300 gifts for their home! The new couple writes letters to thank each person who gave a gift—otherwise people will think the young couple is rude. Most people have some custom that lessens the financial burdens of those who marry.

Q 29 *What 3 things will help the couple decide where to live?*

The location of the home will usually depend on three things.
- The work of the couple may require a certain location.
- The money or income of a couple will guide them to choose a home.
- The responsibilities to the larger family may influence the choice of a home.

Talking about these three factors will help the couple decide where to live. The husband and wife should discuss these three matters and come to an agreement.

G. Prepare for the wedding by gaining knowledge about sexual union.

Q 30 *How should an engaged man or woman learn about sexual union?*

The closer they come to the time of marriage, the more sexual knowledge the couple needs. God has given sexual union as a marriage gift. It is a treasure He desires for the husband and wife to enjoy. In order for both to enjoy this gift fully, it is important for them to understand the sexual ways of their bodies. It is important for the man to know how to prepare his wife for sexual union. The couple will continue to learn about sexual matters throughout marriage. But knowledge can increase the enjoyment of learning in the first days of marriage. Lack of knowledge by the man or woman can make things difficult. Each engaged person should seek a godly, married person to discuss sexual matters. They may also refer to books written by believers about sex in marriage. Two good books are: *The Act of Marriage* by Tim and Beverly LaHaye [2] and *Intended for Pleasure* by Ed and Gaye Wheat.[3] Perhaps there are other good books written by believers in your area. In chapter 5, we will discuss the topic of sex in marriage. The sexual union of a husband or wife will be better as the couple understands the ways God has created their bodies for each other.

Figure 3.7   There are good Christian books for both men and women that discuss sex in marriage.

H. Prepare for the wedding by making a plan for pregnancy.

Some couples desire to limit the number of children they will have. Others may desire many children, but they want to have time to adjust to marriage *before* becoming parents. These couples must know how to prevent pregnancy while having sex in their marriage. Education about birth control is necessary for these couples. For birth control to work, three things are necessary.

- The couple must choose a trustworthy method. A doctor, nurse, or teacher from the community can explain several methods of birth control. In a Bible school, a teacher may invite a person to come and teach about various methods of birth control.
- The couple must follow the directions, using the method as the maker directs.
- The couple must, in some cases, use the method every time they have sexual intercourse.

Q 31 When must a couple learn about birth control?

> **RIDDLE:** WHAT DO YOU CALL A HUSBAND AND WIFE WHO DO NOT PLAN FOR BIRTH CONTROL?
>
> **ANSWER:** PARENTS!

The engagement period is the time to prepare for birth control. Waiting until marriage to plan for children in the family is too late; it is like waiting until the Rapture to plan for it.

The couple should educate themselves about pregnancy even if they use birth control. If the wife becomes pregnant, the couple must be ready for this change in their marriage. Pregnancy will affect the wife's body. She must eat more food and get more rest. Doctors recommend that pregnant women take *vitamins*. When a woman is pregnant, she may feel sick in her stomach, and even vomit. Sometimes this is called *morning sickness*.

Q 32 Summarize a wife's physical, emotional, and mental changes during pregnancy.

Likewise, other things change during pregnancy. The wife's emotions may change quickly during pregnancy. She may suddenly begin to cry! Or she may feel nervous from noise or work. In contrast, the husband's attitude should change when his wife is expecting a child. He must prepare mentally to be kind to his wife while she is pregnant. She cannot escape from the changes in her body. So he must be kind to her. And he must prepare to be a father and provide for a bigger family. The more knowledge the couple has about pregnancy, the better they are prepared for children in marriage.

Q 33 Why must a husband show special kindness to a wife who is pregnant?

I. Prepare for the wedding by remaining sexually pure.

The engagement period is a time to prepare for marriage and a time to grow in knowledge of each other. But it is also a time for the couple to be pure in their sexual lives. The biblical principle is clear—God intends the sexual union for marriage alone. Engagements can be broken. Some engagements fail because of unfaithfulness. Some fail because of deceit. Sometimes family agreements are broken. Perhaps the man or woman has a change of mind. Sometimes, a young man will want to have sex with a girl before marriage. But if she agrees and has sex with him, he often loses respect for her and leaves. Accidents, sickness, and even death can break an engagement. Because of all these possibilities and because of God's Law, the couple should be sexually pure as they look toward their marriage.

Q 34 State 3 reasons an engaged couple must remain sexually pure.

In chapter 2 we studied some about sexual purity. This is a very important topic. So let us consider four keys to remaining pure during the engagement period.

1. Walk in the Spirit. *"Live by the Spirit, and you will not gratify [fulfill] the desires of the sinful nature"* (Gal. 5:16). The easy way to overcome the lust of the flesh is to enjoy the presence of God. Isaiah saw a vision of God and a wonderful thing happened (Isa. 6:1-8). The prophet began to see sin as God saw it. When he saw the holiness of God, things that had not troubled him before brought guilt. At once, he knew that his

Q 35 Summarize 4 principles to stay sexual pure.

Figure 3.8
As we abide in Christ, His Spirit produces fruit, such as self-control and patience, which enable us to win the battle over fleshly lusts.

Q 36 A couple should avoid most physical affection because it is like putting _____ on a _____.

own lips—lips that he had used every day—were unclean with sin. He longed to be clean and to be God's servant. Walking in the Spirit and being in God's presence causes us to want to be like Him. When we are near God, we desire to be holy. The knowledge of His holiness strengthens us against sin. We become more like Joseph. He ran from sexual sin because he could not bear to sin against God (Gen. 39:1-12). When we serve our sexual desires, we become more like David. He gazed upon Bathsheba and fell into sin (2 Sam. 11:2-5). If there are two targets, a man can only hit the one he aims at. Will you aim at being like Joseph, or David? **Submit** to the Spirit—enjoy His presence through singing, praying, and praising. Then you will be like Joseph, not David! A fruit of the Spirit is self-control. Depend on the Spirit to produce this fruit in you.

2. Avoid a long engagement period. Long engagements make sexual purity more difficult. If the engaged people live near each other, they must often deal with their sexual desires for each other. When a couple agrees to marry, sexual temptation gets stronger. They know that in the future they will become one flesh, so they are more tempted by sexual attraction. Paul says that if self-control is getting weak, get married (1 Cor. 7:8-9).

3. Do not practice physical affection that increases sexual desire. A little fire can be put out with a cup of water. But if a person feeds a fire with small sticks and then logs, no one can put it out. Ecclesiastes 3:1 and 5 says, [1]*"There is a time for everything ... *[5]*a time to embrace and a time to refrain."* When a person is seeking to control sexual desires, it is **not** the time for long kisses or long hugs.

4. Place limits on time alone. An engaged couple can spend time together without being alone. They can walk together in a park. They can sit at a table-for-two in a restaurant. If they want to be together in their homes, they need to invite others to join them. The presence of other people protects them from acting on their desires, and from harming their reputation.

When God requires us to do something, He always enables us to obey. God has commanded us to live sexually pure. An engaged couple can remain pure by following the four guidelines of this lesson. Couples do not need more knowledge or more guidelines to live holy lives—they just need to practice the four guidelines mentioned.

Conclusion

The engagement period is an important time. It gives time to prepare all the things necessary for the wedding. It allows time for the engaged couple to grow in their knowledge of one another. And it is a time when the engaged couple is to be pure as they approach their holy wedding.

The Wedding Celebration—A Time to Plan With Balance
Goal A: *Comment on the balance between being generous and sensible at the wedding celebration.*
Goal B: *Explain the balance between pleasing the new couple and pleasing others at the wedding.*

Setting

Jesus loves weddings. He said heaven would include the joy of a great wedding feast. We believers—as a virgin bride—will be joined for all eternity with Jesus Christ, the Groom who loves us. When He returns, there will be a great wedding supper (Rev. 19:6-9).

Weddings are a time to rejoice and celebrate! But weddings are also a time to plan wisely. Let us examine two areas of the wedding that call for wisdom.

How to Plan the Engagement and Wedding   59

A. A couple needs wisdom to celebrate well without spending money they need for their marriage.

The path of wisdom is often between two mountains. The wise will not spend too little, or too much. Rather, wisdom will guide them to the balance between these two mistakes.

 Q 37 Explain the 2 mistakes a new couple must avoid when planning their wedding.

No one wants the reputation of being stingy. Some squeeze a coin so much that the person on it cries! In the opposite direction, some spend money too freely. A modern proverb says that a fool and his money are soon parted. God Himself prefers generous people (Prov. 11:24-26; 2 Cor. 9:7). *"One man gives freely, yet gains even more; another withholds unduly, but comes to poverty"* (Prov. 11:24). A wedding celebration is a time to be generous. But it is foolish to borrow money to be generous. Proverbs 22:26-27 warns against borrowing money. Proverbs also tells us that a borrower becomes a slave to the one who lends. God does not want us to be slaves.

It is foolish to borrow money for a wedding. It is also foolish to spend so much on the wedding that there is not enough money left to care for the new family. First Timothy 5:8 tells us that the person who does not provide for his family is worse than an unbeliever. Our generosity must not hurt our ability to provide for the family after the wedding. The Bible guides us to live by the principle of modesty—balance in living—avoiding extremes to the left and to the right (1 Tim. 6:6-10).

Generosity and quantity are not twins. Remember when Jesus watched people give offerings at the temple? Jesus said that the most generous person was the widow who put in the least amount (Luke 21:1-4). The rich person gave the most, but was not generous. Generosity is not measured by how much we give—it is measured by how much we keep. Generosity is an attitude of the heart. A rich man who hosts a big wedding may be stingy (Prov. 23:6-8). A poor man who hosts a small wedding may be generous. This is God's wisdom. So in planning a wedding, spending should match income and savings. Doves are beautiful, but they should not try to fly with the eagles!

Q 38 Explain the saying: Doves are beautiful, but they should not try to fly with the eagles.

B. We need wisdom to balance the concerns of family members with the desires of the couple.

It seems like everyone has an opinion about a wedding. There are many voices about when and where the wedding should occur. People have different ideas about the food and whom to invite. There are many opportunities for conflict.

Sometimes it is good for the new couple to listen to all, but make their own choices. People of honor in the family deserve to give some guidance. It is wise to consider the concerns of others.

Customs vary. Matthew 22:2 tells of a great king who planned a wedding banquet for his son. In some places, parents will help plan much of the wedding. In other places, it is the custom for the new husband and wife to plan almost everything. Tension between people about the wedding plans may rob the wedding of its joy. The Bible teaches that we should submit to one another (Eph. 5:21). James 1:5-8 promises the gift of wisdom to those who ask and believe. God can give wisdom to balance the wedding concerns of others with the desires of the couple.

Situation 1: Joko was looking forward to his wedding. He wanted all of his family to attend—especially his father's brother. This uncle had helped him through school. The uncle had always shown a special interest in Joko. But Joko's father did not want the uncle to come. "He has cheated me. I will not have the brother who stole my money eat my food!" said the father.

 Q 39 What advice would you give Joko?

Situation 2: The bride wanted to look beautiful for her wedding. She had been working on just the right wedding dress. But one day, her grandmother took her aside to show

Q 40 *Should the new bride wear the old dress? Explain.*

Q 41 *Should the wedding be changed because of Omogo's death? Explain.*

Q 42 *What counsel would you give the Funatsus?*

her the dress she had worn at her own wedding, 50 years earlier. "It has always been my dream to see you, my favorite granddaughter, wear this dress at your wedding," the old woman said. The bride smiled at her grandmother. But the smile hid her sorrow. The dress may have been beautiful for her grandmother. But this old garment was not the type of dress the bride wanted.

Situation 3: The bride and groom were ready for the wedding. It was still 2 weeks away, but all the plans had been made. Their home was ready. Some of their guests had made their travel plans. The place for the wedding was reserved. The food was ordered. Then they received the bad news—Omogo, the groom's grandfather had died. The groom's family insisted to delay the wedding. But the bride's family wanted it to happen as planned. They would lose all the money they had paid for the building if the wedding date changed.

Situation 4: Who will perform the wedding ceremony for the new couple, the Funatsus? This was the question that caused problems. The bride's uncle was a fine minister—the bride's mother insisted on him. An elderly pastor was the choice of the groom's father. The groom wanted the younger pastor, who had baptized him, to conduct the ceremony. The bride was afraid that if she said whom she wanted, someone would get angry with her!

Figure 3.9 **People need wisdom to balance the desires of those getting married, and the concerns of family members.**

Conclusion

Some may ask if we need to bother God with our wedding plans. Is He concerned about our traditions, our finances, and our joy at a wedding?

One day Jesus went to a wedding. He did not hesitate to join in the celebration. And when He saw that the drink was low and the host would be embarrassed, Jesus performed His first miracle (John 2:1-11). God is happy for us to talk with Him about our wedding plans. In fact, He desires to be the honored guest at every wedding!

How to Plan the Engagement and Wedding

 **Chapter Summary**

 Local Customs—A Time to Evaluate With Biblical Principles

Goal: *Explain 5 principles to evaluate local customs.*

Honor the Bible above customs. Honor local customs that do not contradict the Bible. Honor your conscience. Avoid customs that cause others to stumble. Do not judge others for customs they feel free to practice.

 The Engagement Period—A Time to Prepare, to Grow, and to Be Pure

Goal A: *Describe matters to consider when choosing a wedding helper and a date for the wedding.*

Choose a person who will: represent you with honor, listen well, follow your instructions, plan the order of the wedding, see and solve problems, spend only the amount you decide, show patience and kindness, and fulfill the responsibilities agreed on.

Goal B: *Explain how to prepare for marriage matters that are legal or financial, including a new home.*

The engaged couple must know the laws in their area—such as health tests or a marriage license.

Financial matters such as debts, a dowry, bride-price, and wedding rings are only the beginning of financial concerns. In a new marriage, a couple must support themselves, and not depend too much on parents

Goal C: *Summarize what a couple should learn about each other, sexual union, pregnancy, and sexual purity.*

Review Figure 3.4—Ways engaged couples can learn more about each other in three different situations.

- The closer they come to the time of marriage, the more sexual knowledge the couple needs. Each engaged person should seek a godly, married person to discuss sexual matters, or refer to books written by believers about sex in marriage.
- The engagement period is the time to prepare for birth control. Waiting until marriage to plan for children in the family is too late; it is like waiting until the Rapture to plan for it. Pregnancy will affect the wife's body and emotions.
- The engagement period is a time to be pure. We mentioned four keys to remain pure. Walk in the Spirit. Avoid a long engagement period. Do not practice physical affection that increases desire. Place limits on time alone.

 The Wedding Celebration—A Time to Plan With Balance

Goal A: *Comment on the balance between being generous and sensible at the wedding celebration.*

The path of wisdom is often between two mountains. The wise will <u>not</u> spend too little, or too much. It is foolish to borrow money for a wedding, or spend so much on the wedding that there is not enough money left to care for the new family. Doves are beautiful, but they should not try to fly with the eagles!

Goal B: *Explain the balance between pleasing the new couple and pleasing others at the wedding.*

Sometimes it is good for the new couple to listen to all, but make their own choices. People of honor in the family deserve to give some guidance. It is wise to consider the concerns of others. God can give wisdom to balance the wedding concerns of others with the desires of the couple.

Test Yourself: Circle the letter by the *best* completion to each question or statement.

1. Which statement is TRUE about local customs?
a) Believers should honor all local customs.
b) Believers should avoid all local customs.
c) Believers should honor Scripture, not customs.
d) Believers should honor the Bible over customs.

2. When celebrating customs, believers must honor
a) their parents.
b) their conscience.
c) their family.
d) their friends.

3. At a wedding, who guides all of the details?
a) The bride
b) The groom
c) The pastor
d) The coordinator

4. You can learn a lot about a person by watching
a) the way he eats dinner.
b) the way he treats others.
c) the way he studies.
d) the way he testifies.

5. An important thing to plan is the
a) date of the wedding.
b) color of the bride's dress.
c) length of the wedding vows.
d) time to begin the wedding.

6. The most important test before marriage is
a) a Bible test.
b) a mental test.
c) an emotional test.
d) a health test.

7. Which financial statement is always TRUE?
a) A dowry is a blessing to a marriage.
b) Bride-price is a good custom.
c) Do not depend too much on parents.
d) Honor parents financially above your family.

8. When should a couple learn about pregnancy?
a) Before marriage
b) During the first week of marriage
c) After the first child
d) When the wife becomes pregnant

9. A great key to remaining sexually pure is
a) a long engagement.
b) much time alone.
c) walking in the Spirit.
d) memorizing Scripture.

10. A key word in planning a wedding is
a) size.
b) balance.
c) location.
d) condition.

Introduction to Unit 2

Jesus told a parable about workers in a vineyard. At the end of the day, some were angry. They complained because they worked longer than others but received the same pay. Their destiny depended on the way they reacted to the unexpected—their fate depended on adjusting. Much of life depends on the way a person reacts, responds, and adjusts to surprises.

There are two groups of people: those who adjust well, and those who adjust poorly. Cain did not expect God to reject his offering. Cain adjusted poorly and turned his anger toward Abel. Matthew did not expect Jesus to call him. But he adjusted well and became an apostle. Judas did not expect to feel guilty after betraying Christ. Then, he adjusted poorly and refused to repent. Peter did not expect to deny the Lord. But he adjusted well and became a great apostle. Paul did not expect a thorn in the flesh. But he adjusted well and became better instead of bitter.

The success of a marriage depends on adjusting to surprises that come from your spouse.
- All weddings are happy. But living together after the wedding causes some to be unhappy!
- The most difficult years of marriage are those after the wedding!
- Succeeding in marriage is like working on a farm—you must start over every morning!
- Marriage is inspired by love—but it is secured by hard work, kindness, respect, and good cooking!
- Arguing with your spouse is as foolish as trying to blow out a light bulb! A wise person learns to adjust, rather than argue.
- "Marriages are made in heaven, but they are lived on earth."[1]

Unit 2: Adjusting to Marriage

In this Unit we will study keys to help you adjust well and enjoy the treasure of your marriage.

Chapter 4 is about communication. We will guide you to:
- *Identify the five parts of the circle of communication.*
- *Explain how body language, social setting, and differences in people affect communication.*
- *Summarize eight temptations that a good listener must overcome.*
- *Describe the role of feelings when men and women communicate.*
- *Explain how the purpose of communicating differs for men and women.*
- *Identify three common mistakes women make when talking with men.*
- *Identify three common mistakes men make when talking with women.*
- *Explain five causes of conflict, and illustrate each.*
- *Summarize 15 bad things to avoid when communicating during conflict.*
- *State five good things to do when communicating during conflict.*

Chapter 5 teaches you about the sexual experience in marriage. We will enable you to:
- *Summarize four reasons for sex in marriage.*
- *State four sexual differences in the desires of men and women.*
- *Comment on expectations, acceptance, and the past in relation to sex in marriage.*
- *Explain how a husband can avoid the most common sexual error in marriage.*
- *Summarize the need for sexual faithfulness and satisfaction in marriage.*
- *Explain four things a wife should know about her husband's sexual desires.*
- *Explain four things a husband should know about his wife's sexual desires.*
- *Describe guarding time together and adjusting to change in marriage.*
- *Identify three reasons for difficult sexual problems in marriage.*
- *Examine three solutions for sexual problems in marriage.*

Chapter 6 discusses three key questions each couple must answer. You will learn to:
- *State three ways of honoring God when making decisions.*
- *Explain how spouses may differ in the way they make decisions.*
- *Contrast basing decisions on the wrong reasons and on priorities. Illustrate each.*
- *Analyze the role of perseverance after making good decisions.*
- *Summarize ten principles for handling finances wisely in marriage. Illustrate each.*
- *State at least four ways for children who marry to honor their parents.*
- *Explain the biblical order in caring for family and relatives.*
- *Summarize the need to protect children from family members.*

Chapter 4:
How to Practice Good Communication

Introduction

Once, everyone in the world spoke the same language. During that time, the people decided to build the Tower of Babel. Day by day they moved toward their goal—talking, planning, and working. But God had a different plan. He wanted the people to scatter and fill the earth. So, He hindered their ability to communicate by giving them many different languages. The people became confused and could no longer work together. They left the tower, separated from one another, and scattered across the earth (Gen. 11:1-9).

Like the people in Genesis 11, family members need to communicate to live together. Communication allows us to understand each other, work together, and solve problems in the family. But sometimes, husbands and wives do not communicate well. Although they speak the same language, at times they do not understand each other. So in this chapter we will study guidelines to communicate better.

Figure 4.1 Good communication in marriage requires the cooperation of two people!

Lessons:

Basics of Good Communication

Goal A: *Identify the 5 parts of the circle of communication.*
Goal B: *Explain how body language, social setting, and differences in people affect communication.*
Goal C: *Summarize 8 temptations that a good listener must overcome.*

Communication—Differences Between Men and Women

Goal A: *Describe the role of feelings when men and women communicate.*
Goal B: *Explain how the purpose of communicating differs for men and women.*
Goal C: *Identify 3 common mistakes women make when talking with men.*
Goal D: *Identify 3 common mistakes men make when talking with women.*

Good Communication During Conflict

Goal A: *Explain 5 causes of conflict, and illustrate each.*
Goal B: *Summarize 15 bad things to avoid when communicating during conflict.*
Goal C: *State 5 good things to do when communicating during conflict.*

 Key Words

internal noise

Basics of Good Communication

Goal A: *Identify the 5 parts of the circle of communication.*
Goal B: *Explain how body language, social setting, and differences in people affect communication.*
Goal C: *Summarize 8 temptations that a good listener must overcome.*

Setting

People cannot change their height. They may wish to be taller or shorter. But they cannot change their height by wishing or studying it. Communication is not like our height. We can improve the way we communicate—but not by wishing. We must study the process of communication and try new ways of listening and speaking. This may feel awkward at first. It might even feel like pretending. But little by little, with practice, new skills feel natural.[1] Change may also seem odd for your spouse at first. So, let him or her know that you are working on improving. In this lesson, you will learn knowledge and skills to help you communicate better.

Q 1 *How will you feel when you begin to practice new skills of communication?*

A. The circle of communication

A process takes place as people speak and listen to each other. There are five parts to the process of communication. Understand these parts, and you will communicate better with others. Let us go through the five steps.

Q 2 *Draw a picture that shows the 5 steps in the circle of communication.*

1. The sender begins the circle of communication. For example, a wife desires to share thoughts with her husband.

2. The message is what the sender communicates to the receiver. The message includes the words and meaning. For example, the wife may ask her husband what he would like for supper.

3. The method is the form of communication. The method includes words, tone of voice, and body language (non-verbal communication). For example, the wife may choose to use a soft voice and a smile, while sitting close to her husband.

4. The receiver interprets the message in personal ways. The person receiving a message understands it by what he has learned before. Also, the present situation affects the way a receiver interprets a message. For example, the husband may know from past experiences that his wife desires to please him by cooking the food he likes best.

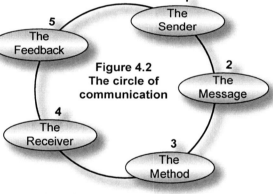

Figure 4.2
The circle of communication

5. Feedback completes the circle of communication. *Feedback* is the response the receiver gives back to the sender. For example, the husband may say that he would like chicken and rice. Some people do all of the talking. But a wise person encourages his or her spouse to talk. This enables two people to understand each other.

B. Three things affect understanding in communication.

Definition: to *communicate* is to share facts, thoughts, or feelings in a way that another can understand. Communication is not just talking. The goal is for two people to understand each other. The sender must find the words to express thoughts and feelings. The receiver must interpret the message. Good communication is harder than most people realize. It requires the efforts of both the speaker and the listener—like two people throwing a ball back and forth to each other.

Q 3 *What is the goal of communication?*

Words are important. But they are only one part of the process of communication. Let us look at three more things that affect how people understand one another.

Q 4 *Give an example of body language, and explain what it means.*

65

Q 5 *Give an example of how the social setting can affect communication.*

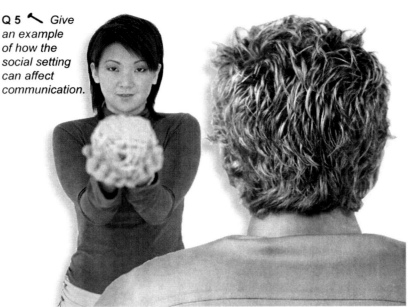

Figure 4.3 Good communication is like throwing a ball back and forth—it requires the effort of two people. For example, Mary asks John a question. This is like throwing the ball to him. John answers (catches) the question and discusses it a little. Then, he asks Mary a related question, throwing the conversation back to her. Talking too much is like holding the ball too long. Saying things that are rude or too direct is like throwing the ball too hard. Talking about things that do not interest the other person is like playing "*keep away."

Q 6 *Give an example of the different ways people interpret a word or an action.*

Q 7 *In your own words, summarize the error of Proverbs 18:13.*

Q 8 *How often do you listen poorly because of thinking about your response?*

Q 9 *Explain: The words 'never' and 'always' cause internal noise.*

1. **Body language affects understanding.** Body language includes such things as expressions of the face, use of the hands, and body posture. Words should match body language. For example, if a husband says he cares about what his wife is saying, he should look at her and pay attention to her words. Otherwise, if he says he cares, but is looking away, he is communicating two different messages. Likewise, if someone says, "I am sorry" while smiling, we do not believe him.

2. **The social setting affects understanding.** All communication happens in some kind of social setting. The setting affects the communication.[2] Are you at home or in public? Are the two people talking alone, or can others see and hear? These are important questions. People are less direct and less open when others are present. For example, a husband and wife will be more careful what they say if children or others are listening.

3. **The differences between people affect understanding.** People interpret words in different ways. For example, two people who see the word *tree* may think of different types of trees. Common words like *Christian, holy, good,* and *soon* mean different things to different people. Likewise, husbands and wives interpret words and actions in different ways.

A wife and husband were at home alone. She smiled at him and put her hand on his shoulder. He thought she wanted to have sex. But she was just feeling thankful for their marriage.

A husband and wife sat together in their home. The wife asked him a question. The husband was silent for about a minute. The wife thought he had not heard her, or was upset. But the husband was just thinking about how to answer her question.

The goal of communication is to understand each other. But many things can cause confusion. If we want to improve communication, we must work at the process. Effort is needed whether we are speaking or listening. Now let us look at some skills that will help us improve.

C. A good listener must overcome eight <u>temptations</u>.[3]

Good listening is the foundation of good communication. Several common things prevent a person from being a good listener. If you want to improve your communication, you must overcome eight temptations.

1. **As a listener, you may be tempted to think you know what a person is going to say, before he or she has said it.** This error causes you to interrupt the speaker. Proverbs 18:13 says, *"He who answers before listening—that is his folly and his shame."*

2. **You may be tempted to think about what *you* are going to say while the other person is talking.** This error prevents good listening.

3. **You may be tempted to react to untrue words the person speaks.** You may feel attacked by sentences that begin with "You" or include words like *always* or *never*.

"You always…" or "You never…" Such words cause *internal noise—reactions inside us that are louder than the speaker's words. It takes a person with great skill to remain silent and listen in such cases. Even in silence, anger may distract you from what the other person is trying to say. But a skilled, mature listener can hear the message, even if the speaker does not choose the best words to use.

4. You may be tempted to stop listening if your spouse acts in a certain way. If your spouse becomes loud, you may become annoyed and quit listening. If your spouse uses the whip of criticism or sarcasm, you may turn away and stop listening. A good listener learns to listen in spite of these harsh actions.

5. You may be tempted to stop listening because you think of something else. Some say that a person only listens for 7 seconds before his thoughts turn away. Perhaps the speaker is talking about an accident, and this causes you to remember another accident. You may still be looking at the speaker, but your mind has wandered into the past—thinking about something else. This is a common error to overcome by disciplining yourself to listen with your face *and* your mind.

Q 10 How long do you usually listen before your thoughts wander away?

6. You may be tempted to stop listening if you lack interest. Your spouse may want to talk about something that you find boring. Perhaps your child wants to talk about a friend at school, but you do not care. Being selfish or self-centered causes this error. Each of us must practice caring about others (Gal. 6:2; Phil. 2:4).

7. You may be tempted to listen poorly because you do not agree with the speaker. Perhaps you are judging what the person is saying instead of listening carefully. To conquer this error, learn to listen well before coming to a conclusion. It takes great skill to practice seeing things from the view of another person.

8. You may be tempted to listen to the speaker's words, but not pay attention to his feelings. If you are a good listener, you can repeat what a person has said, and explain what you think he or she is feeling. This kind of listening requires using your ears, eyes, and heart. You clarify what the speaker means by repeating back the message in your words. You pay attention to the speaker's tone of voice and body language. You ask questions to be sure you understand what the speaker is saying and feeling.

Q 11 In communication, how can you tell what a person is feeling?

D. Example: Listen well and affirm a person's feelings.

A wife came into the room with her head down.

"My Dear," she said, "I am so discouraged. The children do not seem to respect me. Perhaps I am not a good mother. I am wondering if it was a mistake to get married."

"No, no," replied the husband. "The children love and respect you. You are a wonderful mother. You are just tired. Let me fix you some food. Then get a good night's sleep and everything will be fine in the morning."

In this illustration, the husband was not a good listener. Perhaps he wanted to encourage his wife. But he rejected her feelings and words. He said that the children respected her. He said that she should not question herself, because she is a good mother. He told her that she felt tired—not discouraged. And he decided the way to solve her problem even though he did not listen well.

Q 12 What mistakes did the husband make as a listener?

The husband's opinion may be right or wrong. But without listening well, he stopped the chance for his wife to share her heart. She may wonder, "Where can I go to find someone to listen?"[4]

This husband could improve his communication in several ways.

1. He could encourage her to share her thoughts by reflecting what he heard. This is called *reflective listening*. For example, he could have said, "So, you think the children do not respect you." Or, "It sounds like you are discouraged." These responses would assure her that he was listening.

Q 13 How could the husband have listened better?

2. He could clarify by asking questions. "What makes you think that the children do not respect you?" "When did you begin to feel this way?"

3. After he has listened, he may respond with his thoughts. He may still think that she is just tired. But he needs to find a better way to say that. He could say, "I may be wrong, but I think you are very tired. Maybe you should get some extra rest. Perhaps things will seem different tomorrow."[5] Notice the tone of these words. His softer tone and support will help his wife remain open to him. He is admitting that he may be wrong. He is suggesting—not demanding. He is also leaving the decision about extra rest to her. And his response has kept open the chance to discuss this matter again.

E. A wise communicator must learn to control his tongue.

Scriptures give special attention to what we say. James 3:1-12 warns that the tongue is the most powerful and harmful part of the human body. The tongue is a great force for good or evil. It can build up or destroy. So, the speaker must learn *when* to speak and *what* to say. The wisdom of Proverbs warns us what to avoid when speaking.

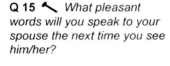

Q 14 ⬉ *Complete the chart in Figure 4.4.*

Proverbs	Things to Avoid When Speaking
13:3; 17:28; 29:20	
16:28; 17:9; 26:20	
17:14; 20:3; 21:9, 19; 27:15	Quarreling/nagging
22:10; 29:8	
26:24, 28	
27:2	
29:11, 22	

Figure 4.4 Proverbs warns of things to avoid when speaking.

Proverbs also teaches us what to say.

Proverbs	Things to Include When Speaking
10:19; 17:27; 20:5; 25:12	Wisdom
16:21-24; 25:11, 15	Pleasant words

Figure 4.5 Proverbs teaches things to practice when speaking.

Q 15 ⬉ *What pleasant words will you speak to your spouse the next time you see him/her?*

There is a reason why God gave us two ears and only one tongue. We should listen twice as much as we speak! We should be quick to listen and slow to speak (James 1:19). Likewise, we should practice obeying Ephesians 4:29: *"Do not let any unwholesome [unpleasant, harmful] talk come out of your mouths, but only what is helpful for building others up according to their needs, that it may benefit those who listen."*

F. Example: Harsh words—how to avoid speaking them and how to respond to them

A wife looked with joy at her healthy children. Smiling, she said, "My dear, these children are healthy, and growing so fast. They will soon need new clothes." Her heart was full of gratitude for her children. She felt close to her husband as she watched their children play. He had provided well for the needs of the family.

Q 16 ⬉ *What mistake did the husband make as a listener?*

But her husband began to feel anxious about her words. Would he have enough money to provide new clothes for his children? He thought that if his wife had married a richer man, she would not have to be concerned about clothes. He felt afraid that he might not be able to meet his duties as a husband and father.

"You are never satisfied," he spoke harshly to his wife. "You always want something more. The kids have plenty of clothes. You will just have to manage!"

How to Practice Good Communication   69

This husband was not a good listener. He heard her words, but did not pay attention to her smile and grateful feelings. He interpreted her words through his own feelings. He thought he knew what she meant, but he did not ask questions to clarify her thoughts. He was quick to speak and quick to become angry. So he missed a chance to share joy with his wife. He also created a problem between them by falsely accusing her. He needed to delay his reactions while he sought to better understand.

A wife might react quickly to such harsh words. She might hide her hurt in silence—or burst out with tears or anger. Then, the husband and wife could have a bad argument.

There are several good ways for the wife to respond.

Q 17 — *How should the wife respond to her husband's harsh words?*

1. A mature, skillful wife will discipline her emotions. She must not react before she thinks. She knows that her husband has misunderstood. That is the first problem she must solve.

2. She needs to look past her husband's harsh words at this time. This is difficult, but Proverbs 19:11 tells us that *"A man's wisdom gives him patience; it is to his glory to overlook an offense."*

3. She needs to return to the subject and make her meaning clear. Her husband's words and body language have warned her that he is feeling unsure and afraid. So, she restates her thoughts using different words. "I'm sorry. I did not make myself clear. I was not thinking about the need for more clothes now. I was feeling blessed that we have fine, healthy children." She may choose to praise him for the things he has done to bless their family. She has refused to react to his harsh words. Instead, she has focused on making her meaning clear. Proverbs 15:1 gives us this wisdom: *"A gentle answer turns away wrath."*

Most husbands would think of the wife's kind words as medicine on a wound. A godly husband would apologize for his harsh words. He might explain what he was thinking when he spoke the harsh words. Many husbands would thank the wife for the things she did to help their children.

After the husband has understood her meaning, the couple may still need to talk. Are they having money troubles? Does the wife demand too much? It may be good for them to discuss the harsh things that he said. In private, she may need to tell him that his harsh words hurt her—they cut like a knife. This will help the husband learn to control his sharp tongue!

Q 18 — *Should the couple talk about the husband's harsh words?*

Communication—Differences Between Men and Women
Goal A: *Describe the role of feelings when men and women communicate.*
Goal B: *Explain how the purpose of communicating differs for men and women.*
Goal C: *Identify 3 common mistakes women make when talking with men.*
Goal D: *Identify 3 common mistakes men make when talking with women.*

Men and women communicate in different ways, and for different reasons. Neither the male nor the female way of communicating is wrong or right—they are just different. All men do not communicate in the same ways, and women differ in the way they talk. Still, knowing the basic ways men and women talk can help communication. As you study the following differences, seek to determine which ones are true of your spouse.

> WOMEN WANT TO TALK ABOUT THEIR FEELINGS,
>
> BUT MEN WANT TO FIX THE PROBLEM!

A. Women want to talk about their feelings, but men want to fix the problem.[6]

God created women to talk more than men. In a day, a woman speaks twice as many words as a man does. She wants to talk more often and for longer periods of time than a man talks. In contrast, God created a man to talk less and focus more on tasks.

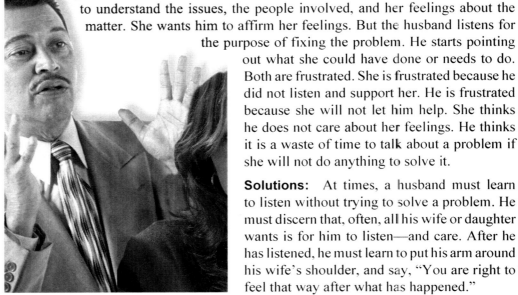

Figure 4.6 A man may not understand that a woman just wants him to listen.

Q 19 ↖ *What often frustrates a wife when she talks about a problem?*

Problems: A woman becomes frustrated when a man wants to fix a problem—when all she wants to do is talk about it. She wants her husband to understand the issues, the people involved, and her feelings about the matter. She wants him to affirm her feelings. But the husband listens for the purpose of fixing the problem. He starts pointing out what she could have done or needs to do. Both are frustrated. She is frustrated because he did not listen and support her. He is frustrated because she will not let him help. She thinks he does not care about her feelings. He thinks it is a waste of time to talk about a problem if she will not do anything to solve it.

Q 20 ↖ *What must a husband learn to do, instead of always trying to fix a problem?*

Solutions: At times, a husband must learn to listen without trying to solve a problem. He must discern that, often, all his wife or daughter wants is for him to listen—and care. After he has listened, he must learn to put his arm around his wife's shoulder, and say, "You are right to feel that way after what has happened."

At times, a wife can remind her husband that she is not looking for a solution. She just wants him to understand how she is feeling. At other times, after he understands her feelings, she might ask if he can think of a way to solve the problem.

B. Women can receive many messages at once, but men focus on one thing.[7]

Problems:

Q 21 ↖ *Do women sometimes discern things that men do not discern? Explain.*

1. Women may think they "know" certain things without being able to explain why. This often frustrates men, because men want to know "the facts." But if a husband and his wife are in the same social situation, the wife may be able to receive many messages at once while her husband is focused on one thing.

For example, a husband and wife visited in the home of Ramon and his family for the first time. After the visit, the husband said, "Ramon is a fine fellow. I think we could be great friends." The husband was remembering that he and Ramon talked about fishing. But the wife answered, "Oh, please be careful. I don't think he is the kind of friend that would be good for you." She was not sure why she thought this. But while her husband was talking about fishing, the wife listened, and also noticed the ungodly magazines in the home, saw the way Ramon ignored his wife's comments, and watched the pet dog crawl away from Ramon in fear. The wife had received many messages, while her husband focused on only one.

Q 22 ↖ *Why does a man get frustrated when his wife changes topics often?*

2. Women can jump from subject to subject in a conversation. A man does not like to do this. He wants to solve one problem before going on to another one. A man grows frustrated by "getting off the topic." He feels that this wastes his energy. If the wife changes topics quickly and often, the husband will not enjoy talking with her.

3. A man does not feel the need to talk while doing other things. If a husband and wife go fishing together, she may be looking forward to talking while they fish. But the husband may feel frustrated, because talking interrupts the fishing.

How to Practice Good Communication

Solutions:

1. A man should learn to value the feelings and perceptions that his wife has about issues. Sometimes, what a woman perceives and feels can guide a man in the right direction.

2. When women talk together, they should feel free to fly from topic to topic. But when a woman talks with her husband, she must walk slowly with him, discerning that God has not created him to fly from topic to topic!

3. Women should respect silence when a man desires it. Men should mature to realize that talking does not conflict with many things husbands and wives do together. Women should learn from men, and men should learn from women.

C. Women are more aware of their emotions than men are aware.[8]

Men and women both have the same emotions. But they are aware of emotions and express them in different ways. It takes men longer to understand what they are feeling. And when they understand, it takes them longer to find the words to express themselves. Husbands and wives can frustrate each other if they do not understand this difference. A wife often asks her husband, "How do you feel?" Many times the genuine answer is, "I don't know." But a woman may think he is unwilling to share. "A man has to think about his feelings before he can share them. A woman can feel, talk, and think at the same time."[9] A woman can learn to help her husband discover his feelings by asking him questions.

D. Women expand information when they talk, but men condense it.[10]

Problem: Women give lots of details when they talk. They give background information. They include feelings. They tell you how each person responded. Men make a long story short. They tend to give the "bare facts." While wives are expanding the story, their husbands say, "Just get to the point."

Solution: A husband can learn to value the details and feelings of a story. He can learn to pay more attention to what others say and feel. He can learn to value a woman's ability to remember so much and describe it so well.

A woman can, at times, skip some details when she tells a story to her husband, if she sees that he does not want to hear a long story. Also, when the husband is describing an event, she can ask him questions to help him give more information.

E. Women talk to develop relationships, but men talk to share information.[11]

Men and women often talk for different reasons. Women talk to bond with people—to get closer. This is why women are better listeners than men. They affirm, nod, encourage, and do not interrupt as much as men. Husbands often confuse this encouragement with agreement. Men do not usually affirm unless they are agreeing with the speaker.

Women explore *feelings* and ask more questions than men ask. Men talk more about topics, such as business, sports, or politics. Men are more interested in the attention they get while speaking than the relationship they may develop.

These differences cause women to create problems they could avoid. Women tend to be indirect in their speaking. A woman may circle around a topic—so her husband must guess how she feels and what she wants him to do. A husband is looking for information. A wife communicates better with her husband when she states what she feels and what she wants.

Q 23 ✎ What can a husband and wife learn from each other about communication?

Q 24 ✎ How can a woman help a man become more aware of his feelings?

Q 25 ✎ How should a husband respond to the way his wife describes an event?

Q 26 ✎ How can a man communicate in a way that interests his wife?

72   Marriage & Family

Q 27 What does a man think when his wife complains about what he has *not* done?

F. Communication mistakes women often make[12]

Mistakes a Wife May Make	What Her Husband Thinks
She offers advice when he does not ask for it.	She does not trust me.
She tries to control him through showing her feelings.	She does not accept me.
She complains about what he has not done.	She does not appreciate the things I do.
She corrects and instructs him.	She does not admire me.
She accuses indirectly, "How could you do that?"	She does not think I am a good person.
She criticizes his decisions or actions.	She does not love me or believe in me, because she does not encourage me.

Figure 4.7 Common mistakes women make in communicating

Q 28 What does a wife think when her husband does not listen well?

G. Communication mistakes men often make[13]

Mistakes a Husband May Make	What His Wife Thinks
He does not pay attention or ask questions to show interest.	He does not care.
He gives advice and solutions.	He does not understand.
He listens, but gets angry and blames her for making him feel upset.	He does not respect my feelings.
He is not sensitive to her feelings and needs.	He does not love me.
When she is upset, he explains why he is right and why she should not feel as she does.	He does not support me.
After listening, he says nothing or walks away.	I am not secure with him.

Figure 4.8 Common mistakes men make in communicating

Good Communication During Conflict
Goal A: *Explain 5 causes of conflict, and illustrate each.*
Goal B: *Summarize 15 bad things to avoid when communicating during conflict.*
Goal C: *State 5 good things to do when communicating during conflict.*

Setting

Conflict occurs in every marriage. It is a normal part of life. But how will a couple deal with conflict? This is an important question. A couple can work through conflict in a way that strengthens their marriage instead of harming it. In this lesson we will look at four things:
- 5 causes of conflict,
- 5 reactions to conflict,
- 15 things to avoid during conflict, and
- 5 good things to do during conflict.

A. Five causes of conflict

Q 29 What are 5 reasons for conflict?

1. Conflict arises from unmet needs.[14] People from every culture have similar needs. They need food and shelter. They need to feel safe. They need to belong and be loved. They need to feel that they are needed. They need to know that their work is important.[15] Tension will grow in a marriage if these kinds of needs are not met.

Q 30 In marriage, what question should a couple ask when conflict arises?

Acts 6:1-7 tells of a conflict that arose in the Jerusalem Church. Believers from a Greek background (Hellenistic Jews) became angry with believers from a Hebrew background. The Grecian Jews felt that their women were not receiving a fair share of food. This caused them to feel angry, less loved, and less important. So a conflict arose. The apostles solved this problem. Believers chose seven deacons—all with Greek names—to minister

How to Practice Good Communication 73

to the needs in the church. The solution provided food for all, and affirmed the value of Grecian Jews. When the people's needs were met, there was no conflict.

Whenever you see conflict in a family, ask yourself, "Which needs of people are not being met?"

2. Conflict arises from emotions controlled by the flesh, not the Spirit.[16] Many people do not manage their emotions in godly ways. Emotions are normal. God created us to have feelings. The problem is not the emotion, but the way we respond to it. For example, it is normal to feel anger at times. But we must allow the Holy Spirit—not the flesh—to guide our feelings. The Bible teaches us to be angry without sinning (Eph. 4:26). Mature believers learn to depend on the Spirit to produce the fruit of self-control over their emotions (Gal. 5:22-23).

Q 31 ✎ Is it wrong to feel an emotion like anger? Explain.

Figure 4.9 lists many feelings or emotions. Some husbands and wives react to their emotions in ways that hurt each other. Spouses may hurt one another on purpose in many ways. They may withdraw from their spouses and refuse physical closeness. They may refuse to provide them with the things they need such as money, love, or sex. They may use words that bring pain. They may dishonor them in front of others. They may have an affair. They may destroy things that are important to their spouses. They may shout, shove, or hit their mates. All of these ways of hurting come from emotions that are controlled by the flesh, not the Spirit.

Emotion	Opposite Emotion
Anger, hostility, annoyance	Calmness, patience, tolerance
Love, friendship	Hate, enmity
Fear, anxiety, nervousness	Confidence, peace, security, trust
Shame, guilt, sinfulness, worthlessness	Forgiven, cleansed, righteous, holy, justified, valuable, important
Kindness, thoughtfulness, tenderness, gentleness	Harshness, cruelty
Pity, mercy, compassion	Unconcern, selfishness
Envy, jealousy, greed	Contentment, gratefulness
Closeness	Distance
Joy, happiness, gladness	Sorrow, sadness
Encouragement, hope	Discouragement
Relaxed	Stressful
Interested	Repelled, bored
Respect, honor	Contempt
Wonder, worship, awe	Commonplace, unimpressed, familiarity
Thankful	Ungrateful

Figure 4.9   List of some basic emotions and opposite emotions[17]

3. Conflict arises from selfish desires.   Our desires and feelings are closely related. James tells us that fleshly desires are a cause of conflict.

Q 32 ✎ According to James 4:1, what is the cause of many conflicts?

*¹**What causes fights and quarrels among you?** Don't they come from your desires that battle within you? ²You want something but don't get it. You kill and covet, but you cannot have what you want. You quarrel and fight. You do not have, because you do not ask God. ³When you ask, you do not receive, because you ask with wrong motives, that you may spend what you get on your pleasures. ⁴You adulterous people, don't you know that friendship with the world is hatred toward God? Anyone who chooses to be a friend of the world becomes an enemy of God* (James 4:1-4).

James 4:1-3 answers the question, *"What causes fights and quarrels among you?"* Conflict comes because people are selfish. They want something selfish, for their own pleasure. But someone or something keeps them from getting what they want. It is not

Q 33 ✎ Is it wrong for a believer to love self? Explain.

wrong to love ourselves. But Jesus taught that we should place limits on the love we have for ourselves. He said we should love others as we love self (Mark 12:31). Likewise, Paul wrote that a husband should love his wife as he loves his own body (Eph. 5:28).

In marriage, conflict comes when a husband or wife thinks only of self. He or she may be willing to fight, *manipulate, deceive, or hurt in order to get what is wanted. Selfish desires are the opposite of loving one another. When conflict arises in a family, ask the question, "Is someone loving self too much?"

Q 34 *Does James say we should be quick to speak and slow to listen? Explain.*

4. Conflict arises from making a quick judgment about what a spouse means. Too often, a spouse jumps to a conclusion. The husband or wife thinks he/she knows what the other means, and answers harshly. Thus a conflict begins. Often, the spouse who speaks harshly has misunderstood. That is why James tells us to be *"quick to listen, slow to speak"* (James 1:19). Joshua 22 tells how a quick judgment almost caused a war.

Joshua sent his soldiers home after they conquered Canaan. Two and a half tribes returned toward their land on the east side of the Jordan River. At the Jordan River they stopped and built a large altar. They wanted to make sure that the descendants of all the tribes would know they worshiped Jehovah. They did not intend to sacrifice on the altar. It was to be a witness that Jehovah was their God. The other tribes heard that the altar had been built. They thought that their brothers had turned to idolatry. They feared God's judgment—so they gathered soldiers and marched to make war against their brothers. Just in time, they talked before they fought. Then the tribes who had wanted to fight—the tribes west of the Jordan—realized that they had made a quick judgment without understanding.

Quick judgments about other people's words and actions almost caused a war. Beware of the conflict that quick judgments may bring to a marriage. A quick judgment is like striking a match—it quickly starts a fire!

Figure 4.10 Look for the cause of the conflict.

Q 35 *What does Proverbs 29:20 say about a person who makes quick judgments?*

- *"Do you see a man who speaks in haste? There is more hope for a fool than for him"* (Prov. 29:20).
- *"A patient man has great understanding, but a quick-tempered man displays folly"* (Prov. 14:29).
- *"Do not be quickly provoked in your spirit, for anger resides in the lap of fools"* (Eccl. 7:9).

Q 36 *Which is better, to be cautious or to be bold? Explain.*

5. Conflict can come from different values. No two people are alike. Each person is shaped in a unique way—by creation, gender, background, and experiences. When the same types of conflict arise again and again in a marriage, it may be a sign that the couple has different values.[18] Many human differences are neither right nor wrong. Spouses can disagree, and both may be right—based on their *values*.

```
←——|————————|————————|————————|————————|——→
 Very cautious person  Cautious   One who balances    Confident   Very confident person
                                  caution and confidence
```

Figure 4.11 People make decisions in many ways. Some value much caution.
Some value a balance of caution and boldness. Others value boldness and confident action.

Figure 4.12 lists seven topics, and contrasts the values of Person A and Person B. However, there are not just two types of people, such as A and B. Rather, there are many types of people, from A to Z! In this chart, we are giving some examples, comparing Person A and Person B, to show that different values can cause conflict.[19] Also, keep in mind that opposite people often attract each other for marriage. So it is normal for one spouse to have the values of Person A, and the other spouse to have the values of Person B. The key to peace in the family is that they be aware of and respect the values of each other.

Q 37 *Is it normal for a married couple to have different values? Give an example.*

Topic	Values of Person A	Values of Person B
1. Security or protection	This person is cautious, careful, doubtful, and wants to avoid all danger.	This person is bold, confident, daring, trusting, and willing to take small risks.
2. Traditions and expectations of others	This person feels an inner sense of duty to do what society expects.	This person has some value for tradition, but is more practical than loyal to old rules.
3. Care or concern for others	This person is aware of and concerned about the feelings of others; cares much about people.	This person thinks little about the feelings of others, but thinks about goals and work to do.
4. Order	This person likes structure, schedules, neatness, routines, and authorities.	This person is more creative, artistic, spontaneous, and less predictable.
5. Social times	This person enjoys a variety of friends and social events.	This person likes to be alone, or with one other person.
6. Communication	This person describes details, tells a complete story, shows emotions, and is dramatic.	This person states the facts, shows little feeling, and uses few words.
7. Decisions	This person is slow to decide, and has doubts.	This person decides quickly and has much confidence.

Figure 4.12 A difference in values can cause conflict in marriage.

A couple with differing values about security might have a history of conflict like this. (Review line 1, Security, in Figure 4.12)

Conflict 1

Wife: "I do not want to move to the city. I do not know anyone there. When you are away, who will help me if I am in danger?" (Note that this wife feels cautious and afraid.)

Husband: "We will make new friends who will help. The city is not that dangerous. You are *always* trying to keep me from improving. In the city, I can earn more money." (Note that this man is confident, but he does not care enough about his wife's feelings. He accuses his wife, and errs by using the word *always*.)

Wife: "You care more about making money than you care about me!" (Note that the wife is afraid, and hurt. She accuses her husband with harsh words.)

Q 38 *In Conflict 1, what could the husband do to show more respect for the values of his wife?*

Conflict 2

Husband: "I am going to send our son to the market tomorrow. He must learn to do business by himself. He has watched me for some time, and now he must go alone."

Wife: "He is still too young. He will be carrying money, and he is still too small to defend himself. The older men will take advantage of him. Wait another year."

Q 39 *In Conflict 2, what smaller step could the husband take to assure his wife and protect his son?*

Conflict 3

Husband: "I want to visit my father and take him a fine gift. It will cost more than I thought, but it will be worth it."

Wife: "But that is half of what we have saved. You should get a less expensive gift. We may need the money for something else."

Husband: "You *never* have liked my father…"

Q 40 *In Conflict 3, does it sound like the husband is honoring his father above his family? Explain.*

The husband and wife may argue about the danger of the city, the maturity of their son, and how the wife feels about her father-in-law. But what is the root of these quarrels and conflict? The root of the conflict is that they have different values about security. The wife is cautious and fearful. The husband is bold and confident. The husband needs to help his wife feel secure. He needs to give assurance, and move ahead slowly. The more secure the wife feels, the more she will support his decisions. We have given three examples on the topic of security. But conflict can arise from any of the topics in Figure 4.12 if a husband and wife have different values.

We have looked at several causes of conflict: unmet needs, emotions controlled by the flesh, selfish desires, quick judgments, and different values. Now let us look at ways people respond to conflict.

B. Five ways people react to conflict

People react to conflict—based on their culture, their nature, and the examples they have seen. Most people react to conflict in one of five ways.

Q 41 ✏ *How do you usually respond to conflict?*

1. My way. This person feels that *his* way is the only way. He keeps pushing until he gets his way or until the other person gets out of the way.

2. No way. This person ignores the problem. Nothing is solved because he walks away from the conflict.

3. Your way. This person wants the other person to be happy. He wants peace or approval so much that he always submits to the other person. This way can be peaceful, for a time, but it is also frustrating.

4. Half way. This person gives up some things, part of the time. Each person gets some of what he wants. But he also loses some of what he wants.

5. Our way. This couple works out problems together. They care about solving problems. But they also care about each other and their marriage. They want each person to be satisfied with the solution. And they each view their spouse as more important than their own personal needs.

In which of the five ways do you respond to conflict? Can you improve? A person can change his response to conflict. He can learn new responses if his ways are not as wise as he desires. God wants us to be at peace with each other. We are to be reconciled with God and with people (Matt. 5:23-24). Paul tells us to protect the unity of the Spirit through the bond of peace (Eph. 4:3). A good response to conflict enables us to live at peace within marriage.

C. Fifteen bad things to avoid during conflict[20]

Q 42 ✏ *How can you learn to obey all of these commandments?*

These 15 commandments for conflict are very important. First, you must read and understand them. Then, you must learn to practice them one by one. Hear this: it is not possible for you to learn to practice all of these commandments quickly. You must pray and choose one of them to practice. As you read them, ask the Holy Spirit to show you which one you break the most often. For example, your worst habit might be bringing up past faults. After choosing one commandment, practice obeying it for a day, two days, and a week. After you have learned to obey that one commandment, it will become a communication skill. Then, you can slowly work on learning to obey another one. In this manner, you can add skills to communicate better in your marriage. For most of us, it does not take long to read and understand these 15 commandments. But it takes time, humility, the desire to improve, the Spirit's help, and practice to learn communication skills.

1. Never speak rashly. Plan what you will say and how you will say it. Be slow to speak. This is very important if you are hurt or angry.

2. Never confront your spouse in public. This is embarrassing for your spouse and for those around you. Nothing will be solved in public.

3. **Never confront your spouse in front of the children.** Your children need to live in peace. They need to love both parents and not choose the side of either.

4. **Never use your children in the conflict.** This develops insecurity within children. For example, do not use a child to testify for you.

5. **Never say "never" or "always."** This makes the other person defend himself. For example, in conflict, a husband told his wife, "You *always* complain." This was not true. By exaggerating, he hurt his wife, and avoided a solution.

6. **Never use name-calling.** This takes a person's flaw and exaggerates it. Names like *liar*, *lazy*, or *stupid* will cause greater problems now and in the future.

Q 43 ✎ *To improve your communication skills, which one of these commandments should you work on first? Explain.*

7. **Never be *historical*—bringing up the past.** Focus on the problem at hand. Bringing up the past causes hurt and confusion. Do not be like the boy who buried his dead cat—except for the tail—and pulled it up from time to time. Digging up bad things from the past will always cause a stink! Forgive and forget, as God does with our sins.

8. **Never walk away unless the other person agrees to a time-out—a few minutes to pray.** Walking away during conflict is rude, and it increases anger in the person left behind.

9. **Never shout.** Remember, the tone of your voice communicates more than your words.

10. **Never bring other people into the conversation unless they are a direct part of the problem.** Comparing someone to another member of his or her family increases the conflict.

11. **Never "win" at the expense of your spouse "losing."** Conflict is not a contest. A problem is not solved when one person wins and the other loses. Both people must feel they have met their needs. Aim at a win/win—a solution in which both spouses win.

12. **Never talk down to your spouse, as if he or she was immature or unwise.** Do not lift yourself higher and make your spouse feel lower. This adds hurt to the problem.

13. **Never accuse your spouse with "you" statements.** Instead of saying "<u>You</u> did this," say something like "I felt ____ when you did not consult me."

14. **Never enter into a conflict when either of you is tired, sick, or taking medicine.** Wait to discuss hard matters until both of you feel well.

15. **Never touch your spouse in a harmful manner.** Do not hit or hurt your spouse!

These 15 commandments are some of the most important things you will ever study. If the only thing you learned from this course was to keep these commandments, you would deserve a grade of A. Learning to be polite and kind to people is among the most important things in life.

D. Five good things to do during conflict[21]

1. **Listen in an active way.**
   - Ask questions.
   - Restate what you are hearing.
   - Be open, rather than defending yourself.

Q 44 ✎ *How can a person listen in an active way?*

2. **Clarify the problem.**
   - Ask yourself and your spouse, "What is wrong?"
   - Ask, "Why is this important to you?"
   - Acknowledge your spouse's point of view. Say, "I can see this is important to you."

Q 45 ✎ *What was the problem in Acts 6?*

3. **Ask for suggestions.**
   - Ask, "What is your solution?" (Too often, people criticize or complain, without seeking a solution. Parents, the time must come in conflict that you turn from

Q 46 ✎ *What happens if people talk about problems but do not seek solutions?*

the problem to the solution. Parents, you should always make it clear to your family members what they can do to please you. Otherwise, they will become discouraged and stop trying to please you.)
- Describe changes in behavior—"What can I do differently?"
- Identify what a time of peace will look like. Ask, "How will we know that things have changed?"

4. **Share your thoughts.**
   - Stay calm.
   - Give information.
   - Clarify your point of view.
   - Find something in your spouse's complaint that you can agree with.

Q 47 *Why is it helpful to write down agreements in the family?*

5. **Agree on a solution.**
   - "I can do _____, but it would help me if you would _____."
   - Affirm that both of you want to solve the problem. Write the agreement in a book, and have all sign it who are concerned. Otherwise, the time may come that someone forgets the agreement.
   - Set a date to review your progress.

Chapter Summary

 Basics of Good Communication

Goal A: *Identify the 5 parts of the circle of communication.*

The sender, the message, the method, the receiver, and feedback

Goal B: *Explain how body language, social setting, and differences in people affect communication.*

Body language includes such things as expressions of the face, use of the hands, and body posture. Words should match body language.

The social setting affects communication. People are less direct and less open when others are present.

Husbands and wives interpret words and actions in different ways—depending on their backgrounds, points of view, and emotional differences.

Goal C: *Summarize 8 temptations that a good listener must overcome.*

You may be tempted to stop listening if you think you know what a person is going to say; if you think about what you are going to say; if you react to untrue words; if your spouse acts in a certain way; because you think of something else; if you lack interest; or if you disagree. Also, you may be tempted to listen to the speaker's words, but not pay attention to his or her feelings.

 Communication—Differences Between Men and Women

Goal A: *Describe the role of feelings when men and women communicate.*

Women want to talk about their feelings, but men want to fix the problem. All must learn to listen to words and affirm feelings.

Goal B: *Explain how the purpose of communicating differs for men and women.*

Women talk to develop relationships, but men talk to share information.

Goal C: *Identify 3 common mistakes women make when talking with men.*

She offers advice when he does not ask for it. She tries to control him through showing her feelings. She complains about what he has not done, without praising what he has done. (Review Figure 4.7.)

Goal D: *Identify 3 common mistakes men make when talking with women.*

He does not pay attention or ask questions to show interest. He gives advice and solutions. He listens, but gets angry and blames her for making him feel upset. He is not sensitive to her feelings and needs. He explains why she should not feel a certain way. (Review Figure 4.8.)

How to Practice Good Communication 79

 Good Communication During Conflict

Goal A: *Explain 5 causes of conflict, and illustrate each.*

Conflict arises from unmet needs, from emotions controlled by the flesh (not the Spirit), from selfish desires, from making a quick judgment about what a spouse means, and from different values.

Goal B: *Summarize 15 bad things to avoid when communicating during conflict.*

Never speak rashly. Never confront your spouse in public. Never confront your spouse in front of the children.

Never use your children in the conflict. Never say "never" or "always." Never use name-calling. Never be historical. Never walk away without a time-out. Never shout. Never bring other people into the conversation.

Never "win" at the expense of your spouse "losing." Never talk down. Never accuse your spouse with "you" statements. Never enter into a conflict when either of you is tired, sick, or taking medicine. Never touch your spouse in a harmful manner.

Goal C: *State 5 good things to do when communicating during conflict.*

Listen in an active way. Clarify the problem. Ask for suggestions. Share your thoughts. Agree on a solution.

 Test Yourself: Circle the letter by the *best* completion to each question or statement.

1. The circle of communication includes:
a) The Interpreter
b) The Outline
c) The Method
d) The Summary

2. Looking away as a person talks is an example of
a) indirect listening.
b) being angry.
c) internal noise.
d) body language.

3. Which words cause internal noise?
a) The words *yours* and *mine*
b) The words *always* and *never*
c) The words *forever* and *ever*
d) The words *you* and *me*

4. Who are more often aware of their feelings?
a) Women
b) Men
c) Youth
d) Children

5. Women often communicate to
a) share information.
b) build relationships.
c) discover feelings.
d) avoid silence.

6. In communication, wives often err by
a) becoming angry and walking away.
b) not paying attention when he speaks.
c) giving him too much praise.
d) giving advice when he did not ask for it.

7. In communication, husbands often err by
a) not paying attention when she speaks.
b) blaming the children for his faults.
c) talking about her family members.
d) explaining why he feels as he does.

8. A common cause of conflict is
a) financial problems.
b) time alone.
c) unmet needs.
d) loving self.

9. A commandment during conflict is:
a) Never mention your parents.
b) Never refer to past sins.
c) Never delay a discussion.
d) Never exclude children.

10. Listening in an active way includes
a) using actions as well as words.
b) raising your voice for expression.
c) asking questions to clarify.
d) remaining completely silent.

Chapter 5:
How to Approach Sexual Life in Marriage
Song of Songs

Introduction

> **Groom to His Virgin Bride:**
>
> ¹⁰*How delightful is your love, ... my bride!*
> *How much more pleasing is your love than wine, and the fragrance of your perfume than any spice!*
> ¹¹*Your lips drop sweetness as the honeycomb, my bride; milk and honey are under your tongue. ...*
> ¹²*You are a garden locked up, ... my bride; you are a spring enclosed, a sealed fountain.*
> ¹³*Your plants are an orchard of pomegranates with choice fruits, ...* ¹⁴*... and all the finest spices.*
> ¹⁵*You are a garden fountain, a well of flowing water streaming down from Lebanon.*
>
> **Virgin Bride:**
>
> ¹⁶*Awake, north wind, and come, south wind!*
> *Blow on my garden, that its fragrance may spread abroad.*
> *Let my lover come into his garden and taste its choice fruits.*
>
> **Groom:**
>
> ¹*I have come into my garden, ... my bride; I have gathered my myrrh with my spice.*
> *I have eaten my honeycomb and my honey; I have drunk my wine and my milk.*
>
> **Choir:**
>
> *Eat, O friends, and drink; drink your fill, O lovers (Song of Songs 4:10–5:1).*

    The Song of Songs has several interpretations. But many overlook the plain, main meaning. In this greatest of songs, we see the pleasure of the husband and wife sharing their love in physical ways. Throughout the song, they seek one another with passion. They become "one flesh." The Bible clearly shows that sexual relations in marriage are meant to bring pleasure to the husband and wife. This chapter will explore how the husband and wife can enjoy their sexual experience throughout marriage.

Lessons:
Beginning Your Sexual Life Together in Marriage

Goal A: *Summarize 4 reasons for sex in marriage.*
Goal B: *State 4 sexual differences in the desires of men and women.*
Goal C: *Comment on expectations, acceptance, and the past in relation to sex in marriage.*
Goal D: *Explain how a husband can avoid the most common sexual error in marriage.*

Continuing Your Sexual Life Together in Marriage

Goal A: *Summarize the need for sexual faithfulness and satisfaction in marriage.*
Goal B: *Explain 4 things a wife should know about her husband's sexual desires.*
Goal C: *Explain 4 things a husband should know about his wife's sexual desires.*
Goal D: *Describe guarding time together and adjusting to change in marriage.*

Dealing With Difficult Sexual Problems in Marriage
Goal A: *Identify 3 reasons for difficult sexual problems in marriage.*
Goal B: *Examine 3 solutions for sexual problems in marriage.*

Beginning Your Sexual Life Together in Marriage

Goal A: *Summarize 4 reasons for sex in marriage.*
Goal B: *State 4 sexual differences in the desires of men and women.*
Goal C: *Comment on expectations, acceptance, and the past in relation to sex in marriage.*
Goal D: *Explain how a husband can avoid the most common sexual error in marriage.*

A. Begin sex together understanding the four reasons for sex in marriage.

The Bible states four reasons why God gave the sexual experience to husbands and wives.

Q 1 *What are 4 reasons for the gift of sex in marriage?*

First, **sexual intercourse—sex between a husband and wife—is the way to create new life.* God created the man and woman. He blessed them and told them to be fruitful and increase in number (Gen. 1:28).

Second, *sex between a husband and wife prevents sexual immorality.* While the marriage bed is holy, sex outside of marriage is sinful (Heb. 13:4). So, 1 Corinthians 7:2 tells us that most people should seek marriage as a holy way to fulfill their sexual desire.

Third, *sex moves husbands and wives to "oneness."* They become "one flesh." *"For this reason a man will leave his father and mother and be united to his wife, and they will become one flesh"* (Gen. 2:24). In sexual intercourse, the husband and wife are drawn away from themselves to concern for each other. They care as much about each other as they care about their own sexual and emotional needs. Sex in marriage unites body, soul, and spirit. *"Has not the LORD made them one? In flesh and spirit they are his. And why one? Because he was seeking godly offspring. So guard yourself in your spirit, and do not break faith with the wife of your youth"* (Mal. 2:15). Sex in marriage renews and refreshes the love between a husband and wife.

Fourth, *sex is for fun and pleasure between a husband and wife.* This pleasure encourages them to delight in each other. Pleasure within the commitment of marriage is like a magnet that keeps them turning to each other. Sex in marriage is a fun, satisfying way of sharing love. A believer who feels guilty about having fun in bed with his mate needs to discern that this guilt is not from God. The Song of Songs teaches us that God wants husbands and wives to have fun together, sexually. It is God's plan for a husband and wife to enjoy sex with each other.

These four reasons show why sexual intercourse is a unique and powerful part of marriage. Marriage allows time for a rich sexual life to grow. But it is good to begin well. So let us look at how to make a good sexual beginning as a newly married couple.

B. Begin sex together agreeing about children and birth control.

Sexual intercourse can create children. But that is not its only purpose. If sex was only for this reason, couples could have sex only a few days each month. Most females in the animal world want sex with a male for just a few days each year—to become pregnant. But the human female desires sex with her husband throughout the year. However, fear of pregnancy can hinder sexual love. An early pregnancy may make marriage difficult. A couple should discuss, agree, and choose a plan for children before sex begins. Many couples desire to wait a few months, and some a few years, until they have children. This gives them time to enjoy each other, gain financial strength, and adjust to the marriage.

Q 2 *In your culture, after marriage, do some like to wait for a time before having children? Explain.*

81

Q 3 *What lesson does Tom illustrate?*

Q 4 *What is pornography, and why is it wrong?*

Q 5 *What is the best way to learn about sex in your culture?*

Q 6 *What are some sexual differences between a husband and wife?*

C. Begin sex together knowing the sexual differences in men and women.

Tom had never driven a car. He had no training, but he had a lot of desire. He did not know how to put in gas or check the oil. He was not sure which pedal controlled the brakes or the speed. And he only knew the meaning of a few road signs. Still, he imagined how much fun it would be to drive. He could see himself racing around curves and driving the car to the top of a hill. Which one of us would want to ride with Tom as he drove? All would prefer that he get some teaching first.

There is a right way and a wrong way to learn about sex. For example, *pornography is the wrong way to learn about sex. It is a sin that Satan uses. Pornographic magazines, pictures/films/videos, and dances bring money to the maker and sexual pleasure to the viewer. The people in the pictures can be shamed, defiled, and hurt. It makes no difference how they are used as long as the viewer is sexually excited. Pornography destroys natural, sexual desires. Users may become totally self-centered about sex. They think of others as objects to be used for their pleasure. They no longer see others as people who are created in the image of God. All of these attitudes bring pain into the marital relationship. Refuse to take even one step on the road of pornography. Do not even look at the food on the devil's table. It is poison.

Some say that people should have sexual experience before marriage. We have already studied the foolishness of this. Learning about sex through practice is only for marriage. However, before the wedding, there is much to learn by talking or studying. In an earlier chapter we mentioned books about sex by LaHaye and Wheat. These books have teachings about sex in marriage. Some cultures may think these books are too open. Parents, before your children marry, you should teach them about sexual matters. Otherwise, they will learn from someone else. A father should teach his son, and a mother should teach her daughter. Also, an elder in the church who counsels can discuss these matters with one planning for marriage. Whatever the source of sexual education, a person seeking marriage should learn about male and female bodies. Figure 5.1 compares men and women on several sexual topics.

Basic Sexual Differences Between Men and Women	
Most Men	**Most Women**
Desire sex often, such as 1 or more times each week	May be content with less sex; Do not desire sex during their *menstrual cycle—their monthly flow of blood
Desire sex because of *seeing* the female body	Desire sex because of *relationship:* touching, talking, and romance
Can enjoy sex almost any time	Must feel closeness to enjoy sex
Have sexual desire that rises quickly, like striking a match	Have sexual desire that rises slowly, like boiling water
Can reach a *climax quickly	Need more time to reach a climax
Can focus on sex easily, no matter what is happening	Are easily distracted by surroundings, odors, uncleanness, noises, or lack of privacy
Need a climax to enjoy sex	May find sex enjoyable without a climax
Can often find extra energy for sex	Have less sexual desire if they feel tired

Figure 5.1   General sexual differences between men and women

Q 7 *If a husband desires sex with his wife in the evening, how can he plan ahead?*

Husband, if you want to have sex with your wife in the evening, plan ahead. Begin to plant seeds of kindness in the morning. Show your love to her throughout the day. Think of sex as not just an event, but as the fruit of your friendship and relationship with your wife. Take time to talk with her. Ask questions about her day, smile at her,

How to Approach Sexual Life in Marriage

and listen carefully when she talks. Do some of her work. Eat with her, and go to bed early before she is too tired. In the bedroom, do not act like a bull in the field! Rather, be gentle. Hold her close to you. Talk softly, and touch her in the places that bring her pleasure. Rub her neck, back, and feet. Ask her what feels good to her. Kiss her slowly in places and ways she enjoys. Thank her for being such a good wife to you. Give her sincere praise for her beauty in character, spirit, and body. Tell her how much you love her. Which of us ever tires of being praised? Your wife will never grow weary of hearing the kind things you can say to her. Slowly, her sexual desires will arise, as a charcoal fire turns from smoke to glowing coals. Your wife can fly, but she needs a long runway![1] Make sex something that your wife enjoys—an expression of your loving relationship. Love her as you love yourself. One wise counselor said it is good for a husband and wife to spend an hour having sex. It is a special, holy time to enjoy together.

Figure 5.2 Husband, sometime, to begin a romantic evening, do some of your wife's work!

D. Begin sex together with realistic, sensible expectations.

Sexual expectations are hopes and ideas people have about sex. Expectations are created in many ways—either good or bad. A person's expectations may be formed through stories of a culture, pornography, movies, dreams, conversations, imagination, or past experiences. The first sexual experiences in marriage may not be what people have expected or imagined. This can bring discouragement. It is best to approach marriage with clear thinking. Below are four truths about the sexual experience in marriage.

1. It takes time for a couple to develop sexual relations that please each other. The biblical plan is that sexual pleasure is for the husband and the wife. Each person—and each couple—is unique. Basic differences between men and women do not describe all. For example, a wife may desire sex more than her husband desires it. This is not true most of the time, but it is possible. Or a certain husband may find little pleasure in sex if his wife does not enjoy him sexually. There is a wide range of healthy sexual behavior in men and women. Each couple will be unique in their experience.

A husband and wife need time to learn what pleases each other. Things that bring pleasure may differ from person to person. Things that bring pleasure may change in a person from time to time. This means that a passionate, perfect, first night between two virgins is rare. The couple should not be discouraged or embarrassed by early experiences. Sex in marriage gets better and better as the years go by. A husband and wife learn to please each other as they talk during sex, and practice new things together.

Deuteronomy 24:5 says, *"If a man has recently married, he must not be sent to war or have any other duty laid on him. For one year he is to be free to stay at home and bring happiness to the wife he has married."*

2. There is still a need for sexual control in marriage. Marriage does not mean that sex is available at all times. Loving couples sometimes wait to fulfill their sexual needs. Sickness, sadness, pregnancy, lack of privacy, being tired, travel, or times of prayer and fasting may limit sex. During such times, a husband or wife must practice sexual control. Remember, Jesus taught us to love each other, not just ourselves (John 15:12)!

3. The whole relationship of a couple affects their sexual relationship. As a bad apple or potato affects the whole bag; as yeast affects the whole loaf of bread; a problem in any part of a marriage relationship affects all of the relationship. Arguments between

Q 8 ➚ *What are some sources of sexual expectations?*

Q 9 ➘ *Is the first sex in marriage the best sex? Explain.*

Q 10 ➘ *How can you apply the principle of Deuteronomy 24:5 in your culture?*

Q 11 ➘ *Should a husband demand sex whenever he desires it? Explain.*

Q 12 ➚ *Why does a wife not enjoy sex soon after an argument?*

a husband and wife will cause coldness in their sexual life. This is especially true for the wife, because she must feel emotionally close to enjoy sex. Things like arguments, harsh words, and financial pressures will affect a couple's sex life. After a quarrel, the husband may want to make peace and have sex—but the wife may need several hours for her emotions to heal. Husband, do not quarrel with your wife. If you want to gather honey, do not kick the beehive.

Song of Songs 5:2-8 tells of a time when a wife rejected her husband. In those days, the king and his wife often slept in separate rooms. She was asleep when he came home late. She was upset because he woke her in the middle of the night—so she refused to open her door. After a few minutes, she awoke fully from her sleep and agreed to welcome him in. But it was too late. He had gone. His male pride was bruised by her rejection. She looked for him to make peace, but she could not find him for a while. So they both felt badly for a time, until they solved the argument.[2] This example teaches us that arguments affect sex within marriage.

> JESUS TAUGHT US TO LOVE EACH OTHER, NOT JUST OURSELVES (JOHN 15:12)!

Q 13 *How will you know what your mate likes the most when making love?*

4. It helps to communicate with each other when making love. Many people find it hard to talk with a mate about sexual feelings. This may come from a cultural idea of modesty. Or, some err by thinking that since sex is natural, the spouse should know what is pleasing. Sometimes, not talking about sex comes from the fear of being honest. For example, a husband might not know how a wife will respond to what he likes. Perhaps she is doing one thing and he likes another, so he is afraid he will hurt her feelings if he speaks. One husband solved this problem by being silent about the things he did not like, but telling his wife when she did something he liked. Some form of communication helps. The couples that enjoy sex most are those who find ways to communicate what pleases them. Each mate should seek to love in the way that pleases the other the most.

E. Begin sex together with acceptance.

Q 14 *Why is acceptance important for sex in marriage?*

When Adam and Eve were first created, they stood before each other naked (Gen. 2:25). Neither was ashamed of the way they appeared, and both accepted each other. This level of acceptance in marriage is good. God is the Creator of each person. So all husbands and wives should feel good about the way God has created them.

There are few perfect bodies. Pornography and fashion magazines use pictures of bodies that are close to perfect. Many of the people in magazines and on television have had their bodies changed by doctors—changes that make them look more attractive sexually. But acceptance means loving yourself and your spouse, knowing that God is the Creator. So do not wish you were taller or shorter, thinner or fatter, darker or lighter. Husband, never compare your wife's body with another woman in a bad way. Accept her just the way she is. Wife, do not criticize your husband's body, or wish he could be like a different man. Accept him as the gift God has given you. Acceptance emphasizes things about a spouse that are delightful.

Marriage is not a place for a husband and wife to judge each other. The sexual act is not to evaluate or to criticize. In sex, a husband and wife are bare before each other—both emotionally and physically. Deep and wonderful sex does not require past experience. It requires openness and acceptance by husband and wife.[3] Lack of acceptance pushes a husband and wife away from each other. For example, if a husband tells his wife that he does not like the way she looks, this will hurt her feelings. Then, she will not enjoy having sex with him. But if he accepts her, and praises the way she looks, this enables her to enjoy being naked before him.

How to Approach Sexual Life in Marriage 85

The Song of Songs shows how the man and the woman accepted each other's bodies. The groom tells his bride about the beauty he sees in her (Song of Songs 4:1-7; 7:1-9). And the bride shows her pleasure in his body (Song of Songs 5:10-16). These spoken words of acceptance bring security to the bedroom. **Acceptance in marriage frees two people to share all of themselves with each other.**

The bride of the Song of Songs knew her skin was different. It had become darker because she worked outside. She felt as if the city girls were staring at her because of her dark skin (Song of Songs 1:5-6). Yet she and her groom found beauty in the thing that others may have rejected. His words of praise caused her confidence to grow. The acceptance by her husband wiped away all of her fear and insecurity about herself.[4]

Q 15 How did the way Solomon accepted his bride encourage her?

Husband, accept your wife and speak sincere words of praise about the way she looks. When a wife knows that her body pleases her husband, she likes to share it with him! Wife, accept your man as he is, and say good things to him about the way he looks. This will encourage him to be a faithful husband, a good lover, and a kind father.

F. Begin sex together with honesty about your past.

Some people will not be virgins when they marry. But the marriage bed is only for two people. The time for talking about the past is before marriage. Then, past experiences and memories must be forgotten. Never compare your spouse to another lover. To have a good beginning, there should be honesty about the past.

Q 16 Can a person be honest without sharing all of the details of the past? Explain.

Q 17 What should a person do if he is entering marriage, but is no longer a virgin?

If you have not been pure, these four actions can help you:
- Repent, if you have not already done this. Turn away from past sins, and turn toward the grace of God.
- Receive forgiveness from the one you will marry.
- Release the affections and memories. This is an act of the will. When bad feelings and thoughts come, do not dwell on them. Each time bad feelings and thoughts come, reject them. Replace them with thoughts of your spouse.
- Reject guilt if it comes. Repeat the truth of forgiveness to yourself. *"If we confess our sins, he is faithful and just and will forgive us our sins and purify us from all unrighteousness"* (1 John 1:9).

There is an old story about a widow who married seven times. She lived longer than her first six husbands, and the seventh left her. When they went to court, the judge asked why he left the widow. He said, "It was not my desire to leave. But there was no place for me to sleep in the bedroom. I got crowded out of the bed by the old husbands she kept bringing into it."

G. Begin sex together by avoiding the most common mistake.

The most common mistake of a new couple is that the husband is in a hurry. The new husband is usually eager, quick, and ready to have sex. But most new wives need time, tenderness, and privacy. It is common to be tired after the wedding celebration. The wife may need time to rest before beginning to make love. The new husband should be patient with his wife. The love act should come after foreplay—taking time to talk, touch, kiss, and hold each other close. The husband should speak words of love to his wife. She must know that the husband's desire is for her—not just for sex. She is not just an object for his satisfaction. He desires her as a person—and her alone. He should show concern for any pain she may feel when he is about to break her *hymen—the seal of her virginity.[5] Still, he should seek to arouse her—to raise her sexual desire above any fear.

Q 18 What is the most common mistake of a young husband?

Beginnings are exciting and a little frightening. Every newly married couple wants their sexual life to begin well. Their shared passion will unite them in a powerful way—that is exciting. But they will be naked to each other, both physically and emotionally—and this may frighten or embarrass one or both of them. The vows of marriage create

Q 19 *How does the security of this little boy relate to security in marriage?*

safety for this new beginning. Your spouse has already promised not to reject you. So, relax and enjoy the beginning.

It was the little boy's first day at school. He had spent every day of his life, until now, with his parents. He had heard some things about school, and he was excited. But as his father walked him to school, he began to feel afraid. What if he did not know anyone? What if everyone else but him knew what to do? What if the teacher thought he could already read? His father took his hand as they neared the school. "See that tree at the corner of the building? When school is over, I will be right there waiting for you." The little boy felt better. Secure in his father's promise, he stepped into the classroom, ready to discover a new world.

**Figure 5.3
A child can face new situations if he is secure in his father's love.**

Continuing Your Sexual Life Together in Marriage

Goal A: *Summarize the need for sexual faithfulness and satisfaction in marriage.*
Goal B: *Explain 4 things a wife should know about her husband's sexual desires.*
Goal C: *Explain 4 things a husband should know about his wife's sexual desires.*
Goal D: *Describe guarding time together and adjusting to change in marriage.*

Setting

It is good to begin a race well; but it is even more important to finish it well. Let us now look at how to continue your sexual life together in ways that satisfy both husband and wife.

A. Remain faithful to your mate.

Q 20 *Compare idolatry and adultery.*

The greatest harm that can come to a marriage is through unfaithfulness. This is such a sin against being one flesh that Jesus allowed divorce for it (Matt. 19:9). Throughout the Old Testament, God said that Israel was committing spiritual adultery by seeking other gods. The Israelites did not get rid of Jehovah—they *added* other gods to their worship. But covenant love demands loyalty to one and only one. The Israelites could not love other gods and also Jehovah. So God turned them over to captivity because they broke the covenant. Likewise, God demands people to be sexually faithful in marriage. *"You shall not commit adultery"* is a command from God (Exod. 20:14). *"What God has joined together, let man not separate"* (Matt. 19:6).

B. Do not refuse to give your mate sexual satisfaction.

Q 21 *When is it okay for a husband or wife to refuse sexual relations in marriage?*

A husband and wife must choose to respond to the needs of each other. Paul wrote these instructions to the church at Corinth: *"The husband should fulfill his marital duty to his wife, and likewise the wife to her husband"* (1 Cor. 7:3-5). Spouses depend on each other for sexual satisfaction in marriage. Neither the husband nor wife has the right to say "no" to the spouse's sexual needs. Each should be sensitive and respond to the other. But each spouse should also be sensitive to the physical condition of the other. True love does not insist on sex when the spouse feels badly.

Sex should never become a ritual or habit, because the couple is alone again in bed. Rather, it should be started because of love and sexual desire.[6] When this happens, a mate should not refuse for a small reason. Sex between husband and wife should **never** be connected to rewards or punishments. A wife must never refuse sex to punish or guide her husband.

Anabella was angry with her husband. He expected her to work too much. He treated her like a servant, rather than a mate. He seldom took time to talk with her. It seemed like the only time he wanted to see her was to eat or have sex. She knew that if she complained he would be angry. So she decided to speak to him through a parable of actions. Each time he wanted sex, she said that her head or back hurt. Weeks passed, but he did not understand the true message she was telling him. What should she do?

Gloria, a foolish young wife, saw a beautiful dress at the market. She told her husband that she liked the dress very much. Weeks passed. The husband went to the market several times, but he never returned with the dress. Still, the wife was determined. One night, when her husband came to her for sex, she turned her back. Pouting, she said, "You do not love me enough to get me a dress. How can I give my body to such a man?" The next night he came to her again. She surrendered herself, but with little response, as if sex was a duty. The next day the young husband went to the market and bought the dress. The bride smiled, took her husband's hand, and led him to the bed. But after the sexual pleasure, the husband felt a root of bitterness growing within him. It is possible to win the battle, but lose the war.

C. Wife, learn more about your husband.

1. A husband desires sex more often than his wife desires sex. The man's sexual desire is usually stronger than the woman's. A woman can increase her readiness for sex by thinking about her husband and the pleasure he brings. Much female desire begins in the mind. The bride in Song of Songs thought about and looked forward to joining with her husband. [2]*"Let him kiss me with the kisses of his mouth— ... [4]Take me away with you—let us hurry! Let the king bring me into his chambers"* (Song of Songs 1:2, 4).

2. A husband enjoys seeing his wife's body. This is a major source of pleasure for men. God created man with a desire to see his wife naked. Some wives are embarrassed by being nude. They do not want to be bare, or wear sexy clothes in the bedroom. They want to make love in the dark. This robs a man of the joy he gets from seeing his wife's body. The body does not have to be perfect to be a source of pleasure. But the wife should care for her body to keep it beautiful. A husband can make his wife feel good about being nude by always saying good things about her body—and never saying anything negative about her. Soft words and soft light—such as a candle—may please both the man and woman.

3. A husband likes his wife to feel free. Shyness and modesty have their worth. But they lose much of their value in the marriage bed. A husband enjoys having his wife explore and love his body. He is pleased when she takes joy in him. The bride in the Song of Songs even takes the lead in seduction. In chapter 6:13–7:9, we see her dancing before her husband. He admires her body as she entices him to love.[7] A wife will feel freer if her husband provides a place where she is sure of privacy—behind a locked door. No wife likes to have sex if children or others might hear, or might enter the bedroom. So a wise and loving husband provides a private, secure place for married love.

How do you decide as a couple what the limits are for sexual experience? *First,* do not do anything that shames or hurts either person. *Second,* anything that breaks marital vows is wrong. *Third,* do not do anything that harms a person's conscience. Within these guidelines, a couple can experiment with many sexual pleasures.

4. A husband likes to be praised when he pleases his wife. Much of a man's confidence is in his sexual ability. He feels stronger and more committed when he knows that he is pleasing his wife. A wife must **never** criticize a man's sexual ability. Do not increase his anxiety if he is unable to perform because of physical or emotional stress. Let him know how to please you. Praise him when he satisfies you emotionally and physically. He will work hard to do it again.

Q 22 *What advice would you give Anabella?*

Q 23 *What is the danger of Gloria's actions?*

Q 24 *How can a wife prepare to enjoy sex?*

Q 25 *Why does a husband enjoy seeing his wife nude?*

Q 26 *What are 2 ways a husband can help his wife feel more freedom in sex?*

Q 27 *What are 3 guidelines for sexual limits in marriage?*

Q 28 *What increases when a woman praises her husband?*

Q 29 How can a husband show that he values his wife for more than sex?

D. Husband, learn more about your wife.

1. A wife likes her husband's attention throughout the day, not just when he wants sex. A woman wants to be valued as a unique person. For her, sex is part of the whole relationship with her husband. If her husband does not show interest in her thoughts and feelings, she will feel 'used' during sex. A husband's willingness to talk, to listen, and to pay attention in other ways brings joy to the wife's sexual love. Husband, show physical love sometimes without seeking sex. Do kind things for your wife when you are not hoping to get her into the bed. This will help her to feel loved, and your sexual life will be better.

Figure 5.4
A woman likes to feel that her husband cares about <u>her</u>, and not just sex.

2. A wife likes help with the work of the home. A husband hates to hear the words, "I'm too tired." But too often, this is not an excuse—it is the truth. Around the world, women often work longer than men. A man usually has a time of the day when his work is over. But a woman often works all day. If you want to see your wife with more energy for sex, help with more of the work. Then she will not be so tired. Also, teach the children to help with work in the home.

Q 30 How can a husband help his wife have more energy for sex?

Dr. Laura is a well-known radio speaker about the family. She says that when her husband helps with housework, she gets excited about sex. For her, the sound of him running the floor sweeper is foreplay!

Q 31 Describe a romantic husband.

3. A wife likes to see more romance in her life. Song of Songs gives good illustrations of how to create romance. All of the senses come alive in a romantic setting. The mind is awakened. A beautiful setting for sex is prepared. The scents of clean bodies and perfumes are present. The taste of the mouth is refreshing. The touch upon the skin is slow, tender, and exciting. The woman is caused to feel beautiful, valuable, and loved. Her husband may even bring her a gift. Her pleasure is valuable to him. A husband who approaches sex like a carpenter on a hot roof—dirty, sweaty, and eager to get the job done—is not a romantic husband. Any husband can learn to approach sex in a romantic way—kind, clean, neat, patient, grateful, cheerful, friendly, tender, thoughtful, generous, interesting, loving.

Q 32 How can a husband know the way his wife likes to be treated sexually?

4. A wife likes to be free to respond as she desires. A wife often desires sexual climax with her husband. Some husbands stir up a wife's desire by kissing and touching, and then go to sleep and leave her in frustration. If a wife desires sexual climax, the husband must not be content with his own satisfaction. Sometimes, a woman can enjoy bonding with her husband without climax. A husband should follow his wife's lead in this. Sometimes the husband pressures his wife to experience a climax. He may feel like a failure if his wife does not reach her highest sexual level. But there are many ways to enjoy sexual love. Sometimes the wife may not feel that a climax is necessary to be satisfied. Some women never experience climax, and yet have sexual relations that satisfy. Let the woman determine the importance of this in her life each time.

E. Plan and protect time together.

Q 33 State 2 ways that a couple can have time alone outside of the routine.

Guard your sexual relationship—it is valuable. Do not allow sex to become just part of a routine. Rather, keep it special. A couple should plan to be alone together each week. Many couples choose one night a week when they do something special together. Perhaps they eat at a restaurant, or go to town together. This strengthens their friendship

How to Approach Sexual Life in Marriage 89

and closeness—and it improves their sexual experience. Surprises also keep romance alive in a marriage. A husband may come home to find that the children are away. The wife has prepared herself for an entire evening to be alone with him. The husband may surprise his wife with a gift, or a day to rest from her work—a day she will be served and treated like a queen. Trips together, away from daily work, will add life to a marriage and increase your sexual pleasure together.

F. Expect changes throughout your marriage.

Stages in life will change your sexual experience. The beginning of married life has fewer responsibilities. The couple has more time for each other. They have more time and chances to make love. There is often great passion in the discovery of sexual life together.

Q 34 *What are the 3 stages that affect sex? State the challenges of each stage.*

When children and other responsibilities come, there may be less time for sex. With children in the home, a husband and wife must plan private time for sex. A couple must take great care to protect their sex life as the family grows. There are three good things you can do. *First,* manage stress and levels of energy. This may mean that you give up some activities, so you will not feel too tired. *Second,* plan regular times to be alone as a couple. *Third,* take care of your appearance. Stay clean, neat, and wise in what you eat. Since the married couple know each other well, it is easier for them to please each other. Still, they must take care to remain close.

As the couple grows older, they can still enjoy sex together. Some men continue to enjoy sex when they are 80 years old! Abraham and Sarah enjoyed their sexual relationship the most when he was 100 (Gen. 17:17)! Remember that the mind is a key to sexual relations. Sexual desire can continue with age, if the couple agrees mentally. Good health is a part of good sex. And, physical love can continue, even if sex is no longer possible. ¹⁸*"May your fountain be blessed, and may you rejoice in the wife of your youth. ¹⁹A loving doe, a graceful deer—may her breasts satisfy you always, may you ever be captivated by her love"* (Prov. 5:18-19).

Life has different stages, but there is joy in every year. Cherish good memories, but never let change prevent you from finding joy in the present.

Dealing With Difficult Sexual Problems in Marriage
Goal A: *Identify 3 reasons for difficult sexual problems in marriage.*
Goal B: *Examine 3 solutions for sexual problems in marriage.*

Setting

Difficult sexual problems can bring pain and confusion. It may be challenging to know the causes of a problem. A person may need to look at many different things to discover the roots and solutions.

Q 35 *Why is it sometimes difficult to identify the problems and their solutions?*

Sexual problems may cause a person to have such doubts as:
- "Am I a real man if I cannot have a good sexual experience with my wife?"
- "How much of a person am I if I cannot satisfy my spouse?"
- "What is wrong with me as a man/woman if I do not like sex—or if I can never get enough?"

These questions are hard to ask ourselves. It is easier to blame our spouse. But a difficult sexual problem belongs to both. The husband and wife are now one flesh. They must work together to solve any sexual problems that are a part of their marriage. So, let us look at some reasons for difficult sexual problems and possible ways to solve them.

A. Reasons for difficult sexual problems

Q 36 *Identify 3 reasons for sexual problems*

There are three general reasons for difficult sexual problems: 1) There is a relational problem between the husband and wife. 2) There is a problem with sexual knowledge and technique. 3) There is a problem within one or both of the spouses. Let us look at each of these more fully.

1. Relationship problems between a husband and wife will often cause sexual problems. We have already studied about the connection between sex and the daily life of a husband and wife.

Q 37 *What caused Nimo's husband to become impotent?*

For example, Nimo often criticized her husband because of the small amount of money he earned. She compared him to other men who were doing better. Then, one day, he was unable to complete the sex act. She ridiculed and laughed at him about that also. It was not long before the husband was *impotent—unable to have sex with his wife. When she was near, he could not get his sexual motor turned on. He could only find sexual release by himself or with other women. (There are many reasons a man may become impotent. Perhaps he works too much or does not get enough exercise.)

Figure 5.5 Sexual problems may come from relationship problems.

Q 38 *Why does pornography destroy a marriage?*

Another husband, Alto, enjoyed pornography. He would become sexually excited and then come to his wife and ask her to do the things he had seen. His wife began to feel like an object of sex. She did not think her husband's desire was for her. He was being unfaithful in his thoughts, and then using her as he thought of the other women he had lusted for. She began to resist his ideas and make excuses for not having sex. Her back ached, her head ached, she was not feeling well, the children might hear. In time, he began to accuse her of being boring and cold.

2. A lack of understanding may lead to sexual problems in marriage. We have already looked at the need to understand the sexual relationship. Ignorance bears bad fruit. A couple may learn a good method for sex through loving practice and good communication. They may learn through wise counsel or good books. But if they do not learn about the needs of each other, one or both of them will find the sex act painful or unhappy. Many wives avoid sex when they can because the couple has not learned to make sex fun for the wife. Many husbands are tempted to seek other ways of sexual release, because their wives do not know how to please them. Some sexual knowledge comes from within. But much must be learned. Happy is the husband who learns to satisfy his wife in bed. A husband and wife should ask each other what each enjoys.

3. A problem *within* one or both of the spouses can cause sexual problems in the marriage. Some sexual problems have physical roots. Some diseases and medicines can cause impotence or low sexual desire. Pain during sex may mean that there are physical problems. Seek help from a medical doctor if there are problems of this kind. When there is a sexual problem, begin by seeing if the cause is a disease or drug.

Q 39 *Why is it wrong to circumcise any female?*

Female circumcision is another cause of sexual coldness. This unwise, unbiblical practice of female circumcision varies. People who do not understand the way God created women cut off part or all of the woman's sexual organs. The more scar tissue is present, the less pleasure a woman will experience in that part of her body. A woman may never experience climax if the *clitoris (a major center of female pleasure) has been completely removed. She can learn to enjoy relations with her husband. But many circumcised women will never experience all of the pleasure that God intended for them. Circumcising a female is like cutting off part or all of the head of a male's sexual organ!

Emotional pain is another cause of sexual problems.[8] This pain may have roots in one or two places. *First,* if parents do not show love and care, it can wound a child's emotions. The child may grow up without learning how to accept love. For example, if a father does not show proper affection to his daughter, she may find it hard to accept love from her husband. Some have twisted this truth to include the sinful teaching that a father should show sexual love toward his daughter. This is wrong. But it is right for a father to hold or hug his children.

> **Q 40** *What are 2 things that can damage the emotions, and cause lasting emotional pain?*

Likewise, quarreling between a father and mother can damage the emotions of children in the home. A small child may decide that sex is bad, after hearing about or seeing sex in marriage. Children who have poor examples and bad experiences will later bring *baggage* into marriage.

> **Q 41** *Describe the baggage an abused child will bring into marriage.*

Second, people may have sexual problems because of sexual experiences or sexual abuse. This is another form of baggage that some bring into a marriage. The sexual wounds of a child or young person are very deep. People who have been used may try to avoid sex. They may experience physical pain during sex in marriage. Or they may think that their value is as a sex object. This may lead to many sexual partners. They may let themselves be used in sexual ways and feel powerless to say "no." They become like a house with no doors to close.

> **Q 42** *Is sexual abuse a common problem in your community?*

Millions of people have physical and emotional wounds that affect their sexual lives. Most of these people will get married. Often, wounded people will marry other wounded people. So, what can married couples do when they discover that their own marriage contains sexual wounds and problems?

B. Solutions for difficult sexual problems[9]

We have looked at several causes of difficult sexual problems. Throughout this course, we examine how to have a good relationship between husband and wife. This can bring healing to many wounds. Besides this, let us look at some other ways to bring sexual healing within marriage.

1. The husband and wife must seek to have the attitude of Christ. It is common to want a quick solution to problems. But it may take time and great care to solve difficult sexual problems. There may be times of sorrow, discouragement, and anger. These problems may test the marriage. But God calls couples to love and serve each other.

> **Q 43** *How can having the attitude of Christ help a husband and wife with sexual problems?*

> [1]*If you have any **encouragement** from being united with Christ, if any **comfort** from his love, if any **fellowship** with the Spirit, if any **tenderness** and **compassion**, [2]then make my joy complete by **being like-minded, having the same love, being one in spirit and purpose.** [3]Do nothing out of selfish ambition or vain conceit, but in humility **consider others better than yourselves.** [4]Each of you should look not only to your own interests, but also to the interests of others. [5]Your attitude should be the same as that of Christ Jesus* (Phil. 2:1-5).

Philippians 2:1-5 can help couples with sexual problems. *First,* it reminds us that God is our source of help. His love gives us encouragement, comfort, fellowship, tenderness, and compassion. We are not the source of these things in a marriage. All good things come from God. In days of discouragement, sorrow, hurt, and need, we can turn to God to help us.

Second, these verses teach that our fellowship with God affects our relationship with others. For example, in marriage, the husband and wife are one in spirit and purpose. A sexual problem in a marriage no longer belongs to just one of the spouses—they share everything. One is not to seek a solution while the other points a finger of blame. They must unite to solve the problem that now belongs to both of them.

Third, neither spouse should be concerned only about self. Each should consider what is best for the other. It is all right to consider your own interests. But you must *also* consider the interests of your spouse. For example, if a spouse is hurt, the husband and wife must seek to heal that wound. But the one who is wounded must not ignore the needs of the other spouse. And the one who is well must be patient with the wounded spouse. Both must think of the needs of each other. This was the attitude of Jesus. He left heaven to bring spiritual life and healing to us. Having the attitude of Christ will help the husband and wife solve their problem with unity and love. They should daily seek to have this attitude.

Q 44 *How can a person with physical problems help meet the needs of the spouse?*

2. Physical problems do not mean the end of physical affection. Physical problems that cause sexual trouble may last for a brief time or a lifetime. But, some love is better than no love. Romance—being tender and kind—and love play can help meet emotional needs even without climax. Kissing and hugging each other gives assurance of attraction and love. Either the husband or the wife may still be able to climax. Each spouse should find ways to meet the other's sexual needs. Oneness needs to be enjoyed in physical ways. A couple that cannot climb the highest mountain of sexual pleasure should still climb the hills that lead to it. One day, they may reach the top.

Q 45 *Why is it unwise to ignore emotional wounds?*

3. Emotional wounds can be healed. Many people try to ignore their emotional wounds. Children who have been sexually abused may repress (ignore, hide, and cover) their memories. But our emotions affect our bodies—even if the emotions or memories are hidden. The only way to solve sexual problems caused by emotional wounds is through inner healing. Let us consider some steps to heal painful memories:[10]

- Invite Jesus and a trusted friend or counselor to walk through your past memories with you.

- Visit the old, painful memories. You must have the courage to remember what happened and how you reacted. Ask Jesus to help you see things in the right way. Strong feelings will probably come as you remember. Tell Jesus exactly what you feel.

Q 46 *Explain the false guilt that an abused person can have.*

- Identify the person who did wrong. Many people with painful memories feel ashamed. For example, a young woman felt shame because her uncle abused her sexually when she was a small child. She remembered that her uncle gave her gifts to remain silent. She felt guilty because she took the gifts and did not tell. But when she went back to those memories as a grown woman, she realized how small and innocent a girl is at the age of 3 years. She could see that it was her uncle who did wrong—and her parents for not protecting her.

Sometimes, a person has shared in the sin and guilt of a painful experience. If that is true, face the truth. Ask for forgiveness, and receive it (1 John 1:9).

Q 47 *Explain: "What someone tells self is as powerful as the painful experience."*

- Examine what you told yourself about the experience. The experience has power. But what a person tells self about the experience has equal power. For example, a young man was deeply in love for the first time. He honored the young woman. Even though his desire was strong, he waited for marriage to have sexual relations with her. While he was away for a summer, the young woman became pregnant by another man. Her unfaithfulness hurt the young man deeply. He told himself, "I cannot trust *any* women. They will give their bodies to someone. It might as well be me." Then, for many years, this young man used women for sex. He told them anything they wanted to hear in order to convince them to surrender their bodies. What he told himself about his hurtful first love twisted his life.

A woman who has been raped must reject her thoughts that sex is ugly. At the same time, she must embrace the truth that sex is a gift from God. Money is not bad because thieves steal it. Likewise, sex is not bad because people abuse it. God created man and woman for each other in Eden. Sex is a part of God's good plan.

A woman who thinks her value is only in giving sex must reject that thought. She must tell herself the truth—she is so valuable that Jesus died for her. The value of something is always seen by the price someone pays. The price Jesus paid for us shows each of us that we have great value!

- Deal with the person who hurt you. You must seek good counsel and wisdom from God to know the best way to deal with this person. Sometimes, you and your husband must face the person who wounded you. This is especially true if the person may be abusing other children. Other times, you may need to break contact with that person. Always, you must forgive. Jesus and Stephen are examples of those who forgave, although no one was asking for forgiveness. And remember, God will still judge those who do not repent, even if we forgive them.
- Seek sexual pleasure and fulfillment with your marriage partner. Do not punish your spouse for what someone else has done to you. Love your spouse with the love God gives you.

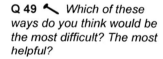

Q 48 *Should we forgive if a person has not asked for it? Explain.*

Q 49 *Which of these ways do you think would be the most difficult? The most helpful?*

These steps may take time. The depth and number of wounds will determine how long a journey this will be. A couple with the attitude of Christ will take the journey together. But how can the mate best help while this process is happening?

Ways to help your wounded mate:[11]
- Pray for healing.
- Help your spouse, but do not try to fix him/her. Your spouse must take responsibility for self.
- Listen more than you talk.
- Accept your spouse completely. Sexual problems and solutions may be difficult to identify. But part of becoming *"one"* means the husband and wife will work faithfully together to seek healing.
- Always speak the truth in love.
- Help your spouse face self and God. God is the primary source for his/her healing.
- Do not react in violent ways when you discover who has wounded your spouse.
- Be patient. Do not rush your mate. You may need to let the spouse lead the direction and the pace.

Figure 5.6 Walk the path of wholeness together.

Chapter Summary

 Beginning Your Sexual Life Together in Marriage

Goal A: *Summarize 4 reasons for sex in marriage.*

Sex in marriage creates new life, prevents sexual immorality, brings oneness, and is fun.

Goal B: *State 4 sexual differences in the desires of men and women.*

Review Figure 5.1.

Goal C: *Comment on expectations, acceptance, and the past in relation to sex in marriage.*

- A couple should *expect* four things: It takes time to develop sexual relations that please each other. There is still a need for sexual control in marriage. The whole relationship of a couple affects their sexual relationship. It helps to communicate with each other when making love.
- Acceptance, not judging, leads to good sex between a husband and wife. No bodies are perfect!
- Begin sex together with honesty about your past.

Goal D: *Explain how a husband can avoid the most common sexual error in marriage.*

A husband can avoid the mistake of being in a hurry by giving time, tenderness, and privacy to his wife.

 Continuing Your Sexual Life Together in Marriage

Goal A: *Summarize the need for sexual faithfulness and satisfaction in marriage.*

- The greatest harm that can come to a marriage is through unfaithfulness. *"What God has joined together, let man not separate."*
- A husband and wife must choose to respond to the needs of each other.

Goal B: *Explain 4 things a wife should know about her husband's sexual desires.*

A husband desires sex more often than his wife desires sex. A husband enjoys seeing his wife's body. A husband likes his wife to feel free. A husband likes to be praised when he pleases his wife.

Goal C: *Explain 4 things a husband should know about his wife's sexual desires.*

A wife likes her husband's attention throughout the day, not just when he wants sex. A wife likes help with the work of the home. A wife likes to see more romance in her life. A wife likes to be free to respond as she desires.

Goal D: *Describe guarding time together and adjusting to change in marriage.*

Many couples spend one night a week together. Perhaps they eat at a restaurant, or go to town together. This strengthens their friendship and closeness—and it improves their sexual experience.

A couple must protect their sex life as the family grows. They must manage stress, plan time together, and take care of their appearance. As the couple grows older, they can still enjoy sex together.

 Dealing With Difficult Sexual Problems in Marriage

Goal A: *Identify 3 reasons for difficult sexual problems.*

Sexual problems may result from relationship problems between a husband and wife, or a lack of understanding, or a physical or emotional problem in one or both of the spouses.

Goal B: *Examine 3 solutions for difficult sexual problems.*

The husband and wife must seek to have the attitude of Christ. Physical problems do not mean the end of physical affection. Emotional wounds must be healed.

How to Approach Sexual Life in Marriage

 Test Yourself: Circle the letter by the *best* completion to each question or statement.

1. A reason for sex in marriage is
a) communication.
b) pleasure.
c) abstinence.
d) sinfulness.

2. In marriage, women like
a) quick sex.
b) sex, almost any time.
c) to be excited by seeing.
d) privacy and security.

3. What affects sex the most in marriage?
a) Cleanliness
b) Communication
c) Relationship
d) Finances

4. A common sexual error of a new husband is
a) being in a hurry in the bedroom.
b) thinking his body excites his wife.
c) talking too much in the bedroom.
d) criticizing the way his wife looks.

5. A biblical reason to end a marriage is
a) financial stress.
b) unfaithfulness.
c) relatives.
d) too many children.

6. In bed, a husband likes his wife to be
a) shy as a dove.
b) free as a leopard.
c) strong as an ox.
d) submissive as a lamb.

7. A husband can help his wife enjoy sex by
a) dancing for her in the nude.
b) being like a bull in the field.
c) taking time to talk with her.
d) showing great confidence.

8. Which is TRUE?
a) The more children, the more time for sex.
b) Appearance means less after marriage.
c) Sex is the most enjoyable early in marriage.
d) A couple can enjoy sex more as years go by.

9. A major cause of difficult sexual problems is
a) emotional pain from childhood.
b) spiritual immaturity.
c) differences in men and women.
d) lack of interest in sex.

10. The worst thing to do with a difficult sexual problem is
a) share it, so others can help you through it.
b) discuss it, to seek a solution.
c) bury it, so no one will remember it.
d) confront it, to bring a quick solution.

Chapter 6:
How to Answer Three Key Questions

Introduction

A man and his wife were traveling to town together. They had not spoken to each other for an hour, because they were angry. They had quarreled, and neither would take a step toward peace. Suddenly the man pointed to a stubborn donkey they passed by.

"A relative of yours?" he asked.

"Yes," the wife replied, "by marriage!"[1]

Quarrels happen in marriage. Many quarrels are about **decisions,** or **money,** or **relatives.** These three subjects stir strong feelings and affect marriage. In this chapter, we encourage couples to answer questions on each of these topics. If a husband and a wife can agree on the answers, their marriage will grow in unity, in prosperity, and in peace.

Figure 6.1 When a husband and wife face conflict in marriage, the foolish fight each other, but the wise seek a solution.

Lessons:

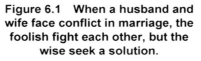

How Will We Make Decisions About Our Lives Together?
Goal A: *State 3 ways of honoring God when making decisions.*
Goal B: *Explain how spouses may differ in the way they make decisions.*
Goal C: *Contrast basing decisions on the wrong reasons and on priorities. Illustrate each.*
Goal D: *Analyze the role of perseverance after making good decisions.*

How Will We Handle Financial Matters?
Goal: *Summarize 10 principles for handling finances wisely in marriage. Illustrate each.*

How Will We Relate to Our Larger Family?
Goal A: *State at least 4 ways for children who marry to honor their parents.*
Goal B: *Explain the biblical order in caring for family and relatives.*
Goal C: *Summarize the need to protect children from family members.*

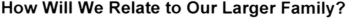

 Key Word

extended family

How Will We Make Decisions About Our Lives Together?

Goal A: *State 3 ways of honoring God when making decisions.*
Goal B: *Explain how spouses may differ in the way they make decisions.*
Goal C: *Contrast basing decisions on the wrong reasons and on priorities. Illustrate each.*
Goal D: *Analyze the role of perseverance after making good decisions.*

Setting

A couple will need to make thousands of decisions about their lives together. Some will be small, but other decisions will affect the future—even generations to come. We do not always know which decisions are small or great. So, we should learn how to make good decisions.

A. Seek God for direction.

The Scriptures can give us God's direction. *"Your word is a lamp to my feet and a light for my path"* (Ps. 119:105). A believer does not need to struggle about decisions that God's Word makes clear. For example, it is easy to decide about attending church. The Bible makes this an easy decision. Likewise, the Bible helps us make the right decisions about tithing, disciplining children, and godly living. *"I gain understanding from your precepts; therefore I hate every wrong path"* (Ps. 119:104). For many decisions, there is a chapter and verse in the Bible.

> **Q 1** ↖ *Give an example of a decision that can be guided by a chapter and verse in the Bible.*

Our faithfulness to God helps us receive His direction. *⁵"Trust in the LORD with all your heart and lean not on your own understanding; ⁶in all your ways acknowledge him, and he will make your paths straight"* (Prov. 3:5-6). Faithfulness pleases the heart of God. God guides the steps of those who trust and honor Him. *"The path of the righteous is like the first gleam of dawn, shining ever brighter till the full light of day"* (Prov. 4:18).

> **Q 2** ↗ *How is holy living related to guidance?*

Prayer helps us receive God's direction. *"If any of you lacks wisdom, he should ask God, who gives generously to all without finding fault, and it will be given to him"* (James 1:5). Jesus, Himself, spent the night in prayer before choosing 12 apostles (Luke 6:12-16). A husband and wife should pray separately and together when they are seeking God's direction.

> **Q 3** ↗ *What promise does James 1:5 give?*

B. Seek agreement with your spouse.

God wants His Church to dwell in unity and peace, having the same mind and purpose (Phil. 2:1-4). And the church is only as united and peaceful as the families in it.

The Bible teaches that the husband is the head of the home, and his wife should submit to him. But a wise husband does not make big decisions without his wife. Remember that God did not create woman from man's foot. He made her from man's rib—a place at his side and near his heart. God's plan is for a husband and wife to discuss important matters together. The husband and the wife each have strengths and weaknesses—but together, they are complete. What the husband does not see, the wife may see. What the wife does not think of, the husband may discern. When they agree about a decision, they are a powerful team.

If a couple cannot agree, they should pray. Each should submit to God. They should delay a big decision until both hear from God and agree. Or they should delay until the wife feels good about submitting her will to her husband, even if she does not agree completely. When a husband is patient, it gives his wife time to receive grace to support him. Otherwise, if a husband demands quick submission, later, the wife will blame him if things go wrong. A husband may be able to force his wife's physical submission. But only the woman can submit her will.

Q 4 *What blessings come when a family agrees on big decisions?*

A minister felt that God was leading him to move from one place to another. His wife and two daughters did not agree. They were happy in the place they were living, and did not want to move to a new place. The husband wanted his wife to feel good about the decision. He talked to an older pastor whose counsel was surprising. The wise pastor said, "Do not move until your wife agrees. Tell her that even though you believe God is leading you to move, you will wait until she approves." The younger pastor was shocked! Should he depend on the agreement of his wife? What if she refused to move? Should he allow her to prevent him from obeying God? But the older pastor knew that the wife was a spiritual person. And he knew that including her in the decision would cause her to pray much. The younger pastor prayed, and in time, he felt peace about the counsel of the older pastor. So he told his wife that he would not move until she agreed. The wife began to pray about God's will. After a few days, she came to him and said that God had spoken to her, and she was ready to move. Together, they presented this decision to their daughters and asked for their support. The girls prayed—and cried for several hours about leaving the people they loved. But after a few days, they agreed to support the decision. So together, in unity and peace, the family moved forward in the will of God. No one was bitter toward the father, because they all agreed on the decision.[2]

C. Have understanding and patience for the way your spouse makes decisions.[3]

Paul reminds us that in relating to each other, we need *"understanding, patience and kindness"* (2 Cor. 6:6).

Q 5 *What should a husband do if his wife takes longer to decide than he takes?*

Slow or Quick? People make decisions at different speeds (Figure 6.2). Some are very slow to decide—so slow that they rarely decide at all! Those who are slow to decide are cautious, and may find it hard to choose. At the other extreme are people who make decisions very fast—perhaps too fast. In between these two extremes we find people making decisions at various speeds. This causes us to realize that the husband and wife may not make decisions at the same speed. So each must understand and show love to the other. Remember, love is patient and kind (1 Cor. 13:4).

Figure 6.2 People make decisions like they drive—at various speeds from very slow to very fast.

If a husband and wife have opposite ways of making decisions, try this. Set a *deadline—a date by which the decision must be made. Then the quick person can relax, knowing the decision will be made by a certain time. The slower one can think about the decision without feeling pressured to hurry. Also, this will allow time for prayer, discussion, counsel, and gathering facts.

Q 6 *What affects your decisions most: feelings or facts? Explain.*

Factual or Emotional? Some are very factual—they want *all* the facts before deciding. They want to research and make sure they have all the information about a decision. Gathering facts can go on forever. In the other direction are those who base their decisions only on their feelings. These are *not* concerned about a lot of facts. It may be hard for them to say why, but they *feel* that a decision is right or wrong. In between these two extremes are people who use *both* facts and feelings to make decisions.

Figure 6.3 People make decisions in different ways, ranging from factual to emotional.

If a husband and wife often decide in different ways, try this. Agree to allow both facts and feelings, but put limits on each. Agree what information will be helpful, and who will find it. Agree on when the research will end. Agree to pray and discuss the decision. Let each person express feelings.

Confident or Doubtful? Those who are steadfast make a decision and stay with it. These are confident after they decide. They are like a post driven in the ground—steadfast and sure. In contrast, some people decide, and then begin to have doubts. New questions or new circumstances cause them to be like a reed blowing in the wind. In between these two extremes are people who are steadfast, but may have some doubts about a decision.

Q 7 ↖ *Do all spiritual persons make decisions quickly, based on facts alone? Explain.*

Figure 6.4 **People make decisions in different ways, ranging from confident to doubtful.**

Concerning decisions, if one spouse is confident and the other is doubtful, try this. Plan for a period of time to review a new decision. Then the person who is steadfast and confident about deciding will know the decision is not final until after the review time. Also, this time for review will give the doubtful person a few days to live with a new decision. At the end of the review time—if both agree on the decision—it will be final. Then, they will both face the future and not discuss doubts about the past decision.

We have considered the ways people make decisions: slow or fast, factual or emotional, confident or doubtful. All may be spiritual, yet they decide in different ways. Discern that a person who decides slowly may be the husband or the wife. And the one who decides quickly may base the decision on facts and/or feelings. Seek to understand the way you and your spouse make decisions, and value each other. Together, you can make better decisions than either could alone. God planned marriage so that two different people can help each other. When a husband and wife decide together, the strengths of both help their marriage.

Q 8 ↖ *Why did God create people to decide in different ways?*

D. Avoid making a decision based on the wrong reason.[4]

Sometimes people make decisions for the wrong reasons. These decisions may cause pain and deep regret. Study the examples in Figure 6.5. Learn to analyze and examine the reasons for which you make decisions in a marriage.

Q 9 ↖ *Complete Figure 6.5 by filling in the 5 empty boxes.*

Scripture	Biblical Examples	Bad reasons for making a decision
1 Sam. 8:5	The families of Israel wanted a king, like other nations.	To conform—to be like others
Gen. 12:10-20	Abram decided to lie about Sarai.	
Acts 5:1-10		Recognition—desire to be praised
1 Sam. 2:12, 22-36	Eli refused to discipline and continue to say 'no' to his sons for their evil acts.	Unable to say 'no' to people
Judges 7:22	The Midianites when they heard Gideon's trumpets	Panic; confusion
John 12:42-43	Many families in Jerusalem at the time of Jesus	
	The families of Israel as they faced the giants of Canaan	Fear of failure
Josh. 7; 1 John 2:16	Achan saw the beautiful robe, silver, and gold and hid them.	

Figure 6.5 Biblical examples of people who made decisions, based on the wrong reasons

E. Base decisions on godly priorities in your marriage.[5]

Priorities are the things that a person cares about most. If people's highest priority is the way they look, they will buy nice clothes instead of books. If a person's highest priority is pleasure, he will spend much time and money seeking fun. People's priorities guide their choices. Believers should seek to match their top priorities with things that please God.

Q 10 ↖ *Name 3 godly priorities.*

Q 11 *How should priorities affect decisions?*

Husbands and wives may have some different priorities. If their *highest* priorities are not the same, this will hinder their ability to agree on decisions. Disagreeing does not always mean that one spouse is right and the other one is wrong. Here is an exercise to help you think about your priorities and compare them to your spouse's priorities.

Space has been left at the bottom of the chart to add any topics you desire to Figure 6.7. Rate your priorities; put a number by each. (Number 1 is the lowest priority rating, and 10 is the highest.) Write the rating you think your spouse would give on each topic. Have your spouse use the other two columns of the chart. Then, talk about your choices. See how well you understand each other. Where are you the same, and different? How do your priorities affect your decisions? Each spouse should seek to understand and value the priorities of the other. Both should seek to grow closer together in the priorities of their marriage. If you are not married, or engaged, ask a friend of the opposite sex to complete the chart. Then discuss it together, except for the topic of sex. Each of you should complete two columns. This discussion will give you good practice at understanding yourself and others.

Q 12 *In Figure 6.7, rate your priorities. Put a number by each. Number 1 is lowest priority and 10 is highest.*

Figure 6.6 Discussing priorities will help you understand each other.

List of Common Priorities	Husband's Responses		Wife's Responses	
	Me	Spouse	Me	Spouse
Relationship with God and His Church				
Relationship with my spouse				
Relationship with my family				
Relationship with relatives				
Health				
Education				
Adventure; recreation				
Ownership of property or wealth				
Security				
Physical comfort				
Tradition				
Personal appearance				
Relaxation, freedom from stress				
Time with people				
Time alone				
Work				
Success				
Recognition				
Sex				
Romance				
Integrity				

Figure 6.7 Examine the priorities in your marriage. Seek to understand and value the priorities of your spouse. Work to bring your priorities closer together in your marriage.

F. Conclusion: Commit to a decision once you agree on it.

We have studied five principles (A–E) above. These are keys to practice in making good decisions within marriage. After you have followed these five principles, one thing is still needed—commitment to the good decision. Many good decisions end in failure because people do not persevere. After you plant a good seed, you must leave it in the garden for it to grow. Then, the young plant will need water and weeding. If you dig it up to examine the roots, you will damage or kill the plant. Likewise, after you make a decision, faithful actions are needed. Do not waste time and energy wondering what would have happened if you had made a different decision. Rather, be steadfast and committed to the decision you and your spouse have made.

Be prepared to face any problems that may come with your decision. Problems do not mean it was a poor decision. Any decision needs to be followed by patience and perseverance.

Q 13 *What must a couple do after making a good decision? Give an example.*

The Hebrews left Egypt and slavery with great joy. They were free! They had wealth from the Egyptians, and God was with them. They had decided to follow Moses to the Promised Land. But it was not a long time until problems arose. Pharaoh's army chased them. Later, there was the need for water and food. Then they got tired of the food God provided. Jealousy arose. With each one of these problems, somebody questioned the decision to leave Egypt. [11]*"Was it because there were no graves in Egypt that you brought us to the desert to die? What have you done to us by bringing us out of Egypt?* [12]*...It would have been better for us to serve the Egyptians than to die in the desert!"* (Exod. 14:11-12). Problems were **not** proof that they had made the wrong decision. Problems are a part of life. Always, we must remain steadfast and committed after a good decision. *"You need to persevere so that when you have done the will of God, you will receive what he has promised"* (Heb. 10:36).

Committing to a decision does not mean that a couple cannot admit a mistake or change their minds. If circumstances change, minds can change. But changing a decision should be an exception. If a couple develops a habit of changing their minds, it may mean they lack commitment and discipline to make their decisions successful. This habit shows they are not making true, lasting decisions. Perhaps such a couple is making decisions based on the wrong reasons. If a couple makes decisions based on godly priorities, they should remain committed to these decisions, most of the time.

② How Will We Handle Financial Matters?
Goal: *Summarize 10 principles for handling finances wisely in marriage. Illustrate each.*

Setting

This section is about money in marriage.
- "Money is like laziness; the more a man has of it, the more he wants."
- "Life is a struggle to keep money coming in and teeth and hair from falling out!"
- "Money you can fold is better than coins, yet it does not go to church as often."
- "Money is a good servant, but a poor master."
- "Money will buy a fine dog, but only kindness will make him wag his tail."
- "*Using* money is the only blessing of having it."
- "Before borrowing money from a friend, decide which one you need more."[6]
- "Money will buy a bed, but not sleep; books, but not wisdom; a house, but not a home; medicine, but not health; pleasure, but not happiness; a church pew, but not heaven; a cross, but not a Savior."[7]

Trouble over money is one of the main causes of an unhappy marriage. Arguments over money cause many conflicts in marriage.
- One is a spender—the other is a saver.

Q 14 *Which financial problems do you think are most common in marriage. Explain.*

- One is always working to make money—the other is lonely.
- Both are always working—they become strangers.
- They disagree on how to use the money—neither will compromise.
- They do not have enough to buy what they need—they blame each other.
- They have faith in their riches—instead of faith in God.
- They become discouraged from their poverty—they lose heart or become angry with God.

The list of problems over money goes on and on. So it is important to see what the Bible can teach us about money in marriage. In this lesson we will study several financial principles, most of which come from Scripture.

Q 15 *List 5 principles in a plan for financial prosperity.*

A. Trust God as the source of all you need (Phil. 4:19).

God is our provider.

25 "Therefore I tell you, do not worry about your life, what you will eat or drink; or about your body, what you will wear. ... 26 Look at the birds of the air; they do not sow or reap or store away in barns, and yet your heavenly Father feeds them. Are you not much more valuable than they? ... 33 But seek first his kingdom and his righteousness, and all these things will be given to you as well" (Matt. 6:25-26, 33).

B. Discern the things in life that are worth more than money.

Q 16 *Complete Figure 6.8.*

Scripture	Things more valuable than money
Matthew 16:26	
Proverbs 15:6	
Proverbs 16:8	
Proverbs 16:16	
Proverbs 22:1	

Figure 6.8   Scriptures give us principles about things more valuable than money.

C. Be honest and faithful with a little (Luke 16:1-15).

Never cheat a customer, boss, or fellow worker. *"Dishonest money dwindles away, but he who gathers money little by little makes it grow"* (Prov. 13:11). *"Honest scales and balances are from the LORD"* (Prov. 16:11). *"Food gained by fraud tastes sweet to a man, but he ends up with a mouth full of gravel"* (Prov. 20:17).

Q 17 *Complete Figure 6.9.*

Scripture	Ungodly ways of getting money
Proverbs 20:17	
Proverbs 21:6	
Proverbs 22:16	
Proverbs 23:4	
Proverbs 28:8	

Figure 6.9   Scriptures give us principles about ungodly ways of getting money.

Q 18 *Summarize the principle of Luke 16:10.*

These Scriptures warn us of the final results of getting money dishonestly. What appears to be a quick way to wealth may be a long road to judgment.

Joseph was faithful as a steward of Potiphar's house—and in the prison—before he became a ruler in Egypt.

David was faithful with a few sheep before God made him ruler over the nation of Israel.

⁹*Honor the* LORD *with your wealth, with the firstfruits of all your crops;* ¹⁰*then your barns will be filled to overflowing, and your vats will brim over with new wine* (Prov. 3:9-10).

D. Work hard (2 Thess. 3:6, 10).

Work is a gift from God. It is the main way God has given us to provide for our needs. Although God calls for compassion for the poor, He does not want us to rescue those who are poor because they refuse to work. ⁶*"... keep away from every brother who is idle ...* ¹⁰*For even when we were with you, we gave you this rule: 'If a man will not work, he shall not eat'"* (2 Thess. 3:6, 10).

Q 19 What is God's main plan to meet our needs?

E. Use each spouse's talents.

Romans 12:3-8 explains the biblical principle of sharing responsibilities and abilities as a team. God supplies the church with the talents and gifts to succeed. Likewise, in marriage, God has created the husband and wife as a team. Together, they have the abilities they need to succeed. A married couple should discern which abilities God has put in each of them. God will give some abilities to the husband that the wife does not have; and He will give some talents to the wife that the husband does not have. The wise couple will use each spouse's gifts to help the marriage prosper.

Ask questions such as: Which of us is better at keeping records? Which of us is wiser at business? The talents you have are God's gifts to you. But what you do with them are your gifts to God. So always seek to improve any ability or skill God has given you.

F. Share all of your wealth.

The husband and wife should have the attitude of partnership and trust. "His" money and "her" money should become "their" money. To fully become one, a husband and wife must share their wealth. As each loves the other as self, this sharing becomes joyful.⁸

Q 20 Should the names of both the husband and wife be on the title deed to their land or home? Explain.

Q 21 Should a husband and wife have separate accounts at a bank?

G. Refuse to spend money quickly, on fleshly desires that arise.

"The plans of the diligent lead to profit as surely as haste leads to poverty" (Prov. 21:5). This verse emphasizes the difference between slow, careful plans for spending and quick spending. Spending without planning wastes a lot of money. For example, one woman plans the meals for her family. She makes a list of what she needs to buy. Then, she goes to the market and buys only what is on her list. Another woman goes to the market without a list or plan. The woman with the plan will save money and have better meals.

Q 22 Quick decisions about money lead to _____ _____.

Figure 6.10
Plan together for future needs.

H. Plan for future needs.

Foolish people think only of the present. *"A sluggard does not plow in season; so at harvest time he looks but finds nothing"* (Prov. 20:4). *"In the house of the wise are stores of choice food and oil; but a foolish man devours all he has"* (Prov. 21:20). Jesus said that we should not worry about the future (Matt. 6:25-34). But this does not mean we should not plan for the future. Scripture teaches us to plan for the future. For example, those who plant seeds are planning for the future.

The foolish, like Esau, think only about today. If they ever have extra money, they spend it. They do not think of the needs they will have tomorrow. When those needs appear,

Q 23 How should a couple prepare for future needs?

Q 24 What are 2 examples of thinking only of the present?

Q 25 How can a person plan for the future, financially?

they have no money. A person who wants to prosper must plan ahead. Will the family need new clothes next month? Will you be able to buy your own home someday? Will you be able to send your children to school? When a couple expects future needs, they will save some money each time they earn it. Saving a little in the present opens doors in the future. It also helps protect your family from the unknown. Maybe someone will lose a job. Maybe someone will need medical care. Money saved will help. Wise people, like the two wise servants in the parable of Matthew 25:14-30, use money in a way that brings blessings in the future.

Q 26 *Is it wise to plan financially for the future? Explain.*

Joseph was so wise that God used him to plan for the future needs of Israel and all of Egypt. He kept good records so that he was sure there was enough food for all (Gen. 41:46-49).

Q 27 *What is a budget?*

I. Create a budget to guide your spending.

Q 28 *Choose a monthly income that is common where you live. Then, complete Figure 6.11, based on that income.*

A budget is a plan to match your spending with your income. A budget helps a couple know how much money to plan for each need. Figure 6.11 gives one way to plan a budget for each month.

Dates paid	Description of Expense	A: Amount you plan to spend	B: Amount you spent	Difference: A - B =
	Tithes			
	Housing			
	Utilities: water, electricity, gas, phone			
	Food			
	Clothing			
	Travel			
	Savings			
	Recreation			
	Debts			
	Totals:			

Q 29 *Discuss this budget with your spouse. What insights does she/he have to add?*

Figure 6.11 Sample budget plan for one month; how you will manage your income

Q 30 *How can envelopes help as part of a budget?*

One married couple used envelopes as a part of their budget. They wrote an expense topic on each envelope, such as tithes, housing, utilities, food, clothing, and savings. As soon as they received money, they divided it into the envelopes. Then the money stayed there until it was used for the purpose written on the envelope. This taught them to use discipline and manage their spending.

Spend less than you earn. It is wise for a married couple to keep a budget. This gives them a record of how to manage their money. The record may show that there is not enough money for needs. Or the record may show that the money is spent on less important things. Then the money is missing for priorities—things that are the most important to you. At the end of a month, you can change the budget. Using a budget will help you manage your money wisely, month by month.

Q 31 *Summarize Proverbs 22:26-27.*

Debts can destroy a marriage. Proverbs says, [26]*"Do not be a man who strikes hands in pledge or puts up security for debts;* [27]*if you lack the means to pay, your very bed will be snatched from under you"* (Prov. 22:26-27).

A farmer was able to care for his family. He owned his land and home. The family could eat from the crops they grew. He sold enough grain to earn money for other needs. But if he had a tractor, he could increase his crop and earn more money. However, it would take a long time to save enough money to buy a tractor. So, he borrowed money with the promise that the lender could have his house if he did not repay. One summer, the crops were poor, and he could not make a tractor payment. Then the farmer got sick. He could not work. He could not pay his debt. The lender came and sold the house to pay back the debt.

Sometimes debt is needed in modern times. A loan may help you purchase a home that will grow in value. It may help you start a new business. Or it may help you get an education. But do not borrow money to meet daily needs or pleasures. If you borrow money, get much counsel. Be sure you deal with honest people. Loans based on a fixed rate of interest are safer. Make sure any agreements about payments or interest are reasonable. Do not guarantee to repay your debt with something that you need to live. When possible, do not borrow. Rather, save money first and then buy.

Q 32 ✎ *When is it wise to get a loan?*

*¹My son, if you have put up security **for your neighbor**, if you have struck hands in pledge for another, ²if you have been trapped by what you said, ensnared by the words of your mouth, ³then do this, my son, to free yourself, since you have **fallen into your neighbor's hands**: Go and humble yourself; press your plea with your neighbor! ⁴Allow no sleep to your eyes, no slumber to your eyelids. ⁵Free yourself, like a gazelle from the hand of the hunter, like a bird from the snare of the fowler (Prov.6:1-5).*

Q 33 ✎ *Read Proverbs 6:1-5. Is it wise to promise to pay the debts of another person? Explain.*

Wise couples use a budget and learn to be content with what they have. Contentment does not come from money, but from our relationship with God and others.

> CONTENTMENT DOES NOT COME FROM MONEY, BUT FROM OUR RELATIONSHIP WITH GOD AND OTHERS.

¹³Someone in the crowd said to him, "Teacher, tell my brother to divide the inheritance with me." ¹⁴Jesus replied, "Man, who appointed me a judge or an arbiter between you?" ¹⁵Then he said to them, "Watch out! Be on your guard against all kinds of greed; a man's life does not consist in the abundance of his possessions" (Luke 12:13-15).

Q 34 ✎ *Summarize the wisdom of Luke 12:13-15 and Philippians 4:11-13.*

¹¹... I have learned to be content whatever the circumstances. ¹²I know what it is to be in need, and I know what it is to have plenty. I have learned the secret of being content in any and every situation, whether well fed or hungry, whether living in plenty or in want. ¹³I can do everything through him who gives me strength (Phil. 4:11-13).

J. Be generous—share with others.

God blesses those who are generous.

Q 35 ✎ *What is your favorite Scripture about being generous? Explain.*

²⁴One man gives freely, yet gains even more; another withholds unduly, but comes to poverty. ²⁵A generous man will prosper; he who refreshes others will himself be refreshed (Prov. 11:24-25).

He who is kind to the poor lends to the LORD, and he will reward him for what he has done (Prov. 19:17).

"Give, and it will be given to you. A good measure, pressed down, shaken together and running over, will be poured into your lap. For with the measure you use, it will be measured to you" (Luke 6:38).

¹⁷Command those who are rich in this present world not to be arrogant nor to put their hope in wealth, which is so uncertain, but to put their hope in God, who richly provides us with everything for our enjoyment. ¹⁸Command them to do good, to be rich in good deeds, and to be generous and willing to share. ¹⁹In this way they will lay up treasure for themselves as a firm foundation for the coming age, so that they may take hold of the life that is truly life (1 Tim. 6:17-19).

⁹"*When you reap the harvest of your land, do not reap to the very edges of your field or gather the gleanings of your harvest. ¹⁰Do not go over your vineyard a second time or pick up the grapes that have fallen. Leave them for the poor and the alien. I am the* LORD *your God"* (Lev. 19:9-10).

⁶*Remember this: Whoever sows sparingly will also reap sparingly, and whoever sows generously will also reap generously.* ⁷*Each man should give what he has decided in his heart to give, not reluctantly or under compulsion, for God loves a cheerful giver.* ⁸*And God is able to make all grace abound to you, so that in all things at all times, having all that you need, you will abound in every good work.* ⁹*As it is written: "He has scattered abroad his gifts to the poor; his righteousness endures forever."* ¹⁰*Now he who supplies seed to the sower and bread for food will also supply and increase your store of seed and will enlarge the harvest of your righteousness.* ¹¹*You will be made rich in every way so that you can be generous on every occasion, and through us your generosity will result in thanksgiving to God* (2 Cor. 9:6-11).

Conclusion

"How will we handle financial matters?" is a key question. It is important that both spouses consider the topics in this lesson. Each spouse should commit to God's principles about money. And both should agree on ways to handle the money that comes to them.

How Will We Relate to Our Larger Family?

Goal A: *State at least 4 ways for children who marry to honor their parents.*
Goal B: *Explain the biblical order in caring for family and relatives.*
Goal C: *Summarize the need to protect children from family members.*

Figure 6.12
The extended family can be a great blessing.

Setting

Marriage is between a man and woman, but they must relate well to the families of the husband and the wife. In some cultures, the bonds to the larger family are very strong. But in all cultures, a couple must answer the question, "How will we relate to the *extended family—the families of the husband and the wife?" Families were created to give strength and security. But the extended family may also put pressure on a marriage. There are many arguments in marriages because of the husband's family or the wife's family. In some cases, the pressures are too great and the marriage fails. So, let us look at three principles that will help us draw strength from the extended family, and protect the marriage.

A. Honor both families.

It is common for husbands and wives to love the families they came from. Bonds of love and experience unite a father and mother with their children and grandchildren. It is natural for a husband to love his parents more than the parents of his wife. And it is normal for the wife to love her parents more than she loves the parents of her husband. Still, spouses must be fair. They must show love to both extended families. There may be fairness without treating everyone the same. For example, one set of in-laws may have less money or poorer health than the other. In some cases, the husband and wife may agree to do more for one side of the family than the other. The most important thing is that the husband and wife agree.

Spending time with the larger family may be a more important issue than spending money. If location allows, the couple should spend a similar amount of time with each

Q 36 ➤ *To honor both families, must you treat both the same? Explain.*

family. The husband and wife should be cheerful with each other's families. Each grandfather or grandmother should be given time to enjoy children born within the marriage. Parents should encourage their children to honor both sides of the family, when possible.

Mother: Will your family come to our house for Christmas this year?

Daughter: I am sorry, mother. We will be with my husband's family on that day.

Mother: Again? It has been 2 years since you came here for Christmas. We have gifts for the children. We miss you. Our grandchildren will forget us.

We should seek to honor all family members, but give special honor to the parents. The command to honor fathers and mothers is for all of life. Jesus rebuked the Pharisees because they did not care for their parents (Matt. 15:1-9).

> *³Jesus replied, "And why do you break the command of God for the sake of your tradition? ⁴For God said, 'Honor your father and mother' and 'Anyone who curses his father or mother must be put to death.' ⁵But you say that if a man says to his father or mother, 'Whatever help you might otherwise have received from me is a gift devoted to God,' ⁶he is not to 'honor his father' with it. Thus you nullify the word of God for the sake of your tradition"* (Matt. 15:3-6).

When a person marries, he or she has another father and mother to honor. The way we honor our parents changes in some ways when we become adults—but God still expects adults to honor parents. It is difficult when parents continue to treat an adult like a child. Sometimes parents become jealous because they still want all of their child's love. Sometimes, parents find it difficult to let their adult children make their own decisions. As children grow up and marry, they must relate as adults to their parents, but still honor them. Here are some guidelines for honoring parents.

- Remember that God used parents to bring you and your spouse into the world. You owe them for your lives.
- Seek counsel from your parents—pay attention to what they say. *"Listen to your father, who gave you life, and do not despise your mother when she is old"* (Prov. 23:22). You still have much to learn from them. Moses gained wisdom from his father-in-law. Ruth gained blessing from listening to her mother-in-law. Affirm their continued place in your life by a willingness to learn from them.
- Forgive your parents for their mistakes. No one is perfect—not even parents. As you grow older, you can see more clearly the mistakes your parents made. If you refuse to forgive, bitterness and strife will hurt all of your family. If you have deep wounds, do not ignore them. Seek help from God and a wise, godly listener. With healing, forgiveness is still the goal. God requires you to forgive all who hurt you (Matt. 6:12; 18:21-35). Why? Because there is only one Judge—and that is God, not any of us (James 4:12). Even after we forgive people, God is still their judge. *"Do not take revenge, my friends, but leave room for God's wrath, for it is written: 'It is mine to avenge; I will repay,' says the Lord"* (Rom. 12:19.).
- Give thanks for the work and sacrifices your parents have made for you. They could have spent their time and money in selfish ways. But most parents care for their children. All of the things they have provided for you were gifts. Let them know that you are grateful.
- Honor your parents in ways that please the Lord. In an earlier chapter, we emphasized that believers must sometimes choose between honoring the teachings of the Bible and tradition. The Holy Spirit can lead a couple to honor both God and their parents.
- Share your life with your parents. Tell them about important things in your life. Some privacy is important, but parents should not feel like strangers in their children's lives. Share your thoughts and plans from time to time. Let them celebrate and mourn with you. Of course, there should be limits. A mother or mother-in-law should not control

Q 37 *What do you think the mother is feeling? How could this problem be solved?*

Q 38 *Is it God's plan for a husband and wife to care for their elderly parents (Matt. 15:3-6)?*

Q 39 *What are some ways to honor our parents?*

the wife's home. A father or father-in-law should respect a husband. A husband must have some power over his own life. Have balance and healthy relationships with the parents on both sides of the marriage.
- Help your parents with their financial needs. We will discuss this more in the next three paragraphs.

B. Care for the needs of both families.

Q 40 *What is one reason Paul wrote about providing for relatives?*

In the culture of New Testament times, the government did not help provide for those in need. This is one reason Paul said, *"If anyone does not provide for his relatives, ... he has denied his faith and is worse than an unbeliever"* (1 Tim. 5:8). In Paul's day, a hungry person could not get food from the government. Many cultures today are like the New Testament culture in this way. The needs of each person are met through a family. It is God's will for a family to help those who need food, clothing, shelter, and medical care. Jesus rebuked the Pharisees for not meeting the needs of their parents (Matt. 15:1-9).

Q 41 *Should believers depend on the government to meet all the needs of their parents? Explain.*

Some governments help care for the financial needs of extended families. In these countries, people may feel that they have met their duty to help others through the taxes they pay. But no government can meet every need. God uses governments, but He has created the family to care for its members' physical, emotional, and spiritual needs. So, married couples from all cultures must be concerned for the needs of their extended families.

Q 42 *In your culture, does the larger family help in times of need? Explain.*

One couple cannot meet everyone's needs. They must rely on other relatives to help. A young husband became ill. He needed much care and attention to get well. At once, the larger family began to help. All of the family prayed. Each month, the families of his brothers, sisters, and parents sent some money to make up for the husband's lost income. Aunts and cousins took care of the children. Some made meals while the wife cared for her husband. The husband's father and brothers visited him day by day. This cheered the husband and gave the wife rest. Little nephews and nieces made small gifts to encourage their uncle. This family was a source of strength and care, just as God intended families to be. In time the husband grew strong again. He was thankful to be part of a larger family. And he was ready to help others in the family when they were in need. For everything there is a time—a time to receive, and a time to give.

C. Put your spouse and children first.

Q 43 *First Timothy 5:8 teaches that the greatest care must be for _____.*

1. Put your spouse and children first in finances. Earlier, we quoted part of 1 Timothy 5:8. The full quote is, *"If anyone does not provide for his relatives, **and especially for his immediate family**, he has denied the faith and is worse than an unbeliever."* Paul puts the immediate family as a priority above the extended family. No couple should allow outside expenses to hinder their ability to care for their own needs. A husband and wife must pay the basic expenses for their home and children first—before responding to the needs of the extended family.

Q 44 *In your culture, do parents sometimes try to control their children after marriage? Explain.*

2. Put your spouse and children first in all matters. Husbands and wives must care first for each other and their children. They must not allow parents or relatives to cause them to neglect their own families. A couple must find their own way. A husband or wife's time and emotional energy is limited. Parents must care for their own children *before* caring for their parents or extended family. Give to your marriage and its children first, and share what remains with the extended family. Do not neglect your own family. Obey the principle of 'leave and cleave.'

Q 45 *Have you heard about a family member who abused a child? Explain.*

Parents must protect their children from any evil in the extended family. Do not allow those in the larger family to influence your children in ungodly ways. Do not allow your extended family members to be cruel to your children, or abuse them in sexual ways. You must protect your children even if this means pulling away from a sinful family member. If your child does not want to be around a family member—either adult or older child—do not insist that the child spends time alone with that person. Your child may know something you do not know. If your child acts in an unusual way after spending time with a family member, find out why. If your child tells you that a family member has hurt him or her, respect your child. Your children must know that you are on their side. God has entrusted parents with the responsibility to protect their children. Remember the strong warnings that Jesus gave about causing children to sin or stumble (Matt. 18:5-9). Protect your children from evil, so God will be pleased with you, and so your children will be safe. There are many sad stories about family members who have abused children. The small, helpless children are often afraid to tell about the sins of adults. So parents must be very careful to protect their children from the evil deeds of family members—even believers. Do not depend on an angel to protect your children. At the end of your days, God will judge you for the way you protected your little ones. Do not assume that family members will not harm your children. Be alert and watchful.

A wife went home to visit her mother, who was dying. While the wife was gone, her husband had sex with one of their daughters. As a result of this *incest—sex with a family member—she became pregnant, and later gave birth to a child. Although the Bible condemns the father's sexual sin, the society accepted it as normal. In the home, it is important for believers to be guided by the Bible, not society. God's Word teaches that sex is only holy between a man and his wife (Heb. 13:4).

Figure 6.13
Listen to your child who does not want to be around a certain adult. Your child may be afraid to tell a secret!

Conclusion

A marriage brings families together. A happy marriage needs to relate well to the larger families. A husband and wife should relate to both families with honor and care. With wisdom, they can do this and still put those in their own home first. So, a couple needs to discuss and watch over this part of their lives.[9] The husband and wife should seek to enrich their extended families instead of stirring up conflict.

Questions for spouses to discuss
1. How do we honor each of our parents?
2. Do we show equal honor to all parents?
3. Have we been able to respond to the needs of our extended family in the way we should?
4. Is there any tension between us about the honor and care of our parents?
5. Does each spouse feel like the marriage has priority over the extended family?
6. Do we make sure that our children are safe around all family members?
7. What must we do to correct any problems related to the extended family?

Figure 6.14 Seven questions to discuss about the extended family

Chapter Summary

How Will We Make Decisions About Our Lives Together?

Goal A: *State 3 ways of honoring God when making decisions.*

Seek God for direction. Seek agreement with your spouse. Seek to understand and appreciate the way your spouse makes decisions.

Goal B: *Explain how spouses may differ in the way they make decisions.*

One may be slow and the other quick; one factual and the other emotional; one confident and the other doubtful.

Goal C: *Contrast basing decisions on the wrong reasons and on priorities. Illustrate each.*

Priorities, not worldly desires, should guide our choices. A husband and wife should agree on their *highest* priorities, and let these guide decisions such as spending money and time.

Goal D: *Analyze the role of perseverance after making good decisions.*

Many good decisions end in failure because people do not persevere. After you plant a good seed, you must leave it in the garden for it to grow. Then, the young plant will need water and weeding.

How Will We Handle Financial Matters?

Goal: *Summarize 10 principles for handling finances wisely in marriage. Illustrate each.*

Trust God as your source. Discern the things that are worth more than money. Be honest and faithful with a little. Work hard. Use each spouse's talents. Share your wealth with each other. Refuse to spend money quickly on fleshly desires. Plan for future needs. Create a budget. Be generous to others.

How Will We Relate to Our Larger Family?

Goal A: *State at least 4 ways for children who marry to honor their parents.*

Remember that you owe your parents for your lives. Seek counsel from your parents. Forgive them for their mistakes. Give thanks for their work and sacrifices. Share your life with them. Help them with financial needs.

Goal B: *Explain the biblical order in caring for family and relatives.*

Care for the needs of both families. Put your spouse and children first in finances and all other matters.

Goal C: *Summarize the need to protect children from family members.*

Do not allow those in the larger family to influence your children in ungodly ways, to be cruel to your children, or to abuse them in sexual ways. You must protect your children even if this means pulling away from a sinful family member.

Test Yourself: Circle the letter by the *best* completion to each question or statement.

1. A verse on honoring God in daily decisions is
a) Psalm 119:105.
b) Revelation 3:20.
c) 1 Peter 2:24.
d) Proverbs 3:16.

2. If a wife disagrees with her husband's decision,
a) he should move ahead, because he is the head.
b) he should ask the church to pray for her.
c) he should remind her about submission.
d) he should give his wife time to pray and discuss it.

3. Decisions in marriage should be based on
a) speaking in tongues.
b) personal prophecies.
c) godly priorities.
d) current needs.

4. Many Israelites died in the wilderness because
a) leaving Egypt was the wrong decision.
b) they did not remain steadfast.
c) Moses struck the rock.
d) there was not enough water.

5. In marriage, the main way God provides money is
a) through parents.
b) through education.
c) through children.
d) through hard work.

6. A key to having enough money is
a) working two jobs.
b) much education.
c) planning ahead.
d) borrowing all you need.

7. The key to handling money in marriage is
a) a budget.
b) tithing.
c) sharing.
d) prosperity.

8. Honoring parents of both spouses means
a) treating all the same.
b) meeting their needs.
c) putting them first.
d) living with them.

9. Which must come first in a marriage?
a) The needs of those in your home
b) The needs of those in ministry
c) The needs of parents
d) The needs of the church

10. Who is often a great danger to children?
a) Thieves
b) Relatives
c) Demons
d) Murderers

Unit 3: Relating in a Family Life

Relating to people is the hardest problem you will ever face. Relating well to people can be hard, whether the person is your boss, relative, spouse, child, or the person you see in the mirror! Success in the family depends mostly on the skills of getting along with others. So the most valuable skills you can ever have are the skills to relate well to others.

Since relationships are so important, it seems that schools would teach courses on relating to others. But students can pass through public school and college without taking one course on relationships! So the lessons in this Unit may be new to you! Study them slowly and often. Learn one principle at a time, and then practice it for a lifetime! Relating to others is one of the most important lessons in life. Learn to relate well to your spouse, children, and relatives so you can enjoy all that God has planned for you.

Chapter 7 emphasizes how to be a loving husband. You will be able to:
- *Explain five ways a husband should love his wife as Christ loved the Church (Eph. 5:25-33).*
- *Give examples of how a husband's love is gentle, respectful, fulfilling, open, patient, steadfast, and thankful.*
- *Analyze the type of leader a husband should be in relation to his wife and family.*
- *Describe the balance a husband should have between his work and family.*
- *Explain the meaning and purpose of the Sabbath.*
- *Summarize the proper use of a husband's time, energy, and money.*

Chapter 8 focuses on how to be a loving wife. We will guide you to:
- *Discuss eight ways a loving wife relates to her husband.*
- *Describe six characteristics of a loving wife in her home.*
- *Describe three ways a wife should relate to those outside her home.*

Chapter 9 is about how to be a good father or mother—Part I. You will learn to:
- *Explain God's point of view on children in relation to: ownership, value, and gifts.*
- *Summarize what a parent should understand about a child's growth and uniqueness.*
- *Describe a parent's responsibilities to be an example and a provider.*
- *Explain a parent's role in a child's education and work skills.*
- *Summarize ten reasons for sex education in the home.*
- *Identify seven guidelines for teaching your children about sex.*
- *Explain how a child's age affects what he should learn about sex.*
- *List ten things a pregnant mother should do to protect the health of her unborn child.*
- *Summarize the need for good food, rules for eating, pure water, and cleanliness in caring for children*
- *Explain the role of vaccines and doctors in caring for children.*

Chapter 10 is about how to be a good father or mother—Part 2. You will be able to:
- *Explain why the examples of parents are so important.*
- *Summarize steps that parents should take to teach their children.*
- *Describe guidelines for daily, family devotions.*
- *Comment on the relationship between security and social growth.*
- *Explain three different ways that parents can show love to their children.*
- *Summarize how parents can help a child feel accepted, and have self-esteem.*
- *Analyze the roles of manners, attitudes, and skills in relating to others.*
- *Explain ten of the fifteen principles on discipline.*
- *Summarize four types of discipline.*

Chapter 7:
How to Be a Loving Husband

Introduction

If you take good care of a car, it might last 200,000 miles. But, it might only run for 300 miles if you do not pay attention to the fuel gauge. Every day, a few cars run out of gas. It is common to see someone walking from a car toward a gasoline station. The owner's manual for the car tells us—most already know this—that we can know when the fuel is getting low. When the gauge points to empty, the car will stop running after a few miles. Whether you are driving a big or a small car, it will stop working if you do not pay attention to the need for fuel.

Likewise, God wants your marriage to keep going. You must take care of your spouse, yourself, and pay attention to the gauges that God gives. You can have a life full of satisfaction with your spouse. On the other hand, if you do not do what the owner's manual (the Bible) tells you to do, your marriage may stop working.

Figure 7.1
A husband should love his wife as Christ loved the Church.

Husbands and wives need to be filled and refilled with the Holy Spirit. They need to study God's Word and remember the principles He gives for the home. Marriage is a partnership that has roles for each spouse. If we live marriage the way God planned, it will succeed and last for a lifetime.

Lessons:

A Husband's Relationship to His Wife—Part 1
Goal: *Explain 5 ways a husband should love his wife as Christ loved the Church (Eph. 5:25-33).*

A Husband's Relationship to His Wife—Part 2
Goal: *Give examples of how a husband's love is gentle, respectful, fulfilling, open, patient, steadfast, and thankful.*

A Husband's Attitude Toward His Wife and Family
Goal A: *Analyze the type of leader a husband should be in relation to his wife and family.*
Goal B: *Describe the balance a husband should have between his work and family.*
Goal C: *Explain the meaning and purpose of the Sabbath.*
Goal D: *Summarize the proper use of a husband's time, energy, and money.*

A Husband's Relationship to His Wife—Part 1
Goal: *Explain 5 ways a husband should love his wife as Christ loved the Church (Eph. 5:25-33).*

Background

How would you summarize the theme of Ephesians 5:25-33 in one word? Some seem to think these verses focus on control, headship, or authority. But the main topic of Ephesians 5:25-33 is *love*. That is why the title of this chapter is "How to Be a Loving Husband."

Q 1 *What is the theme of Ephesians 5:25-33?*

God wants the wife to submit to her husband, as the Church submits to Christ. But why does the Church submit to Christ? Is it because He threatens us? Christ never whips or bullies His bride. We love Him because He first loved us. We love Him because He is kind, gracious, and gentle. Christ's love for the Church is the model for husbands. It is easy for a woman to submit to a husband who treats her like Jesus treats us.[1]

Q 2 *What causes the Church to submit to Christ? Apply this to the home.*

> [25] *Husbands, **love** your wives, just as Christ **loved** the church and gave himself up for her* [26] *to make her holy, cleansing her by the washing with water through the word,* [27] *and to present her to himself as a radiant church, without stain or wrinkle or any other blemish, but holy and blameless.* [28] *In this same way, husbands ought to **love** their wives as their own bodies. He who **loves** his wife **loves** himself.* [29] *After all, no one ever hated his own body, but he feeds and cares for it, just as Christ does the church—* [30] *for we are members of his body.* [31] *"For this reason a man will leave his father and mother and be united to his wife, and the two will become one flesh."* [32] *This is a profound mystery—but I am talking about Christ and the church.* [33] *However, each one of you also must **love** his wife as he **loves** himself, and the wife must respect her husband* (Eph 5:25-33).

In this lesson we will examine five ways a husband should love his wife as Christ loved the Church.

A. A husband's love should sacrifice for his wife (Eph. 5:25).

Jesus *"gave himself up for"* the Church (Eph. 5:25). He loved so much that He died for His bride. *"Greater love has no one than this, that he lay down his life for his friends"* (John 15:13). Jesus gave the greatest sacrifice—His life.

Q 3 *How does a husband follow the example of Christ's sacrifice?*

"Husbands, love your wives, just as Christ loved the church and gave himself up for her" (Eph. 5:25). Husband, give yourself up to save your wife. Be willing to die to protect her. As Chrysostom said, be willing to be cut into pieces for her.[2] Marriage is a privilege and a sacrifice.

Some sacrifices are made through death. But the Bible also speaks of being a living sacrifice (Rom. 12:1). Few husbands are asked to die for their wives—but all are asked to live for them. Love that sacrifices means dying to self. It means putting the needs of your wife above your own needs. Some husbands treat their wives like servants. But the Bible says a husband should love his wife as Christ loved the Church. This means that a husband should sacrifice some things to serve his wife. Husband, sacrifice your desires for other women. Sacrifice some of your time to meet her needs. Sacrifice some of your will and seek what pleases her best.

Q 4 *Husband, what are some sacrifices you make for your wife?*

B. A husband's love should make his wife better (Eph. 5:26-27).

A husband's love should make his wife better spiritually. Jesus' love for His bride led him *"to make her holy, cleansing her..."* The love of Jesus made his bride purer. Wives need to see a pure husband—not one who is a slave to pornography, immorality, dishonesty, or other forms of sin (Eph. 5:26-27).

Q 5 *How can a husband make his wife better spiritually?*

115

A husband should set a holy standard for the language in the home. No unholy words or coarse joking should ever come out of his mouth (Eph. 4:29). Rather, a husband should lead the wife in talking and thinking about godly things.

A love that drags a person down is false, worldly, and ungodly. Is your wife more beautiful in spirit because she has lived with you? A husband's love and devotion toward his wife should encourage her to grow in her spiritual life.

If a husband has a wife who is not a Christian, he is to live the Christian life in front of her. He should pray for her and do all he can to show the love of God to her. At times, some Christians feel that they can divorce a spouse because he or she is not a Christian. The Bible forbids this and tells us; *"If any brother has a wife who is not a believer and she is willing to live with him, he must not divorce her"* (1 Cor. 7:12).

Q 6 *Husband, what can you do to help your wife improve mentally?*

A husband's love should make his wife better mentally. How a husband does this will vary from country to country. In some countries like Bangladesh and Pakistan, up to 85 percent of the women cannot read. In Africa, about 50 percent of the women do not read. In such countries, a husband's love should lead him to help his wife learn to read. In countries where there is a higher standard of education, a husband's love might lead him to help his wife get a diploma, college degree, Masters, or doctorate. Or it might at least guide him to buy various books for her to read; or encourage her to buy books she chooses to read. In other situations, a husband might help his wife study and learn a skill, such as sewing, the work of a secretary, or nursing. A husband's love should make his wife better.

C. A husband's love should care for and nourish his wife (Eph. 5:28-29).

A husband is the shepherd of his home. It is his job to care for the needs of each sheep in his little flock. Husband, where does your wife fit into your daily priorities? After your relationship with God, she is next. You are to care for your wife more than your job or ministry (Eph. 5:29). You are to love your wife as yourself.

Q 7 *Husband, where does your wife think she is in your priorities? Ask her.*

Someone said, "If you treat your family like customers and your customers like family, things tend to work out pretty well." As a business leader, do you treat your customers better than you treat your family members? On the job, men find things like solutions, answers, and the right product for their customers. How much more should we assist our family members with their needs?

Q 8 *What are some needs that each wife has?*

A man's role is not to rule over his wife. The Bible says that a husband should love his wife as Christ loves the Church. This means that as husbands, we must care for our wives as Jesus cares for the needs of the Church.

Q 9 *Husband, do you love your wife as you love yourself? Discuss this.*

A missionary stood before a group of mature pastors and asked them, "How many of you obey Ephesians 5:28 and 33? That is, how many of you love your wife as you love yourself?" Most of the 50 pastors in the room were cautious. Only three raised their hands—and these three were younger pastors. The missionary continued, "I am a visitor in your country, and I do not know your ways well. So I want you to question these three men. They will come to the front and you will ask them questions. Afterward, you will be the jury to decide whether they love their wives as they love themselves."

So the three young pastors came forward and the elders began to ask questions. "After your wife raises the chicken, catches it, cleans it, and cooks it, who eats the first piece?" One of the three pastors immediately sat down without saying a word. Next, an elderly pastor asked, "Whose name is on the deed to your farm?" (This is important to a wife. If her husband's name alone is on the deed to the family property, she will lose the property at his death.) Upon hearing this second question, a second pastor took a seat. Only one pastor was left for the third question: "Do you have a certificate of marriage that the government recognizes?" (This can be important at a husband's death.) It would have been interesting to hear more questions, but no more came because the third young pastor sat down. May the Lord help each of us husbands to love our wives as we love ourselves. A husband and wife are one flesh in the Lord. May each husband discern that what he does to his wife he does to himself and to Christ within her (Eph. 5:28).

D. A husband's love should unite him to his wife (Eph. 5:30-31).

Jesus is one with His Church. We are members of His body (Eph. 5:30). Nothing can separate us from the love of Christ (Rom. 8:35-39). Likewise, a husband and wife are one flesh (Eph. 5:31).

Figure 7.2 In cleaving to his wife, a husband does not reject his mother and father.

In cleaving to his wife, a husband does not reject his mother and father. He leaves the life of depending on his parents. He begins a new family with his wife. Indeed, he continues to love his parents, but his love is the mature love of an adult. His parents can count on him in hard times. They can depend on him as he depended on them as a child. But he does not allow any conflict from parents to harm his relationship with his wife. He cleaves to her, not allowing anything to separate them.

It is strange to see that some couples live together, sleep together, raise children together, yet are emotional strangers to each other. Those involved in the seminars of *Marriage Encounter call such people "married singles." They are legally married, yet without the bond of deep love. In contrast, a husband's love should cause him to be close to his wife. He should seek to understand her feelings and emotions. Jesus cares about His bride. He knows the number of hairs on each head. He cares about the little things of life. Likewise, a husband should become very close to his wife.

How well do you know your wife? Do you know her favorite food? Would *she* rate your marriage as an A, B, C, D, or F? What part of her day does she like the most and the least? Is she your best friend? What does she like most about you? In which area would she like you to improve a little?

Q 10 *After marriage, how does a husband's love for his parents change?*

Q 11 *Explain: "Sometimes a husband and wife live together, but are like strangers."*

Q 12 *What are some things a husband should know about his wife?*

E. A husband's love should be faithful to his wife until death (Eph. 5:25-33).

Jesus was and is faithful to His bride, the Church. He came to die for us, and He was faithful. With His last words He said, *"It is finished"* (John 19:30). He was faithful unto death.

Likewise, a husband's love causes him to be faithful to his wife. A loving husband guards his emotions. He refuses to love other women. In business or friendship, he is faithful to his wife with his words, actions, and private thoughts. The Bible says that each husband should love only one woman. ² *"Each man should have his own wife, and each woman her own husband. ³The husband should fulfill his marital duty to his wife, and likewise the wife to her husband"* (1 Cor. 7:2-3).

The prophet Malachi rebuked some husbands. He explained why God was angry with them.

¹³*Another thing you do: You flood the LORD's altar with tears. You weep and wail because he no longer pays attention to your offerings or accepts them with pleasure from your hands. ¹⁴You ask, "Why?" It is because the LORD is acting as the witness between you and the wife of your youth, because you have broken*

Q 13 *What are some ways a husband must be faithful to his wife?*

Q 14 *What is God's attitude toward an unfaithful husband?*

Q 15 *How should a husband respond to temptations about other women?*

faith with her, though she is your partner, the wife of your marriage covenant. ¹⁵Has not the LORD made them one? In flesh and spirit they are his. And why one? Because he was seeking godly offspring. So guard yourself in your spirit, and do not break faith with the wife of your youth (Mal 2:13-15).

A husband is to be totally committed to his wife—physically and emotionally. Even in his private thoughts, the Bible forbids a man to lust after a woman (Matt. 5:28). Paul teaches us to conquer every stray thought—to present it as a captive at the feet of Jesus (2 Cor. 10:5). Turn away from evil thoughts and sights. Resist the devil and he will flee from you (James 4:7). It is not a sin to be tempted. But pray so that you will not enter into temptation (Matt. 26:41). The flesh is weak, but the Spirit is willing. Walk in the Spirit and you will not fulfill the lusts of the flesh (Gal. 5:16; Rom. 8:8-9). Do not turn an evil thought over and over in your mind, like a person tastes candy in his mouth. Reject evil thoughts. Love what is right and hate what is wrong (Rom. 12:9; Heb. 1:9). Husband or single man, do not gaze at harlots, pictures of beautiful women, or another man's wife. Be true to God and your wife with your thoughts. Then, God will honor you and bless your marriage. Say with Job, *"I made a covenant with my eyes not to look lustfully at a girl"* (Job 31:1).

Q 16 *Explain the proverb: "Drink all the water you want from your own well."*

Scripture condemns using pornography, or becoming involved with another woman. God's plan is for a man to fulfill all of his sexual desires with his own wife.

¹⁵Drink water from your own cistern, running water from your own well. ¹⁶Should your springs overflow in the streets, your streams of water in the public squares? ¹⁷Let them be yours alone, never to be shared with strangers. ¹⁸May your fountain be blessed, and may you rejoice in the wife of your youth. ¹⁹A loving doe, a graceful deer— may her breasts satisfy you always, may you ever be captivated by her love. ²⁰Why be captivated, my son, by an adulteress? Why embrace the bosom of another man's wife? ²¹For a man's ways are in full view of the LORD, and he examines all his paths. ²²The evil deeds of a wicked man ensnare him; the cords of his sin hold him fast. ²³He will die for lack of discipline, led astray by his own great folly (Prov. 5:15-23).

Q 17 *In which 2 cases does the Bible allow divorce?*

Divorce is like a disease that is spreading in much of the world. Most people who divorce do not follow the biblical reasons for divorce. Some say, "We do not love each other any more," or "We have grown apart." There are only two reasons why a couple could consider divorce. One is if a spouse commits adultery (Matt. 19:9). The other is if an unbelieving spouse deserts a believing spouse (1 Cor. 7:15-16). Scripture clearly instructs husbands: *¹¹"A husband must not divorce his wife.... ²⁷Are you married? Do not seek a divorce"* (1 Cor. 7:11, 27).

A Husband's Relationship to His Wife—Part 2

Goal: *Give examples of how a husband's love is gentle, respectful, fulfilling, open, patient, steadfast, and thankful.*

A. A husband's love is gentle.

Love is never harsh (1 Cor. 13:4-5). Jesus is gentle with the Church.

Q 18 *Explain the 2 word pictures of Matthew 12:18-20.*

¹⁸"Here is my servant whom I have chosen, the one I love, in whom I delight; I will put my Spirit on him ... ¹⁹He will not quarrel or cry out; no one will hear his voice in the streets. ²⁰A bruised reed he will not break, and a smoldering wick he will not snuff out, till he leads justice to victory" (Matt. 12:18-20).

Jesus is gentle with us. A bruised reed is so fragile that a slight wind will break it. Some men are so rough that they knock the bark off of a tree. But Jesus is so gentle that he will not break a bruised reed. Some men are so rough that they would knock a candle off of the table. But the touch of Jesus would not disturb or put out a smoking candle. Jesus is the husband's example of gentleness.

> LOVE IS NEVER HARSH. JESUS IS GENTLE WITH US. SO SHOULD A HUSBAND BE GENTLE WITH HIS WIFE.

"Husbands, love your wives and do not be harsh with them" (Col. 3:19). Husbands must be kind, patient, gentle, understanding, and tender with wives. *Sandpaper is a rough paper to use on wood, not people. Physically, a man must avoid scratching his wife's face with his whiskers. Emotionally, he must avoid sanding her feelings with his words, looks, or actions! God created a woman's skin softer than a man's skin; and He created her emotions softer than the feelings of a man. A woman's tender feelings enable her to be a good mother. So a husband must be very gentle with his wife, or he will hurt her feelings.

Q 19 Why does Scripture command each husband not to be harsh with his wife?

Menstrual cycle. There are times in a woman's life when the husband should be even more gentle than usual. Once a month—for 3 or 4 days—during the time of her monthly flow or period (menstrual cycle), life is harder for her. During this time her emotions change due to *hormones in her body. Physically, she may feel bloated and dull. Emotionally, she may feel sad (even crying), nervous, angry, or worth little. During this hard time of the month, a woman may cry because of small things that upset her. A loving husband should treat her as gently as a new baby for these 3 or 4 days. He should show her extra love, tenderness, and kindness. He should avoid talking about money or hard issues until the storm within her has passed. He should keep the home quiet and peaceful during these days. Also, he should do some of her work to make her load lighter. He might need to remind her that life will return to normal after a few days.[3]

Q 20 How can a woman's monthly cycle affect her emotions?

***Menopause is another hard time in a woman's life.** This may occur between the ages of 40–50. The time it begins and lasts varies. It is a time when many women suffer from the lack of a hormone called *estrogen. During these years she may feel sad, angry, worthless, frustrated, nervous, unable to stand noise, unloved, or confused. She may find it hard to sleep or eat. Along with these emotional problems, she may have physical problems such as trouble digesting her food, hot flashes, dizziness, trouble going to the bathroom, trembling, dry skin, little sexual desire, a racing heartbeat, headaches, dark circles around her eyes, or loss of weight. Problems like these may be caused by many things, but one cause may be the lack of estrogen. Doctors give estrogen through shots or pills.[4] A loving husband should see that his wife gets the best medical care possible.

Q 21 What is menopause? How does it affect a wife?

A husband should be aware that menopause comes to all women. He should consider that this is a period God Himself has planned for women. It is a time when the Lord can teach a man many things. During these years, a man can become more thankful for all his wife has done for him. He can learn to be more loving, patient, kind, and understanding. It is a time when he can learn to serve his wife more than ever before. The more needs she has, the more opportunities he has to serve her as Christ serves the Church. Every husband should ask himself, "How can I become more like Jesus?" In fact, some of us whose wives are so godly should pray, "How can I become more like my wife?" During the menopause years, a man can imitate the love and gentleness he has seen in his mother and his wife. There is a lot that men can learn from women.

Q 22 How should a husband treat his wife during the years of menopause?

B. A husband's love is not rude, but shows respect for his wife (1 Cor. 13:5).

There are times that a husband will become angry. This is normal. Still, when he is angry, a husband must control himself and remain gentle. It is not wrong to become angry. But it is wrong to be rude, even during anger. Husbands (and wives) should avoid going to bed angry (Eph. 4:26-27). They should conquer anger quickly, as they would

Q 23 *What are some ways a husband can show respect for his wife?*

quickly put out a dangerous fire with water. Both spouses should forgive each other by the time they go to bed, whether they agree or not.

A husband should be polite and thoughtful. He should show respect for his wife by being a gentleman. He should do such things as open doors for his wife, carry things for her, and help her with the housework.

The Bible tells husbands to *"be considerate as you live with your wives, and treat them with respect as the weaker partner"* (1 Pet. 3:7). A husband should discern that God gave men broad shoulders and narrow hips, but He gave women narrow shoulders and broad hips. In most cases, women are weaker physically than men. So men should use their broad shoulders to do the hardest work and carry the heaviest things (1 Pet. 3:7).

Men need to remember that women are often kinder and speak more softly than men. A husband must avoid ignoring the soft words of his wife. To ignore someone shows a lack of respect and honor.

Q 24 *Have you ever acted like the husband fixing the broken chair? Explain.*

A husband was trying to fix a broken chair. His wife was watching. Softly, in a quiet, gentle voice, she made a suggestion. But he was focused on what he was doing. And he was feeling like the man in charge. So he did not pay attention to what she said. After an hour, he realized the problem. His wife had seen it an hour before, and softly spoke to him. Because he did not respect her words, he hurt her feelings, and he wasted his time! When a husband respects his wife, it makes her smile, and she may shine light on his path.

Q 25 *Husband, when is it the hardest for you to accept advice from your wife?*

Some husbands are foolish. They do not recognize the wisdom God has given wives. A wife is an important member of the family team. God's plan is for her to help her husband make decisions, solve problems, raise children, and build relationships. As a husband respects his wife, she helps him improve and mature in many ways. The husband who cuts himself off from her advice walks a lonely road. Her insights are of great worth. Many men have avoided failure, embarrassment, or financial loss by listening to their wives.

Nabal was a fool. If he had listened to his wise wife, Abigail, he would have lived longer and prospered more (1 Sam. 25).

Q 26 *How are some husbands like Nabal?*

C. A husband's love fulfills her sexual needs and some emotional needs (1 Cor. 7:3-5).

God created a husband to fulfill the needs of his wife—including her needs that are physical, emotional, or sexual.

Q 27 *Describe the sexual and emotional needs of a wife.*

³The husband should fulfill his marital duty to his wife, and likewise the wife to her husband. ⁴The wife's body does not belong to her alone but also to her husband. In the same way, the husband's body does not belong to him alone but also to his wife. ⁵Do not deprive each other except by mutual consent and for a time, so that you may devote yourselves to prayer. Then come together again so that Satan will not tempt you because of your lack of self-control (1 Cor. 7:3-5).

Figure 7.3 God created a husband to fulfill the needs of his wife.

The Scripture is speaking about normal needs for sex within marriage. Sex is for both the husband and wife to enjoy. A husband should fulfill the sexual needs of his wife. He should discern that sex is not just something for him to enjoy. He should learn to please his wife in the bedroom—and other rooms of the house The husband should help his wife feel loved, valuable, appreciated, respected, secure, and fulfilled.

D. A husband's love is honest and open with his wife (Eph. 4:15; James 5:16).

Husbands should speak and receive the truth in love (Eph. 4:15). If your wife is your best friend—and she should be—you will grow to open your life to her. All of us have struggles throughout life. We need to feel free to talk about our faults and concerns. *"Confess your sins to each other and pray for each other so that you may be healed"* (James 5:16). No human knows a husband better than his wife knows him.

Q 28 *Why should a husband discuss his faults with his wife?*

Some husbands hide things from their wives—things that they reveal to their parents and friends. A wife is designed by God to help her husband by listening and making suggestions. It is foolish for a man to reject such help to protect his male pride. Blessed is the man who learns to talk heart to heart with his wife.

E. A husband's love is patient with his wife (1 Cor. 13:4).

A Swahili proverb says, *Haraka, haraka, haina baraka.* A rough translation is: An attitude of hurry, hurry brings no blessings. Jesus is patient with us. He does not push, push, push. He is content when we walk with Him at a peaceful pace. He does not scold us when we are a little slow.

Q 29 *What are some examples of times a husband can practice being patient with his wife?*

One pastor noticed that his love for his wife changed as the years went by. In the beginning, he treated her like a queen. He was kind and patient. He opened the door for her to enter the house. He carried the biggest part of the load and let her walk beside him. He waited patiently while she brushed her hair to make it look just right. But as so often happens, his love began to grow colder, one degree at a time. One day he realized that he was treating her like a slave instead of a queen. He expected her to carry, cook, and clean. He did not help, and he did not say thank you. When it was time to go somewhere, he was not patient. If she was not ready, he yelled at her. Then, one wonderful day, the Holy Spirit spoke to him from the book of Revelation. [4]*"Yet I hold this against you: You have forsaken your first love.* [5]*Remember the height from which you have fallen! Repent and do the things you did at first"* (Rev. 2:4-5). **From that day on, he practiced being the husband God wanted him to be.**[5]

F. A husband's love perseveres—it works through problems (1 Cor. 13:7).

Conflict comes to every marriage. Storms are a part of life outside and inside the home. But biblical love perseveres. A husband must practice using love, patience, prayer, communication, and skills to solve problems in marriage. God has a solution for every problem. But couples who do not agree on a solution will struggle with the same conflicts throughout their married life. There are numerous verses in the Bible that speak about good communication (Prov. 13:3; 15:1; 21:9, 19; 25:8, 23-24; 29:20; Gal. 5:15; Col. 4:6). From time to time, review the chapter on communication in this book. A husband's love causes him to persevere in communication—to keep on discussing a problem until the couple finds a solution.

Q 30 *In what way should a husband persevere to solve a conflict in marriage?*

G. A husband's love praises and thanks his wife (Gal. 6:10).

All of us need to feel appreciated. Words like "thank you" encourage us. They help our self esteem—make us feel valuable. No one should flatter, but sincere praise is a blessing. Both husbands and wives feel good about themselves when people praise them. If you criticize your wife, do it privately. Also, mix criticism and praise together—mixing one spoonful of criticism with nine spoons of praise!

Q 31 *Explain: "Praise brings out the best in all of us."*

Q 32 *Complete Figure 7.4 by filling in the words of praise.*

In public, say something good about your wife to her parents, children, or friends. In time, she will hear about it and hold her head up with joy. Publicly saying gracious things about her strengthens her good qualities. It causes her to want to live up to the good things you say about her. In private, a husband should tell his wife that he loves her—and why.

God created us with a need to be appreciated. Does Jesus praise the Church? Read the letter Jesus sent to the churches in Asia (Rev. 2–3). Notice the Lord used words of praise to encourage believers. Praise brings out the best in all of us. One of the greatest needs in wives, husbands, and children is the need to be praised.

Scripture	Summary of Words of Praise
Jer. 1:12	
Matt. 8:10	
Matt. 16:17	
Matt. 26:10-13	
Rom. 16:1-16	
Phil. 1:3-5	
Phil. 4:10-19	

Figure 7.4 Practice chart on words of praise

Most husbands do not enjoy taking the time to shop for the best bargain in the market. Yet many women work hard to use their money wisely. It takes much wisdom and hard work to feed and clothe a family. A wife filled with wisdom is truly a gift from God. Each husband should show appreciation and respect for the way a wife manages the home. Then, children will follow his example and praise their mother. And she will feel good about herself and spend her days singing as she serves her family.

A Husband's Attitude Toward His Wife and Family

Goal A: *Analyze the type of leader a husband should be in relation to his wife and family.*
Goal B: *Describe the balance a husband should have between his work and family.*
Goal C: *Explain the meaning and purpose of the Sabbath.*
Goal D: *Summarize the proper use of a husband's time, energy, and money.*

The home tests a husband's ability to lead and guide. We know a man is mature after he proves he can manage his home (1 Tim. 3:4-5). Only then does the church open to him larger doors of influence as a wise elder.

A. A husband's style of leadership

The headship of the husband in the home is not something to vote on or debate. God has chosen the husband to lead the family (1 Cor. 11:3, 8-9).

A good leader in any field must lead in the easy times and the hard times. Even within the family, a good wife is not *always* easy to lead. Neither men nor women are perfect. There are days when we feel grouchy, irritable, angry, sad, or sick. A wise husband will find ways of working with his wife and family under all conditions. He will learn to understand people, and use this skill to lead his family.

Some have noted that a husband may relate to his wife in one of five ways. Let us look at each of these.

1. The style of a Dictator. This is an old, worldly type of *authority*. In this style, a harsh husband treats his wife like she is his property. He may force her to obey through beatings if he chooses.

How to Be a Loving Husband   123

Some men think that they can manage a home by being dictators—having absolute power and the right to make every decision alone. Some foolish young husbands try to lead in this style. They tell a wife about the *laws* of the home. These are like James and John when they were young. Jesus called them the *"Sons of Thunder"* (Mark 3:17). They wanted, like Elijah, to call down fire from heaven on the Samaritans when these people did not agree with them (Luke 9:54-56). Jesus rebuked these fiery young apostles. Some versions of the Bible say that the Lord told them *"You do not know what kind of spirit you are of, for the Son of Man did not come to destroy men's lives, but to save them."* Likewise, Jesus is not pleased today by a husband who rules by fire and brimstone. This kind of harsh husband punishes his wife if she breaks one of his rules. This does not lead. Rather, he reigns through terror, force, and threats. The final result is that he will reap a harvest of confusion, bitterness, and hatred. His wife may obey him, but she will not love and respect him. She will despise him. And his children may obey when they are small. But when they grow up, they will escape from the dictator and reject his reign of terror. Husband, do not <u>destroy</u> your family through ruling by force. God's plan is for you to <u>save</u> them as you lead through gentleness, like Jesus (Matt. 12:18-21).

Q 33 ⟋ *How is The Dictator like a son of thunder?*

2. The style of a President and His Wife. This describes the traditional style of leadership in the home. The wife submits to her husband. She fulfills her role of support and the mother of the home. As the children enter school, she may choose to work some outside the home.

This style of leadership is the one we prefer to create harmony in the family. Each voice in the family is heard. The father *is* the leader, yet he leads through consulting and discussing matters with his wife and children. He earns respect in the home—*not* through force and fear—but by being gentle, caring, and righteous.

Q 34 ⟋ *In a family, what results if a husband leads by terror and threats?*

Q 35 ⟋ *How are decisions made if the husband's style is The President and His Wife?*

Many wise men, when facing a hard decision, will tell their friends and relatives: "I must sleep on this matter." Then, they go home to discuss the matter with their wives before sleeping. A wife's counsel helps a husband make a good decision. As we noted earlier, a husband who neglects the counsel of his wife is like Nabal—whose name means *fool!* Today, wives manage their homes, care for their children, and sometimes have a job outside the home. But a wise husband discerns that his wife can think, reason, and add much to leading the family!

Christ is the Head of man, as man is the head of woman (1 Cor. 11:3). Even though Christ is the Head of man, He gives man the privilege of choosing his own destiny and fate. As the Head, Christ is gracious and loving with each man. Likewise, a husband should reccognize his wife and children's part in matters of the home. This is a godly, Christ-like style of leadership.

3. The style of a President and Vice President. This is a side-by-side style of leadership. It allows the woman to seek a job or career as her husband does. Both share in the work of the home. But his work is a higher priority than her work. This style of leadership may work well when there are no children at home. In this style the husband usually has the final word in decisions.

4. The style of Two Presidents. This style of leadership is very new.[+] In it, both the husband and wife are free to have careers. They share household duties, and have <u>equal</u> power in making decisions.[6]

5. The style of No Government. In this style the leader does not help guide the personal choices of the family members. This was a popular style of government for a time in Europe.[++] It reminds us of the dark period in the time of the Judges. Everyone did

Q 36 ⟍ *Summarize the "No Government" style of leadership.*

[+] Some call it the *egalitarian* form (also spelled <u>equalitarian</u>).

[++] Some refer to this in French as the **laissez-faire* style.

as he saw fit (Judges 21:25). Note that it is not a true style of leadership, because no one is leading. This method is foolish in the home! Wives look to their husbands for strength and wisdom. Children are *not* able to make good decisions without guidance. A man is not caring for his family if he avoids leading in family matters. Yet we must confess that some men drift into this style of cowards. They retreat to laziness, work, pleasure, alcohol, or other ways to avoid their family responsibilities.

B. A husband's relationship to his work

The curse of laziness. The Bible gives a healthy, balanced outlook on work. Consider the following passage:

> [30]*I passed by the field of the sluggard, and by the vineyard of the man lacking sense;* [31]*And behold, it was completely overgrown with thistles, its surface was covered with nettles, and its stone wall was broken down.* [32]*When I saw, I reflected upon it. ...* [33]*"A little sleep, a little slumber, a little folding of the hands to rest,"* [34]*then your poverty will come as a robber, and your want like an armed man* (Prov. 24:30-34 New American Standard Bible).

If the head of the family is lazy, laziness—like a disease—will infect his whole family. A close look at some people's attitude toward work is discouraging. Nations that have lazy, dishonest workers face financial ruin and conflicts within. It is sad to see public servants with an uncaring attitude of "don't bother me" during their office hours. Promotion and salary increases should come only to hard-working, committed employees. And those in business for themselves already know that their financial success depends on their work habits.

The blessing of work. A loving husband is a hard worker. Both culture and Scripture require hard work. For instance, Paul wrote in 1 Thessalonians 4:11-12:

> [11]*Make it your ambition to lead a quiet life, to attend to your own business and work with your hands, just as we commanded you;* [12]*so that you may behave properly toward outsiders and not be in any need* (NASB).

Hard work is not our enemy, even though some men think so. If our attitude toward work is positive, then work will be a happy, fruitful experience.

A man's aim should not be to become wealthy—satisfaction does not come from wealth. But it feels good to know that you have done your best; that you are good at what you do. While some men seek to avoid work by their cleverness, others truly enjoy it.

Figure 7.5 It is all right to relax once in a while, but laziness causes neglect.

Every devoted husband must develop a positive attitude toward work. God has promised to bless the work of our hands. A husband who wants God's blessings should work with honesty and diligence. A loving father rejects laziness, ignorance, procrastination, and pride. In turn, his family will love and respect him. By his example, he passes on godly values to another generation of fruitful family members and citizens.

The balance between work and family. Laziness leads to poverty. At the other extreme, however, greed can drive a man to become a *"workaholic"—a man who works too much, like he is a slave to his work. Addicted only to his work, the workaholic

---

Q 37 *Summarize the curse of laziness.*

Q 38 *What does the Bible teach about work?*

Q 39 *How much should a husband work?*

neglects his family's emotional needs by never being home. This does not represent a blessing from the Lord, no matter how large the pay envelope may be. God's blessings come as we live balanced, productive lives in harmony with His own will.

A husband who neglects to provide for his family has failed (1 Tim. 5:8). Men must earn enough money to meet the financial needs of *each* family member. Yet they must also be present in the family as much as possible to provide moral and spiritual guidance. So husbands must find the balance. Men often work many hours to earn a living; some even take two jobs to earn extra money. Such a man is often shocked and hurt when the family complains that he is seldom present in the home.

From the time Tim Burke was a small child he dreamed of being a paid athlete. Because of his athletic talent, discipline, and hard work, a baseball team hired Tim. As a pitcher, he became successful in the "big league." Tim and his wife wanted children, but for medical reasons, they could not have their own children. After much prayer, they decided to adopt four children. This led to one of the hardest decisions in Tim's life.

Q 40 *How does a husband's work affect the number of children he should plan to have?*

Tim discovered that traveling to play ball prevented him from being a good husband and father. After more prayer and thought, he decided to give up professional baseball, so he could spend more time with his family. As he left the stadium for the last time, reporters wanted to know why he was retiring. Tim said, "Baseball is going to do just fine without me. But I'm the only father my children have. I'm the only husband my wife has. They need me a lot more than baseball needs me." [7] Other than knowing Jesus Christ, Tim realized that being a godly, devoted husband and father was the most important thing he had to do in life.

We all want enough money to meet our needs. Money is important, but it is not everything! It is not good for a husband (*or* wife) to work too much making money, and leave the children without a father in the home.

Some men are so busy in the world of work that they so not see their children for several days of a week. They leave the house before the children are awake and return late at night—after everyone is asleep. This kind of lifestyle can affect men in every type of work—from the businessman to the pastor. Most men feel pulled toward their work. Besides money, work makes them feel satisfied and proud.

Among the things that children desire is the presence of happy parents. While mothers are often in the home and available for the children, some fathers are not around. If a father is not in the home much, how will his children learn to respect him? If the father is absent, how will the children benefit from his example, wisdom, and advice? How will the boys in families desire to be like their fathers if these men are not present?

Of course, some men are absent from the home because the home is not a pleasant place for them. If men do not find good food and a clean house, they may spend more time at work. If men do not find an attractive woman to come home to (without being nagged), they may tend to be absent. This does not mean that when a husband is absent it is always the fault of his wife. Yet it may give a woman something to consider as she searches for ways to keep her husband content at home.

Over-commitment is a family killer. Besides work, other things can fill the lives of parents. Even church activities—though they are good—can harm a family when taken to an extreme. Parents should take time to schedule their lives with the interests of their families at heart. It is not easy to balance family needs with the demands of life. But it can be done *if* the family remains a high priority to parents.

A husband must be able to provide well for his family. Still, the ability to earn money is not the most important characteristic of a good husband. Some men succeed in business, but are "total losers" in their homes. A godly husband is able to put the welfare of others ahead of his own—*selflessly* caring for his family responsibilities.

C. God's word to workaholic husbands

A former President of the United States, George Bush, Sr. was once asked, "What is your greatest accomplishment in life?" He could have replied that he was a pilot in World War II—who was shot down, yet lived. He could have boasted that he was President. He could have said that he has two sons who were governors—and one of them became President. Yet George Bush Senior said, "My children still come home."

Q 41 *What is the purpose of the Sabbath day?*

There are many marriages that have absent husbands. These men are driven by their work and are seldom at home because of it. As a result, many marriages end, because the wife feels that she does not have a husband. A wife should not divorce her husband for this reason. Still, husbands need to realize that working too much is not healthy for them, their marriage, or their family. Those who work too much are often living in disobedience to what the Scripture commands. The Bible tells us, ⁸*"Remember the Sabbath day by keeping it holy. ⁹Six days you shall labor and do all your work, ¹⁰but the seventh day is a Sabbath to the LORD your God. On it you shall not do any work"* (Exod. 20:8-10).

What is the Bible talking about? What does the *Sabbath* mean, and why does God command us to be careful to observe it? The *Sabbath* means "rest." Jesus said, *"The Sabbath was made for man, not man for the Sabbath"* (Mark 2:27). God is saying that the Sabbath is for our benefit. One of the purposes of the Sabbath is to prevent us from being too tired (burnout). Every 7 days we need to get physical, emotional, and spiritual renewal. Like batteries, we run down every few days.

Islam, Judaism, and Christianity all celebrate a Sabbath. Muslims celebrate it on Friday, the Jews celebrate on Saturday, and the Christians celebrate on Sunday.

Q 42 *What are 3 parts of keeping the Sabbath?*

What do you do on the Sabbath? Keep it holy. How can you keep it holy? Scripture gives three guidelines:

Rest your body. *"In vain you rise early and stay up late"* (Ps. 127:2). God wants us to rest our bodies. In fact, He took 6 days to create the world and on the seventh day He rested. There is an old American Indian parable that says, "You break the bow if it is always bent." The Scripture tells us *"A fool's work wearies him"* (Eccl. 10:15).

In the French Revolution, the government tried to get rid of old laws. One of the old laws was that everyone should take Sunday off. Harsh leaders said that every day would be a work day. Within months they had to revive the Sabbath law—to rest one day each week. The health of the French people was being destroyed. The government's idea that 7 days of work was better than 6 days did not work. Why? Because it went against the way God created us. We are made to live better if we rest one day each week. *"Remember the Sabbath day by keeping it holy"* (Exod. 20:8).

Q 43 *How does the Lord restore our emotions?*

Take time to be quiet. Quiet restores the soul. Psalm 23:2-3 says, ²*"He makes me lie down in green pastures, he leads me beside quiet waters, ³he restores my soul."* This Psalm tells us how God restores our soul—which includes our emotions. He restores us by causing us to rest and relax in quiet places. Rest and quiet re-create peace, joy, and happiness within us. A missionary wrote in his journal, "We're going to rest today so that our souls can catch up with our bodies."

Take time for family. In history, Sunday has often been a day for two things: church and family. Ecclesiastes 9:9 tells husbands to *"Enjoy life with your wife, whom you love."* Sunday is a great day to be with family and enjoy getting in touch with each other's lives. A lot of families take the effort to make Sundays special for their families. If you are in the ministry, you will need to choose a day other than Sunday to rest.

Figure 7.6 Quiet can help restore the soul.

Avoid working too much. Burnout and always being tired will harm you physically, emotionally, and spiritually. Too much work will hinder you from being a good husband or father. Obey Ecclesiastes 9:9—this will guide you to be the husband and father that God wants you to be.

D. A husband's investments—time, energy, and money[8]

Time. To lead his home well, a man must spend *time* at home. He must invest time in the same way he invests money. His loving presence in his home—for a part of each day—will help enable his family to be what God intends.

Time is an investment that can pay a high interest rate! Some fathers neglect their small children. They are too busy with work, friends, and other things to play with their children. So they do not know each child's needs and desires. Later, as the children come into conflict with teachers and the law, these fathers must spend *a great deal of time* trying to keep children in school and out of prison. Their homes are filled with conflict. The family bond may be torn beyond repair. An investment of time—at the proper time—can help produce the kind of family a husband hopes for.

One of the most important areas in which a father can invest his time is in leading regular family devotions or family worship times. A man who attempts to lead his family without the presence and help of God is walking a hard, dangerous road. Walk with God, and lead your family to walk with Him. It *is* true that the family that prays together stays together! Be a loving husband who gives his family spiritual leadership. You will produce a future generation of moral, responsible men and women—and they will become leaders in many areas of life.

Energy. In a similar way, a man must be willing to invest his *energy* in family living. At work, if people do not work hard, they are likely to be dismissed, sacked, or demoted. Sadly, some dads need to be "sacked" in their homes! A good husband/father spends part of his energy on family projects, household chores, and repairs. In this way, the house will stay in good repair, his wife will be happier, and the father will have opportunity to teach his children some practical skills. Later, after the children become adults, they will use these skills to repair their own houses. Examples are better than words. Also, a father should spend some of his energy to play games and talk. This means that a man must not use all of his strength at work. If he comes home too tired, he will not feel like giving energy to the family. So a father must save part of his energy for his family.

Q 44 *Why should a husband not use all of his energy at work?*

Do not be a stranger in your home. Time is costly. Invest the greater part of your free time in nurturing and developing your home life. Do not spend more time with your friends than you spend with your family. Be willing to work around the home. Reject the foolish idea that household chores are beneath the *dignity* of a man. Such foolish ideas are often an excuse for laziness, and add to the wife's burden.

Q 45 *In your culture, is it good for a man to help work in his home? Explain.*

Frances Johnson, at the age of 46, started tying pieces of string together. The string (twine) he liked most came around bales of hay. He never dated or married, and died over 80 years old. But 30 years of collecting string resulted in a huge ball, 13 feet high (4 m), 44 feet around (13.5 m), and 21,000 pounds (9,545 kilograms) in weight! Stretched out, it was long enough to reach over 1,000 miles (1,609 kilometers). The huge ball of string brought Johnson fame. It got him into *The Guinness Book of Records*. Near death, Johnson was quoted as saying, "I still like to look at it. It is the greatest thing I ever did." He lived for more than 80 years, and the greatest thing he did was make a smelly ball of string—a ball that helped no one and could burn up in a minute. Husband/father: What will be the greatest thing you do in your life?[9]

Q 46 *What will be the greatest thing you do in life?*

Money. Outside of salvation, the family is the most precious, valuable thing a man has. Many men are busy investing money in housing estates, business, farms, and education. For sure, it is good to invest money wisely. Yet, some find it difficult to invest in the things that will give them a "profit" of good families and homes.

Q 47 *How should a husband invest money on his family to gain profits at home?*

Q 48 *What are the top priorities for family money?*

Children need shoes, clothes, and other things. They need three balanced meals a day. They need money for their education. So clothing, food, housing, and education should be top priorities for family money.

A man should spend money to buy books to strengthen his family life. He should invest in tools that save labor. These will help him and his wife with work in the home. A man may become wealthy from his investments in the world. But he is a financial failure if he does not spend money wisely to build a strong and happy family.

Transition

In this chapter we have looked at a husband's love for his wife and family. In chapters 9 and 10 we will study the way parents should raise their children. In many ways a husband should love his children as he loves his wife. Also, the children will watch the way he treats their mother. They will learn from his example. If he is gentle, kind, thoughtful, respectful, patient, helpful, and godly, they will imitate him. The dad is the leader of the home, and the children will follow in his footsteps.

Figure 7.7 A husband must put God first, family second, and work third.

 Chapter Summary

 A Husband's Relationship to His Wife—Part 1

Goal: *Explain 5 ways a husband should love his wife as Christ loved the Church (Eph. 5:25-33).*

A husband's love should sacrifice for his wife. His love should make his wife better. A husband's love should care for and nourish his wife. His love should unite him to his wife. His love should be faithful until death.

 A Husband's Relationship to His Wife—Part 2

Goal: *Give examples of how a husband's love is gentle, respectful, fulfilling, open, patient, steadfast, and thankful.*

A husband must be kind, patient, gentle, understanding, and tender with his wife at all times, and especially during the menstrual cycle and in menopause. When he is angry, a husband must control himself and remain gentle. A husband should be polite and thoughtful—open doors for his wife, carry things for her, and help her with the housework. He should seek to fulfill the physical, emotional, and sexual needs of his wife. A husband should speak and receive the truth in love. He should not push a wife to be in a hurry. He should praise her in private, in the home, and in public. This will help her feel appreciated and valued.

A Husband's Attitude Toward His Wife and Family

Goal A: *Analyze the type of leader a husband should be in relation to his wife and family.*

A husband should lead the family under God, valuing the wisdom, feelings, and counsel of his wife.

Goal B: *Describe the balance a husband should have between his work and family.*

If the head of the family is lazy, laziness—like a disease—will infect his whole family. A loving husband is a hard worker. He who neglects to provide for his family has failed. So a godly husband works hard, but does not spend too many hours away from his family. He puts the welfare of others ahead of his own—*selflessly* caring for his family responsibilities.

Goal C: *Explain the meaning and purpose of the Sabbath.*

The *Sabbath* means "rest." The Sabbath is a day to rest your body, take time to be quiet, and take time for family.

Goal D: *Summarize the proper use of a husband's time, energy, and money.*

To lead his home well, a man must spend *time* at home. He must invest time in the same way he invests money.

In a similar way, a man must be willing to invest his *energy* in family living. A good husband/father spends part of his energy on family projects, household chores, and repairs.

A husband must also invest *money* in his family. Clothing, food, housing, and education should be top priorities for family money.

 Test Yourself: Circle the letter by the *best* completion to each question or statement.

1. Ephesians 5 says that a husband should love his wife as
a) he loves his children.
b) he loves the Lord.
c) the Father loves the Son.
d) Christ loved the Church.

2. The Bible says that a husband should
a) rule over his wife.
b) submit to his wife.
c) sacrifice for his wife.
d) discipline his wife.

3. A man who loves right and hates wrong
a) rejects evil thoughts when they come.
b) cannot be tempted by evil thoughts.
c) welcomes evil thoughts in secret.
d) thinks only about good thoughts.

4. A husband should be the most gentle with his wife
a) the first hour of each day.
b) every day of the week.
c) three or four days each month.
d) on Sundays and holidays.

5. A husband shows a lack of respect if he
a) disagrees with his wife at times.
b) ignores his wife at home.
c) teaches his wife in private.
d) rebukes his wife in love.

6. What brings out the best in a wife?
a) Praise
b) Diligence
c) Holiness
d) Children

7. The leadership style that the authors recommend is the style of
a) a Dictator.
b) a President and His Wife.
c) Two Presidents.
d) t No Government.

8. In the home, the right attitude toward work is:
a) A husband should guide others to work.
b) A husband should inspect the wife's work.
c) A husband should rest while children work.
d) A husband should help work at home.

9. The word *Sabbath* means
a) "Sunday."
b) "holiness."
c) "law."
d) "rest."

10. Spending money on your family is like
a) saving to reduce debt.
b) investing to bring profit.
c) hoeing weeds in a garden.
d) reaping a great harvest.

Chapter 8:
How to Be a Loving Wife

Introduction

Chapter 7 described the loving husband. How, then, shall we describe the loving wife? Proverbs 31:10-31 lists the characteristics of a loving wife. She is a wise woman who manages her house well. She is trusted by her husband, and respected by her children. *"Charm is deceptive, and beauty is fleeting; but a woman who fears the LORD is to be praised"* (Prov. 31:30).

> **¹The sayings of King Lemuel—an oracle his mother taught him:**
> ²*"O my son, O son of my womb, O son of my vows,*
> ³*do not spend your strength on women, your vigor on those who ruin kings."*
>
> **Epilogue: The Wife of Noble Character**
> ¹⁰*A wife of noble character who can find? She is worth far more than rubies.*
> ¹¹*Her husband has full confidence in her and lacks nothing of value.*
> ¹²*She brings him good, not harm, all the days of her life.*
> ¹³*She selects wool and flax and works with eager hands.*
> ¹⁴*She is like the merchant ships, bringing her food from afar.*
> ¹⁵*She gets up while it is still dark; she provides food for her family and portions for her servant girls.*
> ¹⁶*She considers a field and buys it; out of her earnings she plants a vineyard.*
> ¹⁷*She sets about her work vigorously; her arms are strong for her tasks.*
> ¹⁸*She sees that her trading is profitable, and her lamp does not go out at night.*
> ¹⁹*In her hand she holds the distaff and grasps the spindle with her fingers.*
> ²⁰*She opens her arms to the poor and extends her hands to the needy.*
> ²¹*When it snows, she has no fear for her household; for all of them are clothed in scarlet.*
> ²²*She makes coverings for her bed; she is clothed in fine linen and purple.*
> ²³*Her husband is respected at the city gate, where he takes his seat among the elders of the land.*
> ²⁴*She makes linen garments and sells them, and supplies the merchants with sashes.*
> ²⁵*She is clothed with strength and dignity; she can laugh at the days to come.*
> ²⁶*She speaks with wisdom, and faithful instruction is on her tongue.*
> ²⁷*She watches over the affairs of her household and does not eat the bread of idleness.*
> ²⁸*Her children arise and call her blessed; her husband also, and he praises her:*
> ²⁹*"Many women do noble things, but you surpass them all."*
> ³⁰*Charm is deceptive, and beauty is fleeting; but a woman who fears the LORD is to be praised.*
> ³¹*Give her the reward she has earned, and let her works bring her praise at the city gate.*

Figure 8.1 Proverbs 31 lists the characteristics of a loving wife.

This chapter focuses on the characteristics and behavior of a loving *wife*. Proverbs 31 describes the ideal woman. We recognize that a loving wife is neither perfect nor ideal. This chapter paints a picture for a wife to imitate—a goal for women to aim at. Some women are more capable than others, but every woman can be *a loving wife* in the eyes of her husband and children.

Lessons:

A Wife's Relationship to God and Her Husband
Goal: *Discuss 8 ways a loving wife relates to her husband.*

A Wife's Relationship to All in Her Home
Goal: *Describe 6 characteristics of a loving wife in her home.*

A Wife's Relationship to Those Outside Her Home
Goal: *Describe 3 ways a wife should relate to those outside her home.*

A Wife's Relationship to God and Her Husband
Goal: *Discuss 8 ways a loving wife relates to her husband.*

Background

God created *"male and female."* He placed within them the need for each other in marriage. Adam did not feel complete until God created Eve. Husbands and wives should seek ways to "complete" (help, assist, complement, encourage, fulfill, minister to) their spouse. In doing this, a husband and wife help each other become all God planned them to be.

To build His house as He plans, God asks husbands and wives to build up each other. Wives are called to love, submit to, respect, and honor their husbands—to build them up in the Lord.

One woman counselor says that a good husband is hard to find but easy to keep.[1] She says that men are not complex or hard to understand. They have a few basic needs that wives need to recognize and fulfill. Let us consider eight ways a wife can encourage and assist her husband.

Q 1 *Explain: A good husband is hard to find, but easy to keep.*

A. A loving wife maintains her relationship with God.

We mention a wife's *devotional life*, though we will not spend much time on this subject here. We cover it in our course on evangelism and discipleship. Whether we are talking about men or women, the first, most important thing is our relationship with God. To relate well to others, we must <u>first</u> relate well to our heavenly Father.

Q 2 *Identify 8 ways a wife can encourage and assist her husband.*

Bible reading and prayer are strong characteristics of a loving wife. She daily fills her life with God's Word and presence. She builds her home on her knees, seeking invisible strength and wisdom. Thus she is a source of spiritual strength and light in her home. She has peace at all times—for her secure foundation is God (first) and her husband (second). Her fervent prayers take her children through daily dangers and problems. When the family finances are limited, a loving wife prays to *Jehoveh Jireh*, the Lord Our Provider. The husband and children of a praying wife are truly blessed.

Q 3 *How can a wife have peace and strength for herself and her family?*

The godly wife and mother serves as a wonderful example of how to be a follower of Jesus Christ. When a husband or a child looks at the wife and mother, her daily life points them to a closer relationship with God.

Q 4 *How is your daily time with God? How can you improve in this area?*

Susannah Wesley was the mother of John and Charles Wesley. These men became the leaders of a revival that blessed England and many other nations. The revival gave birth to the Methodist Church. But many historians say that the Methodist Church really began in Susannah Wesley's home. She had many responsibilities, caring for her husband, home, and ten children. Still, she was very devoted to spiritual things. Each weekday she read the Bible and taught theology to her children. Each week she devoted one hour alone with each child. During that hour, she sought to know the child better, and taught the child to pray.

Q 5 *In what way did Susannah Wesley start the Methodist church?*

B. A loving wife submits to her husband.

Some err by thinking that *submission* means being inferior—less than another. But the Bible uses the word *submit* in relation to order and purpose, not value. *To submit* means "to be under." Jesus submitted to the Father, but He is not inferior to the Father. As Philippians 2 says, Jesus is equal to the Father, though He submitted to Him (Phil. 2:6). In theology, we learn that the Father and Son are equal in every way. They have the same nature and power. For example, in the book of Revelation, we see that all worship the Father and the Lamb. Still, the Son submits to the Father for order and purpose.

Q 6 *How do we know that a person who submits is not inferior?*

Q 7 *Wife, when is it easiest and hardest to submit to your husband?*

131

Submission is necessary in many parts of society. Without submission, there can be no government, no schools, no armies, no businesses, and no families. Those who submit have a different role than those above them, but they are not inferior. Submission is an attitude of respect to one who leads.

Scripture gives at least two examples of how a woman should submit to her husband.

First, a wife should submit to her husband as the Church submits to Christ. Because of the way Jesus loves us, we as believers submit to Christ. We seek to honor, respect, please, obey, and follow Him as our leader. Likewise, a wife should submit to her husband.

> [22]*Wives, submit to your husbands as to the Lord.* [23]*For the husband is the head of the wife as Christ is the head of the church, his body, of which he is the Savior.* [24]*Now* **as the church submits to Christ,** *so also wives should submit to their husbands in everything* (Eph. 5:22-24).

Author and speaker Joyce Meyer wrote, "A woman's response to proper loving care and nurturing should be, then, to submit and adapt to her husband as the Church would do to the Lord."[2] Meyer emphasizes that a woman is to respect and reverence her husband. This does not mean that she never has an opinion or is afraid to say what she thinks. "Marriage is a partnership, but... someone has to make a final decision when two people don't agree.... The man is to love his wife as Christ loved the Church, and the woman is to submit to her husband and respect him. If both parties do their part, a glorious relationship will result."[3]

The *second* example of how a woman should submit to her husband is in 1 Peter. Earlier, Peter wrote that believers should submit to every authority (for our testimony about Christ). We should submit to kings and governors—whether these leaders are godly or not (1 Pet. 2:13-17). Next, Peter wrote that a servant should submit, even to an unbelieving master (1 Pet. 2:18-21). Then, Peter wrote that wives should submit to husbands, whether the husbands are believers or not. Jesus submitted Himself to harsh leaders, because He trusted in God above them. Peter wrote that a wife should submit to her husband, and trust in God as Jesus did.

> [22]*"He [Christ] committed no sin, and no deceit was found in his mouth."* [23]*When they hurled their insults at him, he did not retaliate; when he suffered, he made no threats. Instead,* **he entrusted himself to him who judges justly.** [24]*He himself bore our sins in his body on the tree, so that we might die to sins and live for righteousness; by his wounds you have been healed.* [25]*For you were like sheep going astray, but now you have returned to the Shepherd and Overseer of your souls.* [1]*Wives,* **in the same way** *be submissive to your husbands* **so that,** *if any of them do not believe the word, they may be won over without words by the behavior of their wives* (1 Pet. 2:22–3:1).

Some wives say, "He's not a Christian, and he does not obey God or His Word. How can I submit to this man?" Peter spoke to wives in this setting (1 Pet. 3:1). God's apostle knew that there is great power in the act of submitting. Without saying anything, a wife can win her unbelieving husband to Christ through her actions.

> WITHOUT SAYING ANYTHING, A WIFE CAN WIN HER UNBELIEVING HUSBAND TO CHRIST THROUGH HER ACTIONS.

Another excuse to avoid submission is, "If I do that, I will lose my rights as a woman, and he will take advantage of me." Peter spoke about this concern, using the example of Sarah and Abraham. The Scripture says, [5]*"For this is the way the holy*

Q 8 *Explain: A wife should submit to her husband as the Church submits to Christ.*

Q 9 *Why should a Christian wife submit to a husband who is an unbeliever?*

Q 10 *Who will uphold the rights of a woman who submits to an unbeliever (1 Pet. 2:23)?*

women of the past who put their hope in God used to make themselves beautiful. They were submissive to their own husbands, ⁶like Sarah, who obeyed Abraham and called him her master" (1 Pet. 3:5-6). Sarah was not afraid to submit because she trusted God. She knew that it was God's plan for her to submit and that He would take care of the results. As a wife determines to obey God and fulfill her role in marriage, she can believe that God will honor her obedience. (All wives and husbands are to submit to God. There may be a few cases where a husband or wife must choose between obeying man or God, as in Acts 4:19. All believers should honor their consciences and God's Word. The priority of every believer is to obey God. We will discuss this in chapter 11, lesson 3.)

Headship and submission are set up in many ways. Couples often establish their pattern of relating during the first 18 months of marriage. They may continue this pattern or change it as they agree and mature.[4]

C. A loving wife respects, honors, and admires her husband.

An important part of submission is showing respect. Just as a wife needs love, a husband needs respect. Think of how you would feel if your husband stopped loving you? That is how he feels when he thinks you do not respect him. Being respectful means several things:

Q 11 *What are 4 ways a wife shows respect for her husband?*

- A wife shows respect by <u>not</u> strongly disagreeing with her husband in front of the children or others.
- She shows respect by <u>not</u> discussing her husband's faults in public.
- She shows respect by doing things that please her husband.
- She shows respect by supporting her husband's choices and decisions.

Figure 8.2
A smart wife looks for the right time to share her feelings with her husband.

When a wife respects her husband, it makes him stand tall like a man. It encourages him to be the husband and father God wants him to be. Respect inspires a man to be and do better—his very best.

Q 12 *Wife, what do you admire about your husband? How often do you tell him?*

D. A loving wife communicates with her husband.

We discussed communication in an earlier chapter, so we will only review it here. A wise wife tells her husband how she feels. She does not *expect* her husband to know—she *tells him* about her concerns. If she is worried, tired, sad, lonely, angry, hurt, or happy, she looks for the right time to share her feelings with her husband.

Q 13 *Why should a wife tell her husband how she feels about various matters?*

E. A loving wife lets her husband be the head of the home.

When a wife takes over one of her husband's responsibilities, he often surrenders other duties as well. Her action might not bring a problem at once, but it can cause long-term damage in his ability to lead. She needs to encourage him to lead and <u>not</u> *take over* if she thinks he is not leading well. Her encouragement, support, and faith in him will help him develop as a leader. The Bible tells us that *"The wise woman builds her house, but with her own hands the foolish one tears hers down"* (Prov. 14:1). Building a house includes encouraging the husband to be the leader. When you disagree with his leadership, ask God to give you wisdom about how to wisely discuss his wrong decisions.

Q 14 *What results when a woman takes the leadership away from her husband?*

She recognizes him as the main provider. God intends for men to work and supply the needs of their family. There are times when wives work for money. The wife should care for the children when they are small. She should not feel pressured to earn money and be away from them.

Some wives take a job to earn money after the children enter school. Such a wife should be careful to emphasize that her husband is the main provider for the family. Likewise, she should be sure that her husband understands that he and the children are more important than her career.

She recognizes him as the spiritual leader of the family. God created the husband to be the spiritual leader in the home. If a wife respects another leader and depends on him for spiritual advice, her husband may be offended and jealous. So a wife must act wisely if her spiritual growth is greater than her husband's. She cannot neglect the spiritual growth and education of her children. But she must be careful not to cause her husband to be jealous of other spiritual leaders. A wise wife says many good things about her husband, and very few good things about any other man.

Q 15 *Why does a wise wife say very few good things about another man?*

An unwise wife shows more respect to a family member, relative, friend, Bible teacher, or a pastor than she shows to her husband. This causes the husband to feel disrespected. Paul wrote: *"If they [wives] want to inquire about something, they should ask their own husbands at home"* (1 Cor. 14:35). Christian men need to be sensitive to this as well, and ask God to give them wisdom as they lead their homes spiritually. A wife can greatly encourage her husband by showing that he is the spiritual leader of the home.

Q 16 *What lesson did Lucy learn?*

Lucy complained to her pastor. She said: "I am so tired. Please pray that the Lord will give me more strength. I am so tired!" The pastor asked, "What is making you feel tired and weak?" She replied, "Every day I take the Bible and read it to my husband. At night, I always lead him in prayer. Day by day I try to push him to come to church, but he refuses. All of this effort makes me tired." The pastor thought for a moment. Then he said, "I will pray for you, but I think your husband is also tired!" Lucy asked, "Why should he be tired? I am the one making all of the spiritual effort!" The pastor explained that men make good leaders, but poor followers in the home. "So how can I get him to lead?" asked Lucy. The pastor answered, "Do your best to preach to him through your actions. Cook his favorite food. Be cheerful, and never nag. Smile at him often. Show that you respect him. Do whatever you can to please him. Let your actions say 'Jesus has made me the best wife possible' (1 Pet. 3:1)." Lucy agreed to try this new approach.

The next Sunday, Hugh came to church with Lucy for the first time. After the service he told the pastor, "My wife has been saved, and I want to meet the Jesus who changed her life." This was a quick result. Another woman named Wanda practiced this method for 10 years, until it finally brought her husband to Christ.

Wives, consider this proverb: "Two people cannot drive a car at the same time."

F. A loving wife supports the decisions of her husband.

Q 17 *What happens to a husband when his wife affirms, encourages, and supports his goals?*

Encouragement, support, and respect build confidence. As a leader in the home, a husband needs to develop this confidence over the years. A wife can be a great strength to her husband. She can encourage her husband to meet his godly goals. She can help him put his failures behind him. When a wife believes in her husband, he feels like he can succeed. This gives him the emotional strength to try, to grow, and to work hard. Beside most successful men,

Figure 8.3
A loving wife tells her husband that she has confidence in him.

there is a wife who encouraged him—a wife who built him up.

Complaining often—or challenging a husband's goals, dreams, and good plans—discourages a man (Prov. 27:15). Bringing up his past failures or mistakes injures his self-worth. It will cause him to hesitate or stop being the leader God created him to be. Few things in life can encourage a husband more than a wife who sees this truth. Blessed is the man whose wife affirms, affirms, and affirms him! Excellent wife, support your man! There is no question that every husband will sometimes make mistakes and be wrong. Still, wives must learn how to *wisely* counsel, challenge, and appeal to their husbands. Otherwise, he will feel like a tire that lost its air.

> BESIDE MOST SUCCESSFUL MEN, THERE IS A WIFE WHO ENCOURAGED HIM.

Q 18 *Wife, do you know your husband's dreams? How can you encourage him?*

G. A loving wife cares about being attractive.

The biblical story of Ruth contains some excellent advice to all women. Ruth desired to become the wife of Boaz, her wealthy relative by marriage. Yet, coming from another culture, she was not sure how to behave. Her mother-in-law, Naomi, instructed her: *"Wash and perfume yourself, and put on your best clothes. Then go down to the threshing floor, but don't let him know you are there until he has finished eating and drinking"* (Ruth 3:3).

Q 19 *How does a wife remain attractive to her husband?*

Wise Naomi knew what a man wants in the home. She advised Ruth that the way to get into the heart of Boaz was to begin by being neat and attractive. After that, she would need to approach him at the right time. Naomi's advice resulted in the marriage of Ruth and Boaz.

Consider the story of Esther, who became a queen.

Before a girl's turn came to go in to King Xerxes, she had to complete twelve months of beauty treatments prescribed for the women, six months with oil of myrrh and six with perfumes and cosmetics (Esther 2:12).

Esther's beauty treatments and baths were extreme—one full year of preparing to see the king! Still, every wife must work at keeping herself attractive to her husband. A wife will also benefit personally from looking her best.

A wife knows that her beauty changes over the years—from the beauty of a young girl to the beauty of a mature mother. The beauty of youth is fleeting. Still, a loving wife seeks to be healthy and as attractive to her husband as she can—even as she grows older. She disciplines her eating and exercises. She uses lotion or oil to keep her skin soft. She wears clothes that enhance her beauty.

These things require money. But the love and affection a woman expresses when she feels beautiful makes this expense worthwhile in the eyes of her happy, contented husband! The wife should not feel guilty about using some of the family's money on herself.

Some men allow their wives to wear old, ragged clothes. Their weak justification for this neglect is that their dear Christian women do not complain about it! A man is blessed to have a wife that does not complain. But the lack of complaints does not mean that a woman does not want to be treated better in her home. Any man should know that no matter how spiritual, dedicated, or humble his wife may be, she still cares about her appearance.

It is true that a loving wife needs a constant supply of clothing and beauty products—within the financial limits of the family. Yet she will avoid the senseless, worldly competition of fashion and beauty. It is important to look good, but keep this in its proper place. Peter reminds us that a woman's greatest beauty is her gentle and quiet spirit (1 Pet. 3:4). This is basic, and we began this chapter emphasizing a woman's *inner* beauty of the spirit. Still, she should care for the *outer* beauty of her body!

H. A loving wife meets the sexual needs of her husband.

Q 20 *Why is it wrong for a wife to bribe or control her husband through sex?*

Some wives try to control their husbands by refusing to have sex until they get what they want. Some women refuse, saying that their head or back hurts. This is, in reality, *a form of prostitution* in the couple's own bedroom. It damages the strength of the marriage.

A loving wife, on the other hand, knows that it is possible to be right in a wrong way. She refuses to use her body as a prostitute—to control or guide her husband. Sexual relations are free and joyful between them, with no bribery.

Q 21 *Explain: Sex brings babies, but it also brings new life into a marriage in other ways.*

Joyce Meyer says that there must be a sacrifice of self even in your sex life. "The plan of God for your marriage is bigger than your *feelings*. If you are too tired to enjoy your husband, you are too tired to enjoy anything else wonderful that God has planned for you. ... Satan hates the purpose of sex because its ultimate expression is new life. Sexual fulfillment releases tension, is enjoyable, and brings a bond of unity that is unlike any other. It truly does minister new life." Sex in marriage may bring babies into the world, but even long after a woman is past the age of bearing children, the marriage bed continues to bring new life to her relationship and union with her husband. God is the One who put a strong sexual desire in men and women, because He loves new life on every level.[5]

If a wife often resists her husband's sexual needs, she can discourage him and injure his spirit. The Bible tells us that the man's body not only belongs to himself, but to his wife as well. The wife's body not only belongs to her, but to her husband as well. Sex in marriage is a gift to enjoy. This activity also provides spiritual protection from the enemy (See 1 Cor. 7:1-6).

Q 22 *How do the sexual desires of men and women differ?*

Most men are more *physical* in their sexual response, while a woman's sexuality is often more *emotional*. A man becomes sexually excited more quickly and tends to be bolder sexually. A husband's desire for sex may arise as quickly as striking a match. In contrast, a wife's desire for sex is more like starting a charcoal fire. A husband may desire sexual relations more often than his wife may. Both partners need to learn to satisfy one another sexually.[6]

Q 23 *Husband, which of these 8 things, A–H, do you need most from your wife? Which ones is she doing?*

One writer says that each man is born of a woman, and spends the rest of his life wanting his woman (wife) to accept and approve of him. It is easy for a woman to guide a man. If she gives him clear communication, respect, appreciation, food, and good loving, he will do most of the things she desires.[7]

A husband is like a horse or an ox. At the end of the day, he is tired from working. If the owner tries to push and beat a tired animal, it will rebel. But if the owner shows the animal love, food, and kindness, it will respond in a good way. So which way should a woman guide her husband—with love and kindness, or force?[8]

Kathryn spoke some wise words about men. She said that men are simple—easy to understand. A man loves to hear that he makes his woman happy. In his home, a man deserves more respect than a visitor. He loves to be praised, admired, and thanked often for working hard for the family. He likes to hear his children say that they love and appreciate him. He feels like a king as his wife listens closely when he opens his heart, and shows interest and respect for the things he cares about. Kathryn gave some good counsel about the way a woman should treat her man.[9] (Likewise, any wife likes to know that she makes her husband happy. In the same way she likes to be praised, admired, appreciated, respected, and listened to, so does her husband!)

How to Be a Loving Wife 137

② A Wife's Relationship to All in Her Home
Goal: *Describe 6 characteristics of a loving wife in her home.*

Setting

A woman's personal ways can be like soothing oil on rough skin. Or her ways can be like the irritation of a mosquito buzzing near the ear at night. Some women set people at ease. Such women have found, either by nature or by hard work, ways of creating a pleasant home. We will talk about the way a mother relates to her children in chapter 10. In this lesson, let us look at six ways a loving wife relates to all in her home.

Q 24 ↗ *Explain the 6 ways a wife should relate to those in her home.*

A. A loving wife is wise with her ways.

The book of Esther reveals the wise manner in which she related to her husband, the king. Few women today are married to kings. Still, they might be treated more like "queens" if they imitated Esther! She approached the king with humility and courtesy. She planned her actions. The respect and honor she showed the king opened his heart to satisfy her request—to save the Jewish people.

Q 25 ↖ *How did Esther open the heart of the king?*

A wise wife studies the moods of her husband. She knows the best time, place, and method to present matters to him. These skills of relating to others also allow her to succeed in managing her home.

Q 26 ↗ *What can a wife learn by studying her husband week by week?*

B. A loving wife is wise with her words.

The apostle James wrote: *"We all stumble in many ways. If anyone is never at fault in what he says, he is a perfect man, able to keep his whole body in check"* (James 3:2). This truth applies to husbands and wives. Gossip, criticism, and sharp words are a common problem of men and women. A wise wife seeks to avoid stumbling and offending with her words. She understands the power her tongue has—both for good and for harm. God holds us responsible for all that we speak (Matt. 12:34-37). Through prayer, a loving wife seeks the grace of God that she needs to speak without offending those whom she loves the most. The Holy Spirit helps her practice self-control over her tongue (Gal. 5:22-23).

Q 27 ↖ *Does your husband consider you a nag? Ask him.*

Some men travel a lot or seek employment in other cities—partly because of the unwise talking and nagging of their wives. *"A quarrelsome wife is like a constant dripping on a rainy day"* (Prov. 27:15). Such women offend in what they say—sometimes without knowing it. Perhaps their unending flow of words is a part of their personal manner. Perhaps they are not aware of how this discourages those around them. Still, they pay a high price for their loose tongues.

Q 28 ↖ *Contrast the words of a wise and an unwise woman.*

In contrast, a loving wife knows how to express herself without offending. She is not silent when things are wrong in her home. She knows the right time and manner to speak. She knows when her husband is receptive, and when he is not. She is aware that he will not receive well any complaints and concerns at the dinner table. Yet he will be open to the same concerns at a more favorable time. Further, she selects the right words and expressions to share her feelings with her husband.

The home of a woman who bridles her tongue is filled with kind, uplifting words. She speaks wisely and apologizes if necessary. By her example, her children learn to speak in the same careful way. Even when she is grieved by something her husband says or does, she refuses to *explode*. Explosions always destroy—they never build or improve. In contrast, she communicates her point of view in a mature and polite manner. The Bible declares, *"A gentle answer turns away wrath"* (Prov. 15:1). A loving wife uses gentle answers wisely. She knows that "If you want to gather honey, don't kick over the bee hive!"[10]

Q 29 ↖ *Explain the proverb: If you want to gather honey, don't kick the bee hive.*

C. A loving wife works hard for her family.

The excellent wife of Proverbs 31 was not lazy. From early morning until late at night, she was working for her family. This is only possible if a woman's attitude toward work is positive. Without this positive attitude, her home suffers.

Having a positive attitude toward work causes a loving wife to be *diligent.* She makes good things happen. She not only has motion, she has direction. She makes profit on the things she sells. She buys wisely, taking time to shop for bargains. She labors not only to please her family, but also to please the Lord—who saved her and called her to be a wife.

Q 30 *Describe the work of a godly wife in your culture.*

Some wives seek full-time or part-time work, while also trying to manage a home. This is difficult, because the job of being a wife and mother is full-time when the children are small. We must not prosper financially at the expense of our home life. If we get great wealth, but produce worldly children, it will all be wasted effort. The excellent wife of Proverbs 31 was a good businesswoman—but her business efforts were *home-centered* rather than *career-centered.* Her positive attitude toward work brought praise from her family, not complaints about her absence. There may be times when a young mother must work outside the home. In such cases, perhaps a grandmother can help with the children. Each woman who brings children into the world should be a mother to them. Children have no choice about being born, but the mother can choose to be with them in their earliest years.

D. A loving wife is wise with her money.

Like a coin, the topic of money has two sides: earning and spending. In some cases, the woman earns more money than her husband. Earning money often brings power to decide how to spend it. A loving wife is wise to protect her husband's self-respect and not use money to gain power over him. She avoids competing with her husband in money matters.

Q 31 *Describe the way a wise wife manages money in your culture.*

A wise woman manages money well. She is careful when shopping for food and clothing. She knows the true value of everything she buys. With an eye on the future, she seeks to save some money for days ahead. As a result, her children are well fed, well clothed, and well educated. As she and her husband work together in harmony, a loving wife helps build financial security for her home.

A wife was driving to the store with her children when she suddenly pulled the car to the side of the road. "Look, children," she said. "Can you believe what they are throwing away?" And to the embarrassment of her children, she loaded the cast-off chair into their car. Later that evening, they helped her repair and clean the chair—then set it in the corner of the kitchen. "Now, your grandmother can sit and visit with me when I am working. And just think of how much money we have saved." The children were impressed. But they still hoped none of their friends saw their mother hauling away broken furniture. They were young, and had not yet learned the proverb: "A dollar saved is a dollar earned."

E. A loving wife keeps her home clean and healthy.

Q 32 *How does a clean home increase good health?*

The words *cleanliness is next to godliness* are not in the Bible—but they are words of wisdom. A wise wife keeps her home clean and neat. She knows that disease spreads through dirty plates, forks, and spoons, flies, and roaches. She is aware that food poisoning comes when food is left for too long. She makes sure that the water is pure, even boiling it if necessary. Her knowledge of health and her love for the family create a high standard of cleanliness for her kitchen.

Q 33 *How can the husband and children help clean the home?*

As the children are big enough to help, she trains them to do things such as wash dishes, sweep, dust, wash clothes, and keep things in their places. This makes her burden lighter and guides them on the right path. Also, helping with the work causes children to feel good about themselves. A big part of the self-esteem of children comes from duties they fulfill.

A clean home includes clean air. This requires regular cleaning and scrubbing, plus strict rules related to the use of bath and toilet facilities. This is a major challenge with small children in the home. Yet it is these same little ones who become sick in the absence of good hygiene practices.

F. A loving wife cooks balanced meals for her family.

Among the great deeds of a loving wife are the good meals she prepares. It is hard work to produce enjoyable, healthy food. A loving wife takes the time to prepare good meals for her husband and children. This is an important way of building a home. When good food is on the table, good conversation often follows. As we saw in the story of Esther, a woman's dining table can become an important tool for building and guiding the home. Some of the best memories of a family are those around the table.

Figure 8.4 A loving wife plans healthy meals for her family.

Q 34 ✎ *Does the average family you know eat healthy meals? Explain.*

The health of any family depends largely on the quality of its diet. Good food—rich in protein, vitamins, and energy—keeps the family happy and away from the doctor's office. Many people pay to doctors the money they saved by eating poor food. Blessed is the family of the wife who plans good, healthy meals! (We will study more about healthy meals in chapter 9 of this course.)

A Wife's Relationship to Those Outside Her Home
Goal: *Describe 3 ways a wife should relate to those outside her home.*

A loving wife cares about her relationships outside the home. The community's opinion about a person is important. A good reputation in society has great value. As the Bible says, *"A good name is more desirable than great riches; to be esteemed is better than silver or gold"* (Prov. 22:1).

A. A loving wife is hospitable to visitors.

Often, a woman's social reputation is based on her hospitality. The Bible commands that we should show hospitality (Tit. 1:8; Heb. 13:2; 1 Pet. 4:8-9). When we love and care for others, the world knows that we are the children of God. So a loving wife works hard to create gracious hospitality in her home.

As a locomotive pulls a train, a wife pulls the family's attitude toward hospitality. No matter how friendly a husband may be, hospitality is only possible with the full cooperation of his wife. Visitors feel at home *only* when the wife welcomes them. A loving wife will plan to be ready to receive guests, and to make them happy and comfortable. However, a loving husband will seek to tell his wife when visitors are coming.

Q 35 ✎ *What things make you hesitate to have visitors in your home? What can you do about this?*

We lose nothing by sharing what we have with others. Some people may think it is foolish to be generous. But a wise wife knows that God rewards all givers. Those who have not learned the joy of giving should practice it every day to learn it. The stranger at the door, the visitor in the house, the employee from the office, the distant relative—all of these people give us opportunities to be hospitable.

A family traveled for several hours to attend a graduation. After the ceremony, the wife of the graduate approached the family and asked them if they would like to come to their home. "We do not have anything prepared, but we can try to find something if you want to come." Are you surprised that the family decided not to accept her invitation?

> "IF THERE IS ROOM IN THE HEART, THERE IS ROOM IN THE HOME."

Barbara Tuttle served many years as a missionary in India. From her early years as a missionary, she tells about a great truth that a woman named Amani taught her. "I am so happy that I can barely stay on the ground," Amani announced. "Why is that?" Barbara asked. "Have you heard some good news?" "Yes," replied Amani. "Next week we have 14 people coming to stay in our house for 3 days!" Barbara was shocked. "In your little house with only two rooms? How will they fit? Where will they sit? Where will they sleep?" Amani was silent for a moment. Then she said, "You are a visitor here, so you do not know us very well yet. But one of our sayings is, 'If there is room in the heart, there is room in the home.'" Thus Amani taught Barbara a lesson that she never forgot. Let us be sure that we make room for people in our hearts. Then it will be easy for us to be hospitable.

B. A loving wife is hospitable to the larger family.

The most important place for hospitality is with the larger family. A loving wife welcomes both her family and his family to sit at her table. She teaches her children to love and respect all grandparents. A loving wife marries a husband and gains his family as relatives for life. She seeks to love his family as she does her own—for they produced the man she loves so much. It is often easier for her to get along and be hospitable to her own family than to her husband's. But if she is wise, she will always be gracious to her husband's family. Her example may help her husband be kind and gracious to her family.

Q 36 *Is your husband satisfied with the hospitality you offer to his family? Ask him.*

A hospitable wife plans ahead. Death is certain, and it often strikes men before women. A wife should always welcome her husband's family, respect his parents, and not quarrel with her mother-in-law or sisters-in-law. Then if her husband dies, she will avoid many difficult family relationships. If his family accepts the loving wife as a daughter and sister, even her husband's death will not break the love-bond holding her in his family. Acceptance after a husband's death may be vital to the wife and her children.

Q 37 *How does a wife plan ahead by being hospitable to the larger family?*

If a woman is unable to be at peace in the same room with her husband's relatives, she should discuss this situation with her husband. Together, they should pray for a change in everyone's attitudes. At times, a couple may need to provide a home to a family member. If a wife cannot welcome all family members, she will be miserable in her own home. She must find grace from the Lord to love his family. It is good for a wife to welcome strangers to her home and table. But her reputation and future will be damaged if she refuses to welcome the members of her husband's family.

A wife had little time for her larger family. She volunteered to work at church and at her children's school. The demands were great, even though she received no pay. When times for rest came, she only wanted to be with her husband and children. Her husband suddenly died. Friends were happy to help for a time, but they began to tire and wonder when her family or her husband's family would come to help. But the families thought that she had managed fine without them for many years. They were sure she must have plenty of other people to help.

C. A loving wife is discreet about social events.

Q 38 *Explain the balance between life at home and social events.*

Social events outside the home can be healthy for women. Being with children for hours can make anyone feel tired. Wives need some time away from home—to be an adult in the world of adults.

At an extreme level, however, a woman's social events can damage her home. Some women avoid household duties by avoiding the home itself. Always busy in the community (even in church activities), they neglect their homes. Their kitchens and bedrooms are abandoned. Many unsaved men are angry at the church (and God) because their wives are too often absent from home to attend church functions. A loving wife knows that she must balance all that she does in order to build a strong marriage.

Everything a woman does in the community—even the things her family does—contributes to her *public image.* A loving wife guards herself against any behavior that would damage her reputation. Refusing to feed her family, quarreling or nagging in public, eating in public without good manners or restraint—all of these contribute to a negative image.

A husband and wife attended a ball game to watch their son play. Although he was only 10, the father took the game seriously. At one point, the referee called a foul on his son. The father stood to his feet and began to criticize the referee. This embarrassed the wife and many people who knew the angry father. He did not realize that he was giving a bad name to himself, his family, and his church. His wife talked to him in a soft voice. Because he valued her counsel and wisdom, he repented at once. Later, he told her he was sorry, and thanked her for being discreet about social events.

Q 39 *How can social events affect a family's reputation?*

Hundreds of women attended a social event as part of an international meeting. Tea and coffee were served, together with small pastry cakes. Enough were provided for one or two cakes per woman. One of the women at the front of the line, after drinking tea, put some of the cakes in her purse. Such selfish behavior and lack of consideration for others can only damage a person's public image. [1]*"When you sit to dine with a ruler, note well what is before you,* [2]*and put a knife to your throat if you are given to gluttony"* (Prov. 23:1-2).

Believers with personal integrity show restraint and self-discipline in public. They are polite, even if someone is rude or insults them in public. This self-discipline is a testimony for Christ. Love behaves kindly when people crowd in line, are rude in the way they drive, or selfish in other ways. A loving wife guards her words (and anger) in public as she guards her money—both are precious!

Likewise, a prudent wife guards her physical appearance in public. She is always careful to dress wisely in the public eye. One woman dressed in a careless way in public—attracting attention. Her reputation followed her home. As a result, her family suffered. Neatness and modesty are the biblical standards for dress and appearance. Self-discipline is the standard for behavior in public (and at home). These biblical standards characterize a loving wife in her public image and social activities.

Conclusion

This chapter focused on *a loving wife.* Some women may shrink back from the standards we have presented, and Scriptures like Proverbs 31. They may fear that they can never measure up to such high standards. It is true that we have described the *perfect* wife! And it is also true that *no* woman on earth is perfect. No woman can

Figure 8.5 *"Her husband has full confidence in her"* (Prov. 31:11).

Q 40 *How can the standards in this chapter help any wife?*

fulfill the role of *a loving wife* every day of her life. The point of this chapter is not to create guilt. But we want to challenge every woman to grow in grace—to develop and strive for excellence.

Trashy magazines, television, and cheap books often show women living in shame, without moral virtue. In contrast, the Bible shines its light on the godly woman, traveling the upward road of excellence and true success in living.

A loving wife, although not perfect, determines to live in a godly way. Her choices affect the values and choices of her family. She may not be the most capable woman in some areas. She may not be the most beautiful by the world's standards. Yet because she has committed herself to God's standards, she stands out with godly virtue. Her integrity shouts her praises in the city or the country. Indeed, in her old age, her children *will* rise up and call her blessed of the Lord. The challenge of excellence, although a difficult one to accept, will lead any woman to a full, rich, and complete life.

Chapter Summary

 ### A Wife's Relationship to God and Her Husband

Goal: *Discuss 8 ways a loving wife relates to her husband.*

A loving wife maintains her relationship with God. She submits to her husband. Such a wife respects, honors, and admires her husband, and communicates with him. A loving wife lets her husband be the head of the home. She supports his decisions, cares about being attractive, and meets his sexual needs.

 ### A Wife's Relationship to All in Her Home

Goal: *Describe 6 characteristics of a loving wife in her home.*

A loving wife is wise with her ways, her words, and her money. She works hard for her family and keeps her home clean and healthy. A loving wife cooks balanced meals for her family.

 ### A Wife's Relationship to Those Outside Her Home

Goal: *Describe 3 ways a wife should relate to those outside her home.*

A loving wife is hospitable to visitors and the larger family. She is discreet about social events.

Test Yourself: Circle the letter by the *best* completion to each question or statement.

1. The key to a wife having peace at all times is
a) the attitude of her husband.
b) having children who obey.
c) being at peace with his family.
d) her relationship with God.

2. Submission means that
a) the weaker submits to the stronger.
b) the inferior submits to the superior.
c) order and purpose can result.
d) one will rule over another.

3. A wise wife
a) praises her pastor often as an example.
b) says few good things about other men.
c) leads her husband in spiritual matters.
d) speaks all her mind in front of the children.

4. What helps a husband succeed?
a) A wife who believes in him
b) A wife who emphasizes his faults
c) A wife who earns more than him
d) A wife who has much education

5. Who teaches wives to remain attractive?
a) Hannah
b) Miriam
c) Esther
d) Mary

6. A key purpose of sex in marriage is
a) to enable a husband to express his emotions.
b) to bring new life into the relationship.
c) to remind a husband and wife they are one.
d) to prevent problems in communication.

7. From Esther, a wife learns that
a) it is easy to guide an unbelieving husband.
b) it is God's will to marry an unbeliever.
c) the goal justifies the path one takes.
d) there is a right time for everything.

8. A wise wife
a) uses gentle words to turn away angry feelings.
b) is like the constant falling of rain on the roof.
c) remains silent if things are wrong at home.
d) uses words like a hunter uses arrows.

9. Relating well to her husband's family is
a) good but not necessary.
b) a form of planning ahead.
c) the most important of all.
d) an example of truth.

10. Concerning social events and activities,
a) a wife should volunteer as much as she can.
b) these matter little to a spiritual wife.
c) balance is needed to relate to her family.
d) these do not affect her reputation.

Chapter 9:
How to Be an Effective Father or Mother—Part 1

Introduction

Two families were studied—the family of Max Jukes, and the family of Jonathan Edwards. This study illustrates the influence of parents upon their children.

Max Jukes was an unbeliever with poor character. He married a woman much like himself. 1,200 of their descendants were studied. 310 became beggars who wandered from town to town; 440 suffered illnesses caused by sinful habits; 130 were sent to prison—7 for murder. Over 100 became alcoholics; 60 were thieves; 190 were prostitutes. Of the 20 who learned a trade, 10 learned the trade in a prison. It cost the government a great amount of money to train them. But there is no evidence that they added anything good to society.

At about the same time as Jukes, Jonathan Edwards began his family. Jonathan Edwards, a man of God, married a godly woman. 300 of their

**Figure 9.1
Godly grandparents—
godly parents—
godly children!**

descendants became ministers, missionaries, and theological professors; over 100 became college professors; over 100 became lawyers, 30 became judges; 60 became doctors; over 60 became authors of good books; 14 became presidents of universities. Many succeeded in business. Four served as government leaders.[1]

Max Jukes, Jonathan Edwards, and their wives acted in different ways. One father and mother were examples of bad behavior and bad character; the other parents were examples of good and excellent character. Parents—through their examples—have a great influence on their children. Their influence will even guide future generations.

In this chapter and the next one, we will consider the serious task of being a parent. One central question occurs throughout these chapters: **What kind of example am I to my children?** With God's help, we will become better fathers or mothers as we consider this question.

Lessons:

Prepare to Help Your Children Grow

Goal A: *Explain God's point of view on children in relation to: ownership, value, and gifts.*
Goal B: *Summarize what a parent should understand about a child's growth and uniqueness.*
Goal C: *Describe a parent's responsibilities to be an example and a provider.*

Help Your Children Grow in Wisdom—Mentally

Goal A: *Explain a parent's role in a child's education and work skills.*
Goal B: *Summarize 10 reasons for sex education in the home.*
Goal C: *Identify 7 guidelines for teaching your children about sex.*
Goal D: *Explain how a child's age affects what he should learn about sex.*

Help Your Children Grow in Stature—Physically and in Good Health

Goal A: *List 10 things a pregnant mother should do to protect the health of her unborn child.*
Goal B: *Summarize the need for good food, rules for eating, pure water, and cleanliness in caring for children.*
Goal C: *Explain the role of vaccines and doctors in caring for children.*

Prepare to Help Your Children Grow

Goal A: Explain God's point of view on children in relation to: ownership, value, and gifts.
Goal B: Summarize what a parent should understand about a child's growth and uniqueness.
Goal C: Describe a parent's responsibilities to be an example and a provider.

In this lesson we will examine seven keys to being a good parent.

A. Remember that children belong to God.

In one sense, parents and their children belong to each other. Children are fruit from the parents' bodies. The child may look, talk, and behave like the parents in many ways. Concern and love is stronger for the child who is "ours." A mother can recognize her own baby's cry. And a father feels pride at the success of his children. But in the highest sense, children belong to God.

*"The earth is the LORD's, and everything in it, the world, **and all who live in it**"* (Ps. 24:1). God owns the world, and all of the people in it. He expects parents to be stewards of His children. Stewards are managers—not owners. An owner entrusts a steward to care for things of value. The steward manages the wealth and seeks to increase its worth. As parents, God expects us to manage children in ways that increase their value. The Lord gives children to parents to love, train, and guide in godly ways.[2]

Some children are called accidents, mistakes, or possessions. Some children are unwanted, abandoned, or abused. But each parent will give account to God as a steward. Because—from the unloved child to the most loved—each child belongs to God. Jesus warned adults: *"See that you do not look down on one of these little ones. For I tell you that their angels in heaven always see the face of my Father in heaven"* (Matt. 18:10).

B. Discern that God places great value on children.

Children belong to God. As people created in His image, they are His greatest wealth. God paid no ransom to redeem the angels who fell. But He gave His only Son to redeem people. The woman in the parable of Luke 15 was not willing for one coin to be lost. A shepherd with 100 sheep is not willing for one sheep to be lost. They are valuable to him. *"In the same way your Father in heaven is not willing that any of these little ones should be lost"* (Matt. 18:14).

Consider the value our Lord placed on children.

- Jesus blessed children (Mark 10:13-16). He was angry with His disciples when they tried to keep children away from Him. Perhaps the disciples thought that children were not important enough for Christ's attention. But Jesus called the children to Himself—He touched them and blessed them. They are a big part of His wealth.
- Jesus desires the worship of children (Matt. 21:14-16). Jesus was angry with the disciples about their view of children. And Jewish leaders were angry with Jesus because of His view of children! Jesus was only a few days away from being crucified. Children worshiped Him in the street and the temple, shouting, *"Hosanna to the Son of David!"* (Matt. 21:9). The Jewish leaders insisted that Jesus stop them, but He accepted their praise. He said, *"From the lips of children and infants you* [God] *have ordained praise"* (Matt. 21:16).
- Jesus identified Himself with children (Matt. 18:1-5). The disciples wanted to know how to be the greatest in the kingdom of heaven. It must have shocked the disciples to hear Jesus say, *"Whoever welcomes a little child like this in my name **welcomes me**"* (Matt. 18:5). What parents do to children, they do to Jesus Himself!
- Jesus will punish all who sin against children, or cause children to stumble (Matt. 18:6). He said, *"But if anyone causes one of these little ones who believe in me to*

Q 1 Do children belong to parents, God, or both? Explain.

Q 2 Why will parents give an account to God for the way they raise their children?

Q 3 What was the attitude of Jesus when his disciples did not welcome children?

Q 4 How does God feel about worship from children?

Q 5 In what way does Jesus identify Himself with children? Explain.

Q 6 How will Jesus respond to those who sin against children?

Figure 9.2 Jesus rejoiced because the children worshiped Him (Matt. 21:1-16).

sin, it would be better for him to have a large millstone hung around his neck and to be drowned in the depths of the sea."

In heaven, the gates of the New Jerusalem are made from 12 different precious stones. And the streets of the heavenly city are made of gold. But God places a special value on children—of all sizes, colors, and ages. So as parents, we must remind ourselves often that children are God's wealth. We must examine our attitudes toward these little ones. We must adjust our customs and beliefs about children to the example and teachings of Jesus. God values people above everything else. And children are tender, helpless little people.

C. Recognize that children are among God's greatest gifts to parents.

Every good and perfect gift is from above, coming down from the Father of the heavenly lights, who does not change like shifting shadows (James 1:17).

Behold, children are a gift of the Lord; the fruit of the womb is a reward. Like arrows in the hand of a warrior, so are the children of one's youth. How blessed is the man whose quiver is full of them (Ps. 127:3-5 NASB).

Q 7 *If you have children, how are they a blessing to you?*

God blesses parents with the gifts of children. No one else can bring the joy, comfort, hope, and help that a son or daughter can bring. Among God's greatest gifts are the blessings of love and loyalty between parents and their children.

The duties of parents are great, but they should never cast a shadow on the blessing of children. A husband and wife were very poor. They loved the Lord, and were members of a local church. They both worked hard, long hours each day. The husband worked in a city nearby. The wife worked in their small garden, and knitted a few clothes to sell. The couple spent their money wisely, tithed, and planned well. But it was impossible to save even 10 percent of their income. It took every penny just to live from day to day. They seldom ate meat, but when they did, the wife always wanted her son and daughter to have the best pieces. She told them that her favorite piece was the back. You see, even though this couple was poor, they felt wealthy. Who could put a price on these wonderful, smiling, laughing, jumping, singing, loving children whom God Himself had given them?

D. Seek to understand how children grow.

Q 8 *Apply this proverb to children: The fate of the farm depends on the farmer.*

A rich man divided a farm into two parts and entrusted each half to a different steward. The first steward knew little about farming, and the crops were poor. But the second steward had studied farming. From his half of the farm, he helped the land produce a great crop. The fate of the farm depends on the farmer.

Likewise, God has entrusted children to parents. What children become depends much on their parents. The more parents understand how children grow, develop, and mature, the better these parents can help children become fruitful.

Children must **grow** into adults. Everyone knows this. No one would look at a small child and confuse him with an adult. But parents often forget that children cannot act or think like adults. When parents expect a child to behave like an adult, it brings pain to the parents and the child.

How to Be an Effective Father or Mother—Part I 147

Martha decided that this morning her son would dress himself. Although he was 4 years old, he still wanted her to help button his shirt. The young mother thought her son was lazy, and today she would break that habit. She stood over him as his small fingers struggled with the buttons. With each failure, her anger grew. "You are not trying!" she shouted. Her voice grew louder and his tiny fingers began to tremble. Finally, he looked up at his mother and cried, "I am trying, Mama." The mother looked upon his face, turned up to her. She saw his tears and the fear in his eyes. Then, in shame she realized that he was not able to fasten the buttons. He wanted to please her, and he was not lazy. But he had not grown enough to move his fingers in the way buttons demand. As two wise kings, Zebah and Zalmunna, stated in a proverb: *"As is the man, so is his strength"* (Judges 8:21).

Q 9 What mistake did Martha make?

A chart such as Figure 9.3 would have helped Martha. It shows that children can control large muscles in arms and legs from the ages of 3–5. But they cannot fully control small muscles, like the ones in fingers, until the ages of 6–8. This chart also shows some of the ways children grow in their thinking. Children from ages 12–17 begin asking "Why?" to many things they had accepted before. Questions from children cause some parents to fear that their children are losing respect for them. Questions from children may cause unwise parents to become rigid or angry. But Figure 9.3 shows us that children of 12–17 years of age are developing a new way of thinking. They no longer just accept what they hear, but they can think about things as adults think. The apostle Paul said, *"When I became a man, I put childish ways behind me"* (1 Cor. 13:11). Likewise, every child changes from thinking like a child to thinking like an adult. Children grow up and begin to question and examine information. As wise parents, we must discern the changes that take place in our children. We can guide our children to become wise thinkers. As parents, we must not be defensive about the questions of children. Instead, we can lead them to discuss ideas while still showing respect. Study Figure 9.3. It will help you understand the way children grow, as Jesus grew *"in wisdom and stature, and in favor with God and men"* (Luke 2:52).

Q 10 At what age is it normal for children to question the things they once accepted earlier?

Q 11 How should parents respond when children grow to question basic values?

Q 12 At what age can your child begin to learn Bible stories?

Years	Mental	Physical	Spiritual	Social
0–1	Learns much Can feel anger and joy	Grows quickly Learns to sit and stand	Depends on parents	Begins to recognize familiar faces Coos and babbles soft sounds at people
2–3	Learns language and gestures of the hands Thinks only from his own point of view May feel fear or anxiety if separated from those who care for him	Able to walk; begins to run; very active By 2 years has grown to half his adult height	Imitates the way adults worship Can enjoy a Sunday school for his age	Sees himself as the center of the world Plays beside other children instead of with them
3–5	Is curious; loves to explore Can memorize brief items His emotions respond to others Still fearful	Grows more slowly Can control his large muscles like legs and arms Learns much through playing	Accepts whatever he is taught Can sing and learn many Bible stories	Follows older brothers and sisters Still sees himself as the center, but can play simple games with others
6–8	Can learn to read and to do math May be unsure; needs assurance of love and security Eager to please parents	Slow but steady growth Grows adult teeth Can control his small muscles	Able to respond to the gospel; open to accept Christ	Friendly, able to make friends and play games Begins to see others' points of view

Continued on next page

Continued from previous page

Years	Mental	Physical	Spiritual	Social
9–11	Near adult intelligence Watches and asks Shows many emotions; able to give and receive	Very slow growth Full of energy; able to do difficult physical activities	Wants to relate truth to life Wants to know how to apply the Bible to everyday life	Identifies with children of his own sex Socially active in sports, clubs, and church activities
12–14	Questions and examines Tries new mental roles and functions Sudden emotional changes	Puberty; major changes in body and hormones Fast growth	Open to spiritual challenge Ideal view of the world Looking for purpose	Focused on friends; needs friendships Beginning to break away from parents
15–17	Mentally alert; able to think about theories and make conclusions Emotionally, has new feelings—love, rejection, and loyalty	Growing strong Girls reach full height and shape Boys grow more slowly	Looking for reality Critical period—not interested in incomplete answers Time for life commitments	Boys and girls are interested in each other Enjoys sports and clubs
18–22	Mentally organizes all he has learned about life Emotions are more stable Very near adult maturity	Boys reach full adult height and shape Both sexes at the peak of physical ability	Spiritual growth and commitment Seeking to put faith into action	Interest in the opposite sex is more focused on choosing a mate Prepares for life's work

Figure 9.3   Ways children grow mentally, physically, spiritually, and socially[3]

Q 13 *Explain why it is important to know the difference between sin and natural growth.*

Many parents view their child through their own adult experiences. They wrongly interpret a child's natural stages of growth as rebellion. They err by thinking that a small child's desire for attention is sinful. Rather, it is normal, especially during the first 3 years of life.

Punishing a child for curiosity stops healthy mental growth and increases rebellion. An <u>unwise</u> parent will rebuke a child for asking questions about sexual matters. But wise parents understand the way children grow, develop, and mature. They encourage children to ask many questions. Such wise parents realize that questions are the opportunity for a parent to guide a child's thinking. When a child asks a question, he opens the door to his mind.[4]

E. Discern that each child is unique.

The task of parents is not easy. They need to understand the way children grow. But, they must also discern the unique qualities of each child. Perhaps the number one complaint that children have about their parents is "They don't understand me!" We need to study our children and know what makes them unique. Parents who have more than one child understand that their children are different from each other. You cannot guide all children in the same way. They do not have the same strengths or weaknesses, talents, abilities, or interests. It is a bad mistake to compare them to each other. Like adults, all children are unique.

Q 14 *Summarize some ways that children are different.*

Each child is different. One likes to study books; another likes to build or sew. One likes to be guided by another child, but another likes to guide. One likes to talk; another likes to listen. One likes to be alone more; another likes to be with a group. One obeys and agrees quickly; another always asks "Why?" One is a child farmer; another is a child doctor. One is a child teacher; the other is a child carpenter. One is a child businessman; the other is a child pastor. We should study each child and encourage each in the direction that his nature, talents, and abilities guide him. We should not seek to make a child behave like someone else. Would a wise man expect a cat to bark like a dog, or a chicken to act like a sheep? Each child is unique. We should honor the way God created each one. If

Q 15 *How can a parent discover the unique qualities of each child?*

they are shy, we should not try to make them lead singing. If they like to talk a lot, we should not force them to be silent. Even brothers, like Cain and Abel, may have different interests. And twins, like Jacob and Esau, may be as different as night and day.

Some children are like their parents, but others are different. Parents can be frustrated and impatient with both. The Scripture says, *"A patient man has great understanding"* (Prov. 14:29). With patience we can learn to help each child find the path God has planned for him.

Zushya, a Jewish rabbi, is remembered mostly for one statement. He said, "In the world to come, I will not be asked, 'Why weren't you Moses?' I will be asked, 'Why weren't you Zushya?'"[5] God has created each child. He can help us value each one and help that child grow in a special way.

F. Recall that your example teaches your children the most.

Q 16 *How do children learn values?*

Children learn more by example than by words. This is true at school and at home. Parents do not plant values in the hearts of children by talking. Values—both good and bad—grow as children *see* them in their parents. Words of instruction are good and needed. But the advice children hear means more when parents live what they teach. As one poet wrote, "I'd rather see a sermon than hear one any day!"

Figure 9.4 In much of creation, the young learn by following in the footsteps of their parents.

A farmer often talked to his young son about trusting God. One day, a storm destroyed most of the grain—just before harvest time. The father and son walked together through the field, looking at the damage. The boy expected tears and cries of despair from his father. Instead, he heard his father quietly singing a hymn of praise and prayer—"Rock of Ages, cleft for me; let me hide myself in Thee." That morning, the child finally understood the lesson about faith in God that his father had been trying to teach him. The song in the time of trouble moved the lesson from the child's head to his heart.[6] (We will study more about being a good example in the next chapter.)

G. Provide for each child.

Children need care. They are helpless when they enter this world. Parents must provide for all they need. Food, clothing, shelter, security, and love are the most important. The father's role is important. He is the main provider and protector. But the child also needs a father's understanding and love. A husband is a successful father as he provides for the needs of his family.

Parents, do not give birth to a family so large that you cannot provide for their needs. Plan the size of your family. It is true that God told Adam and Eve to multiply and fill the earth. But the earth is already full! Match the size of your family with your time, energy, and money. A father and mother must spend time with each child. If there are too many children, some will be neglected. Wise farmers know that if you plant too many seeds too close together, the harvest will be poor. When seeds are planted too close together, none of them get enough food and water from the soil. Likewise, if you have too many children in the home, none of them will get enough food, clothing, love, spiritual teaching, and education. When there are too many children in a home, some of them may grow up and curse their parents instead of blessing them. These days, there are many methods for planning the size of your family.

Q 17 *Why is it wise for parents to plan the size of their family?*

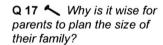

Be wise—fill your quiver with arrows, but do not put so many arrows in that it splits the quiver. And do not put so many arrows in the quiver that it prevents you from getting one out to shoot! Match the number of arrows to the size of *your* quiver (Ps. 127:3-5)!

Q 18 *Explain the proverb: Too many arrows split the quiver.*

150　　　　　　　　　　　　　　　　　　　　　　　　　　　　　　　　　　　　*Marriage & Family*

The importance of the mother's care is great. One teacher said, "Mother is food; she is love; she is warmth. ... To be loved by her means to be alive, to be rooted, to be at home."[7] A child's need for care changes in some ways as he grows—but it never disappears. Even adult children can look to their parents for strength and encouragement.

Conclusion

God entrusts our children to us. We must act as stewards who care for and value each child. We must help each one to grow as a unique person. We can do this by learning how children grow, by providing what they need, and by seeking God's help. The leader of a nation once said that no other success in life—not being president, or being wealthy, or anything else—comes up to the success of the man or woman who succeeds as a parent. Their children and grandchildren will rise up and call them blessed.[8]

Help Your Children Grow in Wisdom—Mentally

Goal A: *Explain a parent's role in a child's education and work skills.*
Goal B: *Summarize 10 reasons for sex education in the home.*
Goal C: *Identify 7 guidelines for teaching your children about sex.*
Goal D: *Explain how a child's age affects what he should learn about sex.*

Setting

The Bible tells us that Jesus grew from a child to a man in several ways. *"And Jesus grew in wisdom and stature, and in favor with God and men"* (Luke 2:52).

Q 19 *In which 4 ways did Jesus grow?*

Jesus grew in at least four ways:
- He grew in knowledge and wisdom (mentally).
- He grew in stature—in body and health (physically).
- He grew in favor with God (spiritually).
- He grew in favor with men (socially).

In this chapter, we will study ways to help your children grow in wisdom and stature (mentally and physically). In the next chapter, we will study how to help your children grow in favor with God and men (spiritually and socially).

A. Teach your children to ask questions and discover for themselves.

Q 20 *How can wise parents encourage a child's desire to learn?*

Children love to learn. From the day they are born, they begin learning about the world. As a dry rag soaks up water, children absorb knowledge. They are even learning when they are playing. It is amazing that children learn to speak an entire language **before** entering school!

Children love to learn. The best way to teach small children is to respond to their natural interests and ways of learning. Pouring water on a fire can put it out. Likewise, a parent can put out the flame of learning by forcing a child to sit still, be quiet, and not touch. Paul warns us not to put out the Spirit's fire (1 Thess. 5:19). We must be careful not to put out the fire of learning that God has lit in each child. Instead, let us guard and feed the fire of a child's interests.

Q 21 *What are the natural ways that children learn?*

Children learn more when they can explore, ask questions, and handle things. For sure, every child needs to learn to cooperate with others. There are times for children to sit, be quiet, and listen. But children learn more—and they have fun learning—when we let them explore, discover, ask questions, and touch things.

When did you learn that your spoon would sit on a table, but it would sink in water? Children do not wait for science class to learn this. Babies begin learning this by banging on everything. When parents try to feed small children, the little ones bang on the table.

When we try to bathe them, they slap the water. Tired parents may be offended. They may think the baby is rebelling. They may tell the baby, "No! No!" again and again. But wise parents laugh with the baby and realize that God created him or her to learn this way.

These are some ways to work with a child's natural way of learning:
- Be patient. Answer the child's questions that come one after the other, like links of a chain.
- Take slow walks with the children and talk about interesting things—trees, flowers, birds, the wind….
- Allow lots of time for play.
- Include children in simple work.
- Try to have easy books with pictures. Begin "reading" to babies as soon as they can sit up.
- Take children to many different places. Help them observe what is happening around them.
- Use teaching moments that arise throughout the day.

When parents take time for such things, they are teaching their children that it is good to learn. They are teaching a child to think—and this will increase a child's ability to learn. You can compare two children from different families. Although the children are the same age, the education of one may be many years ahead of the other because the parents took time to teach the child to learn. Children learn many things the easiest when they are the smallest. Training a small child is an excellent foundation for more education. If we encourage our children to love learning, it will help them grow in wisdom.

Figure 9.5 Take time to answer the questions your children ask.

Q 22 *How can parents work with a child's natural way of learning?*

B. Teach your children to value a good education, and help them get it.

Case Study: Some wealthy men heard about a starving tribe of people who lived far away in rugged mountains. They wanted to help the starving people, but they could not get trucks of food to them quickly enough. So, they decided to use an airplane and drop boxes of food, each under a *parachute. In each box of food, they placed an envelope of chemicals to keep the food fresh. On each packet they wrote, "DO NOT EAT." Also, they began to load trucks with more food for the slower journey up the mountains.

The starving tribe was afraid of strangers. So, when food was dropped from the airplanes, many stayed away from it. But their hunger conquered their fear, and they began eating the food. Some of the food was strange to them, but they ate it all. They also ate the chemicals; for no one in the tribe could read the words, "DO NOT EAT." Within hours, many of the tribe members became sick. Anger arose. What kind of enemy would seek to destroy them through their hunger?

Several days later they saw trucks moving up the mountainside. The trucks carried the same kind of boxes that held the poison. A group of tribesmen attacked the trucks. They killed the drivers and burned the food. When the wealthy people received news of the attack, they were amazed. Discouraged, they stopped all efforts to help. Because they could not read, this tribe did not receive the blessings God wanted to give them.

Illiteracy is a thief that steals food, health, and truth from the poorest 1/3 of the world. If a person cannot read, people will cheat him when he buys and sells. They can cheat him on his wages. Many who cannot read die because they do not understand medicine or health standards. Today, more than 100 million children, over half of them girls, never get a chance to go to school. Education is a ladder to a higher standard of living, but parents must help children climb it. Learning to read is very important. For example, a young mother will provide 25 percent more food for her family if she learns

Q 23 *How did the lack of knowledge prevent the wealthy people from acting with wisdom?*

Q 24 *How did the lack of knowledge prevent the hungry people from acting with wisdom?*

Q 25 *How can a local church help teach children to read?*

Q 26 *How will parents benefit from educating their children?*

Q 27 *Why is work important for children?*

Q 28 *How can you help your children learn skills you do not know?*

Q 29 *What are some attitudes about money you should teach your children?*

Q 30 *What are some financial skills you should teach your children?*

to read. This is why every church should be a literacy center—a place where people in the community can learn to read. (See the *Faith & Action Series* course *Read the Light—Teaching Literacy*).

Reading is the foundation of education. Through good books, people can gain the wisdom of many generations. Books can help a person learn how to run a business or learn how to increase crops. They can help a family learn how to be healthy and how to gain legal protection from people who would cheat them. Other books can help the family learn how to get along better with their neighbors. Reading is a key that unlocks a world of knowledge.

Our children become all God intends as we help them value and get a good education. The more they understand about people and the world, the more they can live wisely.

Parents who keep children away from learning to get more work from them are cheating themselves. A child's ability to add to the health, wealth, and wisdom of a family increases with education. This is true for our sons *and* our daughters. Would the tribe in the story above have been blessed if a little girl had been able to read "DO NOT EAT"? All children do not need the same amount of education. But all children should get a basic education, including skills for reading, writing, math, health, and relating to people. Parents, sow the seeds of education into your children, and you will reap a harvest in your old age. An educated child will care for you better than a child who cannot read!

Important knowledge comes from reading and attending school. But children also learn important things from daily life. Let us look at some areas in which children should gain practical knowledge to help them grow wise.

C. Teach your children skills for work.

Children develop work skills through practice. So every child should share in the family's work. Match responsibilities with each child's age and ability. Even the youngest child should understand that his jobs are important. Work beside the children as they are learning a new skill. Let them watch you. Encourage them. Be patient as they develop good work habits. Help them feel successful, instead of thinking about how much better and faster you could have done the

> EVERY CHILD SHOULD SHARE IN THE FAMILY'S WORK.
>
> BE PATIENT AS THEY DEVELOP GOOD WORK HABITS.

work. Family work develops knowledge and self-discipline needed for wisdom. Parents, teach your children everything you know about preparing food to eat, cooking, sewing, cleaning, gardening, studying, budgeting, banking, buying, selling, building, relating to people, and other skills they need for life.

But do not limit your children to what you know. They can also learn by working beside another skilled person. Perhaps your child can work with a carpenter or a mason. If your daughter shows interest in medicine, she can volunteer to assist in a hospital. If your son likes mechanics, perhaps he can work with a mechanic. It is good for youth to learn computer skills at school or from someone who has such skills. Study your children and plan for them to learn skills that match the things they like. Training can help children develop the wisdom they need to provide for themselves and their families.

D. Teach your children godly attitudes and skills for money.[9]

The Bible teaches us a lot about money, and we should teach that to our children. We studied about money in chapter 6 in relation to husbands and wives. Parents can teach the principles in that chapter to their children. Figure 9.6 lists several attitudes and financial skills to teach children.

How to Be an Effective Father or Mother—Part I 153

Godly attitudes about money	Good skills to manage money
• Stewardship, tithes, offerings • Trusting God • Generosity to others • Contentment • Honesty • Diligence	• Planning • Budgeting • Saving and investing • Spending • Credit and debt

Figure 9.6   Attitudes and skills related to money

Here are some ideas for teaching your children about finances.

- Teach what the Bible says about money. Do this during family devotions. (We will study about family worship in chapter 10.) Let them see you pay your tithes each week. Encourage them to give offerings to the poor and to the church.

- Train each child. Do not just give money to your children. Enable them to earn it. Pay them money each week for work they do, so each may learn how to manage it. Match the work and the pay with the age and ability of each child. Teach all to work as unto the Lord. They will also learn the value of money that comes through labor. One father had little money, but each year he gave a baby goat to one of his children. Each child learned how to manage wealth through caring for the goat.

- Train children in a way that reflects real life. If a child does not complete a job, do not pay him for that job. If a child wastes or loses a coin, make him work to get another coin.

- Be open about how you use finances for the family. Teach your children about your family's budget as they become youth. Encourage them to ask questions. Let them help you buy, sell, and bargain. They will learn through practice.

Q 31 ↖ How can a parent teach his child about finances?

E. Teach your children to understand sexual matters.

1. The need for sex education in the home.[10]   Children will learn about sex. It is just a question of how and what they will learn. If we do not take the lead, then the world will teach them things that are contrary to the Bible. Are we going to be silent and see our children led astray? Is our comfort more important than our children?

Q 32 ↗ Why should children receive sex education at home?

On some sexual matters, a father can teach his son, and a mother can teach her daughter. Figure 9.7 lists ten reasons for sex education in the home.

Q 33 ↖ What makes talking about sex to children difficult in your culture?

1. Sex education helps a child to accept his body and each year of growth. It enables him to discuss sex without fear or shame.
2. Sex education helps a child to understand and be satisfied with his role in life. Children are content to know that boys grow up to be men and fathers, while girls grow up to be ladies and mothers.
3. Sex education answers questions. It takes away the mystery. When children know that their parents will teach them the truth about sexual things, children have no cause for worry or concern. They do not need to turn to dirty stories and pornography to satisfy curiosity.
4. Sex education encourages a child to develop biblical attitudes for life. Good teaching guards against sexual problems later in life. Otherwise, sexual confusion and fears in childhood can carry over into adult life. Bad sexual experiences as a child may produce twisted sexual patterns in life.
5. Christian sex education helps a person spiritually. It clears his mind of distracting sex questions. It brings a deep respect for God and His plan of human growth. Good teaching enables the person to thank God for sex and the way God created us.
6. Sex education builds a child's confidence in his parents. If the parents are honest and helpful about matters of sex, children learn to trust parents about many other things.
7. Sex education given at home is like hoeing the weeds out of a garden. Good teaching at home uproots sinful ideas that reach children through films, friends, magazines, and newspapers.

Q 34 ↖ Which of the 10 reason for teaching about sex are the most powerful? Explain.

Continued on next page

154   *Marriage & Family*

Continued from previous page

8. Sex education in the home makes giving birth to children clear and holy. A child should feel that having children is right. He needs to know—as shown in Genesis 1:24—that God planned for each living creature to produce after its own kind.

9. Sex education helps a child to be proud of his own sexuality and value those of the opposite sex.

10. Sex education helps protect children from sexual abuse. People who sexually use children often take advantage of the child's ignorance. If a child has basic knowledge, he is more likely to go to another adult for help.

Figure 9.7   Ten reasons for sex education in the home

2. The method for sex education in the home.[11]   Talking about sex is sometimes difficult because it is meant to be private. Even a husband and wife may find it difficult to talk with each other about sex. So, it is natural to sometimes feel awkward when talking to our children about such things. Still—for the ten reasons we have studied—parents must teach their children about sex. So, what is the best way to teach them? Figure 9.8 explains seven keys for teaching our children about sexual matters.

Q 35 ⟋ *What is a step-by step approach to teach about sex?*

Q 36 ⟋ *How can a parent use questions and teaching moments to explain sexual matters?*

Q 37 ⟋ *Why should a parent teach about sex with a relaxed attitude and a godly purpose?*

1. Use a long, step-by-step approach. Do **not** wait for one day to tell a child *everything* about sex. Teach children the things that match their ages. Make sure they understand you and then build on that information little by little as they grow. Discern how much the child is ready to learn. Teachings that will satisfy a child who is 3 years old will not satisfy a child who is 5 or 6 years old.

2. Answer questions honestly. Small children will ask sexual questions as they ask questions about all other things. Answer them briefly and honestly. But only give them the information that fits their age. If a parent lies—like saying a big bird brings a baby—the child who discovers the truth will wonder why the parent lied.

3. Use teaching moments. When you and your children see mating between chickens, cows, or goats, explain what is happening. Likewise, a mother has a good opportunity to teach when she or another woman is pregnant. Some pregnant mothers teach their children by letting them feel the baby move in the womb while explaining a little about how it got there. Do not always wait for questions, especially from older children. A child's silence does not mean a lack of interest. A child may find it difficult to ask questions about sex. The parent may need to speak first. Be aware of what your children should know—and talk with them.

4. Use proper words. When children ask questions, they may use vulgar words. Do not be shocked or angry. Children talk with the only words they have heard. Teach children the proper words, and use them yourself. Explain to them why some words are wrong. Explain why we cover our private, sexual parts.

5. Create a relaxed attitude. Encourage your child to always ask questions to you. Never act like any question is a sinful question to ask. A relaxed, open attitude keeps children coming back to their parents for facts and guidance. This attitude helps children understand that sex and sexuality are normal. Use the same tone of voice as always. Relax your face and smile a little, to show that the child has asked a normal question. If a parent becomes embarrassed—and refuses to answer—the child will keep looking for the answer. If you will encourage them, your children will honor you with their questions. If you refuse, they will seek answers from anyone—whether godly or ungodly.

6. Teach with a godly purpose. Good sexual teaching does not just answer questions about *what*. It also teaches *why*. Teach your children that sex is a marriage gift from God to a husband and wife.

7. Be a good example. Show respect, faithfulness, kindness, and love to your spouse. It is good for children to see a father and mother kiss and hug a little. Talk to your children about how much you love your spouse. Plan with the children to do special things for your spouse. Never commit adultery. If you are a single parent, remain sexually pure. Stay away from all pornography. Your example will either underline or erase all your words.

Figure 9.8   Seven keys to teach your children about sexual matters

3. The sexual knowledge each child needs at home.[12]   Parents are not always in control of what their children see and hear about sex. Children may get ideas through friends, television, music, and other things outside the home. Protect children from false or ungodly ideas about sex as much as possible. Be aware of what they see and hear. Protect their innocent, young minds, while teaching them the truth as they grow. Children develop at their own rate within their culture. So, the parent should discern when each child is ready for certain knowledge. Let us study some guidelines for teaching children as they grow.

Children 0–3 years old

- They need to feel loved and accepted by their father and mother. Fathers and mothers should hug their small children, and tell them they love them. And parents should show their love through giving the small children attention and time. This will protect them from becoming sexually active later in life as an attempt to find love that was missing as a child.
- Teach them the names for their sexual parts as you teach them the names for other parts of their bodies.
- They will be curious about the differences between male and female bodies. Give very simple answers.
- They begin wondering where babies come from. They will notice pregnant women and animals. Explain that babies first grow in special sacks in the mothers' bodies.
- They need to develop positive feelings about being a boy or a girl. This usually happens when they look up to their fathers and mothers. If you are a single parent, make sure your children spend time with someone like the missing parent. The best choices are godly people who will be in their lives for a long time—like an aunt, uncle, or grandparents.
- Do not give details about intercourse. If questions arise, just say, "We will talk about that when you are older."
- Leave them in the care of people you trust *completely*. Sexual abuse can happen to children less than 3 years old! The sad truth is that if a very young child is sexually abused, it was usually a friend or a family member who committed this sin.

Children 4–6 years old

- Continue many of the things we mentioned for the smallest children. For example, continue to show that you love and accept each child. As children grow, you will answer their questions more fully. For example, they will now want to know how the baby *gets out* of the mother. But a child still does **not** need to know how the child *got in*—the details of intercourse.
- Teach them about good and bad choices. Encourage them to grow in self-control. This helps them build a foundation for godly, moral living.
- Teach them that God desires babies to be born in marriages with a mother and father. If a child does not have a mother or father living with them, they will begin asking questions about why. Give the simple truth without details. Never make a child feel guilty or at fault over what a parent did. Do not encourage the child to think badly of the missing parent.
- Help them feel that they can come to their parents for answers about sexual things.
- Teach them the difference between private and public body parts. The private parts are not to be shown or touched by others. And they are not to look at or touch another person's private parts. Teach them to come to you quickly if anyone shows or touches his/her private parts. If this has happened with small children who are all the same age, do not become angry. They are just curious. But if someone older is involved, use all your power to protect your child from abuse. Your child's sexual future is at risk. Always let them know that being safe is more important than being polite. Teach them to shout "NO," run away, and tell on **anyone** who touches them in a sexual way.

Q 38 *Explain the way a child's questions about sex differ as he matures.*

Figure 9.9a
Parents should teach some basic truths about sex to small children.

Figure 9.9c
Know the sexual truths to teach children 7–10 years old.

Q 39 ⤳ What is puberty? What sexual lessons should parents teach children at this age?

Figure 9.9d
Prepare your children for puberty, and teach them about sex.

Q 40 ⤳ What sexual lessons should parents teach teenagers?

Figure 9.9e Talk to your older children about sexual issues they need to understand.

Children 7–10 years old

- They will have more questions about the father's part in making babies. They will need to know the role of intercourse in creating a child. At this age, they may not be curious about other purposes of sex, unless they have seen sexual acts in movies, pictures, or elsewhere. Do your best to protect them from understanding sex too early. Children need all their attention and energy to be applied to other areas of growth at this time in their lives.
- They will have more questions about how the baby grows inside the mother and how it is born. Some parents use the process of mating, pregnancy, and birth in animals to teach their children.
- Teach them about the sexual systems of the male and female body. Teach that sex and sexuality are normal and good in marriage. God made all things to reproduce.
- Make sure they understand the ways their bodies are going to change into adult men and women.

Children 10–13 years old

- Prepare them for the physical and emotional changes of *puberty (pronounced PYOO-burr-tee). Every child should know about *menstruation and *nocturnal emissions (wet dreams) before they experience these things. Assure them that people develop at different rates and that variety in human bodies is normal.
- Teach them that sex is for marriage between a man and a woman. Teach them to remain a *virgin—someone who has not had sex until marriage.
- Help them to expect the sex drive to be powerful. But desire does not demand action. Teach them that the Holy Spirit helps us to have self-control over our desires (Gal. 5:13, 16).
- Talk to them about pornography and other entertainment that will harm and twist their thinking about sex.
- Teach them that incest—sex with a family member—is ALWAYS a sin.
- Teach them the value of modesty in dress and interaction with people.
- Educate them about pregnancy and birth control, when others their age are talking about these things. (Parents, do not assume that your children should be as old as you were when you learned these lessons. Find out the ages that children today are discussing these sexual matters.)

Children 14 years and older

- Teach them the purpose of marriage and the other purposes of sex besides *reproduction.
- Teach them how to talk about sex with others—and when it is not acceptable to talk about sex.
- Talk about the results of using and misusing sex as God has commanded. Include information about sexual diseases such as *HIV/AIDS.
- Explain why our church teaches that abortion is wrong, except in rare cases when it threatens the life of the mother. Children belong to God, even when they are still in the womb. Remember, abortion stops a beating heart! (Read the Assemblies of God position on abortion: http://www.ag.org/top/Beliefs/Position_Papers/pp_4196_sanctity_human_life.cfm)
- Help them to understand the opposite sex and respect them.
- Help them develop a personal plan for sexual purity.
- Begin praying with them about wisdom in choosing marriage and a spouse.
- Teach them the steps by which sexual desire gets stronger and stronger so they will be aware.

- Talk with them about *masturbation.
- Details about how to become a good lover should not be shared until engagement. When they become engaged, help them get the information they need to prepare for sex within marriage.

Our children need good knowledge about sex in order to live wise lives. Sexual knowledge helps them understand themselves, protect themselves, and choose wisely.

Conclusion

We want our children to grow in wisdom just as Jesus grew. One of the ways parents can help is to make sure their children are gaining knowledge about themselves and the world. Parents should encourage a love of learning. They should strive to educate all their children. They should teach them practical life skills through everyday work. And parents should not neglect sex education. As our children acquire knowledge, let us pray that their hearts will be turned to God and to wisdom.

A daughter was growing into a woman. As she got older, she began to feel sexual desire. No one had taught her that her desires were normal and could be managed in godly ways. She only heard what adults and other children said. Little by little, she became ashamed of her feelings. She began to feel that she was a bad person. When the first young man she cared for used her sexually, all her fears were confirmed. She spent her life moving from man to man with no understanding of her real purpose in life.

Help Your Children Grow in Stature—Physically and in Good Health

Goal A: List 10 things a pregnant mother should do to protect the health of her unborn child.
Goal B: Summarize the need for good food, rules for eating, pure water, and cleanliness in caring for children.
Goal C: Explain the role of vaccines and doctors in caring for children.

Jesus grew in wisdom. He also grew in *stature—which includes size, weight, and height. Physical growth is the easiest to see. Children's bodies grow, but many children do not grow to their full height and strength. Others face diseases that cripple them or cause an early death. Parents should do their best to provide the things that children need to be healthy. Let us examine some keys to help your children develop the healthy bodies God wants.

A. A healthy pregnancy helps children grow in health.

The physical health of a child begins with the health of his parents. The health of the mother greatly affects the health of her baby. While the child is in the womb, he is nourished or injured—helped or harmed—by the things the mother eats, drinks, and experiences. A woman should do several things to help her child be healthy.

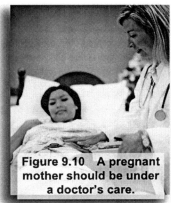

Figure 9.10 A pregnant mother should be under a doctor's care.

1. Stay free from sexual diseases. A mother can pass some of these diseases on to the child. Some sexual diseases may cause *defects in the baby, or even death.
2. Have regular exams by a doctor while pregnant, if possible.
3. Before pregnancy, get a *measles (rubella) *vaccination, if you have not had this disease. Measles during pregnancy may cause death or birth defects—such as problems in the child's eyes, ears, heart, or mind.
4. Talk to a doctor about a *tetanus vaccine. This will protect you and your baby when the *umbilical cord that connects the mother and baby is cut.

Q 41 *Define these important words: defects, measles, vaccination, tetanus, vitamins.*

Q 42 *How can sexual or other diseases in a mother affect the unborn child?*

Q 43 Why should a pregnant mother eat good foods and take vitamins?

Q 44 If a pregnant or nursing mother drinks alcohol or uses drugs, how will this affect the child?

Q 45 Why should a mother be careful about what she eats, drinks, or uses when she is producing milk for her child?

Q 46 What is an _undernourished_ child?

Q 47 What may result if a child eats too little food?

Q 48 What may result if a child eats too much food?

Q 49 Name the four food groups and descibe the purpose of each.

Q 50 Look at the examples of each food group. Are your children eating food from each group each day? Explain.

5. Talk to a doctor about taking anti-malaria pills, if you live in an area where *malaria is common. Malaria during pregnancy is dangerous to the mother and baby.

6. Eat healthy foods and take vitamins if possible. You need to have enough *calories, *vitamins, and *minerals for two—you and the baby. Folic acid (a B vitamin from vegetables, grain products, and fruits) helps prevent some birth defects. Iron is also important, so eat plenty of dark green vegetables. Drink fruit juice with the vegetables to help your body absorb the iron. How the baby's body grows before birth depends on what the mother eats.

7. Avoid ALL alcohol. If a mother drinks alcohol while pregnant, it may cause physical and mental problems for the baby.

8. Be aware of the side effects of x-rays and drugs before receiving any treatment. Sometimes these can cause a *deformity, such as a hand with no fingers, in the baby. Pleasure drugs (such as nicotine in cigarettes, marijuana, heroin, or cocaine) can also cause unhealthy babies.

9. Rest more often. Too much stress may cause the baby to be too small—and may cause the mother to give birth too early.

10. Plan some time between babies. Babies and mothers are healthier if babies are spaced at least 2 years apart. The mother has time to regain and maintain her strength. And both babies receive better care when the first can walk and talk before another is born.

After birth, the mother should continue to take special care about which food, drinks, and drugs she uses while her child is nursing. Mother's milk is the best food for an infant. **It has all the nutrition a baby needs for the first 4–6 months of life. A mother's milk is free of germs. And this milk is more than food.** The first milk (*colostrum) gives a baby special protection against some diseases in early life. Breast milk continues to give some protection until the baby is weaned. But whatever the mother puts into her body can be passed on through her milk. The infant, while in the womb and after birth, has a better chance to be healthy when his mother is healthy.

B. The right food helps children grow in health.[13]

Healthy food is more important for children than for adults. If a child does not get proper food, he may be affected throughout life. We refer to children who do not get enough of the right foods as *_undernourished_ children. The bodies of undernourished children may never grow to their full size and strength. Their mental abilities may be stunted—lessened for all of life. Children may become blind by lack of vitamins.

If a child gets too much food, he may also be unhealthy. Eating too much may cause *diabetes, joint problems, heart problems, and social problems. Parents must do their best to provide the right amount of healthy foods and teach their children about healthy eating (See Figure 9.11).

Food Group	Purpose	How Often?	Sources
Protein	Helps the body grow and be strong.	Every day	Meat, fish, chicken, eggs, insects, soybeans, seafood, milk, cheese, beans, peas, lentils, nuts, dark green leafy vegetables, cereals (wheat, millet, oats)
Starches/ Sugars	Give energy to run, play, and work. The more energy you use, the more of these foods you need.	Every day, but do not eat too much sugar, honey, or molasses.	<u>Starches</u>: maize (corn), rice, cereals, noodles (pasta), potatoes, sweet potatoes, yams, squash, cassava (manioc), plantain, taro (eddo, poi) <u>Sugars</u>: sugar, honey, molasses, fruit, ripe bananas, milk

Continued on next page

Food Group	Purpose	How Often?	Sources
Fats	Stores energy in your body for when it is needed. Large amounts will harm you.	Eat only small amounts of this group every day.	Cooking oil, salad oil, lard, bacon, meat fat, butter, margarine Other sources: groundnuts (peanuts), sesame, soybeans, nuts, coconut, avocado, milk
General—for Protection	Helps your body work properly. Contains many vitamins that your body needs to make healthy blood, bones, and teeth. Vegetables (dark green and orange/yellow) and fruits protect children from blindness.	Every day	Meat (especially liver), chicken, eggs, fish, cheese, milk, fruits, whole grain cereals, seaweed, vegetables (especially yellow and dark green like spinach)

Figure 9.11   Children need various foods to grow in health.

C. <u>Rules for eating</u> can help children grow in health.

Q 51 ↖ Which of these rules do you keep?

1. Always wash your hands with soap or ash before handling food and before eating.
2. Always wash raw fruits and vegetables before eating them.
3. If food smells rotten, do not eat it.
4. If someone in your family is sick, do not eat from the same dish as that person. Do not drink from the cup of the sick person—or use his spoon or fork until washing it in hot water and soap.
5. Protect your food from flies, other insects, rats and mice, and dust.
6. Cook meat. Do not let fruits and vegetables touch raw meat or *utensils used to prepare meat.
7. Eat food as soon as it is prepared. The longer it is unused, the more likely it will collect *germs—tiny things that cause disease. Germs spread through uncleanness, bad water, insects, coughing, and things sick people touch.

Q 52 ↗ What are germs? How do they spread?

8. Keep your cooking area and utensils clean.

D. <u>Pure water</u> helps children grow in health.

Pure water is necessary for a healthy life. But we cannot tell if water is pure by the way it looks or tastes. Most water that comes from lakes, ponds, rivers, and streams has germs in it that can make you sick. Even water from wells and pipes can sometimes have germs or harmful *chemicals. Chemicals, like some sprays that kill insects, build up in the body and harm a person's health over a period of time. This is why we should keep harmful chemicals away from food in the garden and the home. In contrast to chemicals, germs can make people sick quickly. Those who die the most often from bad, impure water are children under the age of 5 years. Everyone around the world should be concerned about water, because we all need pure water for health.

Q 53 ↖ Do you know the quality of water in your community? How can you find out?

Q 54 ↖ Can you tell if water is bad by the way it looks or tastes? Explain.

People who live in towns or cities can have the water that is piped into their homes tested for harmful germs and chemicals. They can buy certain filters to cleanse the water if necessary. People should educate themselves about the use of chemicals in their homes and on their yards. Those who live in less modern areas need to cooperate as a community to have safe water. They also have to commit time and care to provide their children with healthy water. Here are some rules for safe water in **rural or unsafe areas.**[14]

1. No one should *defecate or *urinate in or near drinking water. An old proverb says, "Don't pee where you sleep." An even older proverb says, "Don't pee where you drink!"
2. Keep animals away from water that humans drink. Animals have diseases that will make humans sick.

Q 55 *Why will boiling your water save the lives of your children?*

3. Always boil the water you drink (**bring to a rapid rolling boil, then boil 10 more minutes before cooling it**) or use chlorine in it (chlorine is a chemical that kills germs). Boiling water or using chlorine in it kills germs that cause *diarrhea (watery, loose feces). If the water is cloudy, filter it before boiling or using chlorine. (One man complained that water did not taste good after it was boiled. Add a small amount of salt to water after it is boiled to improve the taste. And remember, disease in water can be like the scroll that the apostle John ate—sweet in your mouth, but bitter in your stomach. So be safe—**boil your water.** Add salt, a little charcoal, and even honey if needed. Be sure to remove the charcoal before you drink the water!)

4. Keep water you will drink in a clean container. Cover the container to protect the water from insects and dust. Be sure that hands do not touch the water inside. Use a clean dipper—that no one drinks from—to move water from the large container. This insures that no one's germs will get into the water that all drink. Clean the container and change the water regularly.

Q 56 *Why should everyone wash his or her hands after going to the toilet?*

5. Always wash hands with water and soap or ash before drinking, eating, preparing food, or feeding little children. Never forget to wash hands after going to the bathroom, or handling the waste of children or people who are sick.

6. If plumbing is not available, dig a pit for an *outhouse (toilet), or dig a *latrine far away from your water source and at least 20 feet (6 m) from your home.

E. <u>Cleanliness</u> helps children grow in health.

Children who live in clean homes and learn clean habits have a better chance for good health. We have already talked about the importance of clean food and pure water. Let us now look at some other areas of cleanliness for good health.

Q 57 *Why should we get rid of garbage or puddles of water around our homes?*

1. Keep the home clean—inside and outside. **On the inside** of the home, remove dust and dirt—since these contain germs. Keep toilets and cooking areas very clean. Never cook in the same clothes that you wear to clean the toilet. Also, after you use cloths to clean the home, wash them. **On the outside** of your home, do not allow garbage or piles of things nearby. These attract mice and rats that spread disease. Also, water near the home attracts insects, like mosquitoes, that spread disease.

Q 58 *Describe cleaning 3 areas of the body.*

2. Keep bodies clean.
   - *Hands* Because we are touching things all day long, it is very important to keep hands clean. Dry your clean hands on a clean cloth or let them dry in the air. And do not forget to clean under your fingernails every day.
   - *Hair* If people go for a long time without washing their hair, bugs—like lice or mites—can get in the hair—and sores can get on the *scalp. Wash the scalp with the fingertips when you wash the hair. Sometimes bugs can get in the skin and hair—even when you have tried to keep clean. If your child is scratching his head or body often, you may need to get medicine to kill the bugs. If bugs are on people, they are probably on household items made of cloth. In this case, you will need to wash clothes and linens on the same day you use medicine to kill bugs in the hair.

Figure 9.12 Use lots of soap and fresh water to wash hands.

Q 59 *Why is it very important to keep a child's face clean?*

   - *Skin* Regular bathing helps clean germs from the skin. Keep the face of each child clean. Flies and germs infect food on the face or *mucus that drips from the nose. If the germs get into a child's eye, it can cause disease or blindness.

Q 60 *How does disease spread through dirty clothes?*

3. Keep clothing clean. Clothes collect dirt and germs and can smell bad. Germs and bugs on clothes can get on skin and in the mouth. This is how dirty clothes can

spread illnesses. So wash clothes every 2 days. Change underclothing every day or wash it every day.

4. Keep teeth clean. Only take care of the teeth you want to keep! Three basic things will help teeth stay healthy.

    - Eat healthy foods. Do not eat too many sweet foods or sweet drinks.
    - Brush your teeth well twice a day—in the morning and before sleeping. Everyone should have his own toothbrush. If you cannot buy one, you can make one from a stick or cloth. Keep it clean and away from germs. Use toothpaste or a mixture of salt and bicarbonate of soda to clean the teeth. Brush in a circular pattern instead of back and forth. Clean between the teeth.
    - Try to see a dentist twice a year. The dentist can stop decay and save a tooth.

Q 61 *What is needed for healthy teeth?*

5. Handle bodily fluids and waste properly. When people are sick, they may cough, sneeze, or blow their noses. The fluids that come out of bodies when this happens carry germs that can make others sick. Teach children to cover their noses and mouths when they cough or sneeze. If they use their bare hands to cover a cough or sneeze, they must wash their hands at once with water and soap or ashes. If they use a cloth, it must be washed in hot water and soap. If they use a paper product, it should be thrown away. People should wash their hands often when they are sick.

    - Animal waste, whether urine or excreta (poop), is a special health concern. Keep animals away from the water that humans drink. Animal waste is good for the garden, but bad to have near the home. Either keep animals away from the home, or remove their waste from near the home every day.
    - Human waste can also spread disease. Flush, clean, and cover toilets that are inside a home. Those who use outdoor toilets may sprinkle ashes over waste. But they should also cover the waste opening after use. If a family does not have a toilet, they should choose a place away from the water and away from their home to relieve themselves. They should dig a hole and bury the waste. In all cases, teach children to wash their hands every time they use the toilet. The following diagram shows why it is so important to be careful about waste (excreta or *sewage).

Q 62 *Summarize the path of disease that spreads from sewage to people (Figure 9.13).*

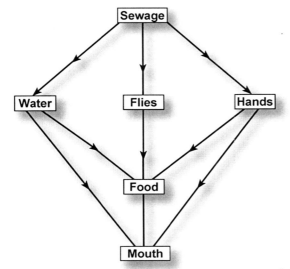

Figure 9.13 Poor planning to get rid of sewage causes sickness.[15]

Workers at one nation's main market killed about 6,000 rats, trucked away 750 tons of garbage, and sucked 70 tons of human waste out of latrines in 3 days. An official said that this was the first major cleanup of the market in 30 years. The Farmers' Market, which supplies fresh food to most of the city's three million people, was a public health hazard.

A local government leader said that garbage was up to 2 meters deep in some places. "Was I shocked? I was traumatized by the rot," the leader told the local newspaper. "We were lucky to be spared from a major outbreak of disease." City workers used 160,000 liters of water in the cleanup. Some traders, who worked at the market for years, were surprised to see that pavement existed below the garbage.[16]

F. <u>Exercise and rest</u> help children grow in health.

Exercise. Small children are usually active. They exercise—walking, running, and playing. They keep their bodies busy. Some are more active than others. But exercise is important for health—for all children and adults. Exercise keeps body weight right, as God planned it. Exercise strengthens muscles and bones—and it lengthens the life of the lungs and heart.

Q 63 — Explain the balance between exercise and rest for children.

Rest follows exercise, as night follows day. The body needs rest to gain strength after working. Children often exercise and then rest throughout the day. They need more times to rest than adults. Infants spend much of their days and nights sleeping. Small children continue to need 12 hours of sleep each night and often a daily nap. Even older children will need 10–12 hours of sleep as they go through various growth spurts. Their lives should balance exercise and rest.

Many children around the world do not balance work and rest. Some adults force their children to work too many hours. They treat their children like they have fully grown adult bodies. Other parents allow their children to sit too much. These children sit many hours in front of a computer or television. So guide your children to a good balance among work, exercise, and rest. Keep your own body fit as a good example.

G. <u>Medical care</u> helps children grow in health.

Q 64 — Where can you get information about vaccines to protect your children?

Vaccines. Many diseases can kill or harm children for life. Some of these diseases are *diphtheria, measles, *polio, tetanus, *cholera, malaria, and *whooping cough. In the past, we were not able to protect our children from these terrible diseases. But today, vaccines are available. Praise the Lord for the good gifts of vaccines. Doctors make a vaccine by taking a germ from a disease. Then, they weaken it so that it will not harm people. Through a small needle, they put this weak germ into a person. Our bodies then build up a defense against the disease. When people receive vaccines, they are safer from the

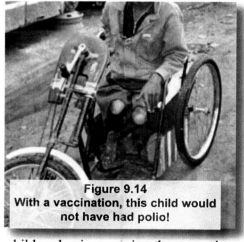

**Figure 9.14
With a vaccination, this child would not have had polio!**

disease. Doctors tell parents to make sure their children begin receiving these vaccines several weeks after birth. See your local Well Baby Clinic or Health Department for their advice about when your child should receive certain vaccines. Do not refuse the good gifts of vaccines that God has given to protect your children. Remember, every good gift comes from our heavenly Father above (James 1:17).

Q 65 — In a group of 100 children, vaccines will protect at least how many of them? Will you protect your child?

Sometimes babies will run a low fever and be sore where the needle entered their bodies. **Rarely,** a child will become sick from a vaccine or shot. Parents may hear these true stories and other false stories and be afraid for their children to receive vaccines. But parents must be wise and know the blessings of vaccines. For example, if a disease came to a school of 100 children, <u>all</u> of the children might get sick. But, if the children had vaccines, probably <u>less than ten</u> children would get sick.[17] So help your child be healthy—use vaccines. Children suffer and die if parents refuse the good gifts, like vaccines, that God has given us (James 1:17).

Long ago, Pentecostal missionaries went to West Africa. They felt spiritual and full of faith. So they did not take vaccines or pills to prevent diseases. Many died. Today, we have learned the difference between faith and foolishness. We should not tempt God by refusing the good gifts He has given to prevent malaria. Jesus did not tempt God by jumping off of the temple. He knew that jumping was not wise. Likewise, today we know that refusing vaccines is foolish, not wise or spiritual.

 Q 66 What foolish mistake did early Pentecostal missionaries make in West Africa?

A father stood weeping over the grave of his son. The dad looked up to the heavens and cried, "God, why did you let a demon kill my child?" The dad did not know it, but the heavenly Father was also crying. The Father looked down and said, "It was not a demon that killed your child. It was a disease! Why did you refuse the vaccine I sent? It was a good gift I gave to protect the health of your child." "*My people are destroyed from lack of knowledge. 'Because you have rejected knowledge ... I also will ignore your children'*" (Hos. 4:6). **Principle:** When parents reject knowledge, it destroys the lives of their children.

 Q 67 What deadly mistake did a loving father make?

Visits to a doctor bless a child's health. They give a doctor the chance to discern small problems before they become big. You can step over a stream when it first begins, but further along it is too wide to cross. Many health problems—in the beginning—are like small weeds to hoe out of a garden. But if we neglect small problems, they grow into big ones.

Q 68 How can parents learn about medical care for their children?

The care of a doctor or nurse is a blessing when problems come to our bodies. Some health problems—such as broken bones—are easy to see. Other dangers—such as *dehydration (loss of fluid in the body)—are hard to discern. Parents should educate themselves about when to seek a doctor. You can find this information at a library, Well Baby Clinic, Health Department, or on the Internet. Sometimes other parents can give good counsel.

But knowing when to seek medical care is not enough. Sadly, good medical care is not available to all. Sometimes clinics and doctors are far away. Sometimes medical care is present, but parents lack money. And then there are the times that the best medicine cannot make our children well. Thank God that doctors are not our only hope. In Jesus, we have hope of healing and the hope of resurrection. God is the One who has given us the precious gifts of our children. He has entrusted them to us, and we, in turn, must trust God with our children. The people of God throughout Scripture trusted God to provide food, water, clothing, and healing for their children. Even though times have changed, we parents stand side by side in faith with the widow of Zarephath (1 Kings 17:7-24) and the ruler of the synagogue named Jairus (Luke 8:40-56). Still, we never ignore or under-value the good gifts God has sent us through doctors and medicine. And we do not tempt God by ignoring the principles of good health.

Q 69 Should those with faith in God neglect doctors and principles of good health? Explain.

Conclusion

Jesus grew in stature. We want our children to have strong, healthy bodies. Health for our children begins with healthy parents. Both parents should be free from disease. And the mother should be very concerned about her health when she is pregnant or nursing her child.

Growing children need healthy food, pure water, and times for exercise and rest. The entire family must be careful to keep bodies and homes clean. Vaccines and medical care also help children grow healthy. As parents, we must do our best to provide these things for our children so they can grow in stature.

Jesus grew in wisdom, in stature, in favor with God, and in favor with men. We have considered how to help our children grow in wisdom and stature. In the next chapter, we will study how to help our children grow in favor with God and men.

Chapter Summary

 Prepare to Help Your Children Grow

Goal A: *Explain God's point of view on children in relation to: ownership, value, and gifts.*

God is the creator and owner of all children. He places great value on them, does not want even one of them to perish, and has charged angels to watch over them. Children are among God's greatest gifts to parents.

Goal B: *Summarize what a parent should understand about a child's growth and uniqueness.*

A parent must discern that each child is different. Still, all children grow are similar ways. Review Figure 9.3 on ways children grow mentally, physically, spiritually, and socially.

Goal C: *Describe a parent's responsibilities to be an example and a provider.*

- Values—both good and bad—grow as children *see* them in their parents. The advice children hear means more when parents live what they teach.
- Children need food, clothing, shelter, security, and love—and a father's understanding and love. Likewise, mother is food love, and warmth. To be loved by her means to be alive, rooted, and at home.
- Match the number of arrows to the size of *your* quiver.

 Help Your Children Grow in Wisdom— Mentally

Goal A: *Explain a parent's role in a child's education and work skills.*

Teach your children to ask questions and discover things. Teach them to value a good education, and help them get it. Teach your children skills for work—all you know about preparing food to eat, cooking, sewing, cleaning, farming, raising animals, buying, selling, building, relating to people and God, and other skills.

Goal B: *Summarize 10 reasons for sex education in the home.*

Review Figure 9.7—Ten reasons for sex education in the home.

Goal C: *Identify 7 guidelines for teaching your children about sex.*

Review Figure 9.8—Seven ways to teach your children about sexual matters.

Goal D: *Explain how a child's age affects what he should learn about sex.*

We studied characteristics of children 0–3 years old, 4–6 years, 7–10 years, 10–13 years, and 14 years and older. Review the teachings for each age group.

 Help Your Children Grow in Stature— Physically and in Good Health

Goal A: *List 10 things a pregnant mother should do to protect the health of her unborn child.*

Stay free from sexual diseases. Have regular exams by a doctor. Before pregnancy, talk to him about vaccines for measles and tetanus, and anti-malaria pills. Eat healthy foods and take vitamins. Avoid all alcohol. Be aware of the side effects of x-rays and drugs. Rest more often. Plan some time between babies.

Goal B: *Summarize the need for good food, rules for eating, pure water, and cleanliness in caring for children.*

Review Figure 9.11 on healthy foods. Obey the rules for eating. Wash your hands. Wash vegetables and fruits before eating them. Do not eat from the same dish as a sick person. Protect your food from flies, other insects, rats and mice, and dust. Cook meat. Eat food as soon as it is prepared. Clean your cooking area and utensils.

Pure water is necessary for a healthy life. But we cannot tell if water is pure by the way it looks or tastes. In rural or unsafe areas, keep the waste of humans and animals away from your water; and always boil the water you drink.

Goal C: *Explain the role of vaccines and doctors in caring for children.*

Many diseases can kill or harm children. But praise the Lord for vaccines that protect our children. Every good gift—such as children and vaccines—comes from above. Visits to a doctor bless a child's health. They enable a doctor to discern small problems before they become big. You can step over a stream when it first begins.

Test Yourself: Circle the letter by the *best* completion to each question or statement.

1. Who owns a child?
a) The parents
b) The child
c) The Lord
d) The family

2. A child begins to learn Bible stories at the age of
a) 1 year.
b) 3 years.
c) 6 years.
d) 8 years.

3. Children learn the most about values through
a) the daily examples of parents.
b) lessons taught at school and at church.
c) discussing matters with other children.
d) stories passed down from age to age.

4. How can a parent guide a child to learn?
a) Force the child to study each day.
b) Encourage the child to ask questions.
c) Teach a child to be seen, but not heard.
d) Avoid letting a child play much.

5. Which is TRUE about sex education at home?
a) It builds a child's confidence in his parents.
b) It is shameful and unbiblical for parents.
c) It hinders the spiritual growth of a child.
d) It awakens a child's interest in sexual matters.

6. Parents should teach their children about sex
a) when they reach the age of 15.
b) because it is easy to teach at home.
c) little by little throughout life.
d) just before they get married.

7. Children enter puberty at the age of
a) 7–9 years.
b) 10–13 years.
c) 14–16 years.
d) 17–19 years.

8. What a pregnant mother eats or drinks
a) should be the same as always.
b) is less important than vaccines.
c) affects the health of the unborn child.
d) causes a child to like certain foods.

9. We know water is safe to drink
a) if it looks clean and tastes good.
b) if animals drink it and are healthy.
c) if it gets very hot and begins to boil.
d) if it boils for more than 10 minutes.

10. Usually, a vaccine will protect
a) 20 children out of 100.
b) 50 children out of 100.
c) 70 children out of 100.
d) 90 children out of 100.

Chapter 10:
How to Be an Effective Father or Mother—Part 2

Introduction

A father prayed one night. "Forgive me, son. I am standing beside you as you sleep. I came to repent. I did not greet you with a smile in the morning. Instead, I scolded you for brushing your teeth too slowly. Then, at breakfast, you were excited about something. I do not know what it was, because I told you to stop talking with food in your mouth. As you left for school, you waved good-bye with joy. But I frowned and told you to stand up straight! Later in the day, you came home from school. I continued noticing the small things and ignoring the big things. I criticized the way you did your chores. When your ball went into the plants, I yelled at you. And do you remember when you interrupted my reading? You came into the room slowly. I was annoyed and asked what you wanted. You said, 'Nothing,' but gave me a big hug. Then you ran out to play. Forgive me, son. I have been a Pharisee, demanding the smallest letter of the law from you. Meanwhile, I have neglected the big themes of love and mercy. Tomorrow will be

Figure 10.1 Children usually grow up to be like their parents.

different. Each time I criticize you for one thing, we will laugh and celebrate over ten things. Sleep well, my son. In the morning, your dad will treat you as God treats us. I will be more patient and less demanding."[1]

Like this father, none of us is a perfect parent. But, thank God, we can repent and become more like our heavenly Father. We can continue to learn how to be a good father or mother.

Jesus grew in favor with God and men. In this chapter, we will study ways to help our children grow in these two areas.

Lessons:

Help Your Children Grow in Favor With God—Spiritually

Goal A: *Explain why the examples of parents are so important.*
Goal B: *Summarize steps that parents should take to teach their children.*
Goal C: *Describe guidelines for daily, family devotions.*

Help Your Children Grow in Favor With Men—Socially

Goal A: *Comment on the relationship between security and social growth.*
Goal B: *Explain 3 different ways that parents can show love to their children.*
Goal C: *Summarize how parents can help a child feel accepted, and have self-esteem.*
Goal D: *Analyze the roles of manners, attitudes, and skills in relating to others.*

Discipline Your Children, So They Will Grow in Favor With God and Men
Goal A: *Explain 10 of the 15 principles on discipline.*
Goal B: *Summarize 4 types of discipline.*

 Key Word

discipline

Help Your Children Grow in Favor With God—Spiritually

Goal A: *Explain why the examples of parents are so important.*
Goal B: *Summarize steps that parents should take to teach their children.*
Goal C: *Describe guidelines for daily, family devotions.*

Setting

God gives families the task of bringing up their children in the ways of the Lord. When He gave the Law to His people, He spoke to families about passing it along to their children (Deut. 6:6-7). Churches, pastors, and teachers all have roles in helping. But parents and families are the main teachers. Parents are powerful teachers. They can have the greatest influence because they live with their children, know them better, and love them so much. Let us look at some ways that parents can guide their children to grow in favor with God.

Q 1 *Why are parents such powerful teachers?*

A. The examples of parents help children grow spiritually.

A father and son were climbing a narrow path up a mountain. The son followed close behind his dad. The boy said, "Choose your steps well father, because I am putting my feet in your footprints."

Q 2 *What are 3 ways, A-C, for parents to help their children grow spiritually?*

Children imitate what they see their parents do. So wise parents seek to set a good example. Children learn from their parents by being together with them, and copying their behavior. So parents must spend time with each child, tell them stories, listen to the stories of their children, and play games with them. In many homes, mothers and their children are together often. But fathers must make a special effort to be with their children. Some dads like to carry small children on a walk. Sometimes a child rides on a dad's back, pretending he is a horse. This brings great joy to a child. One thing you can be sure of—when dad is near his children, they watch him more than he realizes.

Some men fear that a friendly relationship with their children will reduce the respect and honor that they receive. As a result, these fearful men keep a cool, distant relationship with their children. They treat their children like a boss treats employees. The only relationship these fathers have with their children is through rebukes or a rod of discipline. Men like this are afraid to smile and laugh with their children. They do not hold their children on their laps and tell them stories. They fear to play games with them. This is very sad.

Q 3 *Why do some fathers keep a cold, distant relationship with their children?*

Counselors report that most children who rebel come from homes where the father is cold and harsh. A loving, friendly father has very few discipline problems with his children. Often a word of correction is all he needs to give, because the children respect him greatly. Jesus is the best example for all men. He was a strong man who confronted sin and hypocrisy with great courage. Yet children loved to be with Him. He talked with them, held them, and loved them. Still, we find no record in the Bible of a child who did not respect Jesus. We fathers can learn much from Jesus![2] The closer you get to a good man, the more you respect him.

Q 4 *What does the example of Jesus teach us about relating to children?*

Mothers and fathers are the main teachers of children. And they teach most things to their children by example.

Example of personal faith. Before instructing families to teach their children, Moses told the adults, [5]*"Love the* LORD *your God with all your heart and with all your soul and with all your strength.* [6]*These commandments that I give you today are to be upon your hearts"* (Deut. 6:5-6). Children learn by *watching* more than by words. Words without a good example cause children to stumble—and discourage them from following Jesus. Parents must live a life of faith to encourage faith in their children.

167

Q 5 *What is the natural result of a godly marriage?*

Example in marriage. The Bible says that godly children are the result of faithfulness in marriage.

> [14]*The* LORD *is acting as the witness between you and the wife of your youth, because you have broken faith with her, though she is your partner, the wife of your marriage covenant.* [15]*Has not the* LORD *made them one? In flesh and spirit they are his. And why one?* **Because he was seeking godly offspring.** *So guard yourself in your spirit, and do not break faith with the wife of your youth* (Mal. 2:14-15).

God allows divorce for biblical reasons, but it always hurts children. Children often reject a faith that does not bring love to their families. When a husband and wife are faithful to God and each other, the home is filled with love and joy. The natural result is for children to follow in the footsteps of their parents.

Q 6 *Give an example of how children imitate their parents.*

One day, a 3-year-old son followed his dad wherever he went. This made it difficult for him to do his work. The boy was following so closely that sometimes when his dad stopped he bumped into him. His dad encouraged him to go play, but he would just smile and say, "That is all right, Daddy. I want to be here with you." The son continued to follow him, but after the fifth bump, his patience was gone. "Why are you following me constantly?" his dad asked. His little son replied, "My Sunday school teacher told me to walk in the footsteps of Jesus. Since I cannot see Him, I am walking in yours!"[3]

The example of parents is the most powerful influence in the life of a child. A parent should seek to be able to say to children, *"Follow my example, as I follow the example of Christ"* (1 Cor. 11:1).

Figure 10.2 "Dad, I want to grow up to be just like you!"

B. The teaching of parents helps children grow spiritually.

Q 7 *Explain the parable of the 2 fruit trees.*

Consider a parable of two fruit trees. One tree grew without a plan. A man walked in the forest, eating a mango, and threw the seed to the ground. After a few months, a mango tree began to grow. Poor soil, little sunlight, and wild vines prevented the tree from producing good fruit. In contrast, a man planted a mango tree where he lived. He fertilized and watered the plant. As it grew, he pruned certain branches. He guided the growth of the plant until one day it produced good fruit, shade for the house, and beauty to look at.

One man had a vision of what the mature tree would be. This helped him guide the way it grew. In a similar way, parents should have a godly vision of what they want each child to become. Then they should have a plan to fulfill the vision. Let us look at some ways parents should plan to help their children grow spiritually.

Figure 10.3 Use art to teach children about God.

Steps that parents should take to teach their children:[4]

- Dedicate your children to God early in their life (1 Sam. 1:24-28; Luke 2:22).
- Teach your children to love the Lord and to turn away from sin. Help them understand the results of sin in this life and in final judgment. Emphasize God's love and care with small children.
- Nurture your children so they will grow up loving God (Eph. 6:4). Every day is full of chances to teach God's ways. *"Talk about them* [God's ways] *when you sit at home and when you walk along the road, when you lie down and when you get up"* (Deut. 6:7). And answer their questions. *"When your son asks you, 'What is the meaning of the...laws* [of] *the Lord ...?' tell him...."* (Read Deut. 6:20-25).
- Make learning about God fun by using Bible storybooks with pictures. Teach your children happy songs about God and biblical truths. Put biblical pictures on the walls and hang up written Bible verses (Deut. 6:8-9).
- Teach your children to obey you. Show them you are worthy of respect and obedience. This prepares them to respect and obey God (Heb. 12:7-11).
- Protect your children from ungodly influences and friends with poor character. Teach them to walk with God in a world that rejects Him (Prov. 13:20; 28:7; 1 John 2:15-17).
- Help your children understand that God always knows what they do, think, and say (Ps. 139:1-12).
- Lead your children to Christ at an early age and encourage them to be baptized in water (Matt. 19:14) (See Figure 10.5).
- Establish your children in a church that teaches and obeys God's Word.
- Encourage your children to be witnesses for Jesus Christ and to work for God. Be an example of this, and include them in some of your own service to God. Help them understand that they are not of this world but belong to God's kingdom (2 Cor. 6:14–7:1; Phil. 3:20; Col. 3:1-3; Heb. 11:13-16; James 4:4).
- Encourage your children to be baptized in the Holy Spirit (Acts 1:4-5, 8; 2:4, 39).
- Teach your children that God created them, loves them, and has a purpose for their life (Luke 1:13-17; Rom. 8:30; 1 Pet. 1:3-9). Help them discover the spiritual gifts that God has given them (Rom. 12:3-8; 1 Cor. 12; Eph. 4:11-13).
- Encourage your children to read the Bible every day (Dt. 4:9; 6:5-7; 1 Tim. 4:6; 2 Tim. 3:15) and pray throughout the day (Acts 6:4; Rom. 12:12; Eph. 6:18; James 5:16).
- Help your children understand that it is normal for sinners to persecute the righteous (Matt. 5:10-12; 2 Tim. 3:12).
- Pray for your children every day (John 17:1-26; Eph. 6:18; James 5:16-18).
- Never be a stumbling block by your actions and attitudes. Rather, be an example as Paul was to his spiritual children (Phil. 4:9).
- Encourage good character in your children. Second Peter 1:5-9 lists eight godly qualities that the Lord desires for our children and us. The list is followed with a great promise. [10] *"For if you do these things, you will never fall, [11] and you will receive a rich welcome into the eternal kingdom of our Lord and Savior Jesus Christ"* (2 Pet. 1:10-11). We can be certain our children have God's favor if we help them develop these eight qualities.

> 1. **Faith**—trust in God
> 2. **Goodness**—doing what is right
> 3. **Knowledge**—learning about God and His ways
> 4. **Self-control**—allowing the Spirit to rule fleshly desires
> 5. **Perseverance**—enduring and finishing the job
> 6. **Godliness**—being like God
> 7. **Brotherly kindness**—being thoughtful of others
> 8. **Love**—thinking of others (Read 1 Cor. 13:4-8.)

Figure 10.4   Parents should teach their children to bear the fruit of good character.

Q 8 *Which of the steps for teaching children do you think are the most important?*

Q 9 *How can parents make learning fun?*

Q 10 *In your culture, in which areas do parents need to improve the most? Discuss this.*

Q 11 *What are the 8 qualities of character in 2 Peter 1:5-9?*

Q 12 *What are the keys to having the fruit of good character?*

- Teach children to depend on and cooperate with the Holy Spirit to produce the fruit of good character in their life.

  ²²But the fruit of the Spirit is love, joy, peace, patience, kindness, goodness, faithfulness, ²³gentleness and self-control. Against such things there is no law. ²⁴Those who belong to Christ Jesus have crucified the sinful nature with its passions and desires. ²⁵Since we live by the Spirit, let us keep in step with the Spirit (Gal. 5:22-25).

> Often, parents are able to lead their own children to Christ. As parents, we should be sensitive to the Holy Spirit. We should never push our children into spiritual things. But we should always be alert to discern when a child's heart is open to God. Here are some signs that show a child is ready to receive Christ, or grow in grace:
> - When a child feels a need to have his *own* relationship with the Lord.
> - When a child doubts that he will go to heaven.
> - When a child feels guilty about doing something he knows is wrong.
> - When a child is sorry for an action, but fears he will do it again.
> - When a child asks spiritual questions or shows concern about a relationship with the Lord.

Figure 10.5 Watch for signs that show your child is ready to develop a personal relationship with God.[5]

Remember that many children meet Jesus in their own homes. And remember that children should learn much more about God and the Bible at home than during the few hours they are at church.

Missionaries Ken and Trudy Moeckl recall with delight the times their two children received Christ at home. Heidi was 8 years old. The family was singing "He ransomed me." Suddenly, Heidi said, "I want that to happen to me. Please pray with me!" So Ken and Trudy took a few minutes to explain the gospel in simple terms. They prayed together, and then they encouraged Heidi to pray in her own words. And with that simple prayer of a child, Jesus came into her heart and life. Likewise, their daughter Heather was listening to a Bible story in their home. As she heard the story, God opened her heart. She realized that she needed to have Jesus as her Savior. So her parents led her to Christ. What a joy and a wonderful memory![6]

Consider the following parable that describes three ways parents taught their child.

First Parent. "I took a little child's hand in mine. He and I were to walk together for a while. I was to lead him to the Father. It was a task that seemed so big to me. Such a responsibility! So I talked to the child only of the Father. I told the child that God becomes very angry when we displease Him. I told the child to be good so God would not be angry. We walked under tall trees, and I warned the child that the Father could send lightning and thunder to destroy the trees. We walked in the sunshine together. I emphasized that God makes the blazing, burning sun. Then, one evening, we met the Father. The child hid behind me. He was afraid to take the Father's hand. I was between the child and the Father. I wondered. Had I been too serious?"

Second Parent. "I took a little child's hand in mine. I was to lead him to the Father. I felt the burden of so many things to teach him. So we did not waste any time. We hurried from place to place. We compared the leaves of different trees. Quickly we moved on to examine a bird's nest. The child began to ask questions about the nest. But I hurried him on to catch a butterfly. Sometimes the child became tired and fell asleep. But I woke him up so he would not miss a lesson. We spoke of the Father often and quickly. I told the child all the stories he ought to know. But so many times things interrupted us. Once the wind blew and I had to stop a story to explain the wind. In the middle of another story the child asked a question about a river. So I explained as much about the river as I could. Then one evening we met the Father. The child only glanced at Him, and his thoughts wandered in several other directions. The Father stretched out His hand toward the child. But the child was not interested enough to take it. Instead, the child lay down to rest. I wondered. Had I tried to teach him too many things?"

Third Parent. "I took a little child's hand in mine. I was to lead him to the Father. My heart rejoiced for this privilege. We walked slowly. I took short steps to match those of the child. We talked about the things the child noticed. Sometimes we picked the Father's flowers. We touched their soft petals and loved their bright colors. Sometimes we watched one of Father's birds build its nest. We saw the eggs that were laid. Later, we marveled at the way the bird cared for its young. Often we told stories of the Father. I told them to the child, and the child told them again to me. We told them, the child and I, over and over again. Sometimes we stopped to rest, leaning against one of Father's tall trees. We stood in silence, feeling His cool wind blow softly on our faces. Then one evening we met the Father. The child's eyes shone with joy. Eagerly, he looked with love and trust into the Father's face. He put his hand into the Father's hand. For the moment, I was forgotten, but content."[7]

Parents, do not let your children grow spiritually like a fruit tree in the forest. At home, guide them to fulfill the vision God has for each one.

C. Daily family devotions help children grow spiritually.[8]

Every family should have a time of daily *devotions together in the home. This is a time when the family comes together to read the Bible, pray, sing, and worship. This short time each day is a good habit that strengthens the family spiritually. The family that prays together stays together.

Family devotions link faith to every day—not just church services. Daily devotions remind the family that every day is lived in the presence of God. These few minutes each day help the family to stay close, forgive each other, and pray for each other. Let us look at some keys to having family devotions.

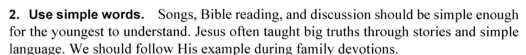
Figure 10.6   Every family should take time to have devotions together.

1. Select a good time. The habit of family devotions is easier at the same time each day. Together, parents and children can agree on the best time. Many families meet after the evening meal. Others come together before bedtime. The length of devotions should be brief, especially for small children in the family. But it should be consistent—about the same time each day.

Q 13 *What time do you think is best for family devotions? Explain.*

2. Use simple words.   Songs, Bible reading, and discussion should be simple enough for the youngest to understand. Jesus often taught big truths through stories and simple language. We should follow His example during family devotions.

3. Aim at balance in teachings, songs, prayer, and praise.   Serve a balanced spiritual diet. For example, balance teachings on mercy with teachings on judgment. An excellent way to do this is to study through an entire book of the Bible over a period of time. Then you will have many topics to discuss. Likewise, aim at balance in other areas. For example, sing old songs and new songs; read prayers in the Bible, and pray prayers from the heart. Teach children how to praise God. For example, one evening, teach them to praise Him as Creator. Another evening, teach them to praise Him because He loves

Q 14 *What causes family devotions to be balanced?*

us, is holy, or merciful. Balance your time on each part of the devotions—teaching, singing, praying, and praising.

Q 15 *How can children do something in family devotions?*

4. Include everyone. Children like to have a part. Give them something to do. They like acting out stories from the Bible. And do not forget that even very young children can pray. Some can lead in a song. You can include older children by changing leaders of the family devotions from time to time—but always under the leadership of the parents. Parents must be the examples of love for God and others. Take time to plan *before* the family sits down for devotions.

5. Show respect for God. The time of family devotions is relaxed. It does not require the same behavior as church. All members should be free to act their age level. Small children may need to move about some. But, parents should always encourage respect for God.

6. Avoid negative experiences. Family devotions is a time to focus on God. This is not the time to discuss regular family matters. It is not the time to settle quarrels or complaints. If this begins to occur, family members become confused about the purpose of family devotions, and children become discouraged. There can be other times to discuss family matters. But devotions must remain a positive time—where all face the heavenly Father and enjoy the presence of God.

Conclusion

The Bible emphasizes the importance of helping children grow in favor with God. Parents help children grow spiritually by being good examples, teaching about God, and having daily family devotions.

Help Your Children Grow in Favor With Men—Socially

Goal A: *Comment on the relationship between security and social growth.*
Goal B: *Explain 3 different ways that parents can show love to their children.*
Goal C: *Summarize how parents can help a child feel accepted, and have self-esteem.*
Goal D: *Analyze the roles of manners, attitudes, and skills in relating to others.*

Setting

Q 16 *Is it wrong to seek favor with men? Explain.*

Jesus grew in favor with men. This is different than living <u>only</u> to please others. Those who live only to please others conform to what others think they should be. But people have little respect for those who live <u>only</u> to please others. Jesus rebuked those who sought favor with men, <u>and not</u> favor with God. *"How can you believe if you accept praise from one another, yet make no effort to obtain the praise that comes from the only God?"* (John 5:44). So remember that Jesus grew in favor with God <u>and</u> man (Luke 2:52).

Q 17 *What are 3 inner strengths that Jesus showed we should have?*

True favor with men comes to those who have **inner strengths**.
- They have a strong knowledge of their values and purpose.
- They have a strong ability to understand others.
- They have a strong concern for others.

Jesus showed these three inner strengths by the time He was 12 years old. He knew His values and calling. He understood the questions and comments of others in the temple. And He was willing to submit to His parents (Luke 2:41-52). We should seek to help our children develop these inner strengths.

Q 18 *What causes people to seek the approval of the crowd or the world?*

Relating well to others depends on a child's emotional health. Those who seek to please <u>only</u> people have unmet, unfulfilled emotional needs. Perhaps these weak people were not loved, accepted, or safe as a child. Our families should meet our basic emotional needs while we are young. If these needs are not met, a person searches for others to satisfy those needs. This search for emotional support affects our relationship with people. But a person with good emotional health relates well to others.

Case Study: Omollo was 15 years old. Some of the other boys at the *boarding school invited him to a party. They said there would be fun, food, alcohol, and drugs for everyone. Also, several popular girls were coming. Omollo smiled. He said thank you for the invitation, but that he did not use alcohol or drugs. He explained that he and several of his friends were followers of Jesus Christ.

Q 19 *What kind of family do you think Omollo came from?*

Let us look at five ways children develop inner strengths and mature socially.

A. To grow socially, children must feel safe and secure.

To relate well to people, a child must learn to trust. Children learn to trust when their parents help them feel secure. Here are some things that parents must do to help their children feel secure and safe.

- Respond quickly when an infant cries.
- Pay attention when your child says he or she is afraid.
- Protect your children from physical, sexual, verbal, and emotional abuse.
- Control your emotions. An angry adult terrifies children.
- Be consistent. Children feel safe within routine.
- Be present in the life of your children.
- Keep your promises.
- Do not place adult burdens on young children.
- Teach your children that God is always present.

Q 20 *Explain: A child will not trust others if he does not feel safe at home.*

Q 21 *How can parents help children feel safe and secure?*

A child who feels secure will learn to trust his parents. Then, he will be able to enter other relationships with trust instead of doubt. The ability to trust good people helps children grow socially.

B. To grow socially, children must feel loved.

Most parents love their children. But some parents use their children to satisfy their own needs and dreams. Other parents feel angry towards their children, or do not care about them. Children who **feel** unloved by their parents are deeply wounded socially.

Most parents love their children. But that is not enough. Each child must **know** that his parents love him. Small children do not recognize love by the sacrifices parents make to provide for them. While still young, children feel loved by the way their parents *relate* to them. It is the parents' task to show love in ways that children understand. In other words, parents must speak a language that children understand. The emotional and social health of your children depends on **knowing** they are loved. There are three ways to assure your children that you love them.

Q 22 *How do children know they are loved by their parents?*

Q 23 *Which of these do you do well?*

Parents show love through underline{touching}. The gentle touch of a father or mother is like food to the emotions of a child. This is not sexual touching; it is the godly, natural love of a parent. This touching includes carrying, holding, rocking, hugging, kissing on the cheek or forehead, patting on the back, rubbing the feet or back, holding hands while walking, and playful wrestling. All of these kinds of touching say, "I love you, my dear child." The way you touch your child may change as the child grows. But never stop touching your child. A touch of love is something we need throughout our life. Parents who were not touched as children may feel strange or awkward about touching their children. But all can learn to show love through touching. Refusing to touch your child is like refusing to give them food.

Q 24 *Did your parents show their love through touching you? Explain.*

Q 25 *What are some good ways for a parent to touch a child?*

Mothers tend to touch more and show more love than fathers. But fathers must also show their love by touching their sons and daughters in the right ways. A father's gentle touch helps children grow socially.

Q 26 *Explain how to show a child love through speaking words of praise.*

Q 27 *What will happen if you tell your child he is lazy, stubborn, and rebellious?*

Q 28 *Which words do children need to hear often?*

Parents show love through <u>telling</u>—speaking kind words. We show love to our children by the way we talk to them daily. The way we talk can affirm and build up children instead of tearing them down. Parents must never say negative things to their children, discourage them, or ridicule them. Why? Because children believe what you tell them! If you tell a child he is slow, dumb, bad, and ugly, the child will believe you and act that way. Instead, parents can bring out the best in their children through kind words of encouragement. Praise children when they do something well. Praise them for the way they smile. Tell them they are beautiful. Teach a child to say please and thank you. And then, when he uses these good manners, praise him for being polite. Teach a child to dry a dish, and then praise the child for helping. Brag on a child who does well in school, or who gets along well with other children. Teach a child to share—by sharing with him, or letting him see you share. Then, when the child shares, praise him for being generous. <u>Always underline the positive</u>—emphasize the good things that you like in a child. And if the child falls or gets hurt, speak kind words of love to the child. Then, the child will learn to be kind, as you are kind.

Our children need to feel that it is okay to take risks in life and even fail at times. If a child fails at a task, praise the child for trying and say, "Each failure is a step up toward success." Children discover their talents and interests when they try new things. When they fail, encourage them and help them try again. By the way we talk to them, they know we love them when they succeed *and* when they fail. Love always listens and responds with comfort and hope. And remember that the simple words, "I love you," are words children need to hear often.

Believe in your children, and they will learn to believe in themselves. Jacob named one of his sons *Joseph*—which means "fruitful." He gave him a special coat to show his love. The love Jacob showed to Joseph through kind words and deeds helped Joseph grow up to be a social blessing to others. His father loved Joseph so much, that it helped him forgive the way others treated him.

Q 29 *Complete Figure 10.6 on the word pictures Jacob used (Gen. 49:8-27).*

Use word pictures to say kind things to your child. Pray and ask God to give you these word pictures about each child. Read Genesis 49:8-27. Notice all of the kind, encouraging things Jacob said about his children. Jacob encouraged most of his children with word pictures.

Child of Jacob	Word pictures Jacob told his children
Judah	
Zebulun	
Issachar	
Naphtali	
Joseph	

Figure 10.7 Jacob used word pictures to encourage his children (Gen. 49:8-27).

One mother prayed several hours each day for her son. God showed her a puzzle that was missing one piece in the middle of the picture. Then the Lord said that her son was the missing piece—formed to connect with all the pieces around it. She shared this insight with her son. He remembered this all of his life. His mother's kind words encouraged him to fulfill God's plan for his life in society.

Parents show love through <u>time</u>—paying attention to a child. Psalm 145:18 says, *"The LORD is near to all who call on him, to all who call on him in truth."* God listens to us and desires to spend time with us. Let us follow His example by paying attention to our children.

A child may use **words** to ask for attention:
- "Can you play with me?"
- "May I go with you?"
- "Can you help me?"
- "Will you tell me a story?"

A child may use **actions** to ask for attention:
- He may follow you around the house.
- He may try to help you.
- He may climb on your lap.
- He may excel at something that is important to you.

Q 30 *What are some ways children ask for time and attention?*

Paying attention to a child sends a loud, clear, wonderful message to a child. Your attention says, "I LOVE YOU!" In contrast, when a parent continually refuses to pay attention, a child hears the message, "You are not important, and I don't care about you." So be careful what message you are sending your child.

Q 31 *What message does paying attention send to your child?*

If you ignore your child, he may do bad things to get your attention. Children would rather have attention for bad things than have no attention at all. Quarrels with other children or trouble at school may be a sign that a child feels ignored.

Q 32 *Why do some children disobey parents or teachers?*

A minister had a burden from God to help drug addicts. He spent so many hours in this ministry that he neglected his own sons. Each night the boys would ask when their father was coming home. Most nights, they were already asleep when he arrived. As the years passed, they quit asking. The family and people of the church were shocked when one of the minister's sons began using drugs. It just did not make sense. Surely the young man knew what a terrible thing it was to use drugs. It was sad, but the young man found a way to get his father's full attention.

We need to be alert to respond to our children's requests for attention. But a child should not always need to ask for a little of father's time or mother's time. What a delight it is for a child when a parent says, "Grab your ball and let's play awhile." Or, "You had better run—I'm going to tickle you!" Or, "Teach me that new game you like so much." Children understand that they are loved when parents volunteer to give them time and attention. Parents say, "I love you!" through *touching*, *telling* kind words, and taking *time* to be with children.

There are at least two other ways that parents also show love. Some show love through kind deeds, even sacrificing. But as we noted earlier, children may not always recognize that the work fathers and mothers do for the family is a form of love. Likewise, parents show love through giving

Figure 10.8 Show your child you enjoy being with him.

gifts. For example, Jacob gave Joseph a special coat. Our heavenly Father loved us so much that He gave His Only Son to die for us (John 3:16).

C. To grow socially, children must feel accepted.

Each child is different from others in appearance, talents, and personality. Parents should accept each child without trying to force him or her to be like someone else. As parents, we should accept all of our children equally. Each one is a gift from God. Whether they are born to us, part of a stepfamily, adopted, or come to us through foster care, children are a gift from God. Your goal should be for each child to fulfill God's

176 *Marriage & Family*

Q 33 What are some ways that parents cause a child to feel rejected?

plan. Socially, a child grows stronger when accepted. Acceptance helps children face relationships with confidence, instead of fear of rejection. We communicate acceptance to a child through touching, words of praise, and paying attention.

It is possible to show your child both love *and* rejection.[9] Love is personal—between a parent and child. But acceptance may deal with the child in relation to others. For example, maybe something about your child's appearance embarrasses you. So you explain this weakness to others. Children see and hear these things. They begin to understand that although you love them, you wish they were different.

None of us is perfect. Our heavenly Father has adopted us as His children. We have received amazing grace. Surely, we can pass it on to children. The Scripture says, *"Accept one another, then, just as Christ accepted you"* (Rom. 15:7). It is good to change things to become better. But many times, a child cannot change his height, nose, teeth, intelligence, or personality. So accept each child the way God has created him. Then the child will grow to have the social confidence he needs.

Q 34 What is the difference between pride and healthy self-worth?

D. To grow socially, children must have self-worth and self-esteem—feel respected by self and others.

The Bible warns against pride; it is a deadly sin. A proud person does not relate well socially. Scripture teaches us: *"Do not think of yourself more highly than you ought, but rather think of yourself with sober judgment, in accordance with the measure of faith God has given you"* (Rom. 12:3).

A wise person avoids two errors about himself—he does not think of himself too highly or too lowly. A person who is healthy socially does not feel superior or inferior. He knows his true height—he does not think of himself as taller or shorter than he is. How a person feels about himself affects how he relates to others (See Figure 10.8).

Q 35 Describe the actions of a person with low self-esteem.

Q 36 How does a person with a healthy self-worth act?

A Person With a Healthy Self-Worth	A Person With a Low Self-Worth
Acts independently	Is easy to influence
Assumes responsibility	Blames others for his own faults
Attempts new tasks and challenges	Avoids trying new things
Sees value in his work	Looks down on his own talents and abilities
Tolerates frustration	Is unable to tolerate frustration
Offers help to others	Feels unwanted and unloved
Handles positive and negative emotions	Feels, or pretends to feel, like he does not care

Figure 10.9   A person's self-worth affects his actions and relations.[10]

How can we help our children feel valuable—develop a healthy self-worth?[11] A child's view of himself is influenced in two ways: by those in the home and those outside of it.

We must be realistic. Parents can love, accept, and affirm their children. But outside of the family, people can be cruel. In the world, our children may meet emotional pain, rejection, and hateful actions. But parents are not powerless. Let us look at five principles for parents to help their children feel good about themselves.

Q 37 List 5 ways to build a child's self-worth.

Q 38 What should a parent do about things a child cannot change?

1. Minimize—talk little about—things your child cannot change. If my child is ugly, we will not emphasize physical beauty in our home. If my child is clumsy, we will not emphasize athletics. If my child is a slow learner, we will not praise quick students in our home. Everyone can succeed at important things in life. Discover the things your children can do well and rejoice in each child. Do not insist that all the children do well in the same things. Never compare children with each other. Do not underline or shine a light on weaknesses that your child cannot change.

2. **Help your child improve as much as possible.** Society may value areas in which your child is weak. People may value things your child does not have, such as beauty, intelligence, athletic ability, good speaking, and good clothes. Many values of the world are not godly. Still, since we live in the world, we must try to relate well to people. Help your child change the things he can change to relate well to others. For example, if his feet turn in, try to have them corrected. If his clothes are too old, seek to get him clothes that are more in style. If he is struggling in studies, try to find a tutor. If he stutters, seek a speech teacher. Teach him to be clean, care for his teeth, and comb his hair. As you are able, give your child the best chance to succeed and relate well to others. Surround him with stories of other people who have overcome weaknesses. Remind your child of his great value to God by the price God paid for him. The value of something is always determined by the price someone will pay for it. God paid a great price to redeem each of us. He gave His only Son! This shows that each of us has great value!

Q 39 Should a child ignore his weakest areas? Explain.

3. **Maximize—talk much about—ways your child can have strengths to succeed.** Help your child *compensate—balance and make up for weak areas. We compensate for a weakness by using a strength. If the left arm is weak, but the right arm is strong, the right arm can compensate for the left. Parents can help a child find his strengths and use them. Then, when he is criticized or rejected because of a weakness, the child can say, "Well, I may not be a good athlete, but I can sing well!" A strength may be a skill, such as singing, cooking, sewing, encouraging, teaching, organizing, guarding, talking, selling, building, fixing, or doing math. A child who may not be athletic—but one who knows all the rules of a sport—may find a place with a team. Help your child discover and develop his strengths. As a child recognizes his strengths, he feels good about himself. Likewise, others value a person who has strengths, such as knowledge and work skills. Underline the strengths of your child. Emphasize the best things about him.

Q 40 Give an example of how a parent can emphasize a child's strengths.

4. **Emphasize good values that your child can have.** Teach your children to value things like hard work, honesty, good character, and good attitudes. These values can encourage all family members, without focusing on the weaknesses they cannot change. Teach a child to feel good about himself because he has good character.

Q 41 How does praising good values in a child affect his or her self-esteem?

A pastor called the young people to help clean the church property. Soon, the pastor saw that his main job for the day would be to get the young people to work. Most were distracted and did a poor job. But three young people were different. They worked hard, well, and cheerfully. The pastor saw the difference in these young people and began to train them for leadership.

5. **Teach your child to do things for himself.** Parents can do too much for their children. They do not want them to face failure, danger, or unkindness. They want life to be easy. But too much protection and care weakens our children and causes them to think badly of themselves. So teach your child to do things for himself.

Q 42 What happens to self-worth as children do things for themselves? Explain.

All of the family took care of the youngest child. When she wore her shoes, there was someone to tie them for her. Each time she tried to do it herself, a family member did it for her. One day at school, her shoe came untied. She asked the teacher for help, and some children began to tease her. She was startled to learn that all the other children could tie their shoes. "Is something wrong with me?" she began to ask herself.

Self-worth grows when children do things for themselves. They need to learn to take care of themselves and to solve their own problems. The parents should always be ready to advise and assist when needed. But to develop self-worth, parents must insist that children do the things that they are able to do for themselves, such as cooking, cleaning, working to make money, and studying. As the child grows, the parents must give him more responsibility for his own life and decisions. Allow the child to learn, though he will make a few mistakes. Self-worth will grow as ability grows. As our children succeed at doing things, they feel confident, valuable, and good about themselves. This helps them relate to others in healthy ways and grow in favor with men.

6. Teach your child social skills. A young man went to apply for a job. He was able to do the work and had good character. But he went to the interview dressed in clothes he would wear to a party. And he talked to the businessman as if he were a friend. So he did not get the job. His skills and character were not enough. He needed to present himself in ways that fit the business world.

At home, parents must teach their children the social skills needed for good relationships. Let us look at three areas.

Q 43 *List 3 areas of social skills needed to relate to others.*

Manners. Each child must learn rules of courtesy. For example, in your culture, teach your child whether it is polite to look at the eyes of an adult. Should a child stand when an adult walks into the room? Should a child say "please" and "thank you"? Parents must teach children the good manners of their culture if they are going to live wisely. People do not want to be near children who are rude. But when children are polite, they will be blessed by the presence of adults and other children.

Q 44 *What is the best way to teach children manners, good attitudes, and personal skills? Explain.*

> THE BEST WAY TO TEACH CHILDREN THESE SOCIAL RULES AND MANNERS IS THROUGH THE FAMILY.

The best way to teach children these social rules and manners is through the family. Insist that each family member treat the others with respect and courtesy. Teach boys to never hit a girl. Be a good example of good attitudes and good communication for your children. In the home, they can learn that relationships are important. They can learn that people talk kindly to solve problems. And they can see that forgiving others and asking forgiveness is part of a wise life.

Q 45 *How does a child feel about himself when he relates poorly to others?*

Attitudes. Each child should develop social attitudes. Teach your child to greet others with a smile. Teach him to be hospitable. Through your example, teach children to pay attention when someone speaks. Teach them to ask questions about the interests of others. They must learn to value and respect the thoughts of others. Show children how to respond in a polite way when they do not agree with another person. Teach your children the good attitude of waiting—of being patient. Patience is an attitude they will need often, before and after marriage. Teach them the value of cooperation and responsibility in the home and the community.

Another important attitude is the <u>heart of a servant</u>. Young children think they should be the center of attention. When they cry, loving parents help them. This is good. But children should not remain infants in their attitudes. We must guide our children to care about the needs of others in the same way they care about their own needs. Children can learn to serve tea or coffee to visitors. They can learn to serve the family by cleaning, cooking, and working. The examples of parents can teach children to serve. And the Holy Spirit can help them with all of their attitudes. Selfish living separates people. But those who are willing to serve relate well to others.

Skills. Each child should learn personal skills. Two important skills are communicating and managing emotions during conflict. Chapter 4 has teaching about these skills for adults. But children can also learn these skills as they grow. Your child can learn anything that you have learned, if you take time to teach him.

We should help our children grow in favor with men as Jesus grew socially. We need to help them develop inner strength that keeps them from being "men-pleasers." Children relate well socially when they feel secure, loved, accepted, and valuable. Parents should teach children right manners, attitudes, and social skills. Jesus grew in favor with men, and so can our children.

Children learn to relate to God and others by watching the examples of their parents, and through *discipline—which is our next lesson.

Discipline Your Children, So They Will Grow in Favor With God and Men
Goal A: *Explain 10 of the 15 principles on discipline.*
Goal B: *Summarize four types of discipline.*

In this lesson we emphasize the word *discipline,* **not** punishment. (The King James Version often uses the words *chasten* or *chastise,* which mean "to instruct.") We do this, because in the New Testament, the emphasis for believers is on words like *disciple* and *discipline.* In contrast, the words *punish* and *punishment*—in the New Testament—are usually related to God's enemies. The New Testament relates *discipline* to instruction and training; *punishment* tends to relate to justice for those who refuse to repent.

Q 46 In the New Testament, how do the words "discipline" and "punishment" differ?

The purpose of *discipline* is to bring blessings such as *growth.* Discipline focuses on the future. We discipline our children to correct, train, improve, and guide them. We discipline because we want our children to succeed as godly adults.

Q 47 What is the purpose of discipline? Explain.

A. 15 guidelines or principles on discipline[12]

1. Discipline because of love. God is our example. We should discipline our children as our heavenly Father disciplines us. God says:

Q 48 How many times does Hebrews 12:5-11 refer to discipline?

⁵*"My son, do not make light of the Lord's **discipline**, and do not lose heart when he rebukes you,* ⁶*because the Lord **disciplines** those he loves, and he punishes everyone he accepts as a son."* ⁷*Endure hardship as **discipline**; God is treating you as sons. For what son is not **disciplined** by his father?* ⁸*If you are not **disciplined** (and everyone undergoes **discipline**), then you are illegitimate children and not true sons.* ⁹*Moreover, we have all had human fathers who **disciplined** us and we respected them for it. How much more should we submit to the Father of our spirits and live!* ¹⁰*Our fathers **disciplined** us for a little while as they thought best; but God **disciplines** us for our good, that we may share in his holiness.* ¹¹*No **discipline** seems pleasant at the time, but painful. Later on, however, it produces a harvest of righteousness and peace for those who have been trained by it* (Heb. 12:5-11).

Figure 10.10 Discipline in love.

God loves us and disciplines us for our good. Our heavenly Father—and earthly fathers—know that discipline brings blessings in the future. God is gracious, gentle, merciful, forgiving, and kind as He disciplines. We are to discipline our children with the same love that our heavenly Father shows us.

Q 49 Does God discipline His children in anger? Explain.

The Scripture tells us, *"The Lord disciplines those **he loves**"* (Heb. 12:6). Discipline is a sign of love. If we do not correct our children's wild and ungodly behavior, it shows

Q 50 *How does discipline save children?*

Q 51 *How does discipline add security to a child?*

Q 52 *Consistent discipline gets rid of _____ _____ in children.*

that we do not love them enough. If you love your children, discipline them when they know they do wrong.

2. Discipline to save your children. Proverbs 19:18 says, *"Discipline your son, for in that* [in discipline] *there is hope; do not be a willing party to his death."* Lack of discipline can lead to physical and spiritual death. Destruction will find the child who refuses to obey. An undisciplined child may choose crime and violence—choices that lead to destruction. The purpose of the Law was to lead us to salvation. *"The law was put in charge to lead us to Christ that we might be justified by faith"* (Gal. 3:24). Likewise, discipline guides children away from destruction to safety.

3. Discipline to give children security. Young parents may be surprised to learn that their children desire their authority over them. Children are confused and frightened when an adult is not over them. Rules and guidelines enable a child to have order in his world. Otherwise, if a child does not learn right and wrong, he does not know when to stop and when to move ahead. Children without discipline are like a house with no walls.

Still, children may express some rebellion. And they may want freedom before they are ready for it. But in their hearts, children desire their parents—especially their fathers—to be strong enough to enforce limits with love. Children do well when there is proper discipline. They feel secure and at peace when they know their parents protect them with boundaries that are fair and right. Children feel secure and safe when they know someone bigger than them is in control of their life. This security at an early age gives children confidence to accept more freedom as they mature and the boundaries decrease.

4. Discipline (correct) consistently. In matters of discipline, parents must be consistent—regular, dependable, unchanging, steadfast, the same. For example, if you discipline a child for stealing on Monday, then you must discipline the child if he steals on Tuesday. Imagine the confusion we would have if the laws changed from day to day! Yet, this is how some children must live. One Sunday they must go to church. The next Sunday it does not matter. One month they must use good manners. The next month the parents do not care about good manners.

What if the laws were the same each day, but the police ignored an offense one day and punished it the next? Most children (and adults) decide if a rule is real by how it is enforced. Many times, children ignore rules because they think the parents do not mean what they say.

For example, a mother told her two small children—David and Daniel—to share their candy with the visitors. David shared, but Daniel kept all his candy for himself. The mother ignored the selfish actions of Daniel. What do you think David, who shared, will do the next time his mother tells him to share?

A consistent schedule also helps children learn to practice self-discipline (self-control). Practice builds good habits. Chores, study, prayer, brushing teeth, and regular rest are examples of good habits. Teaching and learning these habits is easier when each one has its own time during the day. Children and parents will remember and practice good habits more easily when the family has a regular schedule.

Consistent discipline helps children know how to please their parents. Firm, steadfast rules and consistent discipline eliminate confusion. And a consistent schedule makes self-discipline easier. Good discipline must be consistent.

5. Discipline to teach respect for authority. A child should respect authority in the home and outside of it. In the home, God commands children to honor their parents. This is the only command that God gives directly to children (Exod. 20:12; Eph. 6:1-3).

Children must learn to respect authority—so they can do well at school, at work, at church, and in society. The child who grows up saying, "Nobody tells me what to do!" will fail. There are many times people must obey authority—whether they like it or not.

Every child should learn two things about authority.
- **Disobedience brings pain.** God's Word teaches that bad things happen to those who disobey. For example, read all of the curses for disobedience Moses wrote in Deuteronomy 28:15-68.
- **Obedience brings blessings.** The more we obey God and the principles in His Word, the more He blesses us.

Parents, teach your children to respect authority. Obedience leads to life, but disobedience leads to death.

> [11]*Now what I am commanding you today is not too difficult for you or beyond your reach.* [12]*It is not up in heaven, so that you have to ask, "Who will ascend into heaven to get it and proclaim it to us so we may obey it?"* [13]*Nor is it beyond the sea, so that you have to ask, "Who will cross the sea to get it and proclaim it to us so we may obey it?"* [14]*No, the word is very near you; it is in your mouth and in your heart so you may obey it.* [15]*See, I set before you today life and prosperity, death and destruction.* [16]*For I command you today to love the* LORD *your God, to walk in his ways, and to keep his commands, decrees and laws; then you will live and increase, and the* LORD *your God will bless you in the land you are entering to possess* (Deut. 30:11-16).

Respect for authority is a matter of choosing life or death.

6. Discipline as a team—work together as parents. A father and mother must agree on discipline. Let your children see that you are united as parents—especially about things that affect them. They will love and respect you for it. To work together, parents should agree on the goals and methods of discipline. When disagreements arise between you and your spouse, settle them in private. Do not interfere when your spouse is disciplining a child (unless the child is in danger). When parents disagree about discipline, children use a method called "divide and conquer." So parents must be united about discipline. Otherwise, a child will talk to one parent and contradict the authority of the other parent. Do not let your children divide you. God has joined you together as one flesh, so agree and be united on matters of discipline.

Parents can help each other be fair and balanced. One parent may need the counsel of the other to know if rules are too harsh or too strict. Questions parents can ask each other are:
- Is either of us reacting to our children in anger? (Never discipline a child when you are angry. Take time to cool down first.)
- Is the behavior we expect from our children reasonable?
- Do we show equal love and affection to all of our children?
- Are we good examples to our children?

Parents should be united on matters of discipline. You will do a better job together than either of you would do alone. In matters of discipline, two heads are better than one.

Jacob and Esau hated each other. Jacob, by deceit, robbed Esau. Esau, full of anger, desired to kill Jacob. Jacob fled for his life (Gen. 27). This is a sad story about two brothers. What caused them to be so divided? Their parents sowed the seeds of division. Each parent had a favorite son, and the favor was clear. *"Isaac, who had a taste for wild game, loved Esau, but Rebekah loved Jacob"* (Gen. 25:28). This resulted in division

Q 53 *Why is it so important for children to learn respect for authority?*

Q 54 *What is the bad method of "divide and conquer"? How can parents prevent this?*

Q 55 *What 4 things harm discipline?*

between the parents and the sons. A healthy family needs parents who will be united and work as a team.

7. Discipline calmly.[13] We are not to *spank out of anger. Proverbs 29:11 says, *"A fool gives full vent to his anger, but a wise man keeps himself under control."* If we fully express our anger, we are hurting our children and ourselves. Ephesians 6:4 says, *"Fathers, do not exasperate your children; instead, bring them up in the training and instruction of the Lord."* We can discourage our children by nagging them, pushing them, and frustrating them. This often causes rebellion against parents and against God. There may be one or two times in a lifetime that a parent must delay discipline because of anger. Be calm *before* you discipline.

Q 56 ⬉ *What are 2 rare times that discipline should not follow quickly after rebellion?*

8. Discipline quickly. Do not delay correction, unless you are angry. Children learn better when they receive a quick response. The younger the child, the faster the response should be. Discipline will teach better if it occurs close to the time of the child's action. However, parents do need to be concerned about the social setting. Discipline should rarely occur in public. Most discipline should be in private—even away from brothers and sisters. You want the child to focus on the matter of discipline, not on his embarrassment. But, correct as quickly as it is wise to do.

Correct rebellion *immediately,* whenever it occurs. Parents lose the respect of their children when the parents seem helpless. Rebellion towards either parent must be disciplined—at once! Discipline the child for the *behavior,* while still loving and accepting the child himself. It is good to say, "You did a bad thing." But parents should not say, "You are a bad child!" Correct the behavior, but affirm your love for the good child God has given you.

Q 57 ⬉ *Why should parents overlook little faults, and correct children only once in a while?*

9. Discipline sparingly. This means "not all the time." Colossians 3:21 says, *"Fathers, don't scold your children so much that they become discouraged and quit trying"* (Living Bible). Home should be a place to enjoy, not a prison. Children need healthy amounts of freedom and fun.[14] Overlook small things, and only discipline a child once in a while. Try to say at least ten good things about a child between the times you must correct him. In fact, it is better if you can say 100 good things about a child in between the times you must correct him! Encouragement brings out the best in all of us. When children think of you, it is best if they remember a face that is smiling, not frowning.

Q 58 ⬉ *Explain: Some children need only a word of rebuke, but others need a rod.*

10. Discipline to match the child. No two children are the same. Every child sees the world in his own way. Parents must guide a child according to his personality and needs. A stubborn child needs different methods than a tender child. A shy child needs a different approach than a bold child. Each child should also be disciplined according to his age. Discipline must change and decrease as the child grows. Spanking an older child creates bitterness (See Figure 10.12). Fairness means treating each child according to his age, *temperament, and needs.

Figure 10.11 Match the discipline to the child.

11. Discipline to match the crime. In the Bible, God does not give the same discipline for every sin. As Jesus told Pilate, some sins are greater than others (John 19:11). Stealing a chicken is bad, but it does not deserve the death penalty! Likewise, there are times when it is enough discipline for a parent to shake his head "No" and show a stern face. At other times it is enough discipline for a parent to speak a few words to correct a child. In a few cases, a greater form of discipline may be necessary. So as a parent, do not over-react. You do not need a shovel to remove a fly from your tea.

Q 59 ⬉ *Explain: The discipline should match the crime.*

How to Be an Effective Father or Mother—Part 2 183

12. **Discipline (correct) only if a child chose the wrong, and rejected what he knew was right.**[15] Let children know *exactly* what they should or should not do. Children must understand this *before* being judged guilty of disobedience. Parents should *instruct* a child who does wrong—but did not know it was wrong. For example, a father was shocked to hear his child repeat a bad word he heard at school. But the boy did not know the word was bad, so the dad did not spank him. Rather, the father taught the boy what the word meant, and why he should not use it. Never spank a child for a wrong he does in ignorance or innocence. Wise parents will make sure their rules are clear, reasonable, and fair.

Q 60 *Should a parent spank if a child did not know something was wrong? Explain.*

13. **Discipline (correct) for rebellion, but never for accidents.** Parents should seek to discern why children act the way they do. A child who cries at bedtime may be rebellious, OR he may be afraid of the dark. It is harmful to punish a child for his fear. We should spank for *rebellion,* not childish behavior or accidents—even if these upset us as parents. We might require a child to clean up something he spilled on the floor (a logical result). But we should not punish a child for such a childish mistake. It is foolish to expect a child to think, speak, or act like an adult. One foolish mother spanked her infant—who was only 9 months old—for moving around while she tried to dress him. A foolish father disciplined his boy who was 10 for not working as quickly as his brother who was 18.

Q 61 *Should a parent spank a child for an accident? Explain.*

Do not spank a child who spills his drink, wets his bed, misses a section of the garden when he hoes, or forgets where he puts his hat. These are just childish things. Many things call for grace, not spanking.

14. **Discipline to teach.** After giving discipline to a child, a parent has the duty to assure the child that he is loved, valued, and forgiven for the wrong. Good parents will hold their child, and even pray with him that God will forgive him. These may be the most important few minutes parents will ever spend with their child. Love from the parents—during and after discipline—shows the child that his behavior was rejected, but he is loved.

Q 62 *What should a parent teach at the time of, or after, correction?*

15. **Discipline in a way that is fruitful and helpful.** The test is how children respond to discipline. Consider three questions.
    - **Are my children afraid of me?"** It is normal for children to cry during some discipline. But a child should never fear that the discipline would cause injury or pain that is too great. Parents must remember that they are much bigger and stronger than their tender children. It is better for the discipline to be too light than too heavy. If you err as a parent, err on the side of mercy.
    - **Do my children feel rejected?"** A child will not feel accepted by parents when they criticize and punish him over and over, constantly. Discipline is like salt; a little is enough.
    - **Is the discipline having a good, positive effect on my child?"** If a child's attitudes or actions do not improve over time, discipline has lost its power to help. Instead, it has become a source of rebellion. If discipline is unfair, too harsh, or too often, it can cause a child to become bitter or discouraged. So wise parents must examine their methods of discipline to see which ways work best.

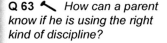
Figure 10.12 After discipline, reassure the child of your love.

Q 63 *How can a parent know if he is using the right kind of discipline?*

184   Marriage & Family

These 15 principles give us basic guidelines for discipline. Now let us look at some methods to discipline.

B. Methods to discipline

Parents and cultures are not perfect. Each parent and culture makes mistakes in discipline. Sometimes we are too soft; other times we are too harsh. Sometimes we neglect what is best for our children, because we **fear** the opinions of others. All parents make mistakes. But parents can learn from each other. We can learn from the failures and successes of other parents. So let us look at four methods that wise parents from all cultures use.

Q 64 How do "natural results" discipline? Give an example.

1. ***Natural results discipline by experience.*** An old proverb says, "Experience is the best teacher." Parents can let experience teach their children through natural results. Some call this "learning the hard way!" God tells us not to worry. If we disobey Him and worry, the natural results are tooth decay, bad blood pressure, sleeplessness, and ulcers. We reap what we sow (Gal. 6:7-10). The natural results of sexual sins are sexual diseases, lasting shame, heartache, and unplanned children. The natural result of touching a hot stove is that it will burn you. The natural result of pulling a dog's tail is that the dog will bite you. It is good for a parent to tell a child not to pull a dog's tail. But a parent does not need to repeat this teaching or warning. The natural results will teach the child who does not obey the warning![16]

> AN OLD PROVERB SAYS, "EXPERIENCE IS THE BEST TEACHER."

A little girl was playing with a kitten. She would chase the kitten and pull its tail. The child's mother called out to the girl, "Don't hurt the kitten!" But the girl was having too much fun to listen. The mother decided not to spank the little girl. Instead, she decided to let natural results teach her child to obey. When the kitten had enough, it turned on the little girl, hissed, and scratched her. The startled girl cried and ran to her mother. "That is what happens when you hurt a kitten by pulling its tail. A kitten only likes to play when you are kind to it. I knew that when I told you to stop. If you listen to your mother, you will avoid the natural results of disobeying. Now you know that mother knows best!" Then the mother cleaned the scratches and put medicine on them.

The father did not punish the prodigal son when he returned. The natural results of his actions had already taught him the lessons he needed to learn. Hunger, shame, and poverty led him to repentance. The natural results were all the discipline that was needed (Luke 15:11-24).

Parents must consider the age of the child and the danger of the results when using this method. The prodigal son's father gave his son the money he requested and let him leave home. A good father would not do the same thing for a boy who was 12 years old. And a parent would never teach a child the danger of crossing the street by allowing a car to hit him. Still, there are times when a parent should use natural results as a method of discipline.

Q 65 Give an example of discipline by logical results.

2. ***Logical results discipline by experience.*** The second method of discipline used around the world is called logical results. Logical results of an action do not happen on their own. The parent must control the logical results. But a logical result is connected to the child's action. Let us look at an example.

A father asked each of his three children to do a task around the house—and to finish these tasks before the dad returned from work. Two of the children completed their tasks. Although the oldest youth planned to do the job, the sun was hot and he did not get started. When his father returned from work, the grass was not cut. The boy had disobeyed his father by doing nothing. Then the boy learned that his father had planned to take him and his brothers swimming that evening. But the grass still needed to be cut. For two, the logical result of obedience was blessing. But for the other, the logical result was that the boy was left behind. He cut the grass while the rest of the family went to swim, play, and have fun.

All three of the children learned a lot from this experience! One boy was disciplined, without anger or a harsh word from his father. This one lesson taught the children that blessings come through obedience. Any parent who has wisdom and patience can use natural and logical results to teach children. The home can become a more pleasant place for everyone. In every culture, parents can use natural results and logical results to teach their children.

3. Encouragement disciplines (trains, guides) by strengthening the good. Encouragement is a form of training children. Although some might not call it discipline, it is a powerful way to guide children—so we want to emphasize it. Children repeat actions or attitudes that parents praise. This is true of human nature in all cultures. So, parents must praise and encourage children when they express good actions or attitudes. Parents around the world use encouragement to train their children.

Q 66 *Give an example of disciplining or training through encouragement?*

Words to encourage are like water on a young plant. Some parents are constantly correcting and nagging their children. They are always seeing the bad, but they are blind to the good. But positive, encouraging words often have more power than negative words of criticism. Watch for good things in your children, and then praise them. Sometimes it is good to ignore what a child does wrong, and brag about what he does right.

A boy arose from the evening meal. He turned to his mother and thanked her for the food. Later that evening his father took the boy aside and said, "I heard you thank your mother for your food. You are wise to be grateful for what others do for you, and you are kind to tell them. I am thankful to have a son who is wise and kind." That was the first time the father had heard his son thank his mother. But you can be sure it was not the last time! Soon, the boy thanked his mother again. Then, he looked toward his father, who smiled and nodded his head in approval.

> A CHILD IS NOT LIKELY TO FIND A FATHER IN GOD UNLESS HE FINDS SOMETHING OF GOD IN HIS FATHER!

A mother was watching her daughter struggle with her schoolwork. She said to her, "I see you are working on your math problems even though it is hard for you. You do not quit when things get hard. You have the godly quality of perseverance. You must feel good about that."

One father made it a habit to praise his son to others. If the son brought a friend home from school, the father looked for a good chance to tell the visitor something good about his son. He knew the friend would tell his son.

A baby who is learning to walk gets lots of encouraging attention. Parents do not scold him when he falls. Instead, they cheer for every sign of progress. One may say, "He pulled himself to his feet. *Hurray! He stood up without holding on to anything. Hurray! He took his first step. Hurray!" We will be better parents if we practice this method of praising our children. As a dog wags his tail when you pet him, a child does his best when you praise him.

Rewards to encourage guide a child as the smell of food guides us to the table. A reward may be extra time with the parent. It may be a special food. It may be attention or privilege. It may be a gift or money. The reward is proof to the child that his actions or attitudes are good. On the other hand, if parents use too many rewards, they may corrupt a child's attitude. Still, there is a time to guide children with rewards. Remember that God promises rewards to His children. He promised rewards to the believers in the seven churches (Rev. 2–3). And He promised the reward of eternal wages to those who win the lost (John 4:36).

Q 67 *What is the danger in using rewards?*

A little girl surprised her father by bringing coffee to him while he rested. She had seen him working hard and wanted to do something special for him. In his delight at her love, the father gave her a coin. Another day she brought more coffee and received another coin. As the habit progressed, the girl thought less and less of her father as she prepared the coffee. Her desire was for more coins.

We must use caution in giving rewards for behavior. A way to use the power of rewards with less chance of damaging attitudes is to give *random rewards—once in a while.

Here is how one mother used random rewards to encourage her son's good actions and attitudes. Each day the son showed good actions and attitudes, but each day did not bring a reward. And the reward changed each time.

Day	Child's Action	The Reward Mother Gave
Day 1	He did all his chores cheerfully.	She let him choose his favorite food for supper.
Day 4	He helped watch his little brother.	She spent extra time reading his favorite book to him.
Day 6	He defended a child that was being teased.	She wrote a note to him about his courage.
Day 11	He worked in the garden.	She gave him some money.

Figure 10.13   Example of random (occasional) rewards

Paul wanted to discipline John Mark when he was a young man. Paul used logical results. Since John Mark left the team during the first mission trip, Paul would not let him go on the second trip. But Barnabas—whose name means "son of encouragement"—wanted to encourage Mark. He formed another ministry team that gave John Mark a second chance. Mark became a fruitful, faithful minister and wrote one of the four Gospels (Acts 15:36-40; 2 Tim. 4:11). As we have already said, encouragement brings out the best in people.

4. Physical discipline can correct with love. Most of the time, it is best to train a child through natural results, logical results, and encouragement. But there are times when physical discipline is necessary. Parents must carefully consider how to use physical discipline without sinning against their children.

> THE GOAL OF PHYSICAL DISCIPLINE IS NOT TO HURT THE CHILD—THE GOAL IS REPENTANCE.

Q 68 *What attitudes should guide physical discipline?*

The Bible allows parents to discipline their children physically with love. People disagree about the use of physical discipline. Some people believe that hitting a child's body is *always* child abuse. There are some places where striking a child in any way is illegal. But the Bible teaches that physical discipline is a valid tool for parents. *"Do not withhold discipline from a child; if you punish him with the rod, he will not die"* (Prov. 23:13). Physical discipline is unpleasant at the time—for both parents and children. But when done *in love,* it can be a helpful tool.

Good parents discipline their children because of wisdom and love, NOT because of anger. Angry parents sometimes are out of control. Physical punishment loses its value if it is driven by anger rather than love. In fact, discipline given by anger harms children emotionally.

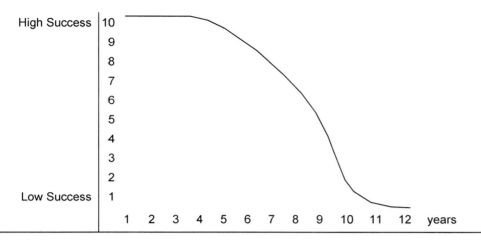

Figure 10.14 The success of physical discipline decreases as a child's age increases.

Remember that physical discipline is for small children, not youth. The bigger a child grows, the less effective physical discipline is. Physical discipline may help a child in his early years, and perhaps once in a while up to the age of 12. But the older a child is, the less helpful physical discipline will be. Physical discipline may create resentment and bitterness in children during *adolescence.

Q 69 *Should a parent use physical discipline on a teenager? Explain.*

If you feel that you must use physical discipline, be careful not to injure your child. Do not hit your child with anything that will cause a bruise or break the skin. If you must strike your child, use something like a small switch, which is short, limber, and less than ¼ the thickness of your smallest finger. And do not hit the child many times. One mother only struck her child once or twice. The child usually cried tears. And the mother herself always cried tears when she struck her child. It is good for a child to see a father or mother cry when they strike their child. Then the child knows the parent's heart is full of love.

If you strike your child in discipline, be sure to hit only the child's backside, the place he sits on—the place God has put the most flesh. Never strike a child on the back, legs, arms, stomach, or face. A parent can harm a child by striking him on the lower back. And avoid striking a child with your hand, except perhaps to give a light swat to a very small child. When the child sees your hand, he should remember the times you touch him softly. You want the child to associate or link discipline to an object—like a switch—and not your hand.

> *After you discipline a child physically, take a few minutes to teach the child. Hug your child or hold him on your lap. Ask the child, "Do you know why daddy (or mommy) had to discipline you?" Explain why the behavior was wrong. Remind the child of the teachings and warnings he had received. Emphasize that the child is good, and that you never expect to see this type of bad behavior again. Tell the child how much you love him. Lead in a prayer of forgiveness and ask the Lord to strengthen and bless your child.*

(For more suggestions on guidelines for physical discipline, see Dr. James Dobson's book, *The Strong-Willed Child,* chapter 2, "Shaping the Will").[17]

The Bible does not allow child abuse. Abuse from parents is a form of hatred, rejection, cruelty, and anger. Scripture does not justify a parent who beats a child. Children are people—just as their parents are—with feelings, emotions, and dignity. Parents must remember this as they train their children. Follow the example of our heavenly Father, who is gentle with us.

Q 70 *What does abuse do to the heart and mind of a child?*

It is possible to destroy children through physical discipline. The Bible warns: *"Fathers, do not exasperate* [dishearten or discourage] *your children; instead, bring them up in the training and instruction of the Lord"* (Eph. 6:4). Children know when they are receiving correction in love. And they know when they are the victims of their parent's anger and greater strength. Love leads to a soft, repentant heart. Abuse leads to a hard heart toward all authority.

The goal of physical discipline is not to hurt the child—the goal is repentance. Some children can be led to repent with only a word of rebuke. Other children need stronger measures. Still, a parent must never abuse a child through deeds or words. No parent should say, "I wish you were never born—I didn't want you in the first place. You are a bad, evil child." Such abusive ideas will remain in a child's mind for a lifetime. Say good things to your child and he will live up to them. Say bad things, and the child will live down to them.

Conclusion

In this chapter we studied how to help children grow in favor with God and with men. We completed our study with a close look at discipline. Neither God nor our children expect parents to be perfect. And parents must not expect perfection from themselves. But as we seek to learn and grow, God will give us the wisdom, grace, and love to be a good father or mother.

Final thoughts for "How to Be a Good Father or Mother"

Q 71 ↖ *What types of things do children learn as they watch?*

Our children are blessings from God, and parents are stewards. God gives us a few years to build a godly foundation for the rest of their life. We pray that they will serve the Lord, marry a Christian, and do their best to raise godly children. Parents have a great influence on children. Children are a reflection of what they see in their home. Dorothy Knolte wrote:

Children learn what they watch.

If children live with criticism, they learn to condemn and judge.

If children live with hostility, they learn to be angry and fight.

If children live with ridicule, they learn to be shy and withdrawn.

If children live with shame, they learn to feel guilty.

If children live with tolerance, they learn to be patient.

If children live with encouragement, they learn confidence.

If children live with praise, they learn to appreciate.

If children live with fairness, they learn justice.

If children live with security, they learn to have faith.

If children live with approval, they learn to like themselves.

If children live with acceptance and friendship, they learn to find life in the world.[18]

So, in the end of this study, we face our original question, "What kind of example am I to my children?"

Chapter Summary

Help Your Children Grow in Favor With God—Spiritually

Goal A: *Explain why the examples of parents are so important.*

Children imitate what they see their parents do. Children learn from their parents by being together with them and by copying their behavior.

Goal B: *Summarize steps that parents should take to teach their children.*

We noted 18 steps. Review them in lesson 1 near questions 8–10.

Goal C: *Describe guidelines for daily, family devotions.*

Select a good time. Use simple words. Aim at balance in teachings, songs, prayer, and praise. Include everyone. Show respect for God. Avoid negative experiences.

Help Your Children Grow in Favor With Men—Socially

Goal A: *Comment on the relationship between security and social growth.*

To relate well to people, a child must learn to trust. Children learn to trust when their parents help them feel secure. Review the 9 ways that parents can help their children feel secure.

Goal B: *Explain 3 different ways that parents can show love to their children.*

Parents show love through touching, telling or speaking kind words, and through time spent with children.

Goal C: *Summarize how parents can help a child feel acepted, and have self-esteem.*

Minimize—talk little about things your child cannot change. Help your child improve as much as possible. Maximize—talk much about ways your child can have strengths to succeed. Emphasize good values that your child can have. Teach your child to do things for himself.

Goal D: *Analyze the roles of manners, attitudes, and skills in relating to others.*

Manners. Each child must learn rules of courtesy. The best way to teach children these social rules and manners is through the family. Insist that each family member treat the others with respect and courtesy.

Attitudes. Each child should develop social attitudes. Teach your child to greet others with a smile. Teach him to be hospitable. Through your example, teach children to relate well to others.

Skills. Each child should learn personal skills Two critical skills are communicating and managing emotions, such as anger.

Discipline Your Children, So They Will Grow in Favor With God and Men

Goal A: *Explain 10 of the 15 principles on discipline.*

Discipline because of love. Discipline to save your children and give them security. Discipline consistently. Discipline to teach respect for authority. Discipline as a team—work together as parents. Discipline calmly, quickly, and sparingly. Discipline to match the child and the crime. Discipline only if a child chose the wrong, and rejected what he knew was right. Discipline for rebellion, but never for accidents. Discipline to teach. Discipline in a way that is fruitful and helpful.

Goal B: *Summarize 4 types of discipline.*
- Natural results discipline by experience.
- Logical results discipline by experience.
- Encouragement disciplines (trains, guides) by strengthening the good.
- Physical discipline can correct with love.

Test Yourself: Circle the letter by the *best* completion to each question or statement.

1. Children learn values by
a) hearing.
b) seeing.
c) doing.
d) memorizing.

2. To teach children well, parents should
a) separate play from religious learning.
b) baptize them at an early age.
c) warn that God knows everything.
d) make learning fun for them.

3. In family devotions, parents should
a) keep the focus on the parents and the Bible.
b) use hard words so that children can learn.
c) encourage children to act out some stories.
d) settle family quarrels and arguments.

4. Parents can help children feel secure by
a) letting infants cry to strengthen independence.
b) placing adult burdens on their shoulders.
c) keeping the promises they make to them.
d) being creative with a new routine each day.

5. A main way that parents should show love is to
a) give each child plenty of money.
b) teach children to be seen and not heard.
c) avoid touching children over 12 years old.
d) speak kind words to each child.

6. Parents build self-esteem in a child by
a) saying little about the child's strengths.
b) underlining things their child cannot change.
c) doing all that they can do for their child.
d) emphasizing qualities of good character.

7. To relate well to others, a person needs
a) manners.
b) education.
c) influence.
d) finances.

8. A parent should discipline a child
a) even if the parent is full of anger.
b) even when a child errs through an accident.
c) in a way that matches the crime and the age.
d) for every small offense.

9. Being scratched by a cat for pulling its tail is
a) discipline through a natural result.
b) discipline through a logical result.
c) an example of emotional discipline.
d) an example of physical discipline.

10. Physical discipline should end by the age of
a) 8 years.
b) 12 years.
c) 16 years.
d) 20 years.

Unit 4: Succeeding as a Family

God promised Abraham that his family would inherit a land flowing with milk and honey. Canaan was a beautiful land. The Mediterranean Sea sparkled on its western border. And the valley of the Jordan River had rich soil that produced much fruit. But to reach the Promised Land, the descendants of Abraham had to pass through the wilderness and conquer many giants.

Likewise, to succeed as a family, there is a wilderness of trials to pass through—and some families must conquer giants. In this Unit we will study how to conquer giants that kill families. The blessings that God has for a family are many. But we live in a world with sin and Satan. So we must be ready to work hard and persevere to inherit the promises of God. For sure, it is God who gives us the victory. And we depend on the Holy Spirit. But no one ever climbed the ladder of success with his hands in his pockets.[1]

Chapter 11 discusses how to overcome threats to your family. We will teach you to:
- *Explain the dangers of feeling alone in a family.*
- *Summarize nine causes and cures of feeling distant in a family.*
- *Explain and apply each of the 11 principles to protect your family from adultery.*
- *Define abuse and state two causes of it.*
- *Summarize four reasons why a wife might continue to live with abuse.*
- *Identify four keys to overcoming abuse.*
- *Define addictions, and explain how people become addicts.*
- *Explain eight keys to being free from all forms of slavery.*

Chapter 12 focuses on tough problems. You will discover how to:
- *Identify the four steps of grief through loss.*
- *Explain and apply the four steps of grief through barrenness, death, or divorce.*
- *Identify three biblical reasons to consider remarriage.*
- *Explain four keys to help a blended family succeed.*
- *Identify three stages in the story of the prodigal son.*
- *Explain three ways parents should respond in stage one of rebellion.*
- *Explain ways parents should respond in Stages 2 and 3 of rebellion.*

Chapter 13 emphasizes the latter years of life. You will learn to:
- *Describe how family expectations should change as children mature.*
- *Explain how the relationship between parents and adult children can deepen.*
- *Summarize the challenges of the years of the empty nest.*
- *Identify three possible roles of grandparents.*
- *Explain five ways a family should care for grandparents.*
- *Describe how the elderly can make peace with their pasts.*
- *Explain why having a purpose is important when you are old.*
- *Describe the physical changes the elderly must face.*
- *Summarize how people should prepare financially for old age.*

Chapter 11:
How to Overcome Threats to Your Family

Introduction

A pastor told of how God helped him overcome a deadly threat to his family. Rejoice at his story.

"Early one morning, I left our home for pastoral duties. When I came home, I found my son—too sick to attend school that day. I left again for ministry. When I returned, I discovered my wife was now ill and in bed with our baby girl. At that time, I turned all my attention to my family. Feeling tired, I lay down in another room to rest. But I heard noise from my son and went to be with him. Standing by his bed, I suddenly felt sick. My knees became weak, and I fell to the floor.

Figure 11.1
Families face many threats.

At church services the Sunday before, we had heard of a sickness (the flu) that had come upon several church members. I thought our family had this sickness. So, I telephoned a church member to ask for help, since all my family was sick. While waiting for the member to come, I tried to sleep. As I lay there praying, I asked, 'Lord, I have known You as my Healer from childhood. I want my children to know You in the same way. Why have You not answered my requests for healing as you did when my parents prayed for me?'

Suddenly, a word from the Lord came to me! He said, 'Your problem is not the flu, it is the furnace. Poison gas—leaking from your heater—is slowly killing your family.' With that word, instant strength filled my body. I jumped to my feet and yelled the news to my wife. I carried my son out of the house. I called out for help, and neighbors carried my weak wife and baby outside.

Later, tests at the hospital revealed the truth. A test of the furnace showed it was leaking a poison gas that had no odor. A word of knowledge from the Spirit had saved our entire family from being destroyed."[1]

Poison gas threatened this pastor's family. Our families also face many threats—from outside and inside the home. Attacks come from demons, the world, and the flesh. Too often, threats come like poison gas—silently, little by little. They spread through a family—while members are unaware of the danger—until the moment of destruction. Like this pastor, we must be alert and in prayer for our families. The Holy Spirit will give us grace to discern the threats, and wisdom to overcome them.

Lessons:

Overcome the Threat of Distance
Goal A: *Explain the dangers of feeling alone in a family.*
Goal B: *Summarize 9 causes and cures of feeling distant in a family.*

Overcome the Threat of Adultery
Goal: *Explain and apply each of the 11 principles to protect your family from adultery.*

Overcome the Threat of Abuse
Goal A: *Define abuse and state 2 causes of it.*
Goal B: *Summarize 4 reasons why a wife might continue to live with abuse.*
Goal C: *Identify 4 keys to overcoming abuse.*

Overcome the Threat of Addictions
Goal A: *Define addictions, and explain how people become addicts.*
Goal B: *Explain 8 keys to being free from all forms of slavery.*

Overcome the Threat of Distance
Goal A: *Explain the dangers of feeling alone in a family.*
Goal B: *Summarize 9 causes and cures of feeling distant in a family.*

Background

Some family members do not relate well to each other. Children raised in these unhealthy families often develop personal problems.[2] And they bring these problems into their own marriages. When they marry, they often repeat what they learned in their homes. Thus they create another unhealthy family (Figure 11.2). Hurt people hurt people.[3] Wounded people wound people.

Many things can create sick families. In this chapter, we will consider four behaviors that produce unhealthy families—distance, adultery, abuse, and addiction. We will also study how to overcome these threats that destroy healthy families.

People need people. God created us to relate to each other. It is God who said, *"It is not good for the man to be alone"* (Gen. 2:18). A terrible moment in the life of Jesus came on the cross. The apostles had been scattered. Jesus felt alone and cried out, *"My God, my God, why have you forsaken me?"* (Matt. 27:46). Although a crowd surrounded him, He felt alone. Likewise, it is possible for people to feel forsaken—even at home. They feel distant from other family members. They do not feel as if they belong. They do not feel as if they are understood or accepted. In this lesson, we will look at the dangers, causes, and cures of feeling *detached—apart from one's family.

Q 1 What are the main sources of unhealthy families—emotionally and spiritually? Explain.

Figure 11.2 The cycle of unhealthy families—emotionally and spiritually

1. Unhealthy parents who do not relate well to family members raise:
2. Children who do not relate well to others. These grow up to be:

A. The dangers of feeling distant within a family.

The desire to belong is strong. One who does not feel a part of the family will turn away from the family and seek to be a part of another group.

- A husband or wife who feels distant may turn to another person for love and acceptance. This often results in a sexual affair that destroys the marriage.
- A young person who feels distant from the family may seek love and acceptance from other youth. This lonely family member is hungry for approval, and may do foolish things to be accepted by a peer group. Feeling distant from parents causes youth to rebel, run away from home, drop out of school, abuse drugs, commit suicide, break the law, and practice violence.[4]
- Family members who feel distant turn inward. They may become sick in body, emotions, mind, or spirit. Loneliness and depression are common as a person feels distant and turns inward. This person's world gets smaller and smaller.

Q 2 Why is it dangerous for a spouse to feel distant?

Q 3 Why is it dangerous for a youth to feel distant?

Q 4 What can result when a family member feels distant and turns inward?

194 *Marriage & Family*

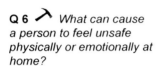 **Q 5** *How is healing related to close relationships?*

Deep connections with others bring blessing. Unity allows love, grace, and encouragement to flow from one family member to another (James 5:16). Good family relationships bring health to the body, soul, mind, and spirit. But family members who feel distant lose the power to heal and be healed of various wounds.[5]

Family members expect to feel close to each other. They do not desire for one or more members to feel distant. Then how does feeling distant happen? It happens when families assume too much. A common error is to think that physical closeness or kinship assures emotional closeness. But this is not true. Family members can live side by side, but feel distant.

Q 6 *What can cause a person to feel unsafe physically or emotionally at home?*

Q 7 *How does a person respond who does not feel safe at home?*

Q 8 *What happens when a family continues to bring up a past wrong?*

B. Nine causes and cures for feeling distant in a family

1. Problem: Failure to make the home a safe place—physically and emotionally—causes family members to feel distant.[6] Feeling unsafe in a family is the main mistake that destroys closeness. The threat of abuse can make a person feel unsafe physically (see lesson 3 of this chapter). Ridicule, criticism, and scorn can cause a person to feel that it is unsafe to share his thoughts and emotions. The home is no longer a safe place for the person who feels used or abused by other family members. When we feel unsafe, we defend ourselves by moving away from those who hurt us.

Solution: Practice the golden rule. Treat others as you would like them to treat you (Matt. 7:12; Luke 6:31). For example, show respect. This shows your family members that you value them. They will feel closer and more open when they feel your respect. People around the world show respect in many different ways. Showing respect often includes: asking the person's opinion; listening without interrupting; praising a person in front of others; treating the person in a kind, gentle, godly manner—as Jesus treats us. Communicating respect with words and actions encourages closeness.

2. Problem: Failure to remain interested in family members causes them to feel distant. When we believe we know all about our spouse and children, we no longer seek deeper knowledge of them. People do not like to share their thoughts with someone who does not care. And the one who is bored may seek out others they find more interesting. How proud we are to think we can know another person completely. George Washington Carver, a famous scientist, spent his lifetime seeking to discover all the hidden qualities and uses of the peanut. How much greater are the mysteries of a human being!

Figure 11.3
Practicing the Golden Rule at home helps family members feel close to each other.

Q 9 *How do children or youth feel when parents do not seem interested in them?*

Q 10 *What types of questions should parents ask their children?*

A teen-age boy began to feel distant, lonely, and rejected by his family. He was learning to play the guitar, but his parents did not care. He knew he could not play well, but no one encouraged him to keep trying. Also, his dad was usually too busy to spend time with him. Sure, the dad was not good at sports, but he could at least play ball with him a little. After 2 years of feeling distant, the boy began to smoke cigarettes. The third year he began using drugs and moved out of the house. Whose fault was it that the son went astray?

Solution: Dig a little. Your family is like treasure hidden in a field. *Each* person is a wonderful creation of God—in God's own image. Ask the Holy Spirit to help you appreciate and understand those in your family. Refuse to look past the wonders under your own roof. Your family is your greatest earthly wealth.

Hold an infant often. Gaze into his eyes and talk to him. As children grow, listen to them and ask them questions. Discover their favorite foods, music, games, topics, jobs, and people. (Review the teachings of chapters 9 and 10 related to this topic.) There is wealth in your home, but you must dig to find it.

3. Problem: Failure to spend time with the family causes members to feel distant.[7] Closeness between family members requires time together. The less time members spend together, the more they will feel distant from each other. Ministry and work will take all the time we have if we allow it. There is always more work to do.

Q 11 What are some ways that parents can spend time with their children?

Solution: Spend time together. Fathers, take a child with you when you can. Mothers, include your children in the things you do. Eat meals together. Attend events together. Take a family vacation. Attend church together. Have devotions at home together. Visit relatives together. Plant a garden together. Work on your home together. Laugh together. Cry together. Create memories together that will be like glue—bonding family members to each other.

Adult brothers and sisters met after several years of living apart. They began to talk about their childhood memories—the walks to school together, the work in the field, the songs they sang as a family. As they remembered, they felt close to each other. Even after all the years, shared memories were a strong bond between them.

4. Problem: Failure to control jealousy between children causes some to feel distant.[8] It is common for a child to want to be the one a parent loves the most. Cain was jealous of Abel. Children compare themselves to each other—to see if parents love all the family members the same. If a child suffers injustice by a *sibling or decides that a parent loves a sibling more, he may pull away from family members. Remember how Esau withdrew from Jacob. And Joseph's brothers sold him into slavery because they were jealous of the favor his father showed him.

Q 12 Give 3 biblical examples of jealousy between children.

A child may try to influence parents to favor him. Even apostles, like James and John, wanted Jesus to favor them above others (Mark 10:35-37). Likewise, a child may seek favor by praising himself. He may describe an event in such a way that his brother looks like a demon, but he himself looks like an angel. As the proverb says, "When a man tells his own story, he always looks like a hero!"

Figure 11.4
Jacob favored Joseph by giving him a coat of many colors. This favoritism caused Joseph's brothers to hate him and feel distant from their father. So they put him in a pit and sold him into slavery.

Solution: Control jealousy and competition in your family. Teach children that being treated fairly does not mean being treated equally. Explain that you treat each child according to his or her age and uniqueness. In general, the older the child, the more privileges and responsibilities he has.

Q 13 Does being fair mean that parents must treat all their children the same? Explain.

When possible, let children solve their own quarrels with each other. Guide them as needed. Have times when the family comes together to discuss family problems. (See number 9 below.) Have a family meeting before Cain kills Abel!

Be careful to show love to each child in special ways. Avoid favoring one child over another, for this is like sowing seeds of hate in the family. Do not give Joseph a special coat.

Q 14 How did Jacob sow seeds of hate among his children?

5. Problem: Failure to adjust to changes causes family members to feel distant. Every family goes through times of change. The birth of children, new jobs, sickness, and aging are only a few of the changes families face. Things seldom stay the same—they are either getting better or worse, either growing or decaying. In the changes of life, if your family is not growing together, it is growing apart. Here are some examples of poor reactions to change that cause family members to separate from each other.

- Some deny change. They say, "My children will always think of me in the same way they did when they were young. Things have not changed."
- Some resist change. They say, "You will never get me to do something like that! I will never try that." "I will never accept that. My children will never dress like that." "These new songs people sing in church are not as spiritual as the old songs. I will not sing them."
- Some resent change. They say, "She is not the same as when we married. I have been cheated, and now I am trapped!" "My children used to obey all I said, without any questions. But now they do not respect me. They want to make their own decisions instead of letting me tell them what to do."

Q 15 Describe a good attitude toward change.

Solution: Do not oppose all change. There are three types of change: bad, neutral, and good. When we do not adjust to changes, family members will grow apart. We cannot control many things in life. So, when change comes, adjust to it. Some win the small battle but lose the war. In a family—and in all of life—we must choose which battles to fight, and which ones to ignore. Adjust to the little things that do not matter much. Learn some of the new songs that youth are singing in church! But stand firm on old, important values, such as honesty, love, kindness, honor, mercy, faith, goodness, holiness, and gentleness.

Q 16 Should a dad tell his son how to comb his hair? Explain.

A father did not like the way his son was combing his hair. It was looking like the other boys at school. The hair was touching the boy's ears and shirt collar. The dad had never worn his hair that way, and he did not want his son's hair to look like that. Still, the dad did not criticize his son. He realized that the boy was changing from a child to a man. As he prayed, the dad decided that this was a small change that did not matter. He was proud of his son's character and love for God. The dad chose to think on these things and accept the change in his son's hair.

Wedding vows in many cultures promise loyalty—even when big changes come. Couples vow to love "for richer or poorer; in sickness or health; for better or worse." Change can be difficult; that is why the wedding promises are necessary.[9] Parents must love their children when big changes come in the family.

Q 17 What caused Lamech's wife to feel distant from him?

6. Problem: Failure to show love and affection causes distance. A wife had plenty of food, but she was starving for affection from Lamech, her husband. She was a good mother and a faithful wife. But he never spoke a kind word to her. She cooked his food, washed his clothes, and fulfilled all of his sexual needs. She worked hard from morning to evening and never complained. But this cold, unfeeling, unthoughtful, wooden man never showed her any love. He never touched her softly and said, "I love you. Thank you for choosing me to be your man." He never offered to rub her aching feet or her tired shoulders. He never greeted her with a smile or asked how her day was. Once, they went to a restaurant to eat. To get good service, he smiled at the waitress and spoke kindly to her. The wife said to herself, "I wish my husband would treat me as nice as he treats this waitress. Instead, he treats me as if I am a servant in his kingdom."

Q 18 In what ways did your parents show love to you?

Solution: Speak the language another understands. What is love and affection? The Bible explains the characteristics of love.

Q 19 In what ways will you try to show love to your children?

⁴*Love is patient, love is kind. It does not envy, it does not boast, it is not proud.*
⁵*It is not rude, it is not self-seeking, it is not easily angered, it keeps no record*

of wrongs. ⁶Love does not delight in evil but rejoices with the truth. ⁷It always protects, always trusts, always hopes, always perseveres (1 Cor. 13:4-7).

The body needs food to be healthy. Likewise, the soul and emotions need attention, tenderness, and touching to be healthy.

People in the same world speak different languages. Likewise, people in the same family speak different languages of love. Consider these five languages of love:[10]
- Some speak love and feel loved through <u>kind words of encouragement.</u>
- Some speak love and feel loved through <u>time together</u>.
- Some speak love and feel loved through <u>gifts.</u>
- Some speak love and feel loved through <u>kind deeds.</u>
- Some speak love and feel loved through <u>touching or hugging</u>.

Study each member of your family. You will find that all do not speak the same language of love, though some may speak several love languages. In fact, a husband and wife often show love in different ways. It is important to speak the language another understands. Suppose Bien speaks only Spanish, and Bon speaks only French. If Bien says, "I love you," will Bon understand him? Likewise, family members must learn to show love in ways that mean the most to each other. A husband may do many kind deeds, thus saying "I love you" to his wife. But if her main love language is kind words, he must at times use words to tell her "I love you." Likewise, he may need to learn the love languages of time and touching for some in his family.

Although a father did many kind things for his family, one of his girls, Deborah, did not feel loved. Her main language of love was touching. Sometimes she gave her dad a hug, or touched his shoulder to say "I love you." But the years went by and Dad touched her very little. When she became a teenager, she sought the love from young men that she had never received from her father.

 Q 20 *Why did Deborah not feel loved by her father?*

Figure 11.5 **An earthly father's love for his daughter helps teach her about the heavenly Father's love.**

Wise parents know that a child's cries may mean "Hold me." A kiss on a bump or bruise does not take away the pain. But the child's soul is soothed—caused to feel better by the connection with his father or mother's love. When the parent reaches out and connects, something happens that makes the pain seem less important.[11] In contrast, the child who is left alone in pain may cry long after the physical pain is gone. He is lonely, and his soul is crying for someone to show love and concern. Likewise, family members of all ages need love and affection.

 Q 21 *What do a child's cries say? Explain.*

7. Problem: Failure to accept, support, and encourage causes family members to feel distant. At the age of 23, a daughter who was married told her parents that she wanted to be a missionary. The parents did not accept this. Instead, they offered her a lot of money to work in the family business. This hurt the daughter's feelings. Still, the parents did not accept their daughter's desire to serve God as a missionary. They hired a lawyer and removed her from the will, taking her inheritance away from her. This caused the daughter to feel very distant from her parents. However, after 10 years, their relationship was healed. The parents showed acceptance and support for their daughter's choice to be a missionary.

 Q 22 *Give an example where failure to accept a family member caused him to feel distant.*

Solution: Communicate acceptance by encouraging the good things that interest members of the family. A mother wanted her daughter to play the piano. The girl practiced many hours, but God had not given her much of a talent for music. In time,

Q 23 *Give an example of someone you feel close to, because he or she accepted your choice.*

the mother discerned that her daughter did not enjoy trying to learn this musical skill. But the girl had fun drawing pictures. So the mother encouraged the child to draw, and paid for some lessons. This encouragement and support caused the mother and daughter to be very close.

A dad wanted his son to continue the family business. But the son felt led to be a teacher. For a time, this was a disappointment to the dad, but he did not tell his son. Instead, after much prayer, he encouraged his son to become a teacher. In this way, the father and son remained close. Otherwise, the son would have felt distant from his father.

When you communicate acceptance, a person wants to share his thoughts and feelings with you. Acceptance does not mean you think your family members are perfect. It means that you love them as they are. In contrast, words of criticism cause people to withdraw or argue. This does not help develop closeness. Acceptance allows people to feel safe to share their hearts (Rom. 15:7).

When you communicate support to your spouse and children, you let them know that you are a real partner. People are stronger when they know they are not alone. They know someone sees their work and values it. They have someone to cheer for them when they are trying to improve. They know someone will encourage and help them. If you communicate support, it will increase your closeness (Phil. 2:4-5).

- **Encourage** and **inspire** family members for what they can become. God treated Gideon in this way. The angel of the Lord came to Gideon as he was hiding from his enemies, threshing wheat. Gideon was the least in his family, and his clan was the weakest in his tribe. But the angel came to him just as he was. He greeted Gideon by saying, *"The LORD is with you, mighty warrior"* (Judges 6:12). God accepted Gideon as he was, but He had a vision of what Gideon would become (Judges 6:7-16).

- **Praise** the good things God has placed in each family member. Remain calm when badness or sin is shown, and have faith in God's work in one another. Speak words of faith, confidence, and encouragement to family members.

Gideon struggled to become the warrior God envisioned. He battled doubt and fear (Judges 6:13, 15, 23, 27, 36-40; 7:10-11). But each time, God encouraged him by reminding Gideon that the Lord was with him.

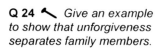

Q 24 *Give an example to show that unforgiveness separates family members.*

8. Problem: Failure to forgive causes family members to feel distant. Refusing to forgive separates people. It builds a wall between them, and makes them feel distant from each other. David and his son, Absalom, became distant because of an offense between them. We were distant from God, separated by the sins we committed against Him. We could not be close to God until He was able to forgive us through Christ.

Likewise in a family, the failure to forgive destroys relationships. Perhaps a parent refuses to forgive a youth for bringing shame to the family. One husband did not forgive his wife for wrecking the family car. Jacob and Esau became distant brothers because of unforgiveness.

Solution: Forgive forever, and bury the offense. Do not ever mention the offense again.

Q 25 *How is bringing up a past wrong like digging up a dead dog?*

A boy named Mike had a dog that died. Mike buried the dog—all except the tail. He left the tail sticking out so he could pull the dog out of the grave from time to time. A week after the dog died, Mike went to visit the grave. He grabbed the tail and pulled out the dog. Phew! What a terrible odor! Mike looked at the dog for a while, and then buried it again, leaving the tail out. But touching the dog had made the boy's hand stink. In the house, his mother asked, "What is causing the house to smell so bad?" Mike explained that it was from the dead dog. His mother wisely told him to bury the dog completely, and then wash his hands. Likewise, when we forgive, we should bury all of an offense and never bring it up again. When we dig up dead things from the past, it causes us and the whole house to stink.[12]

When you forgive, you open the hearts of your spouse and other family members. Parents should be an example of forgiving others. Everybody hurts the feelings of others at some time. But if you refuse to forgive or to admit you need forgiveness, your heart will grow hard. Some flowers close up in the darkness of the night. But in the morning, they open their petals to the sun. The warmth and light of forgiveness opens your family to closeness (Matt. 18:21-35).

A boy was trying to help his mother in the kitchen. He dropped a large, yellow bowl that her mother had given her. The bowl broke in pieces on the floor. The boy began to cry, for he knew how much the bowl meant to his mother. But she held him close and said. "Do not cry over the bowl. Bowls come and go. But you, my son, are the joy of my heart. You will grow strong and bring me great joy by serving the Lord. You are worth more to me than all the bowls in every home!" The boy grew up and became a man. Over the next 20 years, she never mentioned the broken bowl—not even once! Today, the mother is in heaven, but the boy still remembers the forgiveness his mother gave with her inspiring words of encouragement. Because of forgiveness, what could have been a bad memory became a good one.

Imitate God who forgives us (Eph. 5:1-2). And remember, God only forgives those who forgive others (Matt. 6:12, 14-15; 18:21-35). He who forgives releases a prisoner, only to discover that the prisoner was himself.

9. Problem: Failure to be relevant, open, and honest causes distance. Feeling distant occurs when people refuse to talk openly about important matters. Some topics are hard to discuss, so parents may be tempted to avoid them. But this is a big mistake. Consider the parable of the alligator.

Q 26 *What lesson does the parable of the alligator teach?*

A family sat together, eating dinner at a table near a river. The food was good, and all seemed peaceful. Then, two eyes appeared in the river, just above the water. The eyes were big—like a cow's eyes. The parents saw the eyes, and one youth saw them, but the smaller children did not notice. The eyes began to move slowly, closer and closer to the table. Still, no one said anything about the eyes. Then it happened. Suddenly, an alligator leaped from the river. It splashed water on all at the table, and bit deeply into the foot of the teenager. The beast began dragging the boy toward the river. The young man and the alligator wrestled in the mud near the edge of the water. The entire family was shocked, but no one said a word. Some continued to eat, ignoring the problem. Finally, the alligator bit off part of the youth's foot and crawled back into the river. The large, yellow eyes disappeared under the red water. The young man limped and hopped back to the table, feeling great pain. In silence, the whole family began to eat. No one said anything, for in their culture, it was rude and awkward to talk about alligators!

Figure 11.6 Always remember the parable of the alligator.

Each family must answer the questions: "Will we refuse to talk about a topic because it feels awkward or causes pain, embarrassment, or tears? Will we ignore matters that can destroy our family, because talking about these problems feels rude or difficult?"

Solution: Ask God to give you the courage and wisdom you need to discuss hard topics. These might include music, hair, anger, clothing styles, sports, and sex. It is better to make a grade of C than to fail by not trying to discuss these difficult topics.

Q 27 *In your culture, what are some hard—but necessary—topics to discuss at home?*

Speak the truth with love. There will be times when a family must discuss hard topics—such as sexual matters, or the faults of parents and children. When you speak the truth with love, your family will learn to trust you. Discuss to redeem and improve—not to condemn. Closeness grows when family members are open and honest (Prov. 10:11; 15:4). Value doing what is right, more than you value feeling comfortable. Parents, set the example. Confess your mistakes and admit your faults (James 5:16). Be an example of honesty and humility. Whatever example you are, your children will follow in your footsteps.

Q 28 *If someone asks private questions about family members, how should one answer?*

Be open with your family members, but private with others. Families wash and dry their clothes in private—not in public. Likewise, discuss family matters in private, but do not speak about them to others. A wise person is discreet—knowing when to speak and when to remain silent.

Conclusion

One of the harshest ways to punish a prisoner is to lock him alone. Being confined—distant from all other people—often weakens his will and breaks down the health of his spirit, emotions, and body. Even a great prophet like John the Baptist became weak when he was locked up away from people. In a similar way, family members are damaged when they feel distant in the home. We can overcome this threat to our families by practicing the nine keys we have studied.

Overcome the Threat of Adultery
Goal: *Explain and apply each of the 11 principles to protect your family from adultery.*

Nothing destroys a family faster than adultery. In this lesson we will study 11 principles to protect you and your family from this family killer.[13]

A. Recognize the problem and the danger of sexual sins.

Q 29 *Which types of sexual sins are the greatest problem in your culture? Explain.*

Sexual sins are spreading in every society. Many husbands and wives are not faithful to each other. Some have sexual affairs with other spouses. Some use pornography through magazines, videos, or the Internet. We are living in the last days, and sin is increasing (Matt. 24:12-13). So all believers need to beware. *"Your enemy the devil prowls around like a roaring lion looking for someone to devour"* (1 Pet. 5:8).

The Bible records that people who knew God—men like Samson, David, and Solomon—committed sexual sins. *"So, if you think you are standing firm, be careful that you don't fall!"* (1 Cor. 10:12).

Figure 11.7 Satan, like a roaring lion, seeks to destroy people. He continues to destroy many through sexual sins (1 Pet. 5:8).

B. Understand the process from temptation to sin.

Q 30 *What are the 4 steps that lead from temptation to sin?*

[12]*Blessed is the man who perseveres under trial, because when he has stood the test, he will receive the crown of life that God has promised to those who love him.* [13]*When tempted, no one should say, "God is tempting me." For God cannot be tempted by evil, nor does he tempt anyone;* [14]*but each one is tempted when, by his own evil desire, he is dragged away and enticed.* [15]*Then, after desire has*

How to Overcome Threats to Your Family 201

conceived, it gives birth to sin; and sin, when it is full-grown, gives birth to death (James 1:12-15).

Notice that James mentions four steps that lead from temptation to sin.

- *First,* a person is tempted. As a fisherman uses bait to tempt a fish, the devil and the world use bait to tempt a human. Temptation knocks at every door. All people are tempted. Even Jesus was tempted to sin (Heb. 4:15). Temptation is not a sin, but it is a sign that tells us danger is near. People pay attention when a dog growls. Likewise, we should beware when temptation comes. Blessed is the man who perseveres when trials and temptations come. He stands the test and will receive a crown of life(James 1:12). This person in James 1:12 responds to temptation through the Spirit (Rom. 8:4-14; Gal. 5:16-25). He says "no" to temptation. He treats temptation like an evil bird to scare away. He knows that you cannot prevent a bird from flying over your head, but you can prevent it from building a nest in your hair!

  Q 31 ↖ *Is it a sin to be tempted by an evil thought? Explain.*

- *Second,* evil desires (not a demon) within a person respond to a temptation. Unlike the person in James 1:12, the person described in James 1:14 does not stand the test. This person is not led by the Spirit. Rather, his flesh leads him to say "yes" to the temptation. He welcomes temptation into his life, and takes the devil's bait.
- *Third,* as a child is conceived in a woman, sin is conceived in a person. The evil desires within a person unite with temptation to conceive sin. Then, sin begins to grow in a person's thoughts, and finally is born in a person's actions.
- *Fourth,* as a child grows into an adult, sin grows from a small thing into a big one. In the end, sin brings forth spiritual death—eternal separation from God.

C. Walk in the Spirit and you will win the battle over temptation.

Those who understand the process from temptation to sin stop the process at step 1. By the power of the Holy Spirit, they learn to stand firm in the time of temptation (James 1:12). Like Joseph, they run *away from* temptation instead of *toward* it. They depend on the Spirit and cooperate with Him. They say "yes" to things that please the Spirit, and "no" to things that grieve Him. Those led by the flesh produce fruit such as sexual sins (Gal. 5:19-21). In contrast, those led by the Spirit produce fruit such as patience, kindness, gentleness, and self-control (Gal. 5:22-23).

Q 32 ↗ *How does God expect us to have victory over temptation?*

> *⁶The mind of sinful man is death, but the mind controlled by the Spirit is life and peace; ⁷the sinful mind is hostile to God. It does not submit to God's law, nor can it do so. ⁸Those controlled by the sinful nature* [the ⁺flesh] *cannot please God. ⁹You, however, are controlled not by the sinful nature* [the flesh] *but by the Spirit, if the Spirit of God lives in you* (Rom. 8:6-9).

> *So I say, live by the Spirit, and you will not gratify the desires of the sinful nature* [flesh] (Gal. 5:16).

Those who walk in the Spirit recognize that temptation is common. But they allow the Spirit to help them stand firm in times of temptation.

> *No temptation has seized you except what is common to man. And God is faithful; he will not let you be tempted beyond what you can bear. But when you are tempted, he will also provide a way out so that you can stand up under it* (1 Cor. 10:13).

D. Pay attention to outward warning signs in others.

Here are some <u>outward</u> signs to warn you that sexual danger is near if you are working with or counseling a person of the opposite sex.

Q 33 ↗ *What are some outward signs to warn you that sexual danger is near?*

⁺ In the Greek language, the word is *sarx,* which means "flesh" or "fleshly desires."

- The person spends a lot of time with you.
- The person begins to depend on you.
- The person begins to affirm and praise you.
- The person begins to complain about feeling lonely.
- The person talks often about personal matters.
- The person tries to attract you in sexual ways.
- The person begins to touch your body. This may begin with a handshake, a hand on the shoulder, or a hug of thanks. But it soon rises to much more.
- Your spouse begins to feel bad about your relationship with this person.

Figure 11.8 Beware when you see <u>outward</u> signs that warn of sexual danger.

Q 34 *What are some inward warning signs that you need to repent—change directions?*

E. Pay attention to inward warning signs in you.

Here are some <u>inward</u> signs to warn you that sexual danger is near if you are working with or counseling a person of the opposite sex.[14] <u>Discern this</u>: A relationship can be going the wrong direction—long before it becomes sexual.

> A RELATIONSHIP CAN BE GOING THE WRONG DIRECTION—LONG BEFORE IT BECOMES SEXUAL.

- You dress in a way to please the person.
- You are disappointed if you do not see the person; excited when you meet the person.
- You spend a lot of time with the person; you look forward to seeing him or her.
- You think the person understands you better than your spouse understands you.
- You enjoy being with this person more than being with your spouse.
- You imagine what it would be like if this person were your spouse.
- You share private and personal matters with this person, such as problems in your marriage.
- You develop feelings of romantic love for this person.
- You try to hide your feelings and meetings with this person.
- You ignore warnings from others and pretend this person is only a friend.
- You look for ways to be with this person in secret, even if you must deceive others.
- You become angry if your spouse wants more attention, or is jealous.
- You imagine a sexual relationship with this person, and do not reject these thoughts.
- You and the other person focus on each other's needs.
- You commit sexual sins after ignoring all of these inward signs.

Figure 11.9 Beware when you see <u>inward</u> signs that warn of sexual danger.

Q 35 *Do you think most people plan to be unfaithful sexually? Explain.*

Dr. James Dobson, a wise family counselor, describes how people often become adulterers.[15] The affair usually begins with friendship, such as a lunch that lasts too long, or a touch. This first step is enjoyed, so the action is repeated. The next day, or perhaps the next week, the touch or lunch goes further with more pleasant feelings. The two people begin to meet more often, and their attraction to each other grows. Before long, the romantic feelings overcome fears, and the two people commit sexual sin.

F. Guard your heart.

Q 36 *How can you guard your heart?*

"*Above all else, guard your heart, for it is the wellspring of life*" (Prov. 4:23). Your heart is the center of your desires and emotions. Jesus should rule as king over all of our desires. But as weeds grow in a garden, evil desires can take root in the heart. This is why daily devotions, prayer, Bible study, and attending church are so important. People guard their money, their homes, and their reputations. But the most important thing to guard is your heart.

Figure 11.10 The steps down to adultery are many and small.

G. Guard your mind.

The apostle Paul said, *"We take captive every thought to make it obedient to Christ"* (2 Cor. 10:5). Thoughts are like grains of sand—alone they weigh almost nothing, but together, they can bury a person. So if your thoughts are your enemies, they will drag you down to destruction. But if your thoughts are your friends, they will escort you into the presence of God.

How can you practice thinking good thoughts—making good thoughts a habit?

- *First,* be aware of your thoughts—like a mother hen is aware of her chicks. Be as watchful as a business owner in his store. Do not be mentally lazy or sleepy. Roll up the shirtsleeves of your mind. *"Prepare your minds for action; be self–controlled"* (1 Pet. 1:13). Be alert, and keep your thoughts out in front of you, like food on your table.

Q 37 *What are 4 keys to guarding our minds?*

- *Second,* love what is right, and hate what is wrong (Rom. 12:9; Heb. 1:9). Rule over your thoughts—like a judge rules in a courtroom. Love what God loves, and hate what He hates. *"How can a young man keep his way pure? By living according to your word"* (Ps. 119:9). Choose to honor God with your secret thoughts, and He will honor you.

Q 38 *Is it right to hate what is wrong? Explain.*

- *Third,* do not allow your thoughts to travel wherever the flesh and the world lead them. Rather, guide your thoughts as a rider steers a bicycle. Say "no" to fleshly desires and "yes" to the Holy Spirit (Gal. 5:16). Pray so that you do not enter into temptation (Matt. 26:41). Refuse to look at any form of pornography. Make a covenant with your eyes (Job 31:1). Block out evil from your telephone, television, or computer by using filters or other methods. (See the Appendix for a list of Internet helps.)

Q 39 *How can a person guide his thoughts?*

- *Fourth,* replace bad thoughts with good ones. You will become tired if you spend your energy trying to chase away bad thoughts. But remember, your mind can only think on one thought at a time. So when an evil thought knocks at the door of your mind, turn away from it, and welcome a good thought. *"Whatever is true, whatever is noble, whatever is right, whatever is pure, whatever is lovely, whatever is admirable—if anything is excellent or praiseworthy—think about such things"* (Phil. 4:8).

Q 40 *Can a person think two opposite thoughts at the same time? Explain and apply.*

H. Guard your marriage.

Loving your mate is the best protection against sexual sins.

- A married couple should fulfill the needs of each other. God commands them to be faithful. They have vowed to forsake all other lovers, and give themselves only to each other. *"Drink water from your own cistern, running water from your own well"* (Prov. 5:15)!

Q 41 *Summarize 6 keys to guarding your marriage.*

- Avoid touching, shaking hands with, or hugging a person of the opposite sex. Be polite and smile, but avoid touching. This is a good boundary to protect your marriage. You will never commit physical adultery with a person you do not touch!

- Do not praise the way a person of the opposite sex dresses or looks. Save your words of praise for your spouse. This will guard your marriage. Tell your spouse often how much he or she pleases you.

- Avoid being alone with a person of the opposite sex. For example, if you counsel a person of the opposite sex, require either another adult or an elder to be present. Likewise, do not eat a meal with a person of the opposite sex, unless other adults you know are at your table. And do not ride in a car with a person of the opposite sex, unless other adults are in the car.

- Do not discuss your personal matters or problems in your marriage with a person of the opposite sex. This can create an emotional bond. Keep your relationships with the opposite sex strictly business. In contrast, it is wise for a husband to discuss a personal problem with an older man; or for a wife to discuss a marital problem with an older Christian woman whom she trusts and respects.

Q 42 ❮ *Why should a husband and wife seek to understand each other's needs?*

- Guard your non-verbal actions. Without speaking, people give signals of sexual interest. These signals change from culture to culture, but they must stop when you are married. These signals lead to wrong thinking and plant seeds of trouble. Give attention to your spouse, not someone else.

The needs of men and women are not the same! Husbands and wives should continue to learn about each other. A husband and wife should become best friends. Friendship grows deeper and stronger as spouses learn about each other. A wise person practices seeing things through the eyes of another. Compare the needs of husbands and wives (Figure 11.11).[16]

Five Needs of Men	Five Needs of Women
Unconditional love and acceptance	Unconditional love and acceptance
Intimacy: sex	Intimacy: talk and friendship
Admiration, respect, esteem, approval	Affection (love, kindness, tenderness)
Support and praise at home	Security: family commitment; financial support
Friendship	Honesty and openness

**Figure 11.11   Five needs of most men and women.
How well do you know your spouse's needs?**

It is very important to discern that needs and wants are not the same. For example, there may be times when a husband wants sex but the wife is sick or too tired. In such cases, he should realize that although sex is a basic need, he can be patient. He does not have to have sex immediately every time he wants it.

Some say, "But my wife (or husband) is not meeting my sexual needs, so I must seek sex outside of marriage." But God will not accept any reason for committing adultery.

[13]Another thing you do: You flood the LORD's altar with tears. You weep and wail because he no longer pays attention to your offerings or accepts them with pleasure from your hands. [14]You ask, "Why?" It is because the LORD is acting as the witness between you and the wife of your youth, because you have broken faith with her, though she is your partner, the wife of your marriage covenant. [15]Has not the LORD made them one? In flesh and spirit they are his. And why one? Because he was seeking godly offspring. So guard yourself in your spirit, and do not break faith with the wife of your youth. [16]"I hate divorce," says the LORD God of Israel, ... So guard yourself in your spirit, and do not break faith (Mal. 2:13-16).

All the wealth you need is in the field of your marriage. If you are not satisfied, dig a little. Discuss the problems with your spouse, and find solutions. Get some counsel from a pastor or a wise elder if necessary. Do not turn away from your marriage because it is not all you want it to be. Hoe the field you have already bought, and it will produce more.

[15]Drink water from your own cistern, running water from your own well. [16]Should your springs overflow in the streets, your streams of water in the public squares? [17]Let them be yours alone, never to be shared with strangers. [18]May your fountain be blessed, and may you rejoice in the wife of your youth. [19]A loving doe, a graceful deer—may her breasts satisfy you always, may you ever be captivated by her love. [20]Why be captivated, my son, by an adulteress? Why embrace the bosom of another man's wife? [21]For a man's ways are in full view of the LORD, and he examines all his paths. [22]The evil deeds of a wicked man ensnare him; the cords of his sin hold him fast. [23]He will die for lack of discipline, led astray by his own great folly (Prov. 5:15-23).

IF THE GRASS ON THE OTHER SIDE OF THE FENCE LOOKS GREENER, THERE IS OFTEN A SEWER NEARBY!

I. Consider the cost of adultery, so that you will not agree to pay it.

A wise preacher once said that **sin will take you further than you want to go, keep you longer than you want to stay, and cost you more than you want to pay.** Delilah cost Samson his relationship with God and both eyes (Judges 16). For an hour of adultery with Bathsheba, David paid the rest of his life. His payments included the death of his child, a guilty conscience, a sword that never left his house, and a reputation of shame for the whole world to read about (2 Sam. 11). Likewise, sexual sins cost Solomon the kingdom, his reputation, and perhaps his soul. When Satan sells sin, he never mentions the price. There was no price written on the forbidden fruit in the Garden of Eden. And there was no price written on Bathsheba. But do not be deceived; God is not mocked. Whoever commits adultery will spend a lifetime paying the price for those few minutes of sin. The fruit that is sweet in your mouth will become bitter in your stomach.

Q 43 *Did David pay too much for Bathsheba? Explain.*

One man made a list of what sexual sin would cost him. He said, "From time to time I remind myself that for one sexual sin, here are some ways I will pay: [17]

- I will grieve the Lord, who gave His life to redeem me.
- Like David, I will drag the name and reputation of the Lord through the mud.
- I will cause others to stumble and sin. Some may go to hell following my example.
- I will lose—for the rest of my life—the respect and honor of my name. As Scripture says, *"his shame will never be wiped away"* in this life (Prov. 6:33).
- I will lose the trust of my beloved wife.
- I will bring shame and sorrow on my parents, family, and friends.
- I will exchange my self-respect for guilt, tears, bad memories, and shame.
- I may get many sexual diseases, such as gonorrhea, syphilis, herpes, or AIDS; also, I may pass these diseases on to my innocent spouse.
- I will lose the chance to witness to those who know me.
- I will harm or destroy the life and family of the person I commit adultery with.
- I will bring shame on my church—and all believers who know me—and hinder their witness.
- I may cause pregnancy, thus bringing an unwanted child into the world—a lifelong reminder of my sin."

Q 44 *What costs of sexual sin do you think are the most expensive? Explain.*

When we think about the cost of adultery, we realize that it is too expensive. This causes us to turn from sexual sins and think about something good and positive! Sin loses its appeal when we look at the price tag.

J. Guard your health.

Temptations are the strongest when we are the weakest. Satan knew this, so he tempted Jesus when the Lord was the weakest—after fasting for 40 days (Matt. 4:1-11). Likewise, Elijah was tempted the most when he was the weakest. After his ministry on Mount Carmel—and running all the way to town—Elijah was tired. In this weak condition he was tempted to despair (1 Kings 19). Also, John the Baptist was tempted to doubt when he became weak in the prison (Matt. 11:1-6).

Q 45 *How can a person guard his health against sexual sin?*

So, as believers, it is wise for us to guard our health. Sometimes we feel the pressure to work too hard to succeed. But over a period of time, working too hard makes a person weak—either physically, emotionally, mentally, or spiritually. So we must learn to do a day's work, and leave the rest for tomorrow, for others, or for God. If you begin to feel hungry, angry, lonely, or tired, it is time to rest. These feelings are signs that God has given us to guard our health. They are like red lights telling us to stop.

K. Be accountable to others.

Sin grows in the dark, but dies in the light. So plan your life in a way that others know what you are doing and thinking. Each day in prayer, invite the Holy Spirit to search your heart and mind. Respond to any changes He speaks about to you. Also, be a

Q 46 *Do you give account of yourself to a friend? If not, choose one and build that relationship.*

member of a church or group that requires you to give an account of yourself. Talk with your spouse from time to time about your thoughts, temptations, and struggles. Choose a friend or elder to hold you accountable. Invite this person to ask you about your thoughts and actions each week or month. Request this person to ask you questions about your private life and inspect it. Getting temptations into the light makes them weaker and us stronger. So do not fight the battle alone—be open with others who can help you. (See Appendix A for a list of Internet helps that include accountability groups.) *"Though one may be overpowered, two can defend themselves. A cord of three strands is not quickly broken"* (Eccl. 4:12).

Conclusion

Adultery is a family killer. To overcome this threat, we do not need a new revelation. Those who obey the 11 principles in this lesson will never commit sexual sins. Ephesians 5:3 tells us, *"But among you there must not be even a hint of sexual immorality, or of any kind of impurity."*

Overcome the Threat of Abuse

Goal A: *Define abuse and state 2 causes of it.*
Goal B: *Summarize 4 reasons why a wife might continue to live with abuse.*
Goal C: *Identify 4 keys to overcoming abuse.*

The children ran to their hiding place as soon as their father began to hit their mother. Their mother made them promise to stay hidden—no matter how long—until the beating was over. She would come to them whenever she thought it was safe for them. The children had always run—terrified by the yelling, screaming, and loud crying. But what they saw, felt, and heard went deep into their souls. After several years, the oldest son decided that his father would never beat his mother again. So when the father began to yell, the son ran for the gun. One shot stopped his father—just like the son had imagined every time he hid in fear and anger as a child.

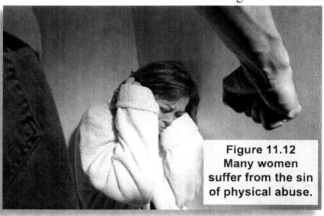

Figure 11.12 Many women suffer from the sin of physical abuse.

The most unusual thing about this story is that the father died. Most often in cases of physical abuse, it is women or children who die. And those who continue to live in a family with abuse carry its scars. To overcome abuse, let us look at four common questions.

 Q 47 *Describe 3 forms of abuse.*

A. What is abuse?

Abuse is causing harm or injury. It takes many forms.

1. Physical abuse is the easiest to recognize. Physical abuse includes such things as hitting, burning, or cutting a family member. This kind of abuse may also include not giving food, water, clothing, or shelter.

2. Sexual abuse is another terrible sin in families. Evil adults sometimes force sexual relations on children. But even the sexual act between husband and wife can be abusive—when it is forced, violent, or unlike God's plan.

Q 48 *Which form of abuse is most common in your culture? Explain.*

3. Verbal abuse causes mental and emotional harm. People use harsh words to make a family member be silent, feel inferior, or become afraid. Verbal abuse includes calling someone an ugly name, cursing, or making threats. The hateful words of verbal abuse harm family members—causing them to think in wrong ways about themselves and others. Verbal abuse causes a person to have an unhealthy, unhappy life. Those who suffer from abuse often struggle with shame, anger, and low self-esteem.

B. Why do some abuse?

Concerning abuse between husbands and wives, there are two main types of abusers.[18]

The *first* type of abuser is usually a man who wants to control the marriage. He will use any method to control a wife. This is the most dangerous abuser. The abuse is fierce, often, and may take any form. This type of abuser believes that a man has the right to rule over his wife. Any action of the wife that he thinks is independent—such as visiting with friends without him—will stir up his fierce anger.

The *second* type of abuser may be a man or a woman. This abuser is not seeking total control over the other person, but wants control over a situation. These abusers will harm their family members as frustration rises out of control. Conflict in marriage may result in violence. It is common for the use of alcohol or drugs to increase the violence.

Most abusers have common things in their past.[19] They grew up in a family where abuse was common. <u>As children,</u> they had three common experiences they saw or heard and felt.

- *First,* their father or mother harmed or shamed them.
- *Second,* their parents abused each other.
- *Third,* their mother was not safe. They saw that she was abused in the home and unable to protect herself.

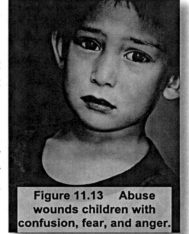

Figure 11.13 Abuse wounds children with confusion, fear, and anger.

Seeing and feeling abuse has a great effect on children. Abuse in the home causes children to feel angry, weak, afraid, and insecure. They become angry if a father abuses the mother. But they may also despise the mother for not protecting herself. Children follow the examples they see in the home. They learn to act like their parents. From the father who abuses, they learn to abuse others. And from the mother who is abused, they learn to accept abuse (Review Figure 11.2 and see Figure 11.14).

C. Why does a woman stay with a husband who abuses her?

Some women are killed by their husbands. Others leave a husband who abuses them. But at times—for several reasons—a woman may continue to live with a husband who abuses her.[20] Let us consider four reasons.

- **Fear** is the main reason a woman remains with a husband who abuses her. Women are afraid of what will happen to them and their children if they leave. A man who seeks to control his wife will follow her if she leaves—and seek to take her home. Then the abuse will be even greater. He may terrorize and threaten the woman, her children, family, and friends. In fact, the most likely time for this kind of husband to murder his wife or children is when they try to leave him.
- **Finances** are a reason that many women continue to live with abuse. A suffering woman asks herself, "How will I support myself and my children if I seek to escape from this abuse?" Many women cannot find a good answer to this financial question.
- **Hope for change** keeps many women under the rod of abuse. They want their marriage to succeed. Some begin to believe the cruel words of their husbands' verbal abuse. These women think that if they try harder to please him, things will get better. The cycle of abuse strengthens this weak hope.[21] Study the common cycle of abuse in Figure 11.14.

Q 49 What are 2 types of abusers?

Q 50 Does a husband have the right to rule over a wife? Explain.

Q 51 How does frustration lead some to abuse?

Q 52 Which 3 past things do abusers have in common?

Q 53 List 4 reasons women stay with abusive husbands?

Q 54 Describe the fears of an abused woman.

Q 55 Summarize 3 common steps in the cycle of abuse.

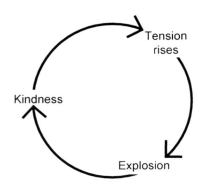

Step	Description
1. Tension rises	Something goes wrong in the husband's life. The wife seeks to please him and keep him from losing his temper. There are repeated minor frustrations. As the wife senses his tension rising, she begins to withdraw in fear. He senses her withdrawal as rejection and feels the need to control her more. Some women think the days and weeks of tension and fear are worse than the beatings.
2. Explosion	This is the shortest phase, lasting 1 or 2 days. He focuses on something his wife did that he does not like. He punishes her. He does not respond to cries for mercy. But his rage is exhausted and the tension is released.
3. Kindness	Out of remorse or guilt or just because he feels better now, the husband will often be tender and affectionate. He may apologize and promise to never hurt her again. It is in this phase that the woman's hope flourishes.

Figure 11.14 Three common steps in the cycle of abuse

Q 56 *How is living in a home with abuse like being in prison?*

- **Lack of support** also keeps many women under a roof that covers abuse. The world of an abused woman can be very small. She may be apart from others who could counsel her. She uses much of her energy to survive from day to day, and finds it hard to discover a solution alone. She may not be able to leave without help. Some societies provide help, but others do not. Churches may provide temporary shelter. But a woman who lacks help will find it very difficult to escape.

D. How can a family overcome abuse?

Help can come in several ways.

Q 57 *List 4 things that are necessary to overcome abuse.*

- **Prayer.** The door of heaven is the first door that believers should knock on to find help for problems. Our heavenly Father invites His children to turn to Him for help. *"Let us then approach the throne of grace with confidence, so that we may receive mercy and find grace to help us in our time of need"* (Heb. 4:16). God helped Hagar when Sarah abused her.

    ⁴He [Abram] slept with Hagar, and she conceived. When she knew she was pregnant, she began to despise her mistress. ⁵Then Sarai said to Abram, "You are responsible for the wrong I am suffering. I put my servant in your arms, and now that she knows she is pregnant, she despises me. May the LORD judge between you and me." ⁶"Your servant is in your hands," Abram said. "Do with her whatever you think best." **Then Sarai mistreated Hagar; so she fled from her.** *⁷The angel of the LORD found Hagar near a spring in the desert; it was the spring that is beside the road to Shur. ⁸And he said, "Hagar, servant of Sarai, where have you come from, and where are you going?" "I'm running away from my mistress Sarai," she answered. ⁹Then the angel of the LORD told her, "Go back to your mistress and submit to her"* (Gen. 16:4-9).

Q 58 *Why should a pastor encourage those suffering abuse to ask for help? Explain.*

- **Asking for help!** The spouse and children must speak the truth. Help seldom comes when abuse is a family secret. So family members must reveal the abuse to others who can help. And when those outside the home hear the truth, they must affirm it. They must not make excuses, or deny the husband's sinful actions. At times, the larger family of the husband or wife can help find a solution. Sometimes it may be best for a wife to return to her parents, with her children, until a solution is found.

Q 59 *Is beating a wife wrong in a culture that says it is right? Explain.*

If the husband is a believer, the church must talk to him about this problem. Church elders must talk in a way to help him solve the problem, not condemn him. The church must do all in their power to lead this believer to a place of repentance. It is the responsibility of the pastor to rebuke those who abuse family members. The church must teach that all abuse is wrong. Husbands are to love their wives as they love themselves, and be gentle with them. God did not make woman from a man's foot, to walk on. Nor did God create woman from man's head to rule over him. The

Lord made woman from man's rib, near his heart. This shows us that God's plan is for a man and woman to live side by side in love. They are joint heirs of the grace of God. As we studied earlier, a man should love his wife as Christ loves the Church; and Christ never abuses His bride, the Church.
- **Repentance.** The abuser must repent. He must show his repentance by stopping all types of abuse. Words of repentance are not enough. Words can be a part of the cycle of abuse as shown in the chart above (Figure 11.14).
- **Counseling.** The abuser and those who have been hurt must find counsel outside the home. Broken emotions must be healed. The abuser must find help to learn how to handle his emotions in a godly way. We will focus on this topic later in this chapter.

Sara sat with her pastor telling her story. She was afraid her husband was going to kill her. She spoke of his rage, violence, and threats. She did not know where else to turn for help. The pastor was shocked. He knew her husband—a friendly, loved, and helpful man in the church. The pastor had not noticed Sara that much. She was quiet. The pastor thought that she must be doing something to irritate her husband. Or maybe she was making things sound worse than they were. So, the pastor encouraged her, and told her to try to be a better wife. Then he sent her back home.

 Q 60 *Did this pastor and church do the right thing?*

The next time he saw Sara, she was in the hospital. Her husband had beaten her and thrown her down some stairs. This opened the pastor's eyes to the truth about abuse. He began preaching more about the love a husband should have for his wife. The church took action and opened a shelter for women and children. They also provided counseling to teach abusive husbands and their victims how to deal with their emotions in godly ways.[22]

Overcome the Threat of Addictions[23]
Goal A: *Define addictions, and explain how people become addicts.*
Goal B: *Explain 8 keys to being free from all forms of slavery.*

A weak, sick man lay on a bed in the hospital. His body was old, though his years were few. Alcohol had destroyed his health. Still, his mind and body cried for a drink—as a tiny baby cries for milk. His time was short, so his wife and son came to see him one final time. They hoped for some kind words from him—after living for years with the pain he had caused the family. Maybe there could be a good moment to remember. As they entered the room, the man looked to them and asked. "Did you bring my liquor?" Then he saw their empty hands. He used his last strength to shake his fist and curse them. The son put his arm around his mother, and they walked out without a word. The father died as he had lived for many years—alone.

A. What is an addiction?

Solomon described one type of addict—a slave to alcohol.

 Q 61 *Describe the addict of Proverbs 23:29-35.*

[29]Who has woe? Who has sorrow? Who has strife? Who has complaints? Who has needless bruises? Who has bloodshot eyes? [30]Those who linger over wine, who go to sample bowls of mixed wine. [31]Do not gaze at wine when it is red, when it sparkles in the cup, when it goes down smoothly! [32]In the end it bites like a snake and poisons like a viper. [33]Your eyes will see strange sights and your mind imagine confusing things. [34]You will be like one sleeping on the high seas, lying on top of the rigging. [35] "They hit me," you will say, "but I'm not hurt! They beat me, but I don't feel it! When will I wake up so I can find another drink?" (Prov. 23:29-35).

At least three verses in the New Testament describe addictions or slavery:
- Jesus replied, *"I tell you the truth, **everyone who sins is a slave to sin**"* (John 8:34).

Q 62 *Does God expect us to be slaves of sin in this life, or does Jesus want to free us? Explain.*

- *"Don't you know that when you offer yourselves to someone to obey him as slaves, you are __slaves to the one whom you obey__—whether you are slaves to sin, which leads to death, or to obedience, which leads to righteousness?"* (Rom. 6:16).
- *"For a man is __a slave__ to whatever has mastered him"* (2 Pet. 2:19).

Q 63 *What is an addiction? Define it and give some examples.*

Definition: An addiction is any form of slavery—anything that controls a person's life, thoughts, emotions, and actions. Slavery can be good or bad. A person can be a slave to God and righteousness (Rom. 6:16). In contrast, a person can be a slave or addict to many forms of sin. Alcohol and other drugs are common masters of slaves. But a person can also be a slave to lust, anger, the desire for power, work, pornography, gambling, gossip, greed, eating too much, violence, or money.

B. How do people become addicts or slaves?

Sometimes people learn to be slaves by following the examples of parents or friends. Other times, mental illness can lead to an addiction. Demons may influence some people to be slaves. But pain and anger are the main things that cause a family member to become an addict.

Q 64 *Explain the 4 steps into slavery (Figure 11.15).*

There are four steps into the bondage of an addiction—a problem that controls a person's life (Figure 11.15).

Step	Description
1. Try it.	I discover that _____(a drug or action) makes me feel good. I do not see any bad results from doing it. I learn to trust _____ to make me feel good or escape from a bad feeling.
2. Use it a little.	I begin to use _____ more often. I use it when others approve. I make rules about it to make me feel "safe." _____ begins to affect my daily choices.
3. Use it daily.	I begin to depend on _____ in a harmful way. I begin to lose control over it. I break my values. I break my "safe" rules. _____ no longer blocks out my emotional pain. My life gets worse in every area.
4. It uses me as a slave.	I lose touch with reality. I may try to escape my problems by running away. I lose control and dignity. I have no desire for God. My family relationships are destroyed.

Figure 11.15   People become slaves by taking four steps over a period of time.[24]

C. Are you in danger of being a slave or addict?[25]

Q 65 *Are you becoming a slave or addict in any area? Examine your life.*

Figure 11.15 shows the steps into slavery. Do you see areas of danger or slavery in your life? Little steps lead to big problems. For example, consider the problem of gossip. Look at gossip through the four steps of Figure 11.15. Step by step, the sin of gossip can destroy family relationships. So what questions should we ask ourselves to test for danger? Here are four:

- Do I hide this action from family and friends?
- Does this action pull me or others away from Christ?
- Does this action express Christian love?
- Do I use this action to escape feelings?

D. How can a person become free from slavery or addictions?

Let us look at eight keys to being free.

Q 66 *What is the first step to overcoming any problem?*

1. Admit the problem. The first step toward solving any problem is to admit it. The worst thing an addict can do is deny or hide his problem. The Pharisees were spiritually blind and would not admit their problem. So their problem remained. *"Jesus said, ...now that you claim you can see, your guilt* [problem] *remains"* (John 9:41).

So an addict should admit his or her problem. Likewise, those who know about an addiction must not hide or deny it. Sin grows in the dark. To get help, we must bring a problem into the light. The Bible offers no help to those who deny their problems. In contrast, Scripture offers help to those who admit their problems. *"If we confess our*

sins, *he is faithful and just and will **forgive** us our sins and **purify** us from all unrighteousness"* (1 John 1:9).

There is a story about an *ostrich that saw a lion nearby. The large bird hid its head in a hole in the sand. It ignored the danger, hoping that it would go away. What do you think happened? Tough love does not hide problems; it discusses them and seeks a solution. If you deny the problem of a fire in your house, it will destroy your home. If you shout FIRE!, you may save the house and those in it. So if there is an addiction in your home, admit it to self, God, and others.

2. Talk about the problem. Often, problems remain because people refuse to talk about them. They do not want to feel ashamed or embarrassed. <u>Remember the parable of the alligator</u>! Perhaps people are afraid that the person with the problem will become angry. Or they are afraid that others will criticize or reject them. For sure, it is difficult to admit and talk about problems. Discussion about problems causes pain and tears. But there is no help for a problem without talking about it. To get help for any problem, we must cross the painful valley of discussion.

Q 67 *Explain: "Help is always beyond the valley of discussion."*

Figure 11.16
In a family, help for any problem comes after the valley of discussion.

3. Refuse to enable a person to continue with the problem. If our child or mate is an addict, we must show tough love. *Tough love* means that we refuse to hide or shelter an addict from the natural results of his behavior. For example, if a son loses a job because of alcohol, a parent should not give money to the son. If a son is selling or using drugs, the parent must not hide this sin from the authorities. If a husband is addicted to anger, and beats his wife, she should not hide his problem. Hiding a problem is called *enabling*—because hiding a problem enables a person to continue as a slave. There may even be a time when a person needs to separate from an addict to provide a safe home for self and children.

Q 68 *Explain "enabling a person to be a slave." Give an example.*

John did not beat his wife or children, but he criticized them. This continued for more than 10 years because the family did not protest. They enabled him to practice this harmful habit by lacking the courage to talk about it. It is possible to show love and respect, but still talk about a problem.

4. Identify and admit your feelings.[26] At the end of the day, a boss rebuked a man in front of other workers. The angry man went home. Instead of greeting his wife, he shouted, "Why isn't the meal ready?" Then he stomped out of the kitchen. The wife turned and scolded the son, "Look at how dirty you've gotten your clothes!" The son went outside and kicked his dog.

Q 69 *What happens when a person does not admit his bad feelings?*

This example shows us the danger of responding to our feelings in the wrong way. No one, except the rude boss, admitted true feelings. The husband, wife, and son were all angry, but they did not talk about it. No one dealt with the real problem. Rather, they expressed their feelings in hurtful ways. Since they did not express their true feelings, those feelings will be present tomorrow, to cause more problems.

People sometimes deny what they are feeling. They want to ignore true feelings because the truth might cause pain or shame. To face the true feelings might mean that they need to forgive or change. But admitting our feelings is important. God has made us as whole people. One part of the whole affects the rest. An egg is made up of the shell, the white, and the yolk. What you do to any part of an egg affects the rest of it. If you crack the shell, it will affect the white and the yolk. Likewise, a human is made up of many parts—such as spirit, mind, body, and emotions. What happens in our emotions—our deepest feelings—affects the rest of us. So, a person must admit what he feels so

Q 70 *Why do some people deny their emotions?*

that his body and spirit will be healthy. *First,* we must admit the truth to ourselves and to God. *Later,* we may desire to speak to others.

You do not need to use careful words with God. He already knows the truth about what you feel. Be honest with Him, as Job was honest about his feelings. Speak to God clearly about what you are feeling. David admitted feelings to himself and to God. Psalm 55:4-8 shows us one of the many times that David told God he was hurting.

Q 71 *How is the root of feeling different from the fruit? Illustrate.*

5. Discover the roots of your feelings. Suppose there is a youth that has a problem with drugs. He may admit that he is feeling lonely, rejected, or angry. Next, he must discover what is causing him to feel this way. Or perhaps a father is a slave to alcohol. Perhaps he feels sad, lonely, or ashamed. This is the fruit, but what is the root? Why is the man drinking? What kind of pain is he trying to cover up or avoid?

6. Repent of any feeling or emotion caused by sin, and ask Jesus to help you. We cannot deliver ourselves from our sins. Evil emotions such as rage, greed, lust, bitterness, and hate are like chains that bind us. We cannot free ourselves from these giants. That is why God sent Jesus to help us. The name *Jesus* means "Savior." Consider the good news of Matthew 1:21— *"She will give birth to a son, and you are to give him the name Jesus, because he will save his people from their sins."* Jesus helps those who repent and turn to him. His name is your invitation. Though you have seven demons, like Mary Magdalene, He will drive them all out (Luke 8:2).

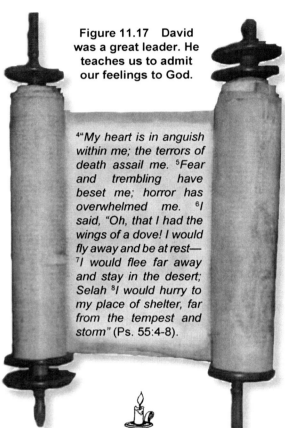

Figure 11.17 David was a great leader. He teaches us to admit our feelings to God.

⁴*"My heart is in anguish within me; the terrors of death assail me. ⁵Fear and trembling have beset me; horror has overwhelmed me. ⁶I said, "Oh, that I had the wings of a dove! I would fly away and be at rest— ⁷I would flee far away and stay in the desert; Selah ⁸I would hurry to my place of shelter, far from the tempest and storm"* (Ps. 55:4-8).

If a person does not repent of sinful feelings, he will make bad choices based on those feelings. A 14-year-old girl named Darla entered the church to worship. When she saw an elderly woman standing nearby, Darla turned away. She wanted to avoid greeting the old woman. Oh, how bitter Darla felt toward that woman! The woman had gossiped about her brother, and this discouraged him from attending church. Darla wished she could correct the

Q 72 *What is repentance? What must follow it?*

woman. But she was too young. It was the responsibility of an elder to talk to the woman about her gossip. So, Darla's anger and malice boiled within. She tried to ignore the old woman during the service.

Later, at the altar, Darla joined others to pray. She sought God's presence and felt the Spirit of God strengthen her. She repented of her attitude toward the elderly woman. As Darla raised her head, through her tears she saw the old woman. With great surprise, Darla realized that her bitterness was gone. In its place she felt concern and compassion. God loved that old woman! Darla arose and gave her a sincere greeting. Then, Darla decided to talk to her parents about the problem.

Q 73 *Is it wrong to feel anger or sexual desire? Explain.*

Q 74 *What is the key to self-control?*

7. Depend on the Holy Spirit to help you express your feelings in ways that please God and others. It is not wrong to feel emotions like anger. Emotions are a part of us. They rise up within us from time to time. But we must learn to respond to our emotions in ways the Spirit leads us. It is not wrong to feel angry. But it is wrong to have a fit of rage. The Bible teaches us that we can be angry, but not allow our anger to lead us into sin (Eph. 4:26). Likewise, it is not wrong to feel sexual desires. God is the One who created sexual desires within us. But it is wrong to lust or fulfill sexual desires outside of marriage. The Holy Spirit wants to rule over our feelings and emotions, as a rider rules over a horse. As we submit to the Spirit, He guides us to express our feelings in ways that please God and others.

16So I say, live by the Spirit, and you will not gratify the desires of the sinful nature. 17For the sinful nature desires what is contrary to the Spirit, and the Spirit what is contrary to the sinful nature. They are in conflict with each other, so that you do not do what you want. 18But if you are led by the Spirit, you are not under law. 19The acts of the sinful nature are obvious: sexual immorality, impurity and debauchery; 20idolatry and witchcraft; hatred, discord, jealousy, fits of rage, selfish ambition, dissensions, factions 21and envy; drunkenness, orgies, and the like. I warn you, as I did before, that those who live like this will not inherit the kingdom of God. 22But the fruit of the Spirit is love, joy, peace, patience, kindness, goodness, faithfulness, 23gentleness and self-control. Against such things there is no law. 24Those who belong to Christ Jesus have crucified the sinful nature with its passions and desires. 25Since we live by the Spirit, let us keep in step with the Spirit (Gal. 5:16-25).

Emotions Produced by the Flesh	Emotions Produced by the Spirit
Hate	Love
Sexual lust	Self-control, patience
Fits of rage	Self-control, patience, kindness
Jealousy, envy, selfish ambition	Love, peace, goodness, faithfulness

Figure 11.18 Galatians 5:16-25 contrasts the emotions caused by the flesh and the Spirit.

Ezekiel received an unusual command from the Lord. God told him that in public he was not to express sorrow for the death of his wife. This was hard—because his wife was *"the delight of* [his] *eyes"* (Ezek. 24:15-16). Still, Ezekiel obeyed and fulfilled God's painful purpose. Through Ezekiel, God gave a prophetic warning to the nation of Israel (Ezek. 24:20-24).

Ezekiel is an example to us. He shows us that it is possible to control strong emotions. Paul teaches us that we may pray in tongues in a loud, public way, or we may pray quietly to ourselves and to God (1 Cor. 14:13, 26-28). And like Ezekiel, we may express our emotions in a loud way, or in a soft way. Ezekiel expressed sorrow to himself and to God as he groaned quietly (Ezek. 20:17-18). He controlled his emotion so that God's greater purpose could be fulfilled.[27]

Likewise, we must control the way we express our emotions. To fulfill God's purposes, we must avoid words or actions that damage others. We are not always free to express our feelings to family members. We must first ask the question, "Will God's purposes be served if I express these feelings?" We may need to wait for a different time to share. We may need to keep these feelings private. We must control how and when we share our emotions. In this way we bring glory to God and fulfill His purposes in our lives.

Learn to make **feeling statements**—polite statements that describe the way you feel. A feeling statement begins with the words, "I feel like...." A husband who feels ignored by his wife—after the birth of their children—might describe that feeling like this: "I feel like a young man who is never chosen to play with the team. All he can do is stand back and watch the others."

Q 75 *What is a "feeling statement"?*

A woman who is being mistreated by her husband's family might describe her feelings like this: "I feel like a spotted chick that is being pecked by the other chickens."

It takes extra thought to describe our feelings, but the result is powerful. People do not like it when you point your finger at them, or accuse them of something. They do not like critical statements that begin with "You." But they will listen with compassion when you begin a sentence with "I feel like... ." So practice the skill of learning to describe your feelings. Talking about the way you feel brings emotional health. And describing your feelings leads you on the path away from addictions and slavery.

Q 76 *Suppose a family member has criticized you. Create a feeling statement as a response.*

8. Seek more help if you need it. We have studied about how to overcome an addiction. If you practice the things we have discussed, but your addiction remains, you need more help. Perhaps there is a Teen Challenge Center near you. You may need counseling through your church or community. Or there may be a local program such as Alcoholics Anonymous. Do not give up. Pray and talk to your pastor. God is faithful. He will help you conquer any addiction.

 **Chapter Summary**

 Overcome the Threat of Distance

Goal A: *Explain the dangers of feeling alone in a family.*

The desire to belong is strong. One who does not feel a part of the family—either a parent or a child—may turn away from the family to seek love and acceptance. This can result in various forms of sin and sickness.

Goal B: *Summarize 9 causes and cures of feeling distant in a family.*

Problems that cause a family member to feel distant	Solutions
Failure to make the home safe—physically and emotionally	Practice the golden rule.
Failure to remain interested in family members	Dig a little. Your family is like treasure hidden in a field.
Failure to spend time with the family	Spend time together.
Failure to control jealousy between children	Control jealousy and competition in your family.
Failure to adjust to changes	Do not oppose all change.
Failure to show love and affection	Speak the love language another understands.
Failure to accept, support, and encourage	Communicate acceptance. Encourage and inspire. Praise family members.
Failure to forgive	Forgive forever, and bury the offense. Do not ever mention the offense again.
Failure to be relevant, open, and honest	Ask God to give you the courage and wisdom you need to discuss hard topics.

Figure 11.19 Problems and solutions related to the threat of distance in a family

 Overcome the Threat of Adultery

Goal: *Explain and apply each of the 11 principles to protect your family from adultery.*

Recognize the problem and the danger of sexual sins. Understand the process from temptation to sin. Walk in the Spirit and you will win the battle over temptation. Pay attention to <u>outward</u> warning signs <u>in others</u>. Pay attention to <u>inward</u> warning signs <u>in you</u>. Guard your heart. Guard your mind. Guard your marriage. Consider the cost of adultery, so that you will not agree to pay it. Guard your health. Be accountable to others.

 Overcome the Threat of Abuse

Goal A: *Define abuse and state 2 causes of it.*

Abuse is causing harm or injury. Abuse may be physical, sexual, or verbal. The desire to control the marriage causes some men to use any method to control a wife. The second type of abuser may be a man or a woman. This abuser is not seeking total control over the other person, but wants control over a situation.

Goal B: *Summarize 4 reasons why a wife might continue to live with abuse.*

A wife may tolerate abuse because of fear, finances, hope for change, or lack of support.

Goal C: *Identify 4 keys to overcoming abuse.*

All in the family can pray. Family members must ask for help. The abuser must repent. Some may need counseling.

 Overcome the Threat of Addictions

Goal A: *Define addictions, and explain how people become addicts.*

An *addiction* is any form of slavery—anything that controls a person's life, thoughts, emotions, and actions.

Sometimes people learn to be slaves by following the examples of parents or friends. Other times, mental illness can lead to an addiction. Demons may influence some people to be slaves. But pain and anger are the main things that cause a family member to become an addict. Review Figure 11.15 on four steps to slavery.

Goal B: *Explain 8 keys to being free from all forms of slavery.*

Admit the problem. Talk about the problem. Refuse to enable a person to continue with the problem. Identify and admit your feelings. Discover the roots of your feelings. Repent of any feeling or emotion caused by sin, and ask Jesus to help you. Depend on the Holy Spirit to help you express your feelings in ways that please God and others. Seek more help if you need it.

 Test Yourself: Circle the letter by the *best* completion to each question or statement.

1. A person who feels distant within a family
a) will cling to family values.
b) will remain loyal to the family.
c) will talk openly about his feelings.
d) will seek others to meet his needs.

2. Closeness in a family is most often ruined by
a) adultery.
b) slavery.
c) feeling unsafe.
d) lack of finances.

3. A guideline for showing love and affection is:
a) Love the way you would like to be loved.
b) Love in the way your mother loved you.
c) Love the way someone wants to be loved.
d) Love in the way that costs you the most.

4. Which statement is TRUE about temptation?
a) Those who are spiritual are not tempted.
b) Even the most spiritual are tempted.
c) Thinking an evil thought is a sin.
d) Jesus is the only one who was not tempted.

5. The steps down to adultery are
a) few and big.
b) rough and steep.
c) many and small.
d) unseen and unknown.

6. Abuse often grows from the root of
a) destruction.
b) bitterness.
c) control.
d) lust.

7. The main reason a wife lives with abuse is
a) fear.
b) love.
c) hope.
d) ignorance.

8. To be free from abuse, family members must
a) remain silent and pray to God.
b) receive a miracle from God.
c) speak the truth about the problem.
d) take matters into their own hands.

9. An addiction is a form of
a) drugs.
b) bribery.
c) adultery.
d) slavery.

10. The first step to freedom from addictions is:
a) Ask God to help you.
b) Be filled with the Spirit.
c) Admit your problem.
d) Talk to your pastor.

Chapter 12:
How to Handle Tough Problems

Introduction

Tough family problems cause *stress. Stress may be good or bad—depending on our response to it. Stress is helpful when a person faces danger. It gives energy and desire to deal with tough issues. But *prolonged stress—pressure that lasts and lasts—can cause impatience, worry, and fear. It may lead to poor work, poor health, poor relationships, and a poor spiritual life.

Some events that cause stress and anxiety are shown in Figure 12.1. Dr. Thomas H. Holmes has made a scale—showing the amount of stress events cause. In one year, stress that adds up to a total of 300 points is dangerous. In the people he studied, 80 percent of those who had stress above 300 became depressed, had heart attacks, or suffered other illnesses.

In this chapter, we will consider some tough issues that bring stress to a family. With God's help, we can deal with these things in faith and hope—and avoid the harmful effects of anxiety.

Event That Causes Stress	Stress Points
Death of a spouse	100
Divorce	73
Marital separation	65
Prison term	63
Death of a close family member	63
Personal injury or illness	53
Marriage	50
Fired from job	47
Marital reunion	45
Retirement	45
Change in health of a family member	44
Pregnancy	40
Sex difficulties	39
New family member	39
Less finances	38
Death of a close friend	37
Change of job	36
Arguments with spouse	35
Failure to pay back a loan	30
Change in work responsibilities	29
Son or daughter leaving home	29
Trouble with in-laws	29
Great personal success	28
Wife starts or stops work outside of home	26
Beginning or end of school	26
Change of personal habits	24
Trouble with boss	23
Change in where you live	20
Change in schools	20
Vacation	13
Disobeying the law in minor ways	11

Figure 12.1 Stress varies with the events of life.[1]

Lessons:

Loss—and the Grief It Brings

Goal A: *Identify the 4 steps of grief through loss.*
Goal B: *Explain and apply the 4 steps of grief through barrenness, death, or divorce.*

Remarriage and Blended Families

Goal A: *Identify 3 biblical reasons to consider remarriage.*
Goal B: *Explain 4 keys to help a blended family succeed.*

Older Children Who Rebel Against God

Goal A: *Identify 3 stages in the story of the prodigal son.*
Goal B: *Explain 3 ways parents should respond in Stage One of rebellion.*
Goal C: *Explain ways parents should respond in Stages Two and Three of rebellion.*

 Key Words

barrenness

infertile

Loss—and the Grief It Brings
Goal A: *Identify the 4 steps of grief through loss.*
Goal B: *Explain and apply the 4 steps of grief through barrenness, death, or divorce.*

Setting

There is no escape from loss in this life. All people of all cultures will experience the loss of something or someone they value. The emotional response to loss is grief. Grief affects every part of who we are—body, mind, soul, and spirit. It can cause the body and mind to slow down. Likewise, grief can cause the soul and spirit to become as dry as a desert. Grief is a strong emotion that often causes people to doubt self, others, and even God. For example, consider the doubts that Job's loss and grief brought to him.

Q 1 How do people you know express grief?

We often express grief through tears, restlessness (poor sleep), and depression. But grief is personal—people grieve in different ways. Some grieve deeper and longer than others. Although we vary in the way we express grief, healthy grief has four parts—four steps to climb through:[2]

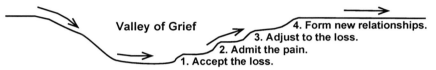

Figure 12.2 Normal life has valleys of grief we must walk through.

1. **Accept the loss.** For example, do not pretend that the person who has died is still there or nearby. Get past the problems of denial or anger.

2. **Admit the pain.** Grief is normal when loss occurs. Do not try to deny or hide your pain. Cry tears of sorrow. Tell God and others how much you hurt. Realize that it will take time for your wounds to heal. People may need to grieve a few days or a few years—depending on the loss.

Q 2 What are the 4 steps of grief to climb through?

3. **Adjust to the loss.** Turn from the past to the present and the future. Do what you must to continue without the one you have lost, and with the ones who remain.

4. **Form new relationships.** Open your heart to meet new people. Make new friends and form new relationships. Plant a new flower or a new tree where the old one died.

In this lesson, we will look at several losses that bring grief. In each type of loss, we will apply the four stages of healthy grief.

A. Loss through *barrenness brings grief.

Most dreams of marriage include children. Children are the fruit of a husband and wife. They are a sign of the love that two people share in marriage. Children are part of our security and hope for the future. They bring mountains of joy to the plains of life. Children extend our lives beyond our time—beyond the grave and into the future. It is a major loss to a couple when they cannot have a child.

Many cultures have wrongly thought that barrenness is always the fault of women. But modern medical science has proven that both males and females can be *infertile—unable to help produce a child.[3]

Q 3 Who causes barrenness, the husband or the wife?

Barrenness can result from sexual diseases. But this is not always the cause. Barrenness may result from problems in the woman's womb or *fallopian tubes. Likewise, the man may not have enough *sperm. A low amount of sperm makes it difficult for a man to make **any** woman pregnant. Also, a husband **or** a wife may have a physical problem that prevents pregnancy. No matter who has the physical problem, both a husband and wife share the loss and grief of barrenness. Since the husband and wife are one flesh, there is a sense in which both are barren if they have no children.

Q 4 What types of problems can cause barrenness?

1. Accept the loss. Barrenness is a difficult loss to accept. People should seek medical care to examine and correct the problem. Doctors may be able to help. Some have erred by turning to ungodly sources of help. This wastes time and money—and causes spiritual problems.

If a couple has no children, they can cry out in prayer to God. Sometimes He answers 'yes' to that cry. God said "yes" to people like Abraham and Sarah, Rachel, Hannah, Zechariah and Elizabeth (Gen. 15:1-5; 18:10; 21:1-3; 30:1, 22-24; 1 Sam. 1; Luke 1:5-25). But sometimes, despite all efforts, barrenness remains.

Q 5 What may happen when barrenness is discovered?

Barrenness may cause a husband and wife to argue and accuse each other. Their sexual life may lose its joy—and become a reminder of their failure. In some cultures, the wife will have not only sorrow but great fear. An ungodly husband may criticize or divorce a barren wife. She may lose her dreams of children, her husband, her home, her self-worth, and her security. Sorrow and fear cause personal pain and strained love between a husband and a wife. But spouses should not allow the strain of barrenness to destroy their love and commitment. The Bible never speaks of barrenness as a reason for divorce.

Q 6 Is barrenness a biblical reason for divorce? Explain.

Figure 12.3
Tears are a language God understands.

Q 7 Is it good to cry about the grief of being barren? Explain.

2. Admit the pain. Tears are a language God understands. Cleanse your heart and emotions by crying tears of sorrow. Bleeding is a step the body takes toward healing. Perhaps tears are the blood of the soul. Share your grief with God. And seek a friend or family member to share the burden of your grief. It is God's plan for believers to share each other's burdens (Gal. 6:2).

Q 8 How can a couple take the third step of grief in being barren?

3. Adjust to the loss. After accepting barrenness, and admitting pain, the third step of grief begins. The couple must adjust—they must change or bend their thinking. Many couples adjust by focusing their attention on each other. Instead of complaining about what they do not have, they give thanks for what they do have. Some people live alone—all of life—with no spouse. It is a great blessing to be married, to have a mate to share life with. A husband and wife have many reasons to rejoice.

Q 9 How can a couple live a fruitful life even though they are barren?

4. Form new relationships. The fourth stage of grief is: Open your life to new people and experiences. Many barren couples have become fruitful through adoption. Every nation has children who long for a home. These orphans are living on the streets, in government shelters, and in refugee camps. *Every* Christian should be concerned about these homeless children (James 1:27; 2:14-17). But a barren couple receives an even greater blessing by opening their hearts and homes to an orphan. Otherwise, a barren couple may seek other ways to enrich their lives. The time and wealth they would have given to children may bless many others.

Q 10 How were the Holts fruitful even though they were barren?

Strangers would not have thought that James and Jean Holt were barren. It is true that they never gave birth to a child. But the people who knew them never used the word *barren* to describe them. A nephew told how he loved their visits. They brought gifts for him and his sisters—things that they needed and a few things just for fun. And when the nephew visited the Holts, they gave him attention and experiences that made him grow into a stronger man. A missionary told how James and Jean spent years of their lives raising funds to help spread the gospel. Only heaven will reveal *all* those the Holts blessed through their work as volunteers. But one young lady told of the way that they opened their home to her. In their old age, they were touched by her need. They adopted her and made her their heir. This couple that never gave birth to a child was very fruitful.

B. Loss through death brings grief.

Death can come to a family in many ways. It may be sudden or expected. Death may take the old or the young. It may come through an accident, sickness, violence, or suicide. Each of these ways brings its struggles. But let us consider <u>the four steps of grief</u> to pass through with any kind of death.

1. Accept the loss. Often a family cannot believe that their family member has died. Feelings of surprise, shock, and unbelief are common. Three things often help us accept the reality that a person we love is dead. *First*, tell and retell the story to many different people. Good listeners are a blessing to those who struggle to accept death. *Second*, bury the dead person. Funerals vary from culture to culture—but most include viewing of the body and burying the dead. *Third*, deal with things the dead person owned. For example, it is good for a wife to remove the clothes of a husband who dies. Selling his clothes, or giving them to someone, helps her accept his death. Still, it may take time for the living to have the courage and strength to sort through the things of one they loved.

Q 11 What are 3 things that help us accept death?

Figure 12.4 Family members can help each other accept their loss.

2. Admit the pain. Allow yourself to cry, and do not be ashamed of your tears. As we said earlier, as blood cleanses a wound to the body, tears help cleanse a wound to the soul.

Q 12 In your culture, do people cry together about a death? Explain.

Cry with a friend. The Bible tells many times of those who mourned together when a loved one died (Gen. 50:1-3; Luke 8:51-52; John 11:30-36). Share your grief with others and your load will be lighter.

3. Adjust to the loss. The first year after the death of a family member, sadness comes during daily life. Also, on special days, the family misses their loved one for the first time. Family members find strength and comfort when they talk to each other about their feelings. Those outside the family continue with life as always. But the family must adjust to the loss. Adjusting to the empty chair at the table takes time. They should be patient with each other and allow time for inner healing. Working day by day can help a family get through this painful time. It is better to work than to sit and do nothing. And, while adjusting, it is wise to avoid other changes or causes of stress. Often people regret big decisions they make in the time of sorrow. For example, one man was very sad after the death of his wife. After a few months, he married again. However, within a year, he wished he had waited longer before making such a major decision. It is common for grief over a family member to last 2 years or more.

Q 13 In the third step of grief, what types of struggles do people have after a death?

4. Form new relationships. The fourth step in grieving is to turn from sorrow to positive things. For example, a mother's child was killed by a drunk driver. The mother joined a group that helped prevent drunk driving. In another case, a child committed suicide. The parents began teaching other parents how to see signs of depression in young people. Healthy grief can guide us to open our lives to good things. We cannot change the past, but we can help change the future.

Q 14 Give an example of the final step in the grieving process.

After grief, our lives will continue, but life will be different. Grief is like a wound that heals. A scar remains, but the pain is gone. God can use grief to help us be a blessing to many people.

Q 15 Do you have an emotional wound that has left a scar? Explain.

Q 16 *Summarize how to help a child after the death of a loved one.*

How to help children after the death of one they love. Grieving adults have the added task of helping the family's children cope with death. Here are some ways to help children have healthy grief.

> 1. Allow children to cry. Give them physical contact and comfort.
> 2. Let them spend time alone if they seem to need it.
> 3. Tell them the truth—that death is final on earth. The person they love will not come back some day.
> 4. Help them understand that death means the person will be absent from now on. Remember that children think differently. Telling them that Jesus took the person can cause a child to be terrified of Jesus. Saying, "He just fell asleep" may make the child anxious about going to bed.
> 5. Let them view the body (after it has been prepared for viewing) if your culture practices this custom.
> 6. Protect young children from public mourning. Let them say good-bye in private.
> 7. Understand that they may be angry because they feel left behind. They may not be able to understand that the person did not have the power to stop death.
> 8. Let them talk about their memories, and tell them about your memories of the person.

Figure 12.5 Eight ways to help children work through grief from the loss of a loved one[4]

C. Loss through divorce brings grief.[5]

God's plan is for a couple to live in love and unity—married for life (Gen. 2:24; Matt. 19:5-6; Rom. 7:2; 1 Cor. 7:39). But some marriages fall short of Gods' plan and end in divorce. Most people who divorce feel loss and grief. Some feel relief from serious problems when they divorce. But even those who are relieved may have grief over their lost hopes and dreams.

Q 17 *How long does it take a family to work through the four steps of grief after divorce?*

Divorce hurts more people than the husband and wife. It affects relationships with the families of the man and woman. It changes many friendships, and even church fellowship. Divorce may affect jobs or business. But children feel the greatest grief from a divorce. When divorce occurs, it takes the family years to work through the four steps of grief.

1. Accept the loss. It is a good thing to fight for the life of a marriage. Breaking a covenant should never be accepted easily. There is a time for hope. But, God does allow divorce for adultery or *desertion (Matt. 5:31-32; 19:1-9; 1 Cor. 7:15).[6] One spouse may not have the power to hold a marriage together, even though he or she hates divorce. Hope is a light to guide us, but it should not blind us to the truth.

A husband told his wife, Agnes, that he loved another woman and planned to move out of their home. Agnes was shocked and began to pray in hope for her marriage. Two months later she received legal papers that her husband wanted a divorce. She continued to hope. Six months later, the divorce was final and he married the other woman. Still, Agnes continued to pray and hope. "Someday," she told others, "his heart will change, and he will return to us." She refused to accept that the time for hope was over.

Q 18 *Was it time for Agnes to accept the divorce and stop hoping? Explain.*

Q 19 *What are 2 issues that could cause a person to prayerfully consider divorce?*

Consider these things to see if it is time to accept divorce.
- Has either spouse taken another lover? When one spouse commits adultery, the Bible says that God allows divorce. Divorce may not be the best answer when a spouse is unfaithful. But unfaithfulness often leads to a problem like sexual disease, or a lack of trust that destroys the marriage.
- Has either spouse deserted or abandoned the other (1 Cor. 7:15)? Paul says that if an unbeliever abandons or divorces a believer, the marriage is no longer binding. This means that the believer who was left is free to remarry.

How to Handle Tough Problems

Children usually take much longer to accept a divorce than the parents. Unless the divorce frees children from great confusion or violence, they will long for their parents to reunite. They may resist a new parent, and try to force their parents to spend time together. When divorce happens, children may have many bad feelings (Figure 12.6).

A child feels:	A child thinks:
Fear	"What is going to happen to me?"
Rejection	"I am being left by one of my parents."
Anger	"My parents could fix the problems if they wanted!"
Powerless	"I cannot do anything to change things. Only my parents have a choice."
Loneliness	"I miss my dad or mom who has left me."
False guilt	"It is my fault. If I had been better, Mom and Dad would have been happier."
Confusion	"Who is wrong? Should I be loyal to Mother or Father?"

Figure 12.6   Divorce causes a child to have many negative feelings.[7]

Q 20 What are the common feelings of children when their parents divorce?

After divorce, do not forget that children have their own struggles. Those who divorce are still parents, and they must minister to the needs of their children. Parents should seek ways to show love to their children. And they should assure the children that it is one or both parents, not the children, who are guilty.

Q 21 How can parents help their children after a divorce?

2. Admit the pain.   A person needs to be honest about what he or she is feeling. As Scripture says,

[1]*There is a time for everything, and a season for every activity under heaven:* [2]*a time to be born and a time to die, a time to plant and a time to uproot,* [3]*a time to kill and a time to heal, a time to tear down and a time to build,* [4]***a time to weep** and a time to laugh, **a time to mourn** and a time to dance,* [5]*a time to scatter stones and a time to gather them, a time to embrace and a time to refrain,* [6]*a time to search and a time to give up, a time to keep and a time to throw away,* [7]*a time to tear and a time to mend, a time to be silent and a time to speak,* [8]*a time to love and a time to hate, a time for war and a time for peace* (Eccl. 3:1-8).

Share your sorrows with God and others. Allow them to listen, talk and pray with you, and share your pain.

A friend loves at all times, and a brother is born for adversity (Prov. 17:17).

Blessed are those who mourn, for they will be comforted (Matt. 5:4).

Q 22 How does Matthew 5:4 relate to divorce?

3. Adjust to the loss.   After the acceptance and pain of a divorce, each spouse must decide how to handle the change. Each person needs to think clearly. *First*, it is wise to get good advice. You need to know your legal position. Be sure that a qualified person will help you receive fair treatment.

Q 23 What 2 things should a person do to adjust to divorce?

Next, you must face the reality of how your daily life will change. The adjustment will take many months. You will have to make many decisions while you still feel hurt. Devote yourself to prayer, and decide to move forward. Mourning is normal. But do not fall into the pit of feeling sorry for yourself. If you got all the pity that you wanted from others, what would you have? A house full of the words, "I am so sorry."[8] So rather than seeking pity, seek the things that will really help you.

One of the biggest challenges after divorce is to become a successful single-parent. Here are some things to consider as you make this change.[9]

Q 24 What are some keys for a single parent after a divorce?

- Do not try to be both parents to your children. You may have to do some of the jobs of the other spouse, but do not try to take over his or her role. Be the best father or mother you can be, but do not try to be both.

- Let your children remain children. Children should not feel the pressure to become a father or a mother. They may have new jobs, but they should see themselves as children whom a parent cares for.
- Be a parent. Children have friends. They do not need you to be another sister, brother, or friend. You need to accept your full duties as a parent.
- Be honest with your children. Speak to them according to their age, but be honest. Though the truth may hurt, it will help your child trust you and deal with reality.
- Do not criticize their other parent in front of them. Do not try to convince them that the other parent is bad. You will lose their respect when they understand what you are doing. It also makes them feel defensive of the other parent and produces conflict.
- Do not use your children to find out what your former spouse is doing. If they spend time with the other parent, let them enjoy it. Do not ask questions when they return.
- Encourage your children and former spouse to spend time with each other, if this is wise. Children need fathers and mothers. Do not use your children to express anger or seek revenge. Do not use time they should have with their other parent as a weapon. If your former spouse is dangerous to the children, you will need help from someone with authority.
- Spend time with your children in a real-life setting. Do not spend your time together trying to entertain them. Do not try to buy their affection with money and good times. Make your life with them as normal as possible.
- Help your children keep their good memories of when the family was together. You have no right to rob them of those precious memories.
- Work together with your former spouse for what is best for the children. Do not use the children as something to fight about with your former spouse.
- Try to keep as many things the same for your children as you can. The same house, school, friends, and church will bring strength, firmness, and stability to them.
- Seek help if your child does not seem to adjust after some time.
- Live in sexual purity. Protect your reputation.
- Consider remaining single until your children are grown. This will save your children much grief. But if a time comes when you desire a new mate, do not hide this from your children.

4. Form new relationships. You must choose to open your life to new things. Be willing to learn everything you can about yourself and other people through the divorce. Seek God about any repentance that is needed on your part. Decide to be a better person because of what you have learned. You may be able to help other hurting people in new ways, because of your suffering.

> YOU MUST CHOOSE TO OPEN YOUR LIFE TO NEW THINGS.

You must be willing to let go of the past with its hopes and its hurts. Focus your mind on living in the present. You may feel of less value because of your painful experience. *"Be transformed by the renewing of your mind"* (Rom. 12:2). God will help you through His Word, His Spirit, and His Church.

Q 25 *Why is it good to avoid romance soon after a divorce?*

Working through the grief process takes time. And time will bring healing as you fight against bitterness and surround yourself with healthy, encouraging people. There will be ups and downs; good days and bad days. But there can be a consistent move into a good future as you open yourself to grow. However, be cautious and beware about romantic love. Many who divorce make the mistake of becoming quickly involved with someone else—to reassure themselves, to avoid loneliness, and to quiet financial fears. Some people will guide you the wrong way when you are weak. But a divorced person is not able to move forward in a healthy way without time for learning, forgiveness, and healing. A romantic relationship—soon after divorce—will make things much harder for your children.

Divorce may bring relief, but it always brings loss and grief. A divorced person can move through the four stages of grief: accept loss, admit pain, adjust, and form new relationships. The marriage is lost, but the man, woman, and their children can be restored to a future of hope.

The opportunity for a good future after divorce is hard. In some cultures, divorce is hardest for women. The lack of power and rights may cause the divorced wife to lose her children, possessions, and her opportunity to remarry.

Q 26 Should your church try to help women who are divorced? Explain.

All of us have sinned (Rom. 3:23). Some have sinned through sexual sins or divorce. The woman at the well had five husbands (John 4:18). This may mean that she had been divorced five times. Also, she was living in adultery. Yet Jesus loved her, even before she repented! He offered her forgiveness and living water. She took it! Another time, some Pharisees caught a woman in the act of adultery. We do not know who the man was that they caught in adultery with her. It could have been anyone from a Pharisee to a beggar. It appears that they let him go free. But they brought the woman for Jesus to condemn. Remember that the law of Moses said to stone her. But Jesus did not condemn her. He offered her forgiveness and said, *"Go now and leave your life of sin"* (John 8:11).

God hates divorce. His plan is for a man and woman to marry for life. But He forgives those with hard hearts who divorce and later repent. Divorce is a terrible sin. It hurts many people and leaves hearts scarred for a lifetime. Still, divorce is a sin that God will pardon. Likewise, the church must love and forgive those whom God forgives. And people who sin through divorce must learn to forgive themselves, as God forgives.

D. Believers have hope during any kind of loss.

We have examined grief from three kinds of loss: barrenness, death, and divorce. But there are many types of loss—including loss of health, freedom, security, money, or position. Believers can face any kind of loss with hope. In this life, we will face tribulation and grief—but our faith in God brings hope. When Paul spoke about death, he said, *"Brothers, we do not want you to... grieve like the rest of men, who have no hope"* (1 Thess. 4:13). With God, we have hope in this life, and beyond the grave.

Q 27 What comfort do the Scriptures give about times of grief?

Hagar lost everything. Abraham and Sarah sent her away. She lost her position, her protection, and her provisions. Finally, the last of her water was gone. Her son lay crying in the desert. Hagar was sure she was losing him to death. Her grief overwhelmed her—it pressed her to the ground—and she began to sob. But God was present. He said, *"What is the matter, Hagar? Do not be afraid; God has heard the boy crying as he lies there"* (Gen. 21:8-20). Hagar discovered, as we also can discover, that no hardship can separate us from the love of God (Rom. 8:28-39).

Remarriage and Blended Families
Goal A: Identify 3 biblical reasons to consider remarriage.
Goal B: Explain 4 keys to help a blended family succeed.

A. Remarriage is an issue to consider with Bible study and prayer.

The Bible allows remarriage for three reasons:

- **Death**

  ²For example, by law a married woman is bound to her husband as long as he is alive, but if her husband dies, she is released from the law of marriage. ³So then, if she marries another man while her husband is still alive, she is called an adulteress. **But if her husband dies, she is released from that law and is not an adulteress, even though she marries another man** (Rom. 7:2-3).

Q 28 For which 3 reasons does the Bible allow remarriage?

So I counsel younger widows to marry, *to have children, to manage their homes and to give the enemy no opportunity for slander* (1 Tim. 5:14).

- **Adultery**

   "But I tell you that anyone who divorces his wife, ***except for marital unfaithfulness,*** *causes her to become an adulteress, and anyone who marries the divorced woman commits adultery"* (Matt. 5:32).

   "I tell you that anyone who divorces his wife, ***except for marital unfaithfulness,*** *and marries another woman commits adultery"* (Matt. 19:9).

- **Desertion**

   *¹⁰To the married I give this command (not I, but the Lord): A wife must not separate from her husband. ¹¹But if she does, she must remain unmarried or else be reconciled to her husband. And a husband must not divorce his wife. ¹²To the rest I say this (I, not the Lord): If any brother has a wife who is not a believer and she is willing to live with him, he must not divorce her. ¹³And if a woman has a husband who is not a believer and he is willing to live with her, she must not divorce him. ¹⁴For the unbelieving husband has been sanctified through his wife, and the unbelieving wife has been sanctified through her believing husband. Otherwise your children would be unclean, but as it is, they are holy. ¹⁵****But if the unbeliever leaves, let him do so. A believing man or woman is not bound in such circumstances;*** *God has called us to live in peace* (1 Cor. 7:10-15).

These verses are a guide to believers who are divorced or widowed. No believer should remarry without careful study and prayer. Before a person remarries, he or she should consider several questions.

- Do I have God's blessing to remarry?
- Do I have the counsel and blessing of my pastor and local church?
- Have I allowed enough time to pass since my last marriage?
- Have I learned the lessons I should learn from my prior marriage?
- Is this a healthy relationship, or am I just looking for someone to fix everything?
- Is it better or worse for my children if I remarry? (Some doctors who study children think that remarriage is almost always worse for the children. The children spend their years dealing with change and conflict, instead of growing healthy in a secure home.)
- How will we form a new family with our children?

Remarriage is a step that a person should only take in harmony with the Scriptures, the Holy Spirit, and the local church.

B. Blending families through remarriage requires patience and wisdom.

A blended family is the result of two families that are joined together through marriage. For example, John's wife died, and he was left with two children. He married Elizabeth, whose husband had died, and left her with a child. In the new, blended family, there were three children.

A blended family is not a natural family. At first it may feel like a collection of strangers. It takes patience and wisdom for members to grow into a loving relationship. Family members must deal with three issues: relationships with former spouses

Q 29 Summarize the questions a believer should consider before remarriage.

Q 30 Before a believer remarries, which 3 blessings should he or she have?

Q 31 Give an example of a blended family.

Q 32 Which 3 issues do blended families deal with?

Figure 12.7 Members of a blended family may not understand each other!

(if there was a divorce); fair treatment of the children on both sides; and there may be financial strain if either previous marriage ended in a divorce.[10] Blending families creates much stress. See Figure 12.9 to identify signs of stress and helps to lessen it.

Figure 12.8 Stress can make you feel like a rope about to break.

Signs to help you recognize stess:	How to lessen stress
• An unusual change in fruitfulness • A person's ability to work varies greatly • A pattern of absence • Colder relationships • Sudden change • Frustration • Fear of losing ability, as age increases • Conflicts • Living against conscience	• Set aside your problems for a time. • Follow a different schedule. • Change your setting. • Find a model to follow. • Find one who can accept and help you. • Show honest concern without judging. • Count your blessings. • Learn to be content in all situations. • Help others with their problems, and you will feel better about yours.

Figure 12.9 Signs of stress and ways to lessen it

Let us consider some keys to help a blended family succeed.

- **Make the marriage a top priority.** The husband and wife must work hard to build a strong marriage. The chances for conflict are great. The chances for failure are great. More second marriages fail than first ones. One couple found that an hour of prayer together each morning became the source for strength in their new marriage. "The decision to arise each morning for a time of prayer and Bible study was the turning point in our marriage, helping us resolve day-by-day tensions and upsets. Prayer forced us to face up to each situation. We could ignore some problems for a while, but not for long."[11]

- **Move forward at the pace of the *stepchildren.** Do not expect to develop a relationship quickly. The children have been hurt, and they feel confused. They are grieving about the loss of their past family. A stepchild may feel negative feelings toward a stepfather or a stepmother. So be patient.

- **Do not try to take the place of the missing parent.**[12] No one can replace a *birth parent, and no one should try. Honor the stepchild's memories. Do not compete or compare yourself to the child's past parent. Form a new kind of relationship with the stepchild.

- **Allow the birth parent to discipline his or her children** until bonding and trust grow between the child and new parent. Talk often with the parent about expectations and discipline, so you can work together.

Q 33 *What are 4 keys to help a blended familiy succeed?*

One stepmother remembered: "I loved all children, I thought. So, I was shocked to feel hatred when one of my husband's children was mean to one of my little angels. Like a mother bear, I defended my own child. Later, I realized that every mother tends to love her own children more than others."[13]

Leah and Rachel competed for Jacob's love. They bargained with each other for a night to sleep with him (Gen. 30:14-16). They wanted to bear children to gain Jacob's favor. Leah's words, after she gave birth to her first son, are very sad. *"Surely my husband will love me now"* (Gen. 29:32). Later, after the birth of her third son, her sadness remained. She said, *"Now at last my husband will become attached to me"* (Gen. 29:34).

The competition between Leah and Rachel spread to their sons. In the end, the brothers of the wives Jacob loved less sold Joseph, the son of Rachel—the wife Jacob loved the most (Gen. 37:23-27). Forming a happy, blended family is a hard task—with much stress. It calls for much love, sacrifice, honesty, patience, and wisdom.

Older Children Who Rebel Against God

Goal A: *Identify 3 stages in the story of the prodigal son.*
Goal B: *Explain 3 ways parents should respond in Stage One of rebellion.*
Goal C: *Explain ways parents should respond in Stages Two and Three of rebellion.*

Setting

An older child who rebels against God brings great pain to Christian parents. Why do children of godly parents go astray? There are no easy answers. The Bible mentions godly parents with children who rebelled. For example, Samuel's sons turned away from God. Today, it is no different. Many godly parents have children who choose the wrong way.

Q 34 What are 2 reasons that the children of believers may not follow God?

Some youth rebel because their parents failed to lead them in spiritual ways. Other youth see a good example but reject it. Every person has the power to choose. Choice is a gift from God to all. Some children and youth choose wisely, but others make foolish choices.

Parents may not know why their child rebels. Godly parents suffer as they seek to understand rebellion. They hurt as they pray about how to respond. Jesus told a story of a rebellious son. In the story, we see three common stages of a young adult's rebellion (Luke 15:11-24).

A. Stage One: The older child rebels.

Jesus tells us,

Q 35 What are 3 stages that usually happen when an older child rebels?

> ¹¹… *"There was a man who had two sons.* ¹²*The younger one said to his father, 'Father, give me my share of the estate.' So he divided his property between them.* ¹³*Not long after that, the younger son got together all he had, set off for a distant country and there squandered* [wasted] *his wealth in wild living"* (Luke 15:11-13).

The story does not tell us how long the younger son grew in rebellion. It does not tell us who whispered in his ear. It does not tell us why he became unhappy with the life of his family. It does not speak of any family quarrels. Perhaps the father wondered about these things—during the long nights his son was gone.

Q 36 What story did Jesus tell about a youth who rebelled?

The story begins with the son's outward rebellion. He made a decision to reject his family and their values. The younger son left his family and lived a life of shame. His decision hurt himself and dishonored his father. But he did it anyway.

There is a struggle for power in the relationship between a parent and a child. When children are born, the parent has complete control. But the child gains more control over his life as he matures. Children often want control quicker than parents want to give it. In this struggle, a young person says, "I want to be my own boss; and I want to have my own money." This struggle for control may be the root of the younger son's request for his inheritance. The father faced a hard decision when his son decided to leave home. The father did three things that all parents can do to older youth that rebel.

Q 37 How do you know when to permit a rebellious youth to go?

1. Let them go. The Bible tells us that the young man *"set off for a distant country"* (Luke 15:13). The father released him. He did not chase after his son or force him to return. Parents must discern when to let a rebellious child go. Sometimes, the more we control our children, the more they resent it and want to be free. Surely this young man's father tried to reason with him. But his son was determined to go. If a young adult will not honor a parent, it may be time to let him go.

2. Let them make their own mistakes. The young man wasted *"his wealth in wild living"* (Luke 15:13). The young man thought, "This is great. I can live like I want." He threw away the values of his family. He rejected the teachings of his father and mother.

How to Handle Tough Problems

He wasted his money and his life. Rebellion is always a waste. The father knew that his son would find trouble when he let him go. But some must choose trouble, before they reject it.

3. Let them experience the results of their choices. There is always a price to pay for rebellion. *"After he had spent everything... he began to be in need"* (Luke 15:14). The young man was not willing to starve to death, [15] *"So he went and hired himself out to a citizen of that country, who sent him to his fields to feed pigs. [16]He longed to fill his stomach with the pods that the pigs were eating, but no one gave him anything"* (Luke 15:15-16). The son reached the bottom of the valley of rebellion. His wild living took everything from him. He had no friends. He had no money to buy a meal.

> **Q 38** *What error must parents avoid when older children rebel?*

Parents are tempted to rescue their youth before these older children reap the harvest of their rebellion. But the father in Luke 15 let his son taste the bitterness of rebellion. He loved his son and wanted him home. The wise parent understood that some people must learn wisdom the hard way. Many times the only way children will learn is through making their own decisions and their own mistakes. We studied this as discipline through natural results.

B. Stage Two: The results of rebellion lead to repentance.

> [17]*"When he came to his senses, he said, 'How many of my father's hired men have food to spare, and here I am starving to death! [18]I will set out and go back to my father and say to him: Father, I have sinned against heaven and against you. [19]I am no longer worthy to be called your son; make me like one of your hired men'"* (Luke 15:17-19).

> **Q 39** *What led the rebellious son of Luke 15 to repent?*

The son had time to think about his sad condition. He realized that his life was a mess. With new light, he saw the value of his family. He repented—turned away from his rebellion, and toward his father. The son was ready to do anything to be home—even if he had to work as one of his father's employees.

We do not know how long it took the son to see the light. Wisdom came slowly to the young man. *First*, he lost his friends and his money. *Then*, he lost his respect, and was willing to work with pigs. For a Jew, this was very shameful. *Finally*, he was losing his health—he lacked the food his body needed to be strong. Sometime—after much pain and great loss—he came to his senses.

What should a parent do while waiting for a young adult to come to his senses?

> **Q 40** *What 3 things should parents do while waiting for an older child to repent?*

1. Parents need to pray. Rebellious children are in a spiritual war. They need the prayers. Parents can commit their children to God. It is a comfort to know that God is in control. He rules over all the earth—including rebellious children. Our heavenly Father can help our children, even when we do not know where they are.

2. Parents need to be patient. Like the son in Luke 15, it may take time for a rebellious child to repent. Remember that patience is a fruit of the Holy Spirit. So do not try to produce patience by your own efforts. Rather, depend on the Holy Spirit to help you be patient as you pray and wait for God to discipline your child.

3. Parents need to love. No matter how far children fall, or how long you wait, continue to love your children. Leave the door to your heart and your home open for them. Letting children reap the harvest of their rebellion is "tough love." Some children must learn the hard way. Much of what they do is out of our control, so we trust God and continue to love them.

C. Stage Three: The child returns and the parent forgives.

> [17]*"When he came to his senses... [20]he got up and went to his father. But while he was still a long way off, his father saw him and was filled with compassion*

Q 41 *How can a parent move past his anger, hurt, and shame to forgive?*

Q 42 *What made it easier for the son of Luke 15 to confess sins?*

for him; he ran to his son, threw his arms around him and kissed him" (Luke 15:17, 20).

The father accepted his son. The dad assured his son that coming home was the right decision. The father ran to him—hugged and kissed him—and welcomed him home. This is what our heavenly Father does to us when we return to Him. God is our example. As the Scripture says, we should imitate Him—forgive as He forgives (Eph. 5:1).

In this stage, there are two things that parents need to remember.

1. **Show them your love.** The Bible tells us, *"His father saw him and was filled with compassion for him"* (Luke 15:20). The father *"ran to his son, threw his arms around him and kissed him"* (Luke 15:20). His son had no doubt that he was welcome. His father showed his physical affection. He did not wait to hear a confession. It is easier to admit wrong when we know someone loves us. The love of parents enables children to confess their unwise decisions.

2. **Forgive them completely.** If a child repents, forgive completely. The Bible tells us,

²²*"But the father said to his servants, 'Quick! Bring the best robe and put it on him. Put a ring on his finger and sandals on his feet.* ²³*Bring the fattened calf and kill it. Let's have a feast and celebrate.* ²⁴*For this son of mine was dead and is alive again; he was lost and is found.' So they began to celebrate"* (Luke 15:22-24).

The father did not criticize his son about his rebellion. This wise father knew that his son had learned his lesson. When the father said, *"Bring the best robe,"* he was saying, "Welcome home, you are back in the family." He also said, *"Put a ring on his finger."* The ring was a sign of responsibility. A ring often had the family name on it. It could be used for buying. The father showed forgiveness by restoring the son to his former place in the family. The father showed God's grace, and the son was grateful.

The older son was not so quick to forgive. Children who stay with the parents see the suffering a rebellious child brings to the family. They may resent the great time and attention the rebellious child receives. It is common for them to forgive more slowly. But the father sought out the older son, who was slow to forgive. The father—through his example and his words—encouraged his other children to celebrate and to forgive their brother (Luke 15:28-32).

Figure 12.10
Continue to love and pray for your children.

This story in Luke 15 has principles to guide parents. It shows how God deals with our rebellion. It is an example of how we can deal with the tough problem of older children who rebel against God. There is a time to let an older rebellious child go. The results of rebellion, prayer, and love of parents can lead a child to repent. Parents must show love and forgiveness to children who return home.

Conclusion

Each family will face tough problems. We have looked at three: loss, remarriage, and older children who rebel. A family may face these problems and many other tough problems. But we can survive all things through the strength God gives (Phil. 4:13). Paul said about his sufferings, ⁹*"...dying, and yet we live on; beaten, and yet not killed;* ¹⁰*sorrowful, yet always rejoicing; poor, yet making many rich; having nothing, and yet possessing everything"* (2 Cor. 6:9-10).

In World War II the *Nazis arrested Corrie ten Boom and most of her family—for helping Jewish people escape the *Holocaust. They sent the ten Boom family to prison camps. All were abused, and many were killed. Only a few survived the war. Corrie survived and said this about the terrible experience of her family: "There is no hell so deep that God is not deeper."[14]

How to Handle Tough Problems 229

Chapter Summary

   Loss—and the Grief it Brings

Goal A: *Identify the 4 steps of grief through loss.*

Accept the loss. Admit the pain. Adjust to the loss. Form new relationships.

Goal B: *Explain and apply the 4 steps of grief through barrenness, death, or divorce.*

- **Accept the loss.** For example, do not pretend that the person who has died is still there or nearby. Get past the problems of denial or anger.
- **Admit the pain.** Grief is normal when loss occurs. Do not try to deny or hide your pain. Cry tears of sorrow. Tell God and others how much you hurt. Realize that it will take time for your wounds to heal. People may need to grieve a few days or a few years—depending on the loss.
- **Adjust to the loss.** Turn from the past to the present and the future. Do what you must to continue without the one you have lost, and with the ones who remain.
- **Form new relationships.** Open your heart to meet new people. Make new friends and form new relationships. Plant a new flower or a new tree where the old one died.

   Remarriage and Blended Families

Goal A: *Identify 3 biblical reasons to consider remarriage.*

Death; adultery; desertion

Goal B: *Explain 4 keys to help a blended family succeed.*

Make the marriage a top priority. Move forward at the pace of the stepchildren. Do not try to take the place of the missing parent. Allow the birth parent to discipline children until children love and trust the new parent.

   Older Children Who Rebel Against God

Goal A: *Identify 3 stages in the story of the prodigal son.*

The younger child rebels. The results of rebellion lead to repentance. The child returns and the parent forgives.

Goal B: *Explain 3 ways parents should respond in Stage One of rebellion.*

Let them go. Let them make their own mistakes. Let them experience the results of their choices.

Goal C: *Explain ways parents should respond in Stages Two and Three of rebellion.*

Parents need to pray, be patient, love, and forgive completely.

Test Yourself: Circle the letter by the *best* completion to each question or statement.

1. The third step in working through grief is to
a) admit the pain.
b) accept the loss.
c) adjust to the loss.
d) pray to God.

2. "Open your life to new people" is the
a) first step in working through grief.
b) second step in working through grief.
c) third step in working through grief.
d) fourth step in working through grief.

3. Barrenness is a result of a problem in
a) both the father and the mother.
b) either the father or the mother.
c) the father.
d) the mother.

4. A key to accepting death is to
a) be present at death.
b) bury the dead person.
c) avoid talking about it.
d) make new friends.

5. A way to help children accept death is to
a) let them talk about memories.
b) wait some years to tell them the truth.
c) tell them that Jesus took the person.
d) explain that it is wrong to feel anger.

6. A biblical reason for divorce and remarriage is
a) unbelief.
b) beating.
c) adultery.
d) all the above.

7. A key to success in a blended family is to
a) proceed at the pace of stepchildren.
b) talk often about the past marriage.
c) try to replace the missing parent.
d) give 110 percent of yourself to the family.

8. The second stage in the rebellion of Luke 15 is
a) the younger son rebels.
b) the father allows the son to leave.
c) the younger son returns.
d) rebellion leads to repentance.

9. When an older child rebels, parents should
a) prevent him from leaving home.
b) allow him to make his own decisions.
c) rescue him from a harvest of rebellion.
d) go with him and bring him home.

10. If a rebellious child repents, a parent should
a) remind him of the shame.
b) love the child from a distance.
c) forgive all the child has done.
d) require him to confess sins.

How To Handle Tough Problems 231

Chapter 13:
How to Live the Latter Years

Introduction

*When as a child
I laughed and wept—time crept!*

*When as a youth
I dreamed and talked— time walked!*

*When I became
A full-grown man— time ran!*

*Then as with years
I older grew— time flew!*

*Soon I shall find
As I travel on— time gone!*[1]

Figure 13.1 As we grow older we walk slower, but time seems to travel faster.

Since Adam's sin, we have struggled with time. Our time on earth is short. As we come to the latter years of our lives, time is like a handshake that is about to end. Our last years are precious and include important tasks to complete. In this chapter, we will look at those final years and final tasks. We will consider how to help our children be mature adults. We will look at the importance of our influence on grandchildren. And finally, we will consider how to finish the journey with peace, purpose, and a plan.

Lessons:

When Our Children Become Adults

Goal A: *Describe how family expectations should change as children mature.*
Goal B: *Explain how the relationship between parents and adult children can deepen.*
Goal C: *Summarize the challenges of the years of the empty nest.*

When We Become Grandparents

Goal A: *Identify 3 possible roles of grandparents.*
Goal B: *Explain 5 ways a family should care for grandparents.*

When We Grow Old

Goal A: *Describe how the elderly can make peace with their pasts.*
Goal B: *Explain why having a purpose is important when you are old.*
Goal C: *Describe the physical changes the elderly must face.*
Goal D: *Summarize how people should prepare financially for old age.*

232

When Our Children Become Adults

Goal A: Describe how family expectations should change as children mature.
Goal B: Explain how the relationship between parents and adult children can deepen.
Goal C: Summarize the challenges of the years of the empty nest.

Setting

Some compare being a parent to flying a *kite.[2] You start by trying to get the kite off the ground, and sometimes you wonder if the kite—like your child—is going to make it. You run as fast as you can with this kite flapping in the wind behind you. Sometimes it crashes to the ground. So to help it fly, you tie on a longer tail and try it again. Suddenly it catches a little wind and almost gets caught in a tree. Your heart pounds as you see the danger. You keep going, leading the kite to safety. Then, in a joyful moment, the kite rises into the sky. It begins to tug on the string, wanting to go higher. You release more string, allowing the kite more freedom. You loosen your grip little by little. Sooner than you expected, you come to the end of the string. You stand on tiptoe holding the last inch of string between your thumb and forefinger. Then you let go, permitting the kite to soar in God's blue sky. Likewise, parents must release their children to become adults.

**Figure 13.2
Being a parent is like flying a kite.**

Nature gives us many illustrations of parents. For example, a male and female bald eagle court in March or April. Then both help build a nest. When the nest is done it is about 3 feet wide and 3 feet deep. The female lays 1 to 3 eggs. Both the male and female take turns sitting on the eggs to keep them warm. The eggs hatch after about 35 days, and out come the tiny babies.

The parent eagles work together to raise their young. The first day the babies sleep the whole day. The second day the babies can eat pieces of meat given by their parents. For the first month or two, the baby eagles are fed by their parents. The second month the parent eagles return to the nest only to feed their young. When the baby eagles are 10 weeks old they can leave the nest, but they do not go far. In this way their parents can help feed them and teach them how to fly. After the summer the baby is alone, left by itself. It will take 4 years for the young eagle to have white feathers on its head and beautiful tail feathers. The eagle lives for about 30 years.[3]

**Figure 13.3
Eagles mate, build a nest, and raise their young together.**

As children become adults, life for a parent is both exciting and scary. All parents face this time in life. Healthy children become healthy adults. They will make mistakes. But the training and example of their parents will guide them. Let us look at some final matters for parents to consider, as their children become adults.

A. Expectations should change, as children become adults.

Cultures expect various behaviors from adult children. Much depends on the view of the larger family. In some places, parents expect their adult children to remain under the authority of the family leader. Other cultures expect the adult to move into his own home and become independent in every way. But all cultures recognize that we should not treat adults as if they were children. And all agree that adults should have more responsibility for their own lives. So as children become adults, both the parents and the mature children think differently about each other.

Q 1 *In your culture, are adults under the authority of their parents? Explain.*

Q 2 *In your culture, what do parents expect from mature children?*

Q 3 *In your culture, what do mature children expect from their parents?*

Q 4 *Should parents demand that mature children have certain beliefs? Explain.*

Q 5 *Give an example of how the relationship can deepen as children mature.*

Q 6 *How does a mature child honor his parents?*

Q 7 *A father was cruel to his wife and son. Later, the mature son did not respect his father's advice or character. How should this son honor his father?*

Q 8 *How can the absence of children in the home cause trouble for a husband and wife?*

1. **Parents expect a mature son or daughter to:**
   - Care for self, manage finances, and be a good citizen;
   - Develop friendships;
   - Find purpose and spiritual meaning in life.[4]
2. **Mature children expect their parents to:**
   - Allow the son or daughter to make their own decisions;
   - Recognize that adult children are responsible for their decisions;
   - Show joy and confidence in their son or daughter;
   - Reduce or stop financial support;
   - Talk to their children as they talk to other adults.

Believers care about the spiritual life of their children. Will their adult children continue to develop, as believers, in their spiritual life? Many young adults question their beliefs, and some turn away from the church.

James Dobson says that once your children are young adults, do not push them too hard spiritually. You can have some expectations for them—as long as they live with you. But you cannot demand that they believe what you have taught them. The door to the world outside must be fully open to adult children. This can be the most frightening time for parents. Most parents want to keep control to prevent their children from making mistakes. But young adults make better choices when rebellion is not the only path to freedom. The plain truth is that love and freedom go together—hand in hand.[5] So parents who love their older children should treat them like adults.

B. Relationships can deepen, as children become adults.

1. **The relationship between parents and children changes, but it can grow.** Parents and children can discover each other in new ways—once they begin to relate as adults.

Ann, a young woman, sat with her mother, Mary. They talked about memories of Ann's early years. Ann remembered a fire in their home. The mother had been brave and rescued the children. Mary talked about her thoughts and fears. She had been afraid that the fire would kill her. Ann was amazed. She had never thought her mother was afraid of the fire. She had only seen her courage. But now she could see her as a person—not just a mother.

A young man came home from college. He began talking with his father about all he was learning. He was surprised to discover the depth of his father's knowledge and interest. The son did not realize that his father thought about anything but the family business.

The relationship between parents and their children changes. But no matter how old children become, they must honor their parents. *To honor* means "to respect, appreciate, and value." God's command to honor parents is for all of life.

Some parents abuse, neglect, or mistreat their children. God does not command us to honor the evil ways of our parents. But all parents deserve a measure of respect—such as polite words, love, and kindness. Jesus commands us to love all people—even our enemies (Matt. 5:44). The relationship between a parent and child changes, but it always requires honor.

2. **The relationship between a husband and wife can grow when children become adults.** For many years, the mother and father spend most of their time, energy, and money on their children. But as children become adults, parents may wonder, "Now what will we do?" For some parents, this question is like a giant standing over them.

Often the marriage goes through pressure when the couple is alone in their home. For decades they have focused their attention on the children. Often, a husband and wife have forgotten to strengthen their relationship with each other. They may need to get to know each other again. Without the children, old problems may resurrect. It is hard to ignore problems when there is no attention on children.

> HUSBANDS AND WIVES CAN HAVE A NEW BEGINNING WHEN THEIR MAIN FOCUS RETURNS TO EACH OTHER.

Husbands and wives can have a new beginning when their main focus returns to each other. Their friendship and love can grow. Facing the past, they can remember the miles they have walked and the mountains they have climbed. There are many memories to discuss. Facing the future, they can walk new paths together. The marriage relationship will change when children become adults. Some call this the time of the empty nest. The husband and wife can make this a good time. And soon—in the nest that once had children—there will be grandchildren!

Q 9 *How can the relationship between a husband and wife deepen during the years of the empty nest?*

When We Become Grandparents
Goal A: *Identify 3 possible roles of grandparents.*
Goal B: *Explain 5 ways a family should care for grandparents.*

Setting

Some say that grandchildren are a reward for the hard work of raising your own children! Grandparents delight in their grandchildren—and influence them greatly. In this lesson we will look at the influence and role of grandparents *around the world*.

A. Grandparents have a special relationship with their grandchildren.

Let us take a quick look at grandparents in different parts of the world.

- In America and much of the West, a new generation of grandparents is younger. They have time and money to spend on their grandchildren. A grandparent is often between the ages of 50 and 85. Because the length of life is increasing, many children get to know their great-grandparents.

Figure 13.4 Grandparents usually have a special relationship with grandchildren.

- In some cultures, like Thailand, a woman is called "Grandmother" when any younger relative has a baby. The grandmother role is not tied to birth by her children.[6]
- The Chinese respect for old people is well known. A son's most important duty is to be sure that his parents have joy and comfort in their old age. Elderly people are treated with honor and respect.
- In the traditional Japanese family, having sons was very important. If a couple had no son to carry on the family name and care for the parents in old age, they adopted a boy. This son was often a brother's son, and they raised him as their own. In Japan, as in Thailand, almost every old person became a grandparent.[7]
- In Fiji, a writer was told, "We do not leave our parents. We stay close, in the same house or nearby. We share. What is mine is yours. What is yours is mine."[8]

In all cultures grandparents can influence grandchildren in many ways. Here are some positive influences:

- Grandmothers who provide physical and emotional care to infants and *toddlers form a bond with them.
- Grandchildren value what grandparents give—such as love, time, attention, teaching, friendship, a godly example, and gifts.

Q 10 *Do grandparents have a special role in your culture? Explain.*

Q 11 *What are some positive ways grandparents can influence their grandchildren?*

- Grandparents can be sensitive. They can be good listeners when grandchildren, as youth, have a hard time talking with their parents.
- A close relationship between grandparents and young adult grandchildren strengthens both.
- Adult grandchildren and great-grandchildren can benefit from the emotional support of grandparents and great-grandparents.[9]

B. Grandparents may fill several roles.

Q 12 *Summarize the 3 roles of grandparents.*

The role grandparents fill depends on culture, personality, location, and the attitude of the family. Grandparents may relate to their children and grandchildren in three ways.

Q 13 *Which of these roles is most common in your culture?*

1. Grandparents may be <u>very close</u>: Substitute parents. Grandmothers often fill this role, especially when a mother works outside the home. The grandmother takes care of and raises the grandchild during the day. This role is also common when the mother is unwed, or if children become orphans. This grandparent has about the same authority as the parent.

2. Grandparents may be <u>close</u>: Traditional role. Grandparents in this role are part of the larger family. They help the parents and give love, time, attention, wisdom, and other gifts to their grandchildren. Sometimes the grandparents visit the home of the parents. Other times, the parents take the children to visit or stay a few days with the grandparents. In either case, the grandparents are careful to let the parents be the parents.

3. Grandparents may be <u>far</u>: Distant people. In this role, the grandparent has little contact with the grandchildren. Perhaps this role occurs because the grandparent lives far away. The grandparent may see the grandchild only at Christmas or on other special days. The grandparent is not part of the grandchild's daily life.[10]

Q 14 *How did Timothy's grandmother affect his life?*

Any grandparent can have a powerful effect on the spiritual life of the grandchildren. Paul wrote in 2 Timothy 1:5, *"I have been reminded of your sincere faith, which first lived in your grandmother Lois and in your mother Eunice and, I am persuaded, now lives in you also."* Grandmother Lois had a strong faith in God. She led Timothy's mother, Eunice, to be a believer. Likewise, Timothy accepted the faith of his mother and grandmother. Faith in God is the greatest inheritance that grandparents can give their children and grandchildren.

Q 15 *Does your church encourage grandparents to have a spiritual role? Explain.*

Grandparents should be concerned about the spiritual life of their grandchildren. They can pray for them, talk to them, and listen to them. Many husbands and wives today can testify that they learned about Jesus sitting on the lap of a grandparent. Children delight to hear grandpa or grandma tell stories from the Bible—or stories of how God has helped in the past. Even as adults, we enjoy hearing grandparents tell stories about God's goodness and faithfulness.

C. Grandparents must receive care from their families.

The Bible commands believers to love and care for their parents and grandparents.

*[1]Do not rebuke an older man harshly, but exhort him as if he were your father... [3]Give proper recognition to those widows who are really in need. [4]But if a widow has children or grandchildren, these should learn first of all to put their religion into practice by caring for their own family and so **repaying** their parents and grandparents, for this is pleasing to God* (1 Tim. 5:1, 3-4).

> IF THE ELDERLY ARE BEING NEGLECTED, THE CHURCH SHOULD FIND WAYS TO HELP THEM.

Family members should care for their parents and grandparents. If the elderly are being neglected, the church should find ways to help them.

Ways to care for our elderly parents and grandparents:

- **Respect their independence,** but be sure they are safe and cared for. Older parents may want to live alone even though this is not safe. Children and grandchildren must help choose what is best for the elderly. Honor your parents and grandparents as long as you are alive. Do not sin—as the Pharisees sinned—by neglecting to repay the love and care the elderly have given (Matt. 15:3-9).

    Watch for changes in their lives—physical, mental, emotional, or spiritual. Our bodies weaken as they grow old. Walking or climbing stairs can become difficult. Infections can take longer to heal. The risk of falling becomes greater. Arthritis, cancer, and other physical problems increase with age. Loneliness can be a trial for a parent or grandparent who has lost a spouse.

    In their final years, grandparents may become weak mentally. Many retain a clear mind to the end. Others lose their memory, or become confused over simple things. There are many causes for forgetfulness. *Alzheimer's disease can be a factor; however, it is not always the case. In some cases, people leave this world much the same way they entered it. A grandparent may become like a baby, depending completely on someone for love and care. Blessed are those who care for their parents and grandparents, for theirs is the favor of heaven.

- **Be sure there is no bitterness between you and them.** God commands believers to forgive. It is common for family members to hold grudges against each other. Old age is a wonderful time to make peace with God and others.

- **Share responsibilities with others.** In the larger family, all children and grandchildren should be aware of the needs of the parents or grandparents. In some societies, brothers and sisters may live hundreds of miles from family. It is common for just one of the children to live near the aging parent. But it is important to contact all the *siblings about the needs. At times, the other children may refuse to help the one caring for the aged parents. In this case, other family members, such as grandchildren, or friends may be able to help. Sometimes, brothers and sisters hire a person to help care for the elderly. A newspaper printed the following letter from a person who was tired of carrying all of the responsibility of an elderly parent:

    > "This letter is for all the sisters and brothers who are too busy with their own lives to lend a hand. Four years ago my life changed—when my mother became ill with an increasing disease. I put all my plans aside. Little by little I gave up visiting my friends, socializing, attending night school, and spending time with my husband. I must now use all my free time to take my parents to their doctors and tend to their needs. I am not complaining—my parents are wonderful people, and I consider it a privilege to care for them. But I am upset because my brothers and sisters do nothing to help me."[11]

- **Visit your parents and grandparents as often as possible.** Listening to the elderly does two things. It brings wisdom to the younger, and it makes the aged feel valuable because someone appreciates them. When you visit the elderly, ask questions and listen carefully. Learn all you can about family history and spiritual times in their lives. Write notes or use a tape-recorder. Get all the family history you can to pass on to your children. Also, ask grandparents to share insights about your life.

- **Pray for your elderly parents and grandparents.** They have needs, struggles, fears, and loneliness just as you do. Let them know that you are praying for them. Pray with them and read the Bible to them (or with them).

Q 16 What are some ways believers should care for grandparents?

Q 17 Why should several share the responsibility of caring for the elderly?

Q 18 Case Study: How would you advise this woman to handle her problem?

Q 19 What are 2 benefits of listening to grandparents?

When We Grow Old
Goal A: *Describe how the elderly can make peace with their pasts.*
Goal B: *Explain why having a purpose is important when you are old.*
Goal C: *Describe the physical changes the elderly must face.*
Goal D: *Summarize how people should prepare financially for old age.*

Figure 13.5
"Come, grow old with me, the best is yet to come."

Q 20 Contrast 2 attitudes about growing old.

Q 21 What are some reasons that the last years can be the best years?

Q 22 How can a person "reconcile the past"?

Q 23 How does making peace with the past affect the present?

Q 24 What are some of the advantages of the older marriage?

Setting

Ptah-hotep—an Egyptian philosopher about 2500 B.C. (500 years before Abraham lived)—said that old age is the worst thing that can affect a man."[12] In contrast, a modern poet named Robert Browning wrote: "Grow old along with me! The best is yet to be." [13] Browning reminds us that we can look forward to old age with joy.

Grandparents often find that their last years together are their best years. They have more time for themselves and being with others. They communicate better. Their sexual relationship is fulfilling, because they have learned to please each other. They enjoy a greater ability to solve problems in their marriage and larger family. They have learned to share power and authority in their home. By the time old age comes, a husband is more concerned about relationships, and has learned to treat his wife with more honor and respect.[14]

Surveys have shown that older people often feel satisfied, content, happy, and fulfilled. However—like any stage of life—there are several challenges that older people face. Let us consider three of these challenges.

A. The old must make peace with the past.

Old people look back over life. This is one of their emotional tasks. The latter years are a time to reflect. Older adults either regret their past, or rejoice over it.

Some believe that they have done well. They accept their faults, and praise God for His grace and presence throughout their lives. But others are in the pit of despair. They are disappointed with their lives, and realize that it is too late to start over. Most elderly people have some despair. It is rare to have no regrets. But wise believers do all they can to *reconcile their past mistakes—to repay, repair, settle, patch, and make old wrongs right. For example, Zacchaeus *reconciled* his past when he paid back those he stole from (Luke 19:8). It is best to reconcile the past before we grow old. But old age gives people a final chance to pay old debts of all kinds.

The gospel gives hope at any age. It always offers peace, forgiveness, and healing. It always helps us to *"put on the garment of praise for a spirit of heaviness"* (Isa. 61:3 KJV). But the gospel also calls us to reconcile—do righteously and justly to those we have wronged. Peace with past mistakes may come when we apologize to those we have hurt. Peace comes when we tear down walls of bitterness and forgive those who have hurt us. Peace comes when we pay debts and forgive those who owe us. In old age, the shortness of time can guide us to deal with these things before it is too late. Making peace with the past brings peace to the present.

B. The old must seek common purposes and interests with their spouses.

Many older couples realize that their marriage is like their home—it needs repairs. Perhaps the couple has drifted apart through the years. Old age is a time for the couple to repair any damage in their relationship and become closer friends. We discussed this earlier in this chapter, in lesson 1, part B. In addition to mending torn fences of the past, the couple should face the future together.

Facing the future includes a refocus—finding a new purpose for their lives. In old age, a couple may struggle with less wealth and health. These struggles can bring discouragement to any marriage. But a vision to serve and to be a blessing brings inspiration and energy to people. Remember, Jesus said that the key to finding life is losing your life to serve others (Matt. 16:24-26). This is true from the womb to the tomb—for grandchildren and grandparents. We are happiest when we serve others.

Q 25 How does having a purpose help the elderly?

What are some purposes that an elderly couple can fulfill?
- Some older couples have learned skills they can teach to others—like reading, telling stories, carpentry, sewing, financial skills, or playing a musical instrument.
- Some older couple can share a ministry to help the church. They can pray, preach, follow up visitors, cook, visit the sick, counsel, or teach. Some can give their time freely to help build, manage, guide, or supervise.

Q 26 What are some purposes grandparents can fulfill in your culture?

These are only a few of the ways that elderly people can be a blessing to others.

Sharing a purpose will bless a couple mentally and socially. It is true that older people walk while the younger run. As the proverb says, "He who once jumped over the creek now wades." Older people take longer to respond, but they have more to say. They think slower, but they think deeper. Their thoughts are easily distracted, but they bring wisdom from many different paths. They are less able to understand new ideas, but they know the value of old ideas. They have trouble learning new skills, but they have old skills that people still need today. They have trouble with short-term memory, and forget things in the recent past. But they remember things from long ago—things that the younger have never learned.[15]

Q 27 What are some ways that grandparents can bless others in your culture?

Many old people continue to inspire and amaze us. For example, Polycarp, the disciple of the apostle John, did not learn Greek until he was 80 years old. Likewise, one pastor, Tom Wilson, began his ministry in the days of tent revivals. As a young preacher in his teens he played the accordion. Today, more than 50 years later, he is in his 60s. But he has never stopped learning. He plays the electric keyboard, and uses the computer and the Internet. And spiritually, he reminds us of Caleb, who conquered his tallest mountain at the age of 80. For Grandpa Wilson, working with his son Scott and others, is planting ten new churches and ten new schools in the big city of Dallas, Texas. Each of these schools in their *Life School* will include three divisions: elementary, middle, and high school. Already, they have established five divisions—including two elementary schools, two middle schools, and one high school. The total number of students is over 2,000! Grandpa Wilson may be walking slower than he used to walk, but it is difficult for a young man to keep up with him! He is not a man who has become bored with retirement. He can tell you about "the good old days," but he says we are living in "the best new days."

Q 28 Summarize the story of Grandpa Tom Wilson.

Grandparent, God has spent all of your life preparing you for your last days. You have climbed tall mountains, crossed rivers, and walked through deep valleys. You have learned to walk softly with the Holy Spirit. And though your physical strength is less, your spiritual strength is more. All that is within you can testify that the battle is not to the swift nor the strong, for the battle belongs to the Lord (1 Sam. 17:47). The church is in great need of your wisdom, patience, presence, and guidance. Make your last years your best years. Find your purpose in the local church, and live your final days as an offering to God. Be like Simeon or Anna, whose prayers and

Figure 13.6 Pastor Tom (Grandpa) Wilson is working with his son (Pastor Scott) to plant ten new churches and ten new schools in the giant city of Dallas, Texas.

Q 29 Give an example of a grandparent who inspires you.

prophecies still bless people today. Be like Daniel whose faith shut the mouths of lions when he was over 70, and whose wisdom counseled kings in his final years.

C. The old must prepare for old age and death.

It is important to have purpose in the present. Still, an older person must recognize that his remaining years are short. Some deny that they will die. This leaves them and their families unprepared for the last issues of life.

There are several kinds of preparation for death—spiritual, emotional, mental, financial, and legal. Your family will avoid arguments and anxiety as you plan for your last days—and communicate your plans to key family members.

Q 30 *What kinds of physical change often come with aging?*

1. Prepare for physical changes. As people age, the body weakens. This differs from person to person—depending on such things as diet, exercise, stress, and your body characteristics. Some people remain strong while aging. Below is a list of some physical changes that the elderly should prepare to face:

- **Change in physical appearance.** Thin and gray hair, teeth loss, shorter height, wrinkles in the skin, and dark spots on the hands—these changes begin many years before a person is 65. People's self-esteem is affected if their culture prizes youth and physical beauty. But remember this truth: *Wrinkles don't hurt!*
- **Changes in the five senses: seeing, hearing, smelling, tasting, and touching.** Older people begin to lose some of their ability to see and hear. Other challenges associated with this stage of life are degeneration of the senses of taste and smell, stiffness of joints, less strength and energy, slower reaction time, poorer circulation of blood—which makes it hard to stay warm—and less ability to tolerate pain. Read Ecclesiastes 12 for Solomon's comments.
- **Sexual changes.** The ability to have children lessens, but sexual ability can continue. It is common for older couples to enjoy sex—in fact, many say this time of life brings more sexual fulfillment.
- **Illness and disease.** "Only a small percent of old people must stay in bed. But about 75 percent of those over 65 years have one or more problems that limit what they do."[16] The common physical problems for those over 65 are arthritis, heart disease, cancer, anxiety, and diabetes. Many also suffer from the breakdown of internal organs.

Q 31 *What comfort do the Scriptures give as we grow old?*

These physical challenges can cause anxiety and discouragement. Still, many old people who suffer are wonderful examples of love, patience, gentleness, faith, and the grace of God. His grace is sufficient for us, and His strength is made perfect in our weaknesses (2 Cor. 12:9). He has promised that we will never be tried beyond our ability to stand firm (1 Cor. 10:13). His name is Faithful and True (Rev. 19:11). He will never leave or forsake us (Heb. 13:5).

Q 32 *In your culture, how do people prepare financially for old age?*

2. Prepare for financial matters. As older people stop working, the money they have coming in goes down. Still, the cost of living keeps climbing up year after year. So elderly people can find it hard to pay for a home, good food, clothing, medicine, doctors, and transportation. If a person or couple has not planned well for old age, or if they have unusual medical expenses, their financial challenge can be very difficult. So people should begin to plan for old age—long before they become old. A farmer puts grain in the barn to plan for the months ahead—when there is no harvest. And Joseph taught the Egyptians to save some from the fat years to help in the lean years (Gen. 41:33-36, 46-49). Likewise, a person must save during the years of work, to have enough during the years when work is not possible.

Q 33 *Why is a legal will important?*

Planning for finances should also include a will—a legal paper about how you want people to divide your wealth after your death. Also, you should have made a legal decision about who will handle your financial and legal matters *if you are still alive* but are unable to make decisions.

Finally, you and your spouse should talk about death before the time comes. In some cultures, it is good to plan some details of your funeral. Unbelievers fear death and what may happen after death. But for the believer, facing death should be a peaceful time of thinking about eternal life with Christ and others.

Q 34 *What plans should an older couple make about death?*

Conclusion

Thank you for studying this course with us. We hope it will be a blessing to you and others.

Prayer: *⁵"May the Lord bless you from Zion all the days of your life; ... ⁶and may you live to see your children's children"* (Ps. 128:5-6).

 Chapter Summary

 When Our Children Become Adults

Goal A: *Describe how family expectations should change as children mature.*

Parents expect a mature child to: care for self, manage finances, be a good citizen, make friends, and find purpose and spiritual meaning in life. Mature children expect their parents to: recognize that adult children are responsible for their decisions, reduce or stop financial support, and talk to them as they talk to other adults.

Goal B: *Explain how the relationship between parents and adult children can deepen.*

Parents and children can discover each other in new ways—once they begin to relate as adults. God's command to honor parents is for all of life.

Goal C: *Summarize the challenges of the years of the empty nest.*

As children become adults, parents may wonder, "Now what will we do?" Parents can have a new beginning when their main focus returns to each other. Facing the past, they have many memories. Facing the future, they can walk new paths together.

 When We Become Grandparents

Goal A: *Identify 3 possible roles of grandparents.*

First, grandparents may be <u>very close</u>: substitute parents. Second, grandparents may be <u>close</u>: traditional role, giving love, guidance, support, wisdom, and gifts. Third, grandparents may be <u>far</u>: distant people.

Goal B: *Explain 5 ways a family should care for grandparents.*

Respect their independence. Be sure there is no bitterness between you and them. Share responsibilities with others in the larger family. Visit them as often as possible. Pray for them.

 When We Grow Old

Goal A: *Describe how the elderly can make peace with their pasts.*

They can reconcile the past—repay, repair, settle, patch—make old wrongs right, as Zacchaeus did.

Goal B: *Explain why having a purpose is important when you are old.*

A vision to serve and to be a blessing brings inspiration and energy. Sharing a purpose will bless a couple mentally and socially. And grandparents have much faith and wisdom to share.

Goal C: *Describe the physical changes the elderly must face.*

Physical changes affect strength, appearance, the five senses, sexual abilities, and health.

Goal D: *Summarize how people should prepare financially for old age.*

A person must save during the years of work to have enough during the years when work is not possible. Planning for finances should also include a will—a legal paper about wealth left for others. Finally, grandparents should talk to each other about death before the time comes.

Test Yourself: Circle the letter by the *best* completion to each question or statement.

1. How should parents relate to adult children?
a) Continue to provide everything for them.
b) In the same ways they have always related
c) Shelter them from the mistakes they make.
d) Allow them to make their own decisions.

2. How should mature children relate to parents?
a) Honor those who deserve honor.
b) Continue to honor them.
c) Rely upon them for their needs.
d) Keep them at a safe distance.

3. In the empty nest years, a husband and wife
a) may choose to walk new paths together.
b) continue to care for their children at home.
c) should ignore the past and face the future.
d) have no problems, for the children are gone.

4. When a mother works outside the home,
a) a grandparent should take children away.
b) a grandparent may serve as a parent.
c) a grandparent should leave and cleave.
d) a grandparent has the most authority.

5. How should parents relate to grandparents?
a) Realize the time for independence is past.
b) Remind them of ways they have failed.
c) Unite as children to care for their parents.
d) Expect things to continue in the same ways.

6. Aged parents often find it hard to
a) climb up stairs.
b) love their children.
c) tell old stories.
d) be with others.

7. An example of one who *reconciled* his past is
a) Nicodemus.
b) Solomon.
c) Zacchaeus.
d) Jesus.

8. A key to being happy in old age is
a) expecting others to be a blessing to you.
b) finding ways to be a blessing to others.
c) measuring past blessings by the present.
d) renewing your desire to receive blessings.

9. Which is usually TRUE about old age?
a) The ability to enjoy sex may remain.
b) The ability to enjoy the Lord lessens.
c) The ability to remember increases.
d) The ability to remain healthy stays the same.

10. To prepare financially for old age, people
a) should follow the example of Enoch.
b) should follow the example of Moses.
c) should follow the example of Paul.
d) should follow the example of Joseph.

Appendix A:

Websites to Help You
Prevent and Conquer Internet Pornography

Focus on the Family, Pure Intimacy (www.pureintimacy.org)

Prodigal International (www.iprodigal.com)

Enough Is Enough (www.enough.org)

Covenant Eyes (www.covenanteyes.com)

EXXit (www.exxit.org)

Literature Ministries International (www.thesafesite.com)

XXXChurch (www.xxxchurch.com)

Appendix B:

Creative Ways to Use This Book

- Teach part or all of it to the whole church.
- Preach a series of sermons based on it.
- Teach a Sunday school class on it.
- Use chapter 2 as a basis for counseling those preparing for marriage.
- Teach a seminar on any of the chapters, one Saturday of each month.
- Give chapter 3 to those planning a wedding.
- Have a woman teach some lessons for women only. Plan time for questions and discussion. (Use chapters 4, 5 and 8.)
- Have a man teach some lessons for men only. Encourage questions and discussion. (Use chapters 4, 5 and 7.)
- Have someone teach some lessons for youth only. (Use chapter 2 for sure.) Lead discussions.
- Advertise and teach chapters 4 and 9 through 13 to the whole community.
- Train people in your church to teach parts of this book in other churches, and within the community.
- Use this book as a resource for counseling.
- Plan some skits or dramas based on the principles and illustrations of this book.
- Plan an outdoor "revival of the home" meeting, and teach parts of this book.
- Ask the local radio or TV station if they would like you to create a series on topics from this book.
- Write a series of articles on marriage and the family for the newspaper.
- Create some tracts based on topics in this book.
- Create some cassettes or DVDs based on topics in this book.
- Offer to teach topics of this book to a business, school, or organization.

Definitions

The right-hand column lists the chapter in the textbook in which the word is used.

	Chapter
adolescence—years between childhood and adulthood; puberty; teenage years	10
Alzheimer's disease—a serious disorder of the brain characterized by loss of memory; a disease that causes a mental decline in the elderly	13
arranged marriage—an agreement between families that two of their youth will marry	2
baggage—things that get in the way and hinder progress	2
barrenness—inability to bear young; sterility; childlessness; infertility	12
birth parent—the biological father or mother of a child	12
boarding school—a school where students live, eat, and sleep during the school term	10
bride-price—a payment given by a husband to the bride's family	2
calorie—a unit to measure the energy value of foods	9
chaperone—an adult who goes with young people to ensure proper behavior	2
chaste—sexually pure, like a virgin, in actions and thoughts	2
chemicals—substances made by man that may be helpful or harmful to the body	9
cholera—a disease that often kills; symptoms are vomiting and diarrhea	9
climax—the point of greatest excitement, the supreme moment; the high point	5
clitoris—a small part of the female genitals at the upper end of the opening of the vagina that can become rigid during sexual excitement	5
colostrum—milk from the breasts for a few days after birth	9
compensate—pay; make up for	10
coordinator—a person who organizes and arranges the wedding plans	3
courtship—trying to win the attention or favor of a member of the opposite sex with a view to marriage	2
dating—social time that a man and woman spend together before marriage	2
deadline—the end of a time limit to complete something	6
defecate—discharge feces from the body; have a bowel movement; poop	9
defects—flaws, imperfections, or shortcoming in key areas, whether physical, mental, or emotional; handicaps	9
deformity—a defect of the body, such as a crippled leg	9
dehydration—the lack of fluid in the body, that can lead to death; usually the result of a disease, and highly dangerous to young children and weak adults	9
desertion—to abandon a person or group to whom one has responsibilities	12
detached—apart from one's family	11
devotions—personal or family time spent in Bible study, prayer, and worship	10
diabetes—a disorder in which the body does not absorb sugar and starch well; signs are thirst, hunger, weakness, loss of weight, and blood in urine	9
diarrhea—a condition of runny poop, very dangerous to young children or weak adults, because it leads quickly to a lack of body fluids	9

244

diphtheria—a disease that affects the throat, breathing, swallowing, and also the heart and nervous system — 9

discipline—to correct, train, improve, and guide, especially our children — 10

Diwali—a Hindu festival of lights between September and November — 3

dowry—wealth from her family that a bride brings into a marriage — 2

estrogen—a hormone that develops and maintains the characteristics of a woman's body — 7

extended family—the broad, larger family that includes grandparents, aunts, uncles, cousins, and in-laws — 6

fallopian tubes—a pair of tubes in a female through which the egg travels from the ovary to the *uterus — 12

fireworks—devices that explode with a loud noise into beautiful colors in the sky — 3

germs—tiny organisms, such as bacteria or viruses, that cause disease — 9

HIV/AIDS—a deadly disease passed on through sex or the blood; HIV stands for human immunodeficiency virus, which causes AIDS (acquired immune deficiency syndrome) — 9

Holocaust—the slaughter of European Jews by the Nazis during World War II — 12

homosexuality—sex between persons of the same gender, as man with man — 1

honeymoon—the first few days a newly married couple spends together — 1

hormones—chemicals to regulate the body — 7

Hurray!—an exclamation of joy or approval — 10

hymen—a thin sheet of flesh that partly closes the opening of the vagina and is usually broken at the time the female first has sexual intercourse — 5

illegitimate—a child born of parent who are not married to each other — 2

impotent—said of: males who are incapable (unable) to have sex — 5

incest—sex between family members; sexual relations between persons regarded as too close to marry each other — 6

infertile—unable to conceive young; barren; sterile — 12

internal noise—reactions inside a listener that distract from a speaker's words — 4

intimacy—thoughts, words, or deeds of a personal or private nature; a close, personal relationship—especially in sexual matters — 1, 2

keep away—a game in which players try to keep a ball away from others — 4

kite—a toy made by stretching paper or plastic over a light frame to fly in the wind, at the end of a long string — 13

laissez-faire—free actions, not interfering with a person's freedom to choose or act — 7

latrine—a pit in the ground to use as a toilet — 9

logical results—outcomes that naturally follow choices — 10

malaria—a disease carried by mosquitoes—signs are chills, and fever—that may lead to death, especially in children and the weak — 9

manipulate—to guide though craft, cunning, and scheming — 4

marriage—the public commitment between a man and a woman to be joined and faithful to each other until death, for the purposes of friendship, fellowship, and family — 1

Marriage Encounter—the name of a seminar for married couples, first made popular in the US, but now available in many countries; the goal is to increase communication in marriage — 7

masturbation—the process of reaching a sexual climax by a means other than having sex — 9

measles—a disease known by red spots on the skin, especially in children, often causing blindness in those who lack vitamin A   9

menopause—the period in a woman's life (usually between 45 and 50) when menstruation stops   7

menstrual cycle—the monthly flow of a bloody fluid from a female's uterus   5

menstruation—the monthly process of discharging blood and other materials from the uterus in sexually mature, non-pregnant women   9

minerals—substances, such as iron, copper, zinc, and magnesium, that are needed in tiny amounts for normal health and development   9

monogamy—being married to only one person at a time   1

mucus—a wet, slimy film that protects in places like the throat and nose   9

naiveté—innocence, childlikeness; lacking in wisdom or judgment   1

natural results—discipline that comes from experience on its own, such as touching a hot stove results in being burned   10

Nazis—members of the German National Socialist party (fascist), who under Adolf Hitler held extreme racist views from 1933 to 1945   12

nocturnal emissions—the natural, involuntary emission of semen during a man's sleep   9

ostrich—a large bird, up to 300 pounds, that runs but does not fly; said to hide its head in the sand and think itself unseen   11

outhouse—an outside building used as a toilet, usually without plumbing   9

parachute—a cloth shaped like an umbrella, that allows a person (or heavy object attached to it) to descend slowly from an airplane   9

plumbing—any system of pipes or tubes that carry fluids   2

polio—a disease that affects the central nervous system and may cause temporary or permanent paralysis, deformity, and defects   9

polygamy—having more than one spouse at the same time   1

pornography—harmful, destructive sexual materials, printed or electronic, designed to arouse sexual desires and addict those who view them   5

pre-marital counseling—training and mentoring a couple that is planning to marry   2

prolonged—continued; lengthy; longer than usual   12

prostitution—selling a human body for sexual purposes   1

puberty—the period in which youth reach sexual maturity and become able to reproduce   9

random rewards—honor or awards for something well done, given at various times rather than as payment for services   10

reconcile—to bring together; to settle or resolve differences; restore harmony   13

reproduction—producing and giving birth to children   9

romantic—having expressions of tender love, affections, or feelings   1, 2

sandpaper—rough paper used to make a board smooth   7

scalp—the skin and hair that cover the top of a person's head   9

sewage—the human waste of urine and poop; these need to be disposed of in a safe way to prevent disease   9

sexual intercourse—sexual union, intimacy, and love making; becoming one flesh   5

sibling—a child who has one or both parents in common with another child   11, 13

single—an unmarried person	2
spank—to slap or strike the buttocks in a mild manner, with a small stick or open hand	10
sperm—semen; the male seed that unites with the female egg to produce a child	12
stature—height or status gained by growth, development, or achievement	9
stepchildren—children of a husband or wife by a previous marriage	12
stress—pressure, tension, or distress	12
temperament—a person's unique nature, character, and personality that affect his actions and emotional state	1, 10
tetanus—a disease that causes continuous muscle spasms	9
toddler—a child who is just beginning to walk	13
umbilical cord—a flexible tube of flesh that connects a baby to the placenta of his mother	9
undernourished—lacking food and vitamins that enable good health	9
urinate—discharge urine; pass water	9
utensils—things to eat with, such as forks, knives, spoons, or chopsticks	9
uterus—the female organ in which a baby is formed; the womb	Def
vaccination—a shot, usually by a needle, to prevent disease or promote health	9
virgin—a person who has never had sexual intercourse	9
virginity—pure, unmarried life, free from sexual intercourse; chastity	2
vitamins—substances, naturally present in food, such as vitamins A, B complex, C, D, K, and M, that are necessary for good health and development	9
whooping cough—a disease, especially in children, known through a series of short, violent coughs followed by a whoop—a gasping intake of breath	9
workaholic—a person who works too much, often at the expense of health or family	7

Scripture List

Genesis
Gen. 1–2 18
Gen. 1:1 17
Gen. 1:26-28 22
Gen. 1:28 . . . . 21, 22, 81
Gen. 1:31 25
Gen. 2 55
Gen. 2:18 . . . . 21, 193
Gen. 2:18, 24 17
Gen. 2:20-23 21
Gen. 2:20-24 17
Gen. 2:20-25 19
Gen. 2:23 22
Gen. 2:24 . . . . 81, 220
Gen. 2:25 84
Gen. 4:19-24 17
Gen. 11:1-9 64
Gen. 12:2-3 16
Gen. 12:10-20 20
Gen. 15:1-5 218
Gen. 16:4-9 208
Gen. 17:17 89
Gen. 18:10 218
Gen. 21:1-3 218
Gen. 21:8-20 223
Gen. 24 33
Gen. 24:3-6 19
Gen. 24:67 19
Gen. 25:28 180
Gen. 26:1-11 20
Gen. 27 180
Gen. 29 33
Gen. 29:1-30 17
Gen. 29:20 31
Gen. 29:32 225
Gen. 29:34 225
Gen. 30:1 218
Gen. 30:14-16 225
Gen. 30:22-24 218
Gen. 37:23-27 225
Gen. 39:1-12 58
Gen. 41:33-36 240
Gen. 41:46-49 . . . . . 104, 240
Gen. 49:8-27 173
Gen. 50:1-3 219

Exodus
Exod. 14:11-12 101
Exod. 20:8 126
Exod. 20:8-10 126
Exod. 20:12 179
Exod. 20:14 86

Leviticus
Lev. 15:16-17 37
Lev. 19:9-10 106

Deuteronomy
Deut. 4:9 169
Deut. 6:5-6 167
Deut. 6:5-7 169
Deut. 6:6-7 167
Deut. 6:7 169
Deut. 6:8-9 169
Deut. 6:20-25 169
Deut. 18:9-13 49

Deut. 24:5 83
Deut. 28:15-68 179
Deut. 30:11-16 180

Joshua
Joshua 22 74

Judges
Judges 1:12-15 33
Judges 6:7-16 198
Judges 6:12 198
Judges 6:13 198
Judges 6:15 198
Judges 6:23 198
Judges 6:27 198
Judges 6:36-40 198
Judges 7:10-11 198
Judges 8:21 147
Judges 16 205
Judges 21:25 124

Ruth
Ruth 3:3 135

1 Samuel
1 Sam. 1 218
1 Sam. 1:24-28 169
1 Sam. 17:47 239
1 Sam. 20 34
1 Sam. 25 120

2 Samuel
2 Sam. 11 205
2 Sam. 11:2-5 58
2 Sam. 13:1, 15 31
2 Sam. 13:1-39 31

1 Kings
1 Kings 17:7-24 163
1 Kings 19 205
1 Kings 21:4 28

Esther
Esther 2:12 135

Job
Job 31:1 203

Psalms
Ps. 23:2-3 126
Ps. 23:6 36
Ps. 24:1 145
Ps. 115:9-11 22
Ps. 119:9 203
Ps. 119:104 97
Ps. 119:105 97
Ps. 127:2 126
Ps. 127:3-5 . . . . 25, 146, 149
Ps. 128:5-6 241
Ps. 139:1-12 169
Ps. 144:12 23
Ps. 145:18 173

Proverbs
Prov. 2:19 121
Prov. 3:5-6 97
Prov. 3:9-10 103
Prov. 4:18 97
Prov. 4:23 202
Prov. 5:15 203

Prov. 5:15-23 204
Prov. 5:18-19 89
Prov. 6:1-5 105
Prov. 6:26 36
Prov. 6:33 205
Prov. 10:11 200
Prov. 11:24-25 105
Prov. 11:24-26 59
Prov. 13:3 121
Prov. 13:11 102
Prov. 13:20 169
Prov. 14:1 133
Prov. 14:26 22
Prov. 14:29 . . . . 74, 149
Prov. 15:1 . . . . . 69, 121, 137
Prov. 15:4 200
Prov. 16:11 102
Prov. 17:17 221
Prov. 17:22 24
Prov. 18:13 66
Prov. 19:11 69
Prov. 19:17 105
Prov. 19:18 178
Prov. 20:4 103
Prov. 20:17 102
Prov. 21:5 103
Prov. 21:9 121
Prov. 21:20 103
Prov. 22:1 . . . . 55, 139
Prov. 22:9 55
Prov. 22:26-27 . . . . . 59, 104
Prov. 23:1-2 141
Prov. 23:6-8 59
Prov. 23:13 185
Prov. 23:22 107
Prov. 23:29-35 209
Prov. 24:3 25
Prov. 24:3-4 55
Prov. 24:30-34 124
Prov. 25:8 121
Prov. 25:23-24 121
Prov. 27:15 . . . . 135, 137
Prov. 27:15-16 26
Prov. 28:7 169
Prov. 28:25 55
Prov. 29:11 180
Prov. 29:20 . . . . 74, 121
Prov. 31:3 37
Prov. 31:10 36
Prov. 31:10-31 130

Ecclesiastes
Eccl. 3:1 55
Eccl. 3:1, 5 58
Eccl. 3:1-8 221
Eccl. 4:9 23
Eccl. 4:12 . . . . 23, 206
Eccl. 7:9 74
Eccl. 9:9 . . . . 24, 126
Eccl. 10:15 126

Song of Songs
Song of Songs 1:2, 4 87
Song of Songs 1:5-6 85
Song of Songs 2:2-3 25

Song of Songs 4:1-7 85
Song of Songs 4:10–5:1 . . . 80
Song of Songs 5:2-8 84
Song of Songs 5:10-16 85
Song of Songs 7:1-9 85

Isaiah
Isa. 6:1-8 57
Isa. 54 17
Isa. 61:3 238
Isa. 62:1-5 17

Ezekiel
Ezek. 16 17
Ezek. 20:17-18 213
Ezek. 24:15-16 213
Ezek. 24:20-24 213

Hosea
Hos. 4:6 162

Malachi
Mal. 2:13-16 204
Mal. 2:14-15 168
Mal. 2:15 81

Matthew
Matt. 1:21 212
Matt. 4:1-11 205
Matt. 5:4 221
Matt. 5:10-12 169
Matt. 5:23-24 76
Matt. 5:31-32 220
Matt. 5:32 224
Matt. 5:44 234
Matt. 6:12 107
Matt. 6:12, 14-15 199
Matt. 6:25-26, 33 102
Matt. 6:25-34 103
Matt. 7:12 . . . . 55, 194
Matt. 11:1-6 205
Matt. 12:18-21 123
Matt. 12:34-37 137
Matt. 15:1-9 . . . . . 107, 108
Matt. 15:3-6 107
Matt. 15:3-9 237
Matt. 16:24-26 239
Matt. 18:1-5 145
Matt. 18:6 145
Matt. 18:10 145
Matt. 18:14 145
Matt. 18:21-35 . . . . . 107, 199
Matt. 19:1-9 220
Matt. 19:4-5 . . . . 18, 21
Matt. 19:5-6 220
Matt. 19:6 . . . . 20, 86
Matt. 19:9 . . . . 86, 224
Matt. 19:14 169
Matt. 21:9 145
Matt. 21:14-16 145
Matt. 21:16 145
Matt. 22:2 59
Matt. 24:12-13 200
Matt. 25:14-30 104
Matt. 26:41 203
Matt. 27:46 193

248

Mark
Mark 2:27 126
Mark 3:17 123
Mark 10:6-7. 18
Mark 10:13-16. 145
Mark 10:35-37. 195
Mark 12:31 74

Luke
Luke 1:5-25. 218
Luke 1:13-17. 169
Luke 2:22 169
Luke 2:41-52. 171
Luke 2:52 . . . . . 147, 150, 171
Luke 6:12-16. 97
Luke 6:31 194
Luke 6:38 . . . . 55, 105
Luke 8:2 212
Luke 8:40-56. 163
Luke 8:51-52. 219
Luke 9:54-56. 123
Luke 12:13-15. 105
Luke 15:11-13. 226
Luke 15:11-24. . . . . 183, 226
Luke 15:14 227
Luke 15:15-16. 227
Luke 15:17, 20 228
Luke 15:17-19. 227
Luke 15:20 228
Luke 15:22-24. 228
Luke 15:28-32. 228
Luke 16:1-15. 102
Luke 16:19-31. 50
Luke 19:8 238
Luke 21:1-4. 59

John
John 2:1-11. 60
John 3:16 . . . . 55, 174
John 4:18 223
John 4:36 184
John 5:44 171
John 8:11 223
John 8:34 209
John 9:41 210
John 11:30-36. 219
John 15:12 83
John 17:1-26. 169
John 19:11 181

Acts
Acts 1:4-5, 8 169
Acts 2:4, 39. 169
Acts 4:1-20 54
Acts 6:1-7 72
Acts 6:4. 169
Acts 15:36-40 185
Acts 16:34. 24
Acts 18:1-3 34
Acts 20:13–21:14 35

Romans
Rom. 2:28-29 49
Rom. 3:23. 223
Rom. 6:16. 210
Rom. 7:2 220
Rom. 7:2-3 223
Rom. 8:4. 37
Rom. 8:4-14 201
Rom. 8:6-9 201
Rom. 8:28-39 223
Rom. 8:30. 169

Rom. 12:1-2 37
Rom. 12:3 175
Rom. 12:3-8 . . . . . . 103, 169
Rom. 12:9 203
Rom. 12:12 169
Rom. 12:19 107
Rom. 13:1-7 54
Rom. 14:13-23 51
Rom. 14:14, 23. 51
Rom. 14:15-21 51
Rom. 15:7. . . . . 27, 175, 198
Rom. 16:1-16 35
Rom. 16:7, 11, 21. 35

1 Corinthians
1 Cor. 6:9-11. 38
1 Cor. 6:9-20. 35
1 Cor. 6:16 36
1 Cor. 7:1-6. 136
1 Cor. 7:1-11. 18
1 Cor. 7:2 81
1 Cor. 7:3-5. . . . . . . 86, 120
1 Cor. 7:4 20
1 Cor. 7:5 20
1 Cor. 7:8-9. 58
1 Cor. 7:10-15. 224
1 Cor. 7:15 220
1 Cor. 7:25-40. 18
1 Cor. 7:39 220
1 Cor. 9:5-6. 35
1 Cor. 9:19-23. 50
1 Cor. 10:12 200
1 Cor. 10:13 . . . . . . 201, 240
1 Cor. 10:18-22. 49
1 Cor. 11:1 168
1 Cor. 11:3 123
1 Cor. 11:3, 8-9. 122
1 Cor. 12. 169
1 Cor. 13:4 . . . . 98, 121
1 Cor. 13:4-7. 197
1 Cor. 13:4-8. 27
1 Cor. 13:6 27
1 Cor. 13:7 121
1 Cor. 13:11 147
1 Cor. 14:13 213
1 Cor. 14:26-28. 213
1 Cor. 14:35 134
1 Cor. 16:15 24

2 Corinthians
2 Cor. 6:6 98
2 Cor. 6:9-10. 228
2 Cor. 6:14–7:1. 169
2 Cor. 6:14-16. 39
2 Cor. 9:6-11. 106
2 Cor. 9:7 59
2 Cor. 10:5 . . . . 37, 203
2 Cor. 12:9 240

Galatians
Gal. 3:6-8 16
Gal. 3:24 178
Gal. 5:1-2, 6 49
Gal. 5:13, 16. 156
Gal. 5:15 121
Gal. 5:16 . . . . 37, 57, 201, 203
Gal. 5:16-25 . . . . . . 201, 213
Gal. 5:19-21 201
Gal. 5:22-23 . . . . 73, 137, 201
Gal. 5:22-25 170
Gal. 6:2 . . . . 67, 218

Gal. 6:7-10 182
Gal. 6:10 121
Gal. 6:15 49

Ephesians
Eph. 4:3 76
Eph. 4:11-13 169
Eph. 4:15 . . . . 28, 121
Eph. 4:15-16. 28
Eph. 4:26 . . . . 73, 212
Eph. 4:29 68
Eph. 5:1 228
Eph. 5:1-2 199
Eph. 5:2–6:3 18
Eph. 5:21–6:4 39
Eph. 5:21 . . . . 25, 59
Eph. 5:22-24 . . . . . . 18, 132
Eph. 5:25 31
Eph. 5:28 74
Eph. 6:1-3 179
Eph. 6:2 19
Eph. 6:4 . . . 23, 169, 180, 186
Eph. 6:18 169

Philippians
Phil. 2:1-4 97
Phil. 2:1-5 91
Phil. 2:4. 67
Phil. 2:4-5 198
Phil. 2:6. 131
Phil. 3:20. 169
Phil. 4:7-9 37
Phil. 4:8. 203
Phil. 4:9. 169
Phil. 4:11-13 105
Phil. 4:13. 228
Phil. 4:19. 102

Colossians
Col. 3:1-3 169
Col. 3:17-21 39
Col. 3:21 181
Col. 4:6 121

1 Thessalonians
1 Thess. 4:11-12. 124
1 Thess. 4:13 223
1 Thess. 5:19 150

2 Thessalonians
2 Thess. 3:6, 10 103

1 Timothy
1 Tim. 2:9 52
1 Tim. 3:4-5 122
1 Tim. 4:6 169
1 Tim. 5:1, 3-4 236
1 Tim. 5:8 . . . . . 59, 108, 125
1 Tim. 5:9 18
1 Tim. 5:14 224
1 Tim. 6:6-10 59
1 Tim. 6:17-19 105

2 Timothy
2 Tim. 1:5 236
2 Tim. 3:12 169
2 Tim. 3:15 169
2 Tim. 4:11 185

Titus
Titus 1:6 18
Titus 1:8 139

Hebrews
Heb. 1:9 203

Heb. 4:15 201
Heb. 4:16 208
Heb. 9:27 50
Heb. 10:36 101
Heb. 11:13-16 169
Heb. 12:5-11 178
Heb. 12:6 178
Heb. 12:7-11 169
Heb. 12:8 36
Heb. 13:2 139
Heb. 13:4 81
Heb. 13:5 240

James
James 1:5 97
James 1:5-8 59
James 1:12 201
James 1:12-15 201
James 1:14 201
James 1:17 . . . . . . 146, 162
James 1:19 . . . . 68, 74
James 1:27 218
James 2:14-17 218
James 3:1-12 68
James 3:2 137
James 4:1-4 73
James 4:4 169
James 4:12 107
James 5:16 . . . . .28, 121,
. . . . 169, 194, 200
James 5:16-18 169

1 Peter
1 Pet. 1:3-9 169
1 Pet. 1:13 203
1 Pet. 2:13-17 132
1 Pet. 2:18-21 132
1 Pet. 2:22–3:1 132
1 Pet. 3:1 134
1 Pet. 3:1-7 39
1 Pet. 3:4 136
1 Pet. 3:5-6 133
1 Pet. 3:7 28
1 Pet. 4:8-9 139
1 Pet. 5:8 200

2 Peter
2 Pet. 1:5-9 169
2 Pet. 1:10-11 169
2 Pet. 2:19 210

1 John
1 John 1:9. . . . 38, 85, 92, 211
1 John 2:15-17 169

Revelation
Rev. 2–3 . . . . 122, 184
Rev. 2:4-5 121
Rev. 7:9 16
Rev. 19:6-9 58
Rev. 19:11 240

Bibliography

Alcorn, Randy. "The real and untold cost: The exorbitant price of sexual sin," *Leadership: A Practical Journal for Church Leaders.* Summer 1996.

Allen, Charles L., ed. *Home Fires: A Treasury of Wit and Wisdom.* Waco, Texas: Word Books Publisher, 1987.

Balswick, Jack O. and Judith K. Balswick. *The Family: A Christian Perspective on the Contemporary Home,* 2nd ed. Grand Rapids, Michigan: Baker Books, 1999.

Barclay, William. *The Daily Study Bible: Galatians and Ephesians.* Philadelphia, Pennsylvania: The Westminster Press, 1976.

Betzer, Dan. *Byline* (radio and e-mail) based on a story by Don Meyer, January 16, 2004.

Bombeck, Erma. "Fragile Strings Join Parent, Child," *Arizona Republic,* May 15, 1977.

Bronfenbrenner, Urie. Testimony before the Senate Subcommittee on Children and Youth, "Hearing on American Families," *Congressional Record.* September 26, 1973.

Burkett, Larry and Rick Osborne. *Financial Parenting.* Colorado Springs, Colorado: Chariot Victor Publishing, A Division of Cook Communications, 1996.

Burkett, Larry and Rick Osborne. *Your Child Wonderfully Made: Discovering God's Unique Plan.* Chicago, Illinois: Moody Press, 1998.

Butrin, JoAnn. *You Can Be Healthy!* Lakeland, Flordia: Healthcare Ministries, 1991.

Carnegie, Dale. *How to Win Friends and Influence People.* London, England: Cedar Books, 1983.

Chapman, Gary. *The Five Languages of Love.* Chicago, Illinois: Northfield Publishing, 1995.

Choi, Sung Kyu. translated by Joo Young Lee, *Survey of the Theology of Hyo.* Sungsanseowon, Korea: Dr. Sung Kyu Choi, 2004.

Cole, Glen D. from a sermon on Revelation 2:1-7.

Collins, Gary R. *Christian Counseling: A Comprehensive Guide,* rev. ed. Dallas, Texas: Word Publishing, 1988.

Crabb, Larry. *Connecting: A Radical New Vision.* Nashville, Tennessee: Word Publishing, 1997.

_____. *The Marriage Builder.* Grand Rapids, Michigan: Zondervan Publishing House, 1992.

Dillow, Joseph C. *Solomon on Sex.* Nashville, Tennessee: Thomas Nelson Publishers, 1977.

Dobson, James. *Bringing up Boys.* Wheaton, Illinois: Tyndale House Publishers, Inc., 2001.

_____. Quoted in *Draper's Book of Quotations for the Christian World,* Edythe Draper, ed. Wheaton, Illinois: Tyndale House Publishers, Inc., 1992.

_____. Quoted in *For Families Only,* J. Allan Petersen, ed. Wheaton, Illinois: Living Books, Tyndale House Publishers, Inc., 1981.

_____. *Dare to Discipline.* Wheaton, Illinois: Tyndale House Publishers, Inc., 1970.

_____. *Straight Talk to Men and Their Wives.* Nashville, Tennessee: W Publishing Group, 1980.

_____. *The Strong-Willed Child.* Wheaton, Illinois: Tyndale House Publishers, Inc., 1978.

_____. *What Wives Wish Their Husbands Knew About Women.* Wheaton, Illinois: Tyndale House Publishers, Inc., 1977.

Douglas, J. D., ed. *The New Bible Dictionary.* Grand Rapids, Michigan: Wm. B. Eerdmans Publishing Co., 1978.

Downs, Tim and Joy. *The Seven Conflicts: Resolving the Most Common Disagreements in Marriage.* Chicago, Illinois: Moody Publishers, 2003.

Draper, Edythe. *Draper's Book of Quotations for the Christian World.* Wheaton, Illinois: Tyndale House Publishers, Inc., 1992.

Dutton, Donald G. "Witnessing Parental Violence as a Traumatic Experience Shaping the Abusive Personality," quoted in *Children Exposed to Domestic Violence: Current Issues in Research, Intervention, Prevention and Policy Development,* edited by Robert Geffner, Peter Jaffe, and Marlies Sudermann. New York, New York: The Haworth Press, Inc., 2000.

Elliot, Elizabeth. *Let Me Be A Woman.* Wheaton, Illinois: Tyndale House Publishers, Inc., 1999.

Ellis, Alfred. *Restoring Innocence: Healing the Memories and Hurts That Hinder Sexual Intimacy.* Nashville, Tennessee: Thomas Nelson Publishers, 1990.

Fromm, Eric. Quoted in *Draper's Book of Quotations for the Christian World,* Edythe Draper, ed. Wheaton, Illinois: Tyndale House Publishers, Inc., 1992.

Gani, Desmond. *The Christian Family,* unpublished lecture notes.

Getz, Gene. Quoted in *For Families Only,* J. Allen Peterson, ed. Wheaton, Illinois: Living Books, 1977.

Gilbert, Marvin, and D. Odunze. *Successful Family Living—An African View.* Unpublished notes.

Gray, Alice, compiler. *Stories for the Heart.* Sisters, Oregon: Multnomah Books, 1996.

Gray, John. *Men Are from Mars, Women Are from Venus.* New York, New York: HarperCollins Publishers, Inc., 1992.

_____. *What Your Mother Couldn't Tell You and Your Father Didn't Know.* New York, New York: HarperCollins Publishers, Inc., 1994.

Green, Holly Wagner. *Turning Fear to Hope: Help for Marriages Troubled by Abuse.* New York, New York: Thomas Nelson Publishers, 1984.

Grunlan, Stephen A. *Marriage and Family: A Christian Perspective.* Grand Rapids, Michigan: Zondervan Publishing House, 1999.

Hamilton, Victor P. *New International Commentary on the Old Testament: The Book of Genesis,* Vol. 1. Grand Rapids, Michigan: Wm. B. Eerdmans Publishing Co., 1996.

Harley, Willard F., Jr., *His Needs, Her Needs: Building an Affair-Proof Marriage.* Grand Rapids, Michigan: Fleming H. Revell Company, 2001.

Harris, Dr. Charles. From his own experience as told by correspondence on September 24, 2004. Used by permission.

Harris, Ralph W., ed. *The Complete Biblical Library: The New Testament Study Bible, Galatians–Philemon,* Vol. 8. Springfield, Missouri: World Library Press, 1995.

Hayes, Steve. *Safe and Sound: Protecting Personal and Ministry Relationships.* Nashville: Tennessee: Broadman and Holman Press, 2002.

Helping Your Child Develop Self-Esteem, http://childdevelopmentinfo.com/parenting/self_esteem.shtml. [accessed July 2005]

Hewett, James S. *Illustrations Unlimited.* Wheaton, Illinois: Tyndale House Publishers, Inc., 1988.

Hiebert, Paul G. *Case Studies in Missions.* Grand Rapids, Michigan: Baker Book House, 1987.

Holmes, Thomas H. Professor of Psychiatry and Behavioral Sciences, University of Washington School of Medicine, developed the stress assessment table.

Howell, John C. *Equality and Submission in Marriage.* Nashville, Tennessee: Broadman Press, 1979.

Hurley, James B. *Man and Woman in Biblical Perspective: A Study in Role Relationships and Authority.* Grand Rapids, Michigan: Academie Books, Zondervan Publishing House, 1981.

Johnson, Carolyn. *How to Blend a Family.* Grand Rapids, Michigan: Pyranee Books, 1989.

Johnson, M. *Journal of Marriage and Family.* Minneapolis, Minnesota: National Council on Family Relations, 1995.

Keil, C. F. and F. Delitzsch. *Commentary on the Old Testament: The Pentateuch,* Vol. 1. Peabody, Massachusetts: Hendrickson Publishers, 1989.

Kitzinger, Sheila. Taken from John F. Ember, *A Japanese Village.* London, England: Kegan Paul, 1946.

_____. Taken from S. Chirawatkul and L. Manderson, "Perceptions of Menopause in Northeast Thailand: Contested Meaning and Practice," *Social Science & Medicine,* 39 (11) (1994): pp. 1545-54.

Koehler, Ludwig Hugo. *Hebrew Man.* New York, New York: Abingdon Press, 1956.

LaHaye, Tim and Beverly. *Against the Tide: How to Raise Sexually Pure Kids in an 'Anything-Goes' World.* Sisters, Oregon: Multnomah Books, 1993.

_____. *The Act of Marriage.* Grand Rapids, Michigan: Zondervan Publishing House, 1976.

Landers, Ann. "Siblings Not Helping with Aging Parents," *Lincoln Journal Star,* 25 November 1997, 8B.

Larson, Craig Brian. *Illustrations for Preaching and Teaching.* Grand Rapids, Michigan: Baker Book House Co., 1993.

Lee, Jimmy Ray. *Insight Group: Facilitator's Guide,* 3rd ed. Chattanooga, Tennessee: Turning Point, 1995.

Leman, Kevin. *Making Children Mind Without Losing Yours.* Grand Rapids, Michigan: Fleming H. Revell Company, 1984.

Marshall, Catherine and Leonard LeSourd. *My Personal Prayer Diary.* New York, New York: Ballantine Books, 1979.

McClaflin, Mike. Sermon illustration of pulling up the dog's tail.

McKenzie, E. C. *Mac's Giant Book of Quips and Quotes.* Grand Rapids, Michigan: Baker Book House, 1980.

Meier, Paul D., Frank B. Minirith, Frank B. Wichern, and Donald E. Ratcliff. *Introduction to Psychology and Counseling: Christian Perspectives and Applications.* Grand Rapids, Michigan: Baker Book House, 1991.

Meyer, Joyce. *Help Me, I'm Married!* Tulsa, Oklahoma: Harrison House, 2000.

Nason-Clark, Nancy. *The Battered Wife.* Louisville, Kentucky: Westminster John Knox Press, 1997.

Nelson, Tommy. *The Book of Romance: What Solomon Says About Love, Sex, and Intimacy.* Nashville, Tennessee: Thomas Nelson Publisher, 1998.

Oliver, Gary J. "The Cult of Success," *New Man,* September 1997.

Petersen, J. Allan, ed. *For Families Only.* Wheaton, Illinois: Living Books, Tyndale House Publishers, Inc., 1981.

Ponzetti, J., and A. Fokrod. "Grandchildren's Perceptions of Their Relationships With Their Grandparents." *Child Study Journal,* 1989. 19:41-50.

Rance, Alver. Assemblies of God missionary, e-mail of May 9, 2003.

Rineas, Gabriele. "Dealing with Conflict," *Enrichment: A Journal of Pentecostal Ministry.* Springfield, Missouri: Gospel Publishing House, Summer 2004, p. 66.

Rubin, Theodore Isaac. *Overcoming Indecisiveness: The Eight Stages of Effective Decision Making.* New York: Avon Books, 1985.

Rutland, Mark. From a marriage seminar taught in West Virginia, 2002.

Sandford, John. *Why Some Christians Commit Adultery.* Tulsa, Oklahoma: Victor House, 1989.

Schlessinger, Laura. *The Proper Care and Feeding of Husbands.* New York, New York: HarperCollins Publishers Inc., 2004.

Sell, Charles M. *Family Ministry.* Grand Rapids, Michigan: Zondervan Publishing House, 1995.

Siak, Neo Soon. Malaysia, e-mail of May 29, 2003.

Bibliography

Simmons, Paul. As told by Karen Burton Mains in *Abuse in the Family.* Elgin, Illinois: David C. Cook Publishing, 1987.

Smalley, Gary. "The Pastor and Family Intimacy," *Enrichment: A Journal for Pentecostal Ministry.* Summer 2004.

Smoke, Jim. *Growing Through Divorce.* Eugene, Oregon: Harvest House Publishers, 1995.

Stamps, Donald C., ed. *The Full Life Study Bible,* NIV. Grand Rapids, Michigan: Zondervan Publishing House. 1975.

Swindoll, Charles R. *The Tale of the Tardy Oxcart.* Nashville, Tennessee: Word Publishing, Inc., 1998.

Sylvester, David, ed. *Great Stories.* Amarillo, Texas. Volume 6/Issue 24, October-December 1999.

Tan, Paul Lee. *Encyclopedia of 7700 Illustrations: Signs of the Times.* Rockville, Maryland: Assurance Publishers, 1984.

Taylor, Anita, Arthur C. Meyer, Teresa Rosegrant, B. Thomas Samples. *Communicating.* Englewood Cliffs, New Jersey: Prentice Hall Publishing, 1992.

Taylor, Cheryl. "The War Within: Maintaining Sexual Integrity," *Rapport,* Summer 2004, Vol. 20, No. 2.

Temple, Todd and Roberta Hromas. *Teaching Your Child to Talk to God.* New York, New York: Inspirational Press, 1994.

ten Boom, Corrie. *The Hiding Place.* Washington Depot, Connecticut: Chosen Books; distributed by Fleming H. Revell Company, 1971.

Thomson, Helen. "The Successful Stepparent," quoted in *For Families Only,* J. Allen Peterson, ed. Wheaton, Illinois: Living Books, 1977.

Trobisch, Walter. *I Married You.* New York, New York: Harper & Row Publishers, Inc., 1971.

Unger, Merrill F. *Unger's Bible Dictionary.* Chicago, Illinois: Moody Press, 1969, 1986.

Vander Ark, Nellie A. *Devotions for Teachers.* Grand Rapids, Michigan: Baker Book House, 1978.

Warren, Neil Clark. *Finding the Love of Your Life.* Colorado Springs, Colorado: Focus on the Family Publishing, 1992.

Wegner, Walter "God's Pattern for the Family in the Old Testament," in *Family Relationships and the Church,* Oscar Feucht, ed. St. Louis, Missouri: Concordia Publishing House, 1970.

Wexler, David B. *Domestic Violence 2000, Group Leader's Manual.* New York, New York: W. W. Norton and Company, 2000.

Wheat, Ed, and Gaye Wheat. *Intended for Pleasure: Sex Technique and Sexual Fulfillment in Christian Marriage,* 3rd ed. Grand Rapids, Michigan: Fleming H. Revell Company, 1997.

Wright, H. Norman. *Communication: Key to Your Marriage.* Ventura, California: Regal Books, 2000.

http://en.wikipedia.org/wiki/List_ of_ emotions [accessed February 18, 2005]

http://link75.org/mmb/Nathist/Birds/eagle.html [accessed April 24, 2005]

http://www.cdc.gov/nip/publications/6mishom.htm [accessed June 2005]

http://www.who.int/water_sanitation_health/hygiene/settings/en/wsh9204.pdf [accessed June 2005]

Endnotes

Unit 1 Page

[1] E. C. McKenzie, *Mac's Giant Book of Quips and Quotes* (Grand Rapids, Michigan: Baker Book House, 1980), p. 420.

Chapter 1

[1] Charles M. Sell, *Family Ministry* (Grand Rapids, Michigan: Zondervan Publishing House, 1995), p. 32.

[2] Stephen A. Grunlan, *Marriage and the Family: A Christian Perspective* (Grand Rapids, Michigan: Zondervan Publishing House, 1999), p. 34.

[3] Grunlan, p. 34.

[4] Walter Wegner, "God's Pattern for the Family in the Old Testament," *Family Relationships and the Church,* edited by Oscar Feucht (St. Louis, Missouri: Concordia Publishing House, 1970), p. 29. See also *The New Bible Dictionary,* J. D. Douglas, ed., (Grand Rapids, Michigan: Wm. B. Eerdmans Publishing Co., 1978), article on "Marriage," pp. 786-791.

[5] Wegner, p. 29.

[6] Ludwig Hugo Koehler, *Hebrew Man* (New York, New York: Abingdon Press, 1956), p. 78.

[7] Merrill F. Unger, *Unger's Bible Dictionary* (Chicago, Illinois: Moody Press, 1969), p. 344.

[8] James B. Hurley, *Man and Woman in Biblical Perspective: A Study in Role Relationships and Authority* (Grand Rapids, Michigan: Academie Books, Zondervan Publishing House, 1981), p. 212.

[9] Sung Kyu Choi, translated by Joo Young Lee, *Survey of the Theology of Hyo* (Sungsanseowon, Korea: Dr. Sung Kyu Choi, 2004), p. 145.

[10] Walter Trobisch, *I Married You* (New York, New York: Harper & Row Publishers, Inc., 1971), p. 19.

[11] Trobisch, p. 15.

[12] Trobisch, p. 21.

[13] Alver Rance, Assemblies of God missionary, e-mail of May 9, 2003.

[14] C. F. Keil and F. Delitzsch, *Commentary on the Old Testament: The Pentateuch,* vol. 1 (Peabody, Massachusetts: Hendrickson Publishers, 1989), pp. 86-89.

[15] Victor P Hamilton, *New International Commentary on the Old Testament: The Book of Genesis,* vol. 1 (Grand Rapids, Michigan: Wm. B. Eerdmans Publishing Co., 1996), p. 175.

[16] Charles R. Swindoll, *The Tale of the Tardy Oxcart* (Nashville, Tennessee: Word Publishing, Inc., 1998), p. 71.

[17] Craig Brian Larson, *Illustrations for Preaching and Teaching* (Grand Rapids, Michigan: Baker Book House Co., 1993), p. 139.

Chapter 2

[1] James S. Hewett, *Illustrations Unlimited* (Wheaton, Illinois: Tyndale House Publishers, Inc., 1988), p. 333.

[2] Desmond Gani, *The Christian Family,* unpublished lecture notes, pp. 14-15.

[3] Jack O. Balswick and Judith K. Balswick, *The Family: A Christian Perspective on the Contemporary Home,* 2nd ed. (Grand Rapids, Michigan: Baker Books, 1999), p. 60.

[4] Gani, pp. 12-13.

[5] Neo Soon Siak, Malaysia, e-mail of May 29, 2003.

[6] Gani, p. 59.

[7] Charles L. Allen, *Home Fires: A Treasury of Wit and Wisdom* (Waco, Texas: Word Books Publisher, 1987), p. 37.

[8] Neil Clark Warren, *Finding the Love of Your Life* (Colorado Springs, Colorado: Focus on the Family Publishing, 1992), pp. 77-78.

[9] Warren, p. 57.

[10] Warren, pp. 48-50.

Chapter 3

[1] Paul G. Hiebert, *Case Studies in Missions* (Grand Rapids, Michigan: Baker Book House, 1987), pp. 84-85.

[2] Tim and Beverly LaHaye, *The Act of Marriage* (Grand Rapids, Michigan: Zondervan Publishing House, 1976).

[3] Ed Wheat and Gaye Wheat, *Intended for Pleasure: Sex Technique and Sexual Fulfillment in Christian Marriage,* 3rd ed. (Grand Rapids, Michigan: Revell, a division of Baker Book House, 1997).

Unit 2 Page

[1] McKenzie, pp. 320-325.

Chapter 4

[1] Anita Taylor, Arthur C. Meyer, Teresa Rosegrant, B. Thomas Samples, *Communicating* (Englewood Cliffs, New Jersey: Prentice Hall Publishing, 1991), chapter 1.

[2] Taylor, Meyer, Rosegrant, and Samples.

[3] H. Norman Wright, *Communication: Key to Your Marriage* (Ventura, California: Regal Books, 2000), pp. 103-105.

[4] Larry Crabb, *The Marriage Builder* (Grand Rapids, Michigan: Zondervan Publishing House, 1992). Pages 80-86 give instructions in how to respond with acceptance when someone shares feelings.

[5] Dr. Kevin Leman advocates beginning many responses with "I may be wrong, but…" He says that this diffuses the common problem of defensiveness.

[6] Wright, p. 129.

[7] Wright, pp. 130-135.

[8] Wright, pp. 135-138.

[9] John Gray, *What Your Mother Couldn't Tell You and Your Father Didn't Know* (New York, New York: HarperCollins Publishers, Inc., 1994), p. 90.

[10] Wright, pp.140-141.

[11] Wright, pp. 139-145.

[12] John Gray, *Men Are from Mars, Women Are from Venus* (New York, New York: HarperCollins Publishers, Inc., 1992), pp. 140-141.

[13] Gray, *Men Are from Mars, Women Are from Venus,* pp. 141-142.

[14] Willard F. Harley, Jr., *His Needs, Her Needs: Building an Affair-Proof Marriage* (Grand Rapids, Michigan: Fleming H. Revell Company, 2001), p. 9.

[15] Abraham Maslow researched human needs and motivations. He found these things to be common human needs.

[16] Harley, p. 15.

[17] http://en.wikipedia.org/wiki/List_of_emotions [accessed February 18, 2005]

[18] Tim and Joy Downs, *The Seven Conflicts: Resolving the Most Common Disagreements in Marriage* (Chicago, Illinois: Moody Publishers, 2003), p. 40.

[19] Tim and Joy Downs, pp. 35-36.

[20] Tommy Nelson, *The Book of Romance: What Solomon Says About Love, Sex, and Intimacy* (Nashville, Tennessee: Thomas Nelson, Inc., 1998), pp. 135-141.

[21] Gabriele Rineas, "Dealing with Conflict," *Enrichment: A Journal for Pentecostal Ministry* (Springfield, Missouri: Gospel Publishing House, Summer 2004), p. 66.

Chapter 5

[1] Mark Rutland, Marriage Seminar in West Virginia, 2002.

[2] Nelson, pp. 109-115.

[3] Alfred Ellis, *Restoring Innocence: Healing the Memories and Hurts That Hinder Sexual Intimacy* (Nashville, Tennessee: Thomas Nelson Publishers, 1990), p. 49.

[4] Joseph C. Dillow, *Solomon on Sex* (Nashville, Tennessee: Thomas Nelson Publishers, 1977), pp. 14, 20-21.

[5] We now know that a virgin may not bleed at first intercourse. The hymen can be broken by vigorous activity like horseback riding. It may be broken by a blow to the pelvic area such as might occur in some falls. It can also be broken by some feminine hygiene products or even by a doctor's exam. Sexual abuse using other instruments besides a sex organ can also break a hymen.

[6] Marvin Gilbert and Don Odunze, *Successful Family Living—An African View* (unpublished notes), chapter 3, p. 6.

[7] Dillow, p. 132.

[8] Ellis, The content of the rest of this section is drawn from his book, *Restoring Innocence.*

[9] It is important to note the problem of homosexuality. This is a complicated subject that does affect marriages. Some people seek marriage to deal with or deny their homosexual desires. There are many ideas about what causes a person to be attracted to those of the same gender. None of these ideas are proven. What we know for sure is that the Bible labels this behavior as sin. We also know that many people have changed their sinful desires. Helping people change is like helping conquer addictions.

[10] Ellis, These steps and illustrations are modified from *Restoring Innocence.*

[11] Ellis, These hints are modified from different sections of *Restoring Innocence.*

Chapter 6

[1] Allen, p. 53.

[2] The older pastor was LaRoi Wood.

[3] Tim and Joy Downs, p. 274.

[4] Theodore Isaac Rubin, *Overcoming Indecisiveness: The Eight Stages of Effective Decision Making* (New York, New York: Avon Books, 1985), summarized from pages 22-72.

[5] Rubin, p. 76.

[6] McKenzie, pp. 340-348.

[7] Paul Lee Tan, *Encyclopedia of 7700 Illustrations: Signs of the Times* (Rockville, Maryland: Assurance Publishers, 1984), p. 832, #3572.

[8] Gilbert and Odunze, chapter 3, p. 16.

[9] Paul D. Meier, Frank B. Minirith, Frank B. Wichern, Donald E. Ratcliff, *Introduction to Psychology and Counseling: Christian Perspectives and Applications* (Grand Rapids, Michigan: Baker Book House, 1991), pp. 333-334.

Chapter 7

[1] Ralph W. Harris, *The Complete Biblical Library: The New Testament Study Bible, Galatians–Philemon,* vol. 8 (Springfield, Missouri: World Library Press, 1995), p. 161.

[2] William Barclay, *The Daily Study Bible: Galatians and Ephesians* (Philadelphia, Pennsylvania: The Westminster Press, 1976), p. 173.

[3] James Dobson, *What Wives Wish Their Husbands Knew About Women* (Wheaton, Illinois: Tyndale House, 1977), pp. 151-153.

[4] Dobson, pp. 143-150.

[5] From a sermon by Pastor Glen D. Cole on Revelation 2:1-7.

[6] Sell, pp. 118-119.

[7] Gary J. Oliver, "The Cult of Success," *New Man,* September 1997, p. 74.

[8] This section is based on the teachings of Gilbert and Odunze, *Successful Family Living—An African View* (unpublished notes), chapter 4, pp. 6-7.

[9] Dan Betzer, *Byline* (radio and e-mail) based on a story by Don Meyer, January 16, 2004.

Chapter 8

[1] Laura Schlessinger, *The Proper Care and Feeding of Husbands* (New York, New York: HarperCollins Publishers, Inc.,

[2] Joyce Meyer, *Help Me I'm Married* (Tulsa, Oklahoma: Harrison House, 2000), p. 69.

[3] Meyer, p. 69.

[4] John C. Howell, *Equality and Submission in Marriage* (Nashville, Tennessee: Broadman Press, 1979), pp. 129-130.

[5] Meyer, p. 136.

[6] Meier, Minirith, Wichern, Ratcliff, p. 215.

[7] Schlessinger, p. xvii.

8 Schlessinger, p. xvii.

9 Schlessinger, p. xx.

10 Dale Carnegie, *How to Win Friends and Influence People* (London, England: Cedar Books, 1983), p. 27.

Chapter 9

1 Swindoll, p. 198.

2 James Dobson in *Draper's Book of Quotations for the Christian World,* edited by Edythe Draper, (Wheaton, Illinois: Tyndale House Publishers, Inc., 1992), p. 62.

3 Grunlan, pp. 228-229.

4 Gene Getz, quoted in *For Families Only,* edited by J. Allen Peterson, (Wheaton, Illinois: Living Books, 1977), p. 49.

5 Larry Burkett and Rick Osborne. *Your Child Wonderfully Made: Discovering God's Unique Plan* (Chicago, Illinois: Moody Press, 1998), p. 79.

6 Gilbert and Odunze, chapter 9, pp. 5-6.

7 Erich Fromm quoted in *Draper's Book of Quotations for the Christian World,* p. 429.

8 Alice Gray, compiler, *Stories for the Heart* (Sisters, Oregon: Multnomah Books, 1996), p. 149.

9 Larry Burkett and Rick Osborne, *Financial Parenting* (Colorado Springs, Colorado: Chariot Victor Publishing, A Division of Cook Communications, 1996).

10 Gani, pp. 64-67.

11 Tim and Beverly LaHaye, *Against the Tide: How to Raise Sexually Pure Kids in an 'Anything-Goes' World* (Sisters, Oregon: Multnomah Books, 1993), chapters 2-7.

12 Tim and Beverly LaHaye, chapters 3-7.

13 Much of the material in sections B–F has been taken from the work of JoAnn Butrin, *You Can Be Healthy!* (Lakeland, Florida: Healthcare Ministries, 1991).

14 http://www.who.int/water_sanitation_health/hygiene/settings/en/wsh9204.pdf [accessed June 2005]

15 http://www.who.int/water_sanitation_health/hygiene/settings/en/wsh9204.pdf [accessed June 2005]

16 Article taken from a national newspaper in 2005. Names changed to avoid embarrassment.

17 http://www.cdc.gov/nip/publications/6mishom.htm [accessed June 2005]

Chapter 10

1 Carnegie, pp. 38-40.

2 Gilbert and Odunze, chapter 4, p. 13.

3 David Sylvester, *Great Stories,* Volume 6/Issue 24, October-December 1999 (Amarillo, Texas), p. 8.

4 Donald C. Stamps, "Parents and Children," *The Full Life Study Bible,* NIV (Grand Rapids, Michigan: Zondervan Publishing House, 1992), p. 1854 (at the end of Colossians) of English translation.

5 Todd Temple and Roberta Hromas, *Teaching Your Child to Talk to God* (New York, New York: Inspirational Press, 1994), p. 17.

6 These joyful events took place while the Moeckl family were missionaries in Tanzania, East Africa.

7 Nellie A. Vander Ark, *Devotions for Teachers* (Grand Rapids, Michigan: Baker Book House, 1978), pp. 79-80.

8 The information about family devotions is adapted from Gilbert and Odundze, chapter 10, pp. 7-9

9 James Dobson quoted in *For Families Only,* p. 50.

10 *Helping Your Child Develop Self-Esteem,* http://childdevelopmentinfo.com/parenting/self_esteem.shtml. [accessed July 2005]

11 James Dobson quoted in *For Families Only,* pp. 50-55.

12 Gilbert and Odunze, chapter 9, pp. 7-14.

13 The three sections on "discipline calmly, discipline quickly, and discipline sparingly" are from *Dare to Discipline* by James Dobson (Wheaton, Illinois: Tyndale House Publishers, 1970).

14 Dobson, *Dare to Discipline.*

15 Numbers 12–14 come from James Dobson, *The Strong-Willed Child,* (Wheaton, Illinois: Tyndale House Publishers, 1978), pp. 31-33.

16 Natural and logical results are from Gilbert and Odunze, chapter 9, pp. 8-10.

17 Dobson, *The Strong-Willed Child,* 1978).

18 Edythe Draper, ed., *Draper's Book of Quotations for the Christian World* (Wheaton, Illinois: Tyndale House Publishers, Inc., 1992), p. 62.

Unit 4 Page

1 McKenzie, p. 479.

Chapter 11

1 Dr. Charles Harris, from his own experience as told by writing on September 24, 2004. Used by permission.

2 Sell, p. 47.

3 Urie Bronfenbrenner, Testimony before the Senate Subcommittee on Children and Youth, "Hearing on American Families," *Congressional Record.* September 26, 1973.

4 Larry Crabb, *Connecting: A Radical New Vision* (Nashville, Tennessee: Word Publishing, 1997), p. xi.

5 Gary Smalley, "The Pastor and Family Intimacy," *Enrichment: A Journal for Pentecostal Ministry* (Summer 2004), p. 52.

6 Smalley, p. 58.

7 Kevin Leman, *Making Children Mind Without Losing Yours* (Grand Rapids, Michigan: Fleming H. Revell Company, 1984), pp. 170-173.

8 Elisabeth Elliot, *Let Me Be a Woman* (Wheaton, Illinois: Tyndale House Publishers, 1999).

9 Gary Chapman, *The Five Languages of Love* (Chicago, Illinois: Northfield Publishing, 1995).

10 Crabb, *Connecting,* p. 27.

11 This is a true story about Mike McClaflin as a child. He shared it in a sermon.

12 Many of the principles and thoughts in this lesson are adapted from an article, "The War Within: Maintaining Sexual Purity," by Dr. Cheryl Taylor in *Rapport* (Springfield, Missouri: Assemblies of God Theological Seminary, Summer 2004), Vol. 20, No. 2, pp. 6-9. Dr. Taylor is a

Endnotes 257

professor at the Assemblies of God Theological Seminary and is available to teach seminars on how to overcome sexual temptation. You can access some of her articles on the Internet at www.agts.edu.

[13] Adapted from John Loren Sandford's book, *Why Some Christians Commit Adultery* (Tulsa, Oklahoma: Victory House Publishers, 1989), and Steve Hayes, *Safe and Sound: Protecting Personal and Ministry Relationships* (Nashville: Tennessee: Broadman and Holman Press, 2002), p. 60.

[14] James Dobson, *Straight Talk to Men and Their Wives* (Nashville, Tennessee: W Publishing Group, 1980).

[15] See these two sources: *Men Are From Mars, Women Are From Venus* by John Gray (New York, New York: HarperCollins Publishers, 1992), pp. 135-137; *The Five Love Needs of Men and Women* by Gary and Barbara Rosberg (Tyndale House Publishers, 2001).

[16] Adapted from an article by Randy Alcorn, "The real and untold cost: The exorbitant price of sexual sin," *Leadership: A Practical Journal for Church Leaders* (Summer 1996), p. 52.

[17] M. Johnson, *Journal of Marriage and Family* (Minneapolis, Minnesota: National Council on Family Relations, 1995) pp. 57, 283-294. David B. Wexler, *Domestic Violence 2000, Group Leader's Manual* (New York, New York: W. W. Norton and Company, 2000), p. 9.

[18] Donald G. Dutton, "Witnessing Parental Violence as a Traumatic Experience Shaping the Abusive Personality," in Robert Geffner, Peter Jaffe, and Marlies Sudermann (eds.) *Children Exposed to Domestic Violence: Current Issues in Research, Intervention, Prevention and Policy Development* (New York, New York: The Haworth Press, Inc., 2000), pp. 59-64.

[19] Nancy Nason-Clark, *The Battered Wife* (Louisville, Kentucky: Westminster John Knox Press, 1997), pp. 12-13.

[20] Holly Wagner Green, *Turning Fear to Hope: Help for Marriages Troubled by Abuse* (New York, New York: Thomas Nelson Publishers, 1984), pp. 48-53.

[21] Constructed from experience of Rev. Paul Simmons as told by Karen Burton Mains in *Abuse in the Family* (Elgin, Illinois: David C. Cook Publishing, 1987), pp. 27-30.

[22] Jimmy Ray Lee, *Insight Group: Facilitator's Guide,* 3rd ed. (Chattanooga, Tennessee: Turning Point, 1995).

[23] Lee, p. 23.

[24] Lee, p. 22.

[25] Crabb, *Connecting,* pp. 68-86.

[26] Crabb, *Connecting,* pp. 70-72.

Chapter 12

[1] Thomas H. Holmes, Professor of Psychiatry and Behavioral Sciences, University of Washington School of Medicine, developed this stress assessment table.

[2] Gary R. Collins, *Christian Counseling: A Comprehensive Guide,* rev. ed. (Dallas, Texas: Word Publishing, 1988), p. 347.

[3] Modern medicine has also discovered that it is the man's sperm that determines whether a child will be a boy or a girl.

[4] James Dobson, *Straight Talk to Men and Their Wives,* pp. 110-111.

[5] Jim Smoke, *Growing Through Divorce* (Eugene, Oregon: Harvest House Publishers, 1995). The portion of material on divorce is drawn largely from the work of Jim Smoke.

[6] *The Full Life Study Bible,* note on 1 Corinthians 7:15, p. 1761.

[7] Smoke, pp. 56-57.

[8] Smoke, p. 15.

[9] Smoke, pp. 58-63.

[10] Smoke, p. 111.

[11] Catherine Marshall and Leonard LeSourd, *My Personal Prayer Diary* (New York, New York: Ballantine Books, 1979), p. xii.

[12] Helen Thomson, "The Successful Stepparent," quoted in *For Families Only,* p. 202.

[13] Carolyn Johnson, *How to Blend a Family* (Grand Rapids, Michigan: Pyranee Books, 1989), p. 101.

[14] Corrie ten Boom, *The Hiding Place* (Washington Depot, Connecticut: Chosen Books; distributed by Revell, 1971), p. 126.

Chapter 13

[1] Anonymous, *Home Fire: A Treasury of Wit and Wisdom,* edited by Charles Allen, p. 114.

[2] Erma Bomback, "Fragile Strings Join Parent, Child," *Arizona Republic,* May 15, 1977.

[3] http://link75.org/mmb/Nathist/Birds/eagle.html [accessed April 24, 2005]

[4] Balswick and Balswick, p. 166.

[5] James Dobson, *Bringing up Boys* (Wheaton, Illinois: Tyndale House Publisher, Inc., 2001), p. 256.

[6] Sheila Kitzinger, taken from S. Chirawatkul and L. Manderson, "Perceptions of Menopause in Northeast Thailand: Contested Meaning and Practice," *Social Science & Medicine* 39 (11) (1994): pp. 1545-54.

[7] Sheila Kitzinger, taken from John F. Ember, *A Japanese Village* (London: Kegan Paul, 1946).

[8] Sheila Kitzinger, *A Japanese Village,* p. 76.

[9] J. Ponzetti, and A. Fokrod, "Grandchildren's Perceptions of Their Relationships With Their Grandparents," *Child Study Journal,* 1989, 19:41-50.

[10] Grunlan, p. 268, research by Neugarten and Weinstein.

[11] Ann Landers, "Siblings Not Helping With Aging Parents," *Lincoln Journal Star,* November 25, 1997, 8B.

[12] Collins, p. 264.

[13] Collins, p. 264.

[14] Meier, Minirith, Wichern, and Ratcliff, p. 220.

[15] Meier, Minirith, Wichern, and Ratcliff, p. 267.

[16] Collins, p. 266.